"Poythress shows how a proper understanding of biblical theology makes possible not just one but many credible harmonizations of biblical and scientific truth. Along the way, he provides an insightful defense of the theory of intelligent design as a viable scientific research program. His examination of the mathematical beauty inherent in the universe gives yet another compelling reason to acknowledge the wisdom and design that lie behind physical reality."

> —STEPHEN C. MEYER, Director, Center for Science and Culture
> Discovery Institute

"With doctorates in both New Testament and mathematics, and with a solid commitment to orthodox Reformed theology, Vern Poythress is uniquely qualified to write on the theology of science. Further, he is one of the most insightful theologians writing today. As you read this book, you will be amazed at the ways in which a biblical perspective illumines the work of science. Poythress deals, of course, with all the traditional science-Bible issues, like the days of Genesis. But he also shows that a biblical worldview is essential to the work of science itself, for scientific law can be nothing other than the law of the God of Scripture. This is by far the most important book you can read on this subject. I recommend it without reservation."

> —JOHN FRAME, Professor of Systematic Theology and Philosophy,
> Reformed Theological Seminary, Orlando

"In this highly original and remarkably insightful work, Vern Poythress demonstrates just how natural the partnership is between science and Christianity. Using examples from a variety of scientific disciplines, Dr. Poythress gives us a prescription for how science and the Christian faith can interact in a way that mutually benefits both and spurs scientific and theological advance."

> —FAZALE RANA, Vice President of Science Apologetics,
> Reasons To Believe

"In the crowded market of theology and science studies this book fills a gap. Not only does it offer a theological perspective rooted in the historic Reformation, but it also attends to strategies of interpretation of Bible texts concerning nature and history that underwrite doctrine but are often left out of the dialogue. The author's approach is nuanced, balanced, and open-minded."

> —JITSE VAN DER MEER, Professor of Biology and History
> and Philosophy of Science, Redeemer University College,
> Ancaster, Ontario

"Sound theology meets sound science in this book as Vern Poythress shows us how to see the beauty of God's character revealed in everything that scientists study in the created universe. A fascinating, comprehensive, profound, yet very readable analysis of all branches of modern science from one of the greatest minds in the Christian world today."

—WAYNE GRUDEM, Research Professor of Theology and Bible,
Phoenix Seminary, Scottsdale, Arizona

"*Redeeming Science* will be welcomed by every thoughtful Christian. Vern Poythress's analysis of the relationship between science and faith proceeds from an unapologetic, undisguised confession of belief in Christ, through personal testimony, clear-minded evaluation of the nature of science, careful analysis of Scripture, and honest reflection on the present state of this debate. This is a book of creational theology and Biblical theology, as well as of apologetics and pastoral instruction. Poythress demonstrates the revelational character of the world around us, especially in his claim that the 'laws' of science are nothing more than descriptions of the sovereign working of an all-wise and all-powerful God. He exposes the unexamined assumptions of the modern scientific enterprise, showing that it, like every worldview, is, at its base, religious in nature. He provides careful and thoughtful exegesis of relevant texts of Scripture, especially Genesis 1–9, demonstrating that Christians can think rationally about the scientific enterprise without compromising their most cherished Biblical convictions. Above all, Poythress points readers beyond the details and doldrums of the debate concerning science and faith to our Lord Jesus Christ, who is the consummation of both redemption and science. Christians committed to pursuing the Great Commission and the cultural mandate will find *Redeeming Science* a most useful resource for their endeavors."

—T. M. MOORE, Pastor of Teaching Ministries,
Cedar Springs Presbyterian Church, Knoxville, Tennessee;
Author, *Consider the Lilies: A Plea for Creational Theology*

REDEEMING SCIENCE

A GOD-CENTERED APPROACH

VERN S. POYTHRESS

CROSSWAY BOOKS
WHEATON, ILLINOIS

Library of Congress Cataloging-in-Publication Data

Poythress, Vern S.
  Redeeming science : a God-centered approach / Vern S. Poythress.
    p. cm.
  Includes bibliographical references and index.
  ISBN 13: 978-1-58134-731-9 (tpb)
  ISBN 10: 1-58134-731-6
  1. Religion and science. 2. Bible and science. I. Title.
BL240.3.P695   2006
261.5'5—dc22   2006009108

ML		18	17	16	15	14	13	12	11	10	09
15	14	13	12	11	10	9	8	7	6	5	4	3

to my wife
DIANE

CONTENTS

Introduction:
Science Mixing with People

When people hear of my love for science and mathematics, some react with enthusiasm, but others with dread. "Not me!" or "I hated math."

Though I classify myself with the enthusiasts, I sympathize with the rest. Somewhere along the way, many of these people started dreading their math or science class, and probably it only got worse with time. They did not understand well what was going on, and they could do the problems only with a hard struggle or not at all. Nothing kills enjoyment like failure.

Of course, it is partly that people differ in aptitude. Some prefer science, others prefer English or history or art. "Live and let live."

Importance of Thoughtful Response

But I believe that this is God's world, and that science and English and art alike reflect his wisdom. Even if we have little personal aptitude in a particular area, we can grow to appreciate and admire what skilled people do and what they experience.

And today our world experiences the continual impact of science, scientific ideas, and technological fruits of science. Whether we like science or not, we all have to deal with it on a practical level.

But then the question arises, "Is this indeed God's world? Or does it all reduce to matter and energy and motion?" And if it is God's world, how does God relate to science?

I myself am a believer in Jesus Christ. So I must ask myself how Christian belief relates to science. People often think that science is antagonistic to Christian belief. Science, it is said, shows that the universe is billions of years old, while the Bible says that it is only thousands of years old. And some people claim science shows that supernatural miracles are impossible.

This thinking in terms of antagonism crops up not only among non-Christians but among some Christians. I sometimes meet Christian people who are afraid of science because they think it is antagonistic to Christianity. The idea of antagonism is widespread, but it rests on a cultural history that has distorted people's understanding of science.

I would like to kindle our appreciation for science as it ought to be, science that could serve as a path for praising God and serving fellow human beings. Have you seen a nature show on TV that followed the story of baby foxes or the life of otters? Often the verbal commentary on such a show invites us to admire "Nature" or "Mother Nature" as the source of wisdom, care, and beauty. But we ought to recognize here the wisdom, care, and beauty of God. A God-centered worldview restores a correct response, where we praise the God who created nature and cares for it.

MY STORY

Soon after beginning school I became fascinated with arithmetic. Practicing addition was like playing in a magical wonderland, because the operation proceeded with such precision, such stability, such consistency. It showed enormous power, because one could add large numbers and obtain still larger ones, on and on as long as one could go. (I did not know it, but I was experiencing the lure of infinity.) Numbers worked like magic, in that the operations carried out on paper matched perfectly what one could find by putting together 13 marbles with 15 more marbles.

My interest eventually expanded to include science and higher mathematics. I was fascinated by the regularity, dependability, and beauty that I saw. I found a sense of rest in the constancy of physical laws, their precision, their harmony.

I pursued my interest by majoring in mathematics at California Institute of Technology and by studying for a Ph.D. in mathematics at Harvard University. I then taught mathematics at Fresno State College (now California State University, Fresno) before turning to pursue a second interest, my interest in the Bible and theology.

Over the years, where did the fascination and the sense of the mystery of science go? To a certain extent they have remained with me. I still enjoy reading *Scientific American*. But learning began to squeeze out the fascination and mystery. To some degree I suppose this is inevitable. Learning brings familiarity, and familiarity can produce lack of attention or even boredom.

But other forces have been at work as well. Science as now taught is influenced by an ideology of "objectivity" that may prefer to sweep under the rug the experience of personal fascination, delight, beauty, and mystery.

Excitement is not communicated as it should be to each new generation, and so they do not see the point. Science gets reduced to a game in which we learn meaningless rules in order to solve artificial problems posed on teachers' tests. Or it is no more than a pragmatic tool by which we produce gadgets that bring comfort, entertainment, and status. Or, for those who excel in science, it is a platform for parading intellectual power and achievement. Where is a vision for the whole world that would draw us into an appreciation of the human significance of science?

My son has been studying conic sections in his high school math class. I think the subject is beautiful. But he does not; and he does not see the point. I asked him whether the teacher or the textbook provided any justification or meaning for it. No. If the teacher were asked, he would say, "We are doing it because it is part of the curriculum." That evasion sounds like saying, "There is no real point, but only an arbitrary decision from the authorities who drew up the curriculum." Such lack of purpose does not produce a good learning atmosphere, despite the fact that the teacher himself has a genuine love for his subject and a commitment to his teaching.

My wife and I observed the trouble with our son much earlier. In about the third grade, he was studying biology by memorizing scientific terminology for the parts of the leaf or for the divisions of the animal kingdom. He was not exploring how animals behave, but just memorizing. I was so appalled by the mauled vision of science that I felt like averting my eyes in shame. I found myself saying lamely, "This is not what real science is like. Real science means exploring and adventuring." And now with more maturity I might add, "And from time to time, after a long, exhausting climb, we catch a breathtaking glimpse of the beauty of God."

I wanted to see my son reading stories about how the bees build their hives and communicate the location of new sources of nectar, or how octopuses catch their prey, or how diamonds are formed. Let him enjoy the written analogue of a nature show, whenever the class cannot manage to get an effective multimedia presentation. Let him also sense some of the excitement in scientific discovery. Let him hear the story of the production of the first vaccine for smallpox and the discovery of penicillin. Have the class go outside and observe ants at work. Let them capture some sow bugs and find out what they like to eat. Let them cut up some large seeds to see what is inside, and let them water some and watch them grow. Let them take apart an old-fashioned wind-up clock and try to figure out how it works. And do not make it into a "lab" project where everyone must come up with the same predetermined results!

I am glad to say that later there were some high points in my son's science education. The sixth grade class set off toy rockets that went 500 feet into the air. The seventh grade took a field trip to a stream valley where they dug out shale and broke it open to find fossils.

We need to reform our thinking about science. And we need to do it in a global way, by tackling on a large scale our conception of what kind of world we live in and what is our human role in it. Western civilization has lost sight of any unified goal, except perhaps the superficial goals of pleasure, prosperity, and tolerance. We have lost our way as a civilization, and the universities have become multi-versities with no center. The grade schools are little better. The atmosphere says, "Work on these apparently meaningless assignments now, so that you will be able to go to college, get a good job, and live the American dream of a large home with two cars and a plasma screen TV." The malaise about science and its meaning is only part of a larger malaise of meaninglessness engulfing us.

So we are taking a long route, to rethink the meaning of science. And I am doing that rethinking as a Christian believer. It would take another book to present the case that the Christian faith is true and that the Bible is the word of God. I am writing this book mostly for Christians who already believe these things. But I believe they are relevant to everyone, because basic truths about God and about science are relevant to all. Even if you are not yet a Christian, you may be interested to see how Christian faith interacts with the scientific enterprise. No, it does not result in the kind of antagonism that popular thinking suggests. And yes, it can liberate us from the tide of meaninglessness.

1

WHY SCIENTISTS MUST BELIEVE IN GOD: DIVINE ATTRIBUTES OF SCIENTIFIC LAW[1]

All scientists—including agnostics and atheists—believe in God. They have to in order to do their work.

It may seem outrageous to include agnostics and atheists in this broad statement. But by their actions people sometimes show that in a sense they believe in things that they profess not to believe in. Bakht, a Vedantic Hindu philosopher, may say that the world is an illusion. But he does not casually walk into the street in front of an oncoming bus. Sue, a radical relativist, may say that there is no truth. But she travels calmly at 30,000 feet on a plane whose safe flight depends on the unchangeable truths of aerodynamics and structural mechanics.[2]

But what about scientists? Do they believe in God? Must they? Popular modern culture often transmits the contrary idea, namely that science is antagonistic to orthodox Christian belief. Recitations of Galileo's conflict and of the Scopes Trial have gained mythic status and receive reinforcement through vocal promotions of materialistic evolution.

Historians of science point out that modern science arose in the context

---

[1] This chapter originally appeared in different form in Vern S. Poythress, "Why Scientists Must Believe in God," *Journal of the Evangelical Theological Society* 46/1 (March 2003): 111-123.
[2] Gregory L. Bahnsen's work on self-deception ("A Conditional Resolution of the Apparent Paradox of Self-Deception," Ph.D. thesis, University of Southern California, 1979) has helped to show how people manage such paradoxical stances. They believe a certain proposition and also believe (as a second-order belief) that they do not believe it. They have hidden from their consciousness what their actions continue to reveal to others. In their actions they tacitly rely on truths about the world, while verbally and consciously they do not believe that they do. This model is helpful. But unbelief and rebellion, as manifestations of sin, produce deep effects on human nature, including its intellectual and practical affairs. Hence, any human account of the evasion of truth remains partial.

of a Christian worldview, and was nourished and sustained by that view.[3] But even if that was once so, twentieth-century and twenty-first-century science seems to sustain itself without the help of explicit theistic underpinnings. In fact, many consider God to be merely the "God of the gaps," the God whom people invoke only to account for gaps in modern scientific explanation. As science advances and more gaps become subject to explanation, the role of God diminishes. The natural drives out the need for the supernatural.[4]

FOCUSING ON SCIENTIFIC LAW

The situation looks different if we refuse to confine God to "the gaps." According to the Bible, he is involved in those areas where science does best, namely areas involving regular and predictable events, repeating patterns, and sometimes exact mathematical descriptions. In Genesis 8:22 God promises,

> While the earth remains, seedtime and harvest, cold and heat, summer and winter, day and night, shall not cease.[5]

This general promise concerning earthly regularities is supplemented by many particular examples:

> You make darkness, and it is night,
>   when all the beasts of the forest creep about (Ps. 104:20).

> You cause the grass to grow for the livestock
>   and plants for man to cultivate,
> that he may bring forth food from the earth (Ps. 104:14).

> He sends out his command to the earth;
>   his word runs swiftly.

---

[3] Reijer Hooykaas, *Religion and the Rise of Modern Science* (Grand Rapids, Mich.: Eerdmans, 1972); Stanley L. Jaki, *The Road of Science and the Ways of God* (Chicago: University of Chicago Press, 1980); Jaki, *The Origin of Science and the Science of Its Origin* (South Bend, Ind.: Regnery-Gateway, 1979); Nancy R. Pearcey and Charles B. Thaxton, *The Soul of Science: Christian Faith and Natural Philosophy* (Wheaton, Ill.: Crossway, 1994); Charles E. Hummel, *The Galileo Connection: Resolving Conflicts Between Science and the Bible* (Downers Grove, Ill.: InterVarsity Press, 1986).

[4] In about 1999 Edward J. Larson and Larry Witham conducted a survey of scientists' beliefs and compared the results with similar 1914 and 1933 surveys by James H. Leuba. They found little change, contrary to the impression that science is a secularizing force. 40 percent believed in God both in Leuba's surveys and today. But they also found that the "elite" of American scientists, represented by the National Academy of Science, contained a higher percentage of disbelief—more than 90 percent of those responding (Edward J. Larson and Larry Witham, "Scientists and Religion in America," *Scientific American* 281/3 [September 1999]: 88-93).

[5] Unless otherwise noted, Bible quotations are from the English Standard Version (ESV).

He gives snow like wool;
   he scatters hoarfrost like ashes.
He hurls down his crystals of ice like crumbs;
   who can stand before his cold?
He sends out his word, and melts them;
   he makes his wind blow and the waters flow (Ps. 147:15-18).

The regularities that scientists describe are the regularities of God's own commitments and actions. By his word to Noah, he commits himself to govern the seasons. By his word he governs snow, frost, and hail. Scientists describe the regularities in God's word governing the world. So-called natural law is really the law of God or word of God, imperfectly and approximately described by human investigators.

Now, the work of science depends constantly on the fact that there are regularities in the world. Without the regularities, there would ultimately be nothing to study. Scientists depend not only on regularities with which they are already familiar, such as the regular behavior of measuring apparatus, but also on the postulate that still more regularities are to be found in the areas that they will investigate. Scientists must maintain hope of finding further regularities, or they would give up their newest explorations.

(I should say here that I am concentrating on the natural or "hard" sciences such as physics, chemistry, geology, biology, and astronomy. To some extent similar observations hold for "human sciences" such as psychology, anthropology, linguistics, and sociology. But the study of human beings brings in additional challenges, because of the way in which one's overall understanding of the nature of humanity vitally influences the investigation. In concentrating on regularities, I am also putting into the background "historical" studies, such as the study of the past history of the large-scale universe [cosmology], the past history of life [paleobiology], the past history of the earth [historical geology], and so on. These studies rely on the assumption of regularities, but they also wrestle with understanding many unrepeatable events, such as the origin of the first cell, or the origin of the first humans. We will focus on the issue of uniqueness versus repeatability later [chapter 13]. And we will consider issues of origins in chapters 18 and 19.)

BELIEF IN SCIENTIFIC LAWS

Now just what are these regularities? For five years in a row a robin appears and builds a nest in the same bush. But in the sixth year no robin appears. Does this show a "regularity" of the appropriate type? It might be a matter of coincidence. Scientists are concerned to observe robins and their nest-building. But in the long run they do not rest with observations of mere coincidence. They want to know whether the recurrence is somehow constrained, whether it occurs according to a general explanatory principle.[6] The principles go by various names: "natural law," "scientific law," "theory." Some of these regularities can be exactly, quantitatively described for each case (within small limits of error), while others are statistical regularities that come to light only when a large number of cases are examined together. All scientists believe in the existence of such regularities. And in all cases, whatever their professed beliefs, scientists *in practice* know that the regularities are "out there." Scientists in the end are all "realists" with respect to scientific laws.[7] Scientists discover these laws and do not merely invent them. Otherwise, why go to the trouble, tedium, and frustration of experiment? Just make a guess, invent a new idea, and become famous!

These regularities are, well, regular. And to be regular means to be regulated. It involves a *regula,* a rule. *Webster's Dictionary* captures the point by defining "regular" as "formed, built, arranged, or ordered according to some established rule, law, principle, or type."[8] The idea of a law or rule is built into the concept of "regularity." Thus it is natural to use the word "law" in describing well-established scientific theories and principles. Scientists speak of Newton's laws, Boyle's law, Dalton's law, Mendel's laws, Kirchhoff's laws. All scientists believe in and rely on the existence of scientific laws.

UNIVERSAL APPLICABILITY OF SCIENTIFIC LAW

What characteristics must a scientific law have in order even to *be* a law? Again, we concentrate on the *practice* of scientists rather than their metaphysical musings. We ask, "Whatever their professed philosophy, what do scientists expect *in practice?*" Just as the relativist expects the plane to fly, the scientist expects the laws to hold.

---

[6] Roy Bhaskar distinguishes carefully between "causal laws" and "patterns of events" (Bhaskar, *Reclaiming Reality: A Critical Introduction to Contemporary Philosophy* [London/New York: Verso, 1989], 16). "Causal laws" correspond to what I call "a general explanatory principle," whereas "patterns of events" may derive from coincidence. Even when a pattern is a direct result of the operation of laws, it is not identical with the laws but is one instance of an effect of the laws. Yet no rigid separation is possible, because no *pattern,* whether coincidental or not, can be recognized by a human being except against the background of the rationality of the word of God. We need to have two distinctions in place: the distinction between God's word and human knowledge of his word; and the distinction between God's word and the things and events it controls. We also need to acknowledge that science involves more than one level of description and explanation. Gathering data about a robin's nest-building involves a more elementary level than analysis of a neurological basis for nest-building instincts. See the later discussion in chapters 13–15.

[7] For a discussion of realism and alternatives to it, see chapter 15.

[8] *Webster's Ninth New Collegiate Dictionary* (Springfield, Mass.: Merriam-Webster, 1987).

Scientists think of laws as universal in time and space. Kirchhoff's laws concerning electrical circuits apply only to electrical circuits, not to other kinds of situations. But they apply in principle to electrical circuits at any time and in any place. Sometimes, of course, scientists uncover limitations in earlier formulations. Some laws, like Newton's laws, are not really universal, but apply accurately only to a restricted situation such as low velocity motion of large, massive objects.[9] In the light of later knowledge, we would say that Newton's laws were always only an approximation to the real pattern of regularity or lawfulness in the world. We modify Newton's laws, or we include the specific restriction to low velocity within our formulation of the laws. Then we say that they apply to all times and places where these restrictions hold.

Thus, within the very concept of law lies the expectation that we include all times and all places. That is to say, the law, if it really is a law and is correctly formulated and qualified, holds for all times and all places. The classic terms are *omnipresence* (all places) and *eternity* (all times). Law has these two attributes that are classically attributed to God. Technically, God's eternity is usually conceived of as being "above" or "beyond" time. But words like "above" and "beyond" are metaphorical and point to mysteries. There is, in fact, an analogous mystery with respect to law. If "law" is universal, is it not in some sense "beyond" the particularities of any one place or time? Moreover, within a biblical worldview, God is not only "above" time in the sense of not being subject to the limitations of finite creaturely experience of time, but he is "in" time in the sense of acting in time and interacting with his creatures.[10] Similarly, law is "above" time in its universality, but "in" time through its applicability to each particular situation.

DIVINE ATTRIBUTES OF LAW

The attributes of omnipresence and eternity are only the beginning. On close examination, other divine attributes seem to belong to scientific laws. Consider. If a law holds for all times, we presuppose that it is the *same* law through all times. The law does not change with time. It is immutable. A supposed "law" that did change with time would not really be "the law," but one temporal phase in a higher or broader regularity that would account for the lower-level change. The higher, universal regularity is the law. The very concept of scientific law presupposes immutability.

---

[9] But not too massive; we get into other limitations when the gravitational fields are strong.
[10] John M. Frame, *The Doctrine of God* (Phillipsburg, N.J.: Presbyterian & Reformed, 2002), 543-575.

Next, laws are at bottom ideational in character. We do not literally see a law, but only the effects of the law on the material world. The law is essentially immaterial and invisible, but is known through effects. Likewise, God is essentially immaterial and invisible, but is known through his acts in the world.

Real laws, as opposed to scientists' approximations of them, are also absolutely, infallibly true. Truthfulness is also an attribute of God.[11]

The Power of Law

Next, consider the attribute of power. Scientists formulate laws as *descriptions* of regularities that they observe. The regularities are there in the world first, before the scientists make their formulations. The human scientific formulation follows the facts, and is dependent on them. But the facts must conform to a regularity even before the scientist formulates a description. A law or regularity must hold for a whole series of cases. The scientist cannot force the issue by inventing a law and then forcing the universe to conform to the law. The universe rather conforms to laws already there, laws that are discovered rather than invented. The laws must already be there. They must actually hold. They must "have teeth." If they are truly universal, they are not violated. No event escapes their "hold" or dominion. The power of these real laws is absolute, in fact, infinite. In classical language, the law is omnipotent ("all powerful").

If law is omnipotent and universal, there are truly no exceptions. Do we, then, conclude that miracles are impossible because they are violations of law? In fact, miracles are in harmony with God's character. They take place in accordance with his predictive and decretive word. Through Moses, God verbally predicted the plagues that came to Egypt, and then brought them about. Through God's word spoken by the prophet Elisha, a spring of water was made healthy:

> "Thus *says* the LORD, I have healed this water; from now on neither death nor miscarriage shall come from it." So the water has been healed to this day, according to the *word* that Elisha spoke (2 Kings 2:21-22).

The real law, the word of God, brings forth miracles. Miracles may be

---

[11] I recently found parallel thinking in Paul Davies, who mentions the eternality, universality, and omnipotence of law (Davies, *The Mind of God: The Scientific Basis for a Rational World* [New York: Simon & Schuster, 1992], 82-83). But Davies then travels in other directions, without further expanding the list of divine attributes.

unusual and striking, but they do not violate God's law. They violate only some human expectations and guesses. But that is our problem, not God's. Just as Newton's laws are limited to low velocity approximations, so the principle that axe heads do not float is limited by the qualification, "except when God in response to a special need and a prophet's word does otherwise" (e.g., 2 Kings 6:5-6).

The law is both transcendent and immanent. It transcends the creatures of the world by exercising power over them, conforming them to its dictates. It is immanent in that it touches and holds in its dominion even the smallest bits of this world.[12] Law transcends the galactic clusters and is immanently present in the chromodynamic dance of quarks and gluons in the bosom of a single proton. Transcendence and immanence are characteristics of God.

The Personal Character of Law

Many agnostic and atheistic scientists by this time will be looking for a way of escape. It seems that the key concept of scientific law is beginning to look suspiciously like the biblical idea of God. The most obvious escape, and the one that has rescued many from spiritual discomfort, is to deny that scientific law is personal. It is just there as an impersonal something.

Throughout the ages people have tried such routes. They have constructed idols, substitutes for God. In ancient times, the idols often had the form of statues representing a god—Poseidon, the god of the sea, or Mars, the god of war. Nowadays in the Western world we are more sophisticated. Idols now take the form of mental constructions of a god or a God-substitute. Money and pleasure can become idols. So can "humanity" or "nature" when it receives a person's ultimate allegiance. "Scientific law," when it is viewed as impersonal, becomes another God-substitute. But in both ancient times and today, idols conform to the imagination of the one who makes them. Idols have enough similarities to the true God to be plausible, but differ so as to allow us comfort and the satisfaction of manipulating the substitutes that we construct.

In fact, a close look at scientific law shows that this escape route is not really plausible. Law implies a law-giver. Someone must think the law and enforce it, if it is to be effective. But if some people resist this direct move to personality, we may move more indirectly.

---

[12] On the biblical view of transcendence and immanence, see John M. Frame, *The Doctrine of the Knowledge of God* (Phillipsburg, N.J.: Presbyterian & Reformed, 1987), especially 13-15; and Frame, *Doctrine of God,* especially 107-115.

Scientists in practice believe passionately in the rationality of scientific law. We are not dealing with an irrational, totally unaccountable and unanalyzable surd, but with lawfulness that in some sense is accessible to human understanding. Rationality is a *sine qua non* for scientific law. But, as we know, rationality belongs to persons, not to rocks, trees, and subpersonal creatures. If the law is rational, which scientists assume it is, then it is also personal.

Scientists also assume that laws can be articulated, expressed, communicated, and understood through human language. Scientific work includes not only rational thought, but symbolic communication. Now, the original, the law "out there," is not known to be written or uttered in a human language. But it must be expressible in language in our secondary description. It must be translatable into not only one but many human languages. We may represent restrictions, qualifications, definitions, and contexts for a law through clauses, phrases, explanatory paragraphs, and contextual explanations in human language.

Scientific law is clearly like a human utterance in its ability to be grammatically articulated, paraphrased, translated, and illustrated. Law is utterance-like, language-like. And the complexity of utterances that we find among scientists, as well as among human beings in general, is not duplicated in the animal world.[13] Language is one of the defining characteristics that separates man from animals. Language, like rationality, belongs to persons. It follows that scientific law is in essence personal.[14]

The Incomprehensibility of Law

In addition, law is both knowable and incomprehensible in the theological sense. That is, we know scientific truths, but in the midst of this knowledge there remain unfathomed depths and unanswered questions about the very areas where we know the most.

The knowability of laws is closely related to their rationality and their immanence, displayed in the accessibility of effects. We experience incomprehensibility in the fact that the increase of scientific understanding only

---

[13] Animal calls and signals do mimic certain limited aspects of human language. And chimpanzees can be taught to respond to symbols with meaning. But this is still a long way from the complex grammar and meaning of human language. See, e.g., Stephen R. Anderson, *Doctor Dolittle's Delusion: Animals and the Uniqueness of Human Language* (New Haven, Conn.: Yale University Press, 2004).

[14] In their ability to undergo transformation and reformulation, scientific laws also show an analogy with the ability of human language to represent multiple perspectives. For more on the language-character of scientific law, see Vern S. Poythress, "Science as Allegory," *Journal of the American Scientific Affiliation* 35/2 (1983): 65-71; Poythress, "Newton's Laws as Allegory," *Journal of the American Scientific Affiliation* 35/3 (1983): 156-161; Poythress, "Mathematics as Rhyme," *Journal of the American Scientific Affiliation* 35/4 (1983): 196-203.

leads to ever deeper questions: "How can this be?" and "Why *this* law rather than many other ways that the human mind can imagine?" The profundity and mystery in scientific discoveries can only produce awe—yes, worship—if we have not blunted our perception with hubris (Isa. 6:9-10).

Are We Divinizing Nature?

But now we must consider an objection. By claiming that scientific laws have divine attributes, are we divinizing nature? That is, are we taking something out of the created world, and falsely claiming that it is divine? Are not scientific laws a part of the created world? Should we not classify them as creature rather than Creator?[15]

I suspect that the specificity of scientific laws, their obvious reference to the created world, has become the occasion for many of us to infer that these laws are a *part* of the created world. But such an inference is clearly invalid. The speech describing a butterfly is not itself a butterfly or a part of a butterfly. Speech *referring* to the created world is not necessarily an ontological *part* of the world to which it refers.

In addition, let us remember that we are speaking of real laws, not merely our human guesses and approximations. The real laws are in fact the word of God, specifying how the world of creatures is to function. So-called "law" is simply God speaking, God acting, God manifesting himself in time and space. The real mistake here is not a matter of divinizing nature, but of refusing to recognize that the law is the law of God, nothing less than God speaking. We are confronting God.

The key idea that the law is divine is not only older than the rise of modern science; it is older than the rise of Christianity. Even before the coming of Christ people noticed profound regularity in the government of the world and wrestled with the meaning of this regularity. Both the Greeks (especially the Stoics) and the Jews (especially Philo) developed speculations about the *logos,* the divine "word" or "reason" behind what is observed.[16] In addition the Jews had the Old Testament, which reveals the role of the word of God in creation and providence. Against this background John 1:1 proclaims, "In the beginning was the Word, and the Word was with God, and the Word was God." John responds to the speculations of his time with a striking revela-

---

[15] In conformity with the Bible (especially Genesis 1), we maintain that God and the created world are distinct. God is not to be identified with the creation or any part of it, nor is the creation a "part" of God. The Bible repudiates all forms of pantheism and panentheism.

[16] See R. B. Edwards, "Word," in Geoffrey W. Bromiley et al., eds., *The International Standard Bible Encyclopedia,* 4 vols. (Grand Rapids, Mich.: Eerdmans, 1988), 4:1103-1107, and the associated literature.

tion: that the Word (*logos*) that created and sustains the universe is not only a divine person "with God," but the very One who became incarnate: "the Word became flesh" (1:14).

God said, "Let there be light" (Gen. 1:3). He referred to light as a part of the created world. But precisely in this reference, his word has divine power to bring creation into being. The effect in creation took place at a particular time. But the plan for creation, as exhibited in God's word, is eternal. Likewise, God's speech to us in the Bible refers to various parts of the created world, but the speech (in distinction to the things to which it refers) is divine in power, authority, majesty, righteousness, eternity, and truth.[17] The analogy with the incarnation should give us our clue. The second person of the Trinity, the eternal Word of God, became man in the incarnation, but did not therefore cease to be God. Likewise, when God speaks and says what is to be the case in this world, his words do not cease to have the divine power and unchangeability that belongs to him. Rather, they remain divine, and in addition have the power to specify the situation with respect to creaturely affairs. God's word remains divine when it becomes law, a specific directive with respect to this created world.

The Goodness of Law

Is the law good? Ah, here we run into struggles. Many people say that the evils in the world are the greatest obstacle to believing in God.[18] Larson and Witham's survey of scientists and religion quotes Albert Einstein as saying, "in their struggle for the ethical good, teachers of religion must have the stature to give up the doctrine of a personal God."[19]

But it is not quite so simple. We may appeal to a standard of good in order to judge that an existing situation is evil. In doing so, we appeal to a standard beyond the confines of the empirical world. We appeal to a standard, a law. To give up the idea of moral law is to give up the very basis on which criticism of evil depends. Moral law is thus indispensable to atheist argument, but at the same time it presupposes an absolute. This absolute, in order to obligate us and hold us accountable, must be personal. The Bible's answer alone gives clarity here. God's character is the ultimate source of moral law. Man made in the image of God is aware of this law but has

---

[17] On the divine character of God's word, see Vern S. Poythress, *God-Centered Biblical Interpretation* (Phillipsburg, N.J.: Presbyterian & Reformed, 1999), 32-36.

[18] Larson and Witham, "Scientists and Religion," 90-91.

[19] Ibid.

rebelled against it (Rom. 1:32). The existing evils are a consequence of that rebellion. Do not cast moral blame on God but on man.

The goodness of God is displayed most clearly in the *moral* law of God. But for many modern people, influenced by Kant and the subsequent history of ideas, moral law is radically subjectified, and radically separated from physical law or scientific law. In order to engage scientists most directly, we need to return to consider scientific law.

Subtle indications of the goodness of God can be seen in the concept of scientific law. One might put it this way: scientists expect "the laws of nature" to be sometimes subtle, but never perverse. Law does not play tricks, deliberately hiding itself and giving anomalous results simply to confound the researcher. "Nature" plays fair. Or, to put it more deeply, God "plays fair." All scientists, to continue with sanity in their research, must believe that the laws of the universe "play fair" with them. There is a fundamental goodness, as opposed to perversity, in the way in which results arise from scientific investigation.

The Beauty of Law

Scientific laws, especially "deep" laws, are beautiful. Scientists have long sifted through possible hypotheses and models partly on the basis of the criteria of beauty and simplicity. For example, Newton's law of gravitation and Maxwell's laws of electromagnetism are mathematically simple and beautiful. And scientists clearly *expect* new laws, as well as the old ones, to show beauty and simplicity. Why? The beauty of scientific laws shows the beauty of God himself. Though beauty has not been a favorite topic in classical expositions of the doctrine of God, the Bible shows us a God who is profoundly beautiful. He manifests himself in beauty in the design of the tabernacle, the poetry of the Psalms, and the elegance of Christ's parables, as well as the moral beauty of the life of Christ.

The beauty of God himself is reflected in what he has made. We are more accustomed to seeing beauty in particular objects within creation, such as a butterfly, or a lofty mountain, or a flower-covered meadow. But beauty is also displayed in the simple, elegant form of some of the most basic physical laws, like Newton's law for force, $F = ma$, or Einstein's formula relating mass and energy, $E = mc^2$. Why should such elegant laws even exist? Beauty is also displayed in the harmony among different areas of science, and the harmony between mathematics and science that scientists rely on whenever they use a mathematical formula to describe a physical process.

The Rectitude of Law

Another attribute of God is righteousness. God's righteousness is displayed preeminently in the moral law and in the moral rectitude of his judgments, that is, his rewards and punishments based on moral law. But moral law, as we have observed, lies outside the area of scientists' special focus. Does God's rectitude appear in physical law, in scientific law?

The traces are somewhat less obvious, but still present. People can try to disobey physical laws, and when they do they often suffer for it. If one attempts to defy the law of gravity by jumping off a tall building, he will suffer consequences. There is a kind of built-in righteousness in the way in which laws lead to consequences.

In addition, the rectitude of God is closely related to the fitness of his acts. It fits the character of who God is that we should worship him alone (Ex. 20:3). It fits the character of human beings made in the image of God that they should imitate God by keeping the Sabbath (Ex. 20:8-11). Human actions fitly correspond to the actions of God.

In addition, punishments must be fitting. Death is the fitting or matching penalty for murder (Gen. 9:6). "As you have done, it shall be done to you; your deeds shall return on your own head" (Obad. 15). The punishment fits the crime. There is a symmetrical match between the nature of the crime and the punishment that fits it.[20] In the arena of physical law we do not deal with crimes and punishments. But rectitude expresses itself in symmetries, in orderliness, in a "fittingness" to the character of law. Symmetries occur in fascinating ways throughout the natural world. Fundamental laws of physics have a deep connection with fundamental symmetries of space, time, charge, and parity. This "fitness" that scientists expect of law is perhaps closely related to beauty. God's attributes are involved in one another and imply one another, so beauty and righteousness are closely related. It is the same with the area of physical law. Laws are both beautiful and "fitting," demonstrating rectitude.

Law as Trinitarian

Does scientific law specifically reflect the *Trinitarian* character of God? Philosophers have sometimes maintained that one can infer the existence of God, but not the Trinitarian character of God, on the basis of the world around us. Romans 1:18-21 indicates that unbelievers know God, but how

---

[20] See the extended discussion of just punishment in Vern S. Poythress, *The Shadow of Christ in the Law of Moses* (Phillipsburg, N.J.: Presbyterian & Reformed, 1995), 119-249.

much do they know? I am not addressing this difficult question,[21] but rather reflecting on what we can discern about the world once we have absorbed biblical teaching about God.

Scientific law is a form of the word of God. So it reflects the Trinitarian statement in John 1:1, which identifies the second person of the Trinity as the eternal Word. In John, God the Father is the speaker of the Word, and God the Son is the Word who is spoken. John 1 does not explicitly mention the Holy Spirit. But earlier Scriptures associate the Spirit with the "breath" of God that carries the word out. "By the *word* of the LORD the heavens were made, and by the *breath* of his mouth all their host" (Ps. 33:6). The Hebrew word here for *breath* is *ruach,* the same word that is regularly used for the Holy Spirit. Indeed, the designation of the third person of the Trinity as "Spirit" (Hebrew *ruach*) already suggests the association that becomes more explicit in Psalm 33:6. Similarly, Ezekiel 37 plays with three different meanings of the Hebrew word *ruach,* namely "breath" (37:5, 10), "winds" (37:9), and "Spirit" (37:14). The vision in Ezekiel 37 clearly represents the Holy Spirit as like the breath of God coming into human beings to give them life. Thus all three persons of the Trinity are present in distinct ways when God speaks his Word. The three persons are therefore all present in scientific law, which is a form of the word of God.

We can come at the issue another way. Dorothy Sayers acutely observes that the experience of a human author writing a book contains profound analogies to the Trinitarian character of God.[22] An author's act of creation in writing imitates the action of God in creating the world. God creates according to his Trinitarian nature. A human author creates with an Idea, Energy, and Power, corresponding mysteriously to the involvement of the three persons in creation. Without tracing Sayers's reflections in detail, we may observe that the act of God in creation does involve all three persons. God the Father is the originator. God the Son, as the eternal Word (John 1:1-3), is involved in the words of command that issue from God ("Let there be light," Gen. 1:3). God the Spirit hovers over the waters (Gen. 1:2). Psalm 104:30 says that "when you send forth your Spirit, they [animals] are created." Moreover, the creation of Adam involves an inbreathing by God that alludes to the presence of the Spirit (Gen. 2:7). Though the relation among the persons of the Trinity is deeply mysterious, and though all persons are involved in all the actions of

---

[21] But see the following chapter, where we at least deal with some of the related issues on the relation of different sources for human knowledge.

[22] Dorothy Sayers, *The Mind of the Maker* (New York: Harcourt, Brace, 1941), especially 33-46.

God toward the world, one can distinguish different aspects of action belonging preeminently to the different persons.

Scientific law stems from the creative activity of God, the "Author" of creation. The activity of all three persons is therefore implicit in the very concept of scientific law. First, law involves a rationality that implies the coherence of a plan. This corresponds to Sayers's term "Idea," representing the plan of the Father. Second, law involves an articulation, a specification, an expression of the plan, with respect to all the particulars of a world. This corresponds to Sayers's term "Energy" or "Activity," representing the Word, who is the expression of the Father. Third, law involves holding things responsible to law, a concrete application to creatures, bringing them to respond to the law as willed. This corresponds to Sayers's term "Power," representing the Spirit.[23]

We may see a reflection of the Trinity in still another way by using the categories that have already been developed in Trinitarian theological meditations on the character of God and his word. According to Trinitarian thinking, the unity and diversity in the world reflect the original unity and diversity in God. First, God is one God. He has a unified plan for the world. The universality of scientific law reflects this unity. God is also three persons, the Father, the Son, and the Holy Spirit. This diversity in the being of God is then reflected in the diversity in the created world.[24] The many instances to which a law applies express this diversity. Moreover, unity and diversity are expressed in another way. The unity of God's plan has a close relation to the Father, the first person of the Trinity, who is the origin of this plan. The Son, in becoming incarnate, expresses the particularity of manifestation in time and space. He is, as it were, an instantiation of God. Thus he is analogous in his incarnation to the fact that the universal law expresses itself in particular instances.

GOD SHOWING HIMSELF

These relations are suggestive, but we need not develop the thinking further at this point. It suffices to observe that, in reality, what people call "scientific law" is divine. We are speaking of God himself and his revelation of himself through his governance of the world. Scientists must believe in scientific law in order to carry out their work. When we analyze what this scientific law

---

[23] See also John Milbank, *The Word Made Strange: Theology, Language, Culture* (Oxford: Blackwell, 1997), on the Trinitarian roots of communication.

[24] See Cornelius Van Til, *The Defense of the Faith*, 2nd ed., revised and abridged (Philadelphia: Presbyterian & Reformed, 1963), 25-26.

really is, we find that scientists are constantly confronted with God himself, the Trinitarian God, and are constantly depending on who he is and what he does in conformity with his divine nature. In thinking about law, scientists are thinking God's thoughts after him.[25]

BUT DO SCIENTISTS BELIEVE?

But do scientists really believe all this? They do and they do not. The situation has already been described in the Bible:

> For what can be known about God is plain to them, because God has shown it to them. For his invisible attributes, namely, his eternal power and divine nature, have been clearly perceived, ever since the creation of the world, in the things that have been made. So they are without excuse (Rom. 1:19-20).

> The heavens declare the glory of God,
>   and the sky above proclaims his handiwork.
> Day to day pours out speech,
>   and night to night reveals knowledge (Ps. 19:1-2).

They know God. They rely on him. But because this knowledge is morally and spiritually painful, they also suppress and distort it:

> . . . for although they knew God, they did not honor him as God or give thanks to him, but they became futile in their thinking, and their foolish hearts were darkened. Claiming to be wise, they became fools, and exchanged the glory of the immortal God for images resembling mortal man and birds and animals and creeping things (Rom. 1:21-23).

Modern people may no longer make idols in the form of physical images, but their very idea of "scientific law" is an idolatrous twisting of their knowledge of God. They conceal from themselves the fact that this "law" is personal and that they are responsible to *him*. Or they substitute the word "Nature," personifying her as they talk glowingly of the works of "Mother Nature." But they evade what they know of the transcendence of God over nature.

Even in their rebellion, people continue to depend on God being there. They show *in action* that they continue to believe in God. Cornelius Van Til

---

[25] See ibid., 31-50.

compares it to an incident he saw on a train, where a small girl sitting on her grandfather's lap slapped him in the face.[26] The rebel must depend on God, and must be "sitting on his lap," even to be able to engage in rebellion.

DO WE CHRISTIANS BELIEVE?

The fault, I suspect, is not entirely on the side of unbelievers. The fault also occurs among Christians. Christians have sometimes adopted an unbiblical concept of God that moves him one step out of the way of our ordinary affairs. We ourselves may think of "scientific law" or "natural law" as a kind of cosmic mechanism or impersonal clockwork that runs the world most of the time, while God is on vacation. God comes and acts only rarely through miracle. But this is not biblical. "You cause the grass to grow for the livestock" (Ps. 104:14). "He gives snow like wool" (Ps. 147:16).[27] Let us not forget it. If we ourselves recovered a robust doctrine of God's involvement in daily caring for his world *in detail,* we would find ourselves in a much better position to dialogue with atheist scientists who rely on that same care.

PRINCIPLES FOR WITNESS

In order to use this situation as a starting point for witness, we need to bear in mind several principles.

First, the observation that God underlies the concept of scientific law does not have the same shape as the traditional theistic proofs—at least as they are often understood. We are not trying to lead people to come to know a God who is completely new to them. Rather, we show that scientists *already know* God as an aspect of their human experience in the scientific enterprise. This places the focus not on intellectual debate but on being a full human being within the context of scientific research.[28]

Second, scientists deny God within the very same context in which they depend on him. The denial of God springs ultimately not from intellectual flaws or from failure to see all the way to the conclusion of a chain of syllogistic reasoning, but from spiritual failure. We are rebels against God, and we will not serve him. Consequently, we suffer under his wrath (Rom. 1:18),

---

[26] I do not know the location of this story in print. For rebels' dependence on God, see Cornelius Van Til, *The Defense of the Faith,* 2nd ed. (Philadelphia: Presbyterian & Reformed, 1963); and the exposition by John M. Frame, *Apologetics to the Glory of God: An Introduction* (Phillipsburg, N.J.: Presbyterian & Reformed, 1994).

[27] See also the discussion in Poythress, "Science as Allegory."

[28] Much valuable insight into the foundations of apologetics is to be found in the tradition of transcendental apologetics founded by Cornelius Van Til. See Van Til, *Defense of the Faith*; and Frame, *Apologetics to the Glory of God.*

which has intellectual as well as spiritual and moral effects. Those who rebel against God are "fools," according to Romans 1:22.

Third, it is humiliating to intellectuals to be exposed as fools, and it is further humiliating, even psychologically unbearable, to be exposed as guilty of rebellion against the goodness of God. We can expect our hearers to fight with a tremendous outpouring of intellectual and spiritual energy against so unbearable an outcome.

Fourth, the gospel itself, with its message of forgiveness and reconciliation through Christ, offers the only remedy that can truly end this fight against God. But it brings with it the ultimate humiliation: that my restoration comes entirely from God, from outside me—in spite of, rather than because of, my vaunted abilities. To climax it all, so wicked was I that it took the price of the death of the Son of God to accomplish my rescue.

Fifth, approaching scientists in this way constitutes spiritual warfare. Unbelievers and idolaters are captives to Satanic deceit (1 Cor. 10:20; 2 Thess. 2:9-12; 2 Tim. 2:25-26; Eph. 4:17-24; Rev. 12:9). They do not get free from Satan's captivity unless God gives them release (2 Tim. 2:25-26). We must pray to God and rely on God's power rather than the ingenuity of human argument and eloquence of persuasion (1 Cor. 2:1-5; 2 Cor. 10:3-5).

Sixth, we come into this encounter as fellow sinners. Christians too have become massively guilty by being captive to the idolatry in which scientific law is regarded as impersonal. Within this captivity we take for granted the benefits and beauties of science for which we should be filled with gratitude and praise to God.

Does an approach to witnessing based on these principles work itself out differently from many of the approaches that attempt to address intellectuals? To me it appears so.

BROADENING OUR AUDIENCE

So far we have focused on scientists as potential recipients of Christian witness. But what implications might we draw for dealing with the broader public?

In a technologized world, every inhabitant depends on the products of science and technology. And people trust some of the tools of technology enough to rely on them. They trust them not only for their information about the world at large but also for the very preservation of their lives. Not everyone travels on airplanes, but most people do travel from time to time in high-speed automobiles, and most buy food from supermarkets that represent the endpoint of a long chain of technological steps in food production and distribution.

What then protects us from disaster? The biblical witness is clear: it is God. We behold day by day God's providential rule. God does "good by giving you rains from heaven and fruitful seasons, satisfying your hearts with food and gladness" (Acts 14:17). The marvels of growing plants manifest the faithfulness of God as he speaks his word to plants. These long-standing marvels are now supplemented by the marvels of chemistry in making fertilizer and pesticides; the marvels of soil science informing and advising the farmers; the marvels of biology in breeding and genetically modifying plants; the marvels of technological complexity in harvesters, processing plants, shippers, and packagers.

Scientists necessarily work daily with the eternality and omnipotence of scientific law right before their eyes. But the rest of us see the faithfulness of God manifested more prosaically in the dependability of the technological apparatus that spins off from science. We assume the reliability of our food sources; we believe the food will grow every year; and we believe that our food will nourish rather than poison us.

RETURNING TO THE ATTRIBUTES OF GOD

To some extent, then, the attributes of scientific law are visible even to ordinary people who enjoy the benefits of technology. Ordinary people believe that technological products will work in the same way at any time and in any place. Thus, in principle they believe in the constancy of technology. And they believe by implication that the laws in back of technology are constant. Of course, an average person may or may not be informed about the details of the scientific laws in back of a particular technological product. But even if he does not know the laws in detail, he believes that even in detail they remain constant. This constancy guarantees the constancy of the functioning of the technological product governed by the laws. The toaster continues to toast bread because the electricity continues to produce heat according to constant laws. The constancy of law in both time and space points to the eternality and omnipresence of the laws.

Of course, the common person may be less aware of the implication of eternality and omnipresence. He is not a theoretician testing the outer limits, theorizing about gamma ray bursts in distant galaxies or about nuclear reactions in the sun. He is much more down to earth. He cares for and believes in the constancy of laws within the practical scope of his personal world.

But in fact a similar observation can be made about the traditional idea of the eternality and omnipresence of God. The teachings of the Bible focus primarily on the common person's world within his limited vision of time and space. The Bible asks people not primarily to believe in eternality and omnipresence as theoretical abstractions, but to trust God in practice in the conduct of their daily lives. The attributes of eternality and omnipresence are theoretical generalizations from this practical experience. Hence, the common person in the biblical world corresponds to the common person today who believes that his toaster will toast bread; the theoretical theologian who speaks of eternality and omnipresence corresponds to the theoretical scientist who speaks of laws in their perfect generality.

God's providence affects us in both spheres. Thus the divine attributes of scientific law offer a platform for witness to both ordinary people and scientists.

2

THE ROLE OF THE BIBLE

Now we need to consider the relation between two different sources of truth, the Bible and science.

As we saw in chapter 1, science can be corrupted by idolatry. Scientists rely on God when they go about their business. At the same time, many scientists think of the law as impersonal. Thus they replace the personal God described in the Bible with an impersonal substitute, as described in Romans 1:18-31. They are then creating an idol according to their imaginations.

The Bible pointedly addresses the temptations to idolatry. It thus addresses the practice of modern science. In what other ways might the Bible be pertinent to science? And in what ways is science pertinent to understanding the Bible? Might modern science also criticize the Bible? Certainly some modern people attempt to criticize the Bible, and they may try to appeal to science as their basis for criticism. But are such moves legitimate? The person who takes his stand wholly in the modern world might suppose that such criticism is obviously legitimate. But the person who takes his stand by being instructed by the Bible goes the other way, and raises critical questions about the modern world.

So what does the Bible say about the relationship? The Bible's teaching about revelation from God gives us a framework for reflection. Roughly speaking, *revelation* is "something revealed by God to man."[1] Within that broad category, theologians speak of *general revelation* and *special revelation*. *General revelation* is what God shows to all human beings through his actions of creation and providence. *Special revelation* is what God shows through redemptive instruction in the Bible.[2]

---

[1] *Webster's Ninth New Collegiate Dictionary* (Springfield, Mass.: Merriam-Webster, 1987).
[2] See Louis Berkhof, *Systematic Theology,* 4th ed. (Grand Rapids, Mich.: Eerdmans, 1941), 37. Actually, "special revelation" as usually understood is broader. It includes verbal communication from God that has not been recorded in Scripture, such as words from Jesus' earthly teaching ministry that did not happen to be included in any of the four Gospels. And it includes special redemptive acts of God, such as the miracles at the time of the exodus from Egypt and during Jesus' earthly life.

Psalm 19 exhibits both kinds of revelation:

[1] The heavens declare the glory of God,
   and the sky above proclaims his handiwork.
[2] Day to day pours out speech,
   and night to night reveals knowledge.
[3] There is no speech, nor are there words,
   whose voice is not heard.
[4] Their voice goes out through all the earth,
   and their words to the end of the world.
In them he has set a tent for the sun,
   [5] which comes out like a bridegroom leaving his chamber,
   and, like a strong man, runs its course with joy.
[6] Its rising is from the end of the heavens,
   and its circuit to the end of them,
and there is nothing hidden from its heat.

[7] The law of the LORD is perfect,
   reviving the soul;
the testimony of the LORD is sure,
   making wise the simple;
[8] the precepts of the LORD are right,
   rejoicing the heart;
the commandment of the LORD is pure,
   enlightening the eyes;
[9] the fear of the LORD is clean,
   enduring forever;
the rules of the LORD are true,
   and righteous altogether.

It is quite difficult to give a definition that precisely distinguishes special from general revelation. One might try saying that special revelation is *redemptive* revelation. But God's speech to Adam before the fall (Gen. 1:28-30; 2:16-17), which precedes the beginning of redemption, is customarily classified as special revelation. And in a loose sense, all of God's works subsequent to the fall are "redemptive," since indirectly they all serve to promote the goal of ultimate cosmic redemption.

Consider another route. One might try saying that general revelation is ordinary, while special revelation is extraordinary. But the difference between the ordinary and the extraordinary is a matter of degree, so such a definition fails to give us a sharp distinction.

Or one may take one's clue from the term "general," and define general revelation as that revelation that comes equally to all people at all times. This attempt gets close to a solution, through its emphasis on the fact that verbal special revelation initially comes to particular people at particular times and places—never just to the world in general. But it overlooks the nonrepeatability of history. Any particular providential act of God, such as bringing a particular storm or a particular blessing of health to a particular person, must count as "special," which is much more inclusive than what theologians want.

For our purposes, we need not possess a precise distinction. In practice, we are concerned with the relation between Scripture and knowledge derived from nature.

[10] More to be desired are they than gold,
   even much fine gold,
sweeter also than honey
   and drippings of the honeycomb.
[11] Moreover, by them is your servant warned;
   in keeping them there is great reward.

[12] Who can discern his errors?
   Declare me innocent from hidden faults.
[13] Keep back your servant also from presumptuous sins;
   let them not have dominion over me!
Then I shall be blameless,
   and innocent of great transgression.

[14] Let the words of my mouth and the meditation of my heart
   be acceptable in your sight,
   O LORD, my rock and my redeemer.

Verses 1-6 show God's revelation through creation and providence. Verses 7-11 focus on his revelation through his law given to Israel. The first of these, general revelation, clearly has a relation to science and its study of the external world. The second, special revelation, has a close relation to the Bible and to the study of the Bible in theology. So the theology of revelation found in the Bible gives us a way of seeing the relation between science and the Bible.

But now we must be careful. Much depends on our conception of revelation. For example, Immanuel Kant argued that phenomena in this world could never directly reveal God, but that human beings find that the idea of God is indirectly necessary as a basis for practical morality. According to Kant God does not "reveal" himself, except in a redefined way. Kant's ideas have exerted tremendous influence in the last 200 years, far beyond those who are directly familiar with his writings. Many ordinary people have picked up from the surrounding culture the firm conviction that the world cannot possibly be as I am describing it. According to their thinking, "our modern world" has shown us that God, if he exists, is inaccessible, and that revelation is impossible.

But growing historical distance from Kant's time, and especially the shift toward postmodernism, has gradually made it more evident that Kant's starting assumptions about the world already presupposed what needed to be demonstrated. Consider a specific example. According to

Exodus 19 and 20 God spoke at Mount Sinai in an audible voice to the people of Israel, and delivered the Ten Commandments (see especially Ex. 20:1, 18-19; Deut. 5:22-27). Because I believe the Bible, I believe that these events actually happened as described. But right now we have a different question, namely whether it is even *possible* for God to act in such a way. Kant's philosophy says no. According to Kant's view, phenomena like thunder and a voice from a mountain are still phenomena of this world, and are the object for scientific investigation, not direct sources of religious truth.

But to make this claim, Kant has to know a great deal about the nature of the world and the nature of God. He has to know not only whether God exists, but how he relates to the world. He has to know whether or not God will choose to make a speech from heaven such as Exodus 20 describes. Kant also has to know about the nature and limitations of human reason, and more broadly the nature of human capacities to know God. Moreover, he assumes that the functioning of the human mind at the present time is normal, rather than being bent by sin and rebellion against God. Thus he has to smuggle in an ontology, a theory of what kind of world we are in. And, paradoxically, this smuggled-in ontology exceeds the bounds of what he himself says that human reason is capable of!

We also need to exercise care in our understanding of the relation between the two kinds of revelation, general revelation and special revelation. For example, some people have argued that the Bible answers questions about "who?" and "why?" while science answers questions about "how?", and that because these are radically different types of questions, they can never really be in conflict. While this position has its attractions, it is too simple.[3] To be sure, the Bible does not directly teach details concerning chemistry. But it does speak about the physical world. And by speaking directly concerning general revelation, it provides a framework for understanding the things about which science occupies itself.

---

[3] Note the evaluation by John Jefferson Davis:
   While such "two realms" approaches may have the apparent advantage of avoiding conflicts between science and religion, they have the grave defect of drawing the lines too sharply between these two areas of human experience. While the biblical writers and modern scientists clearly have markedly differing languages, methods and purposes, they all are making references to a shared physical world existing outside the subjectivity of the speaker (Davis, *The Frontiers of Science and Faith: Examining Questions from the Big Bang to the End of the Universe* [Downers Grove, Ill.: InterVarsity Press, 2002], 13; see also Del Ratzsch, *Science and Its Limits: The Natural Sciences in Christian Perspective* [Downers Grove, Ill.: InterVarsity Press, 2000], 141-159).

REVELATION AND DIVINE SPEECH

First, we need to consider the term *revelation,* which has both strengths and liabilities. Though the word *revelation* has become a common technical term in academic theology, analogous terminology is not as common in the Bible itself. Psalm 19, where we started our thinking about general revelation and special revelation, uses the word "reveal" in verse 2 (ESV). But most of the Psalm talks about verbal communication. The "law of the LORD" (verse 7), "the testimony of the LORD" (verse 7), and "the precepts of the LORD" (verse 8) designate verbal communication from God. The subsequent verses continue with this kind of description of special revelation. Of course, the Bible is verbal communication, so this kind of description fits the second half of the Psalm. But the language of verbal communication extends to the first part of the Psalm as well: "The heavens *declare* the glory of God, and the sky above *proclaims* his handiwork" (verse 1). Even the word "reveal" in verse 2 translates the Hebrew verb *xwh,* which means "tell, declare,"[4] a meaning that seems to indicate an association with verbal communication.

Other parts of the Bible confirm this pattern. In Genesis 1, God creates by *speaking.* "And God said, 'Let there be light,' and there was light" (Gen. 1:3). Psalm 33:6 sums up the pattern: "By the *word* of the LORD the heavens were made, and by the *breath of his mouth* all their host." Providential events take place through God's word of command:[5]

He sends out his *command* to the earth;
 his *word* runs swiftly.
He gives snow like wool;
 he scatters hoarfrost like ashes. . . .
He sends out his *word,* and melts them (Psalm 147:15-16, 18).

When we speak of "the word of God," we may think right away of the Bible. And the Bible is the word of God. But the Bible itself indicates that God speaks words concerning creation and providence, and not all of those words

---

[4] Francis Brown, S. R. Driver, and C. A. Briggs, eds., *A Hebrew and English Lexicon of the Old Testament* (Oxford: Oxford University Press, 1953).

[5] Someone may object that this kind of description is only metaphorical and anthropomorphic. I cannot in this book discuss at length the kind of approach that dismisses or recategorizes biblical truth by appealing to the alleged limitations of human language. (But see John M. Frame, "God and Biblical Language," in John Warwick Montgomery, ed., *God's Inerrant Word* [Minneapolis: Bethany, 1974], 159-177; and Vern S. Poythress, "Adequacy of Language and Accommodation," in Earl D. Radmacher and Robert D. Preus, eds., *Hermeneutics, Inerrancy, and the Bible* [Grand Rapids, Mich.: Zondervan, 1984], 351-376.) Suffice it to say that the objector must have virtually a God's-eye view in order to know the nature of metaphor. We have no more ultimate description of God's ways than what he gives us in language. These descriptions are true precisely in showing us the analogies between human and divine speech.

are recorded in detail in the Bible.[6] God's words comprehensively govern the world, as Lamentations 3:37-38 indicates:

> Who has spoken and it came to pass,
>   unless the Lord has *commanded* it?
> Is it not from the *mouth* of the Most High
>   that good and bad come?

Instead of general and special revelation, we could just as well talk about general and special *speech* from God.[7]

What difference does this alternative terminology make? In one sense, it makes little difference. The reality is the same, and over the centuries theologians have customarily used the word *revelation* as the general word. The word *revelation* even has one advantage: it is vaguer and broader. It can then remind us that when God comes to meet with man, he may speak, but he may *also* give visual or other evidences of his presence, as with the thunder and lightning and cloud at Mount Sinai (Ex. 19). *Revelation,* as a general word, encompasses all the visual and auditory phenomena, as well as the voice of God speaking the Ten Commandments (Ex. 20:1-17).

If we like, we may then speak of *verbal revelation* and *nonverbal revelation.* *Verbal revelation* is what God speaks to mankind or to a part of mankind in human language. *Nonverbal revelation* is what God displays to human beings through means other than human language.[8] But these two cannot be rigidly separated. The experience at Mount Sinai shows that the two kinds of revelation typically complement one another, and each forms a context that helps us to understand the other. The verbal communication helps us to understand who God is, and who it is who is showing himself in the spectacular thunder and lightning. The thunder and lightning helps to show the authority and power of the God who is speaking the Ten Commandments. If there had been no spectacular display, and people had simply heard a quite ordinary, human-sounding voice, the doubters might

---

[6] Genesis 1:3 and Psalm 147:15-18 obviously give us a sample; but from this sample we may infer a much larger whole.

[7] Some readers may feel that my focus on God speaking is one-sided. In a sense it is. I am using God's speaking as a *perspective* on the whole of God's activity. We can do this profitably, as long as we remember that the Bible offers us other, complementary perspectives as well. Rightly understood, the insights attained through one perspective enrich but do not contradict what comes into view from a second perspective. See the further discussion in Vern S. Poythress, *Symphonic Theology: The Validity of Multiple Perspectives in Theology* (Grand Rapids, Mich.: Zondervan, 1987). We need also to distinguish God's word governing the heavens (as in Genesis 1) from what the heavens themselves "declare" in Psalm 19:1. God's word is the more fundamental reality behind the messages that come from things he has created.

[8] Technically, we should add to our list verbal and nonverbal revelation to angels.

simply have scoffed and said that it was Moses' voice, and that he had made everything up himself.

We infer from other passages of the Bible that God's word of command produced the thunder and lightning and cloud. Hence the entirety is an effect of God's words. But only some of it, namely the voice of God speaking the Ten Commandments, is explicitly verbal in character in the form in which it comes to the people at the foot of the mountain.

And now we come to one of the limitations of the word *revelation*. It fails to indicate how much the Bible emphasizes the speech of God, not only when discussing verbal communication to mankind but when talking about events in creation and providence. Moreover, the word *revelation* suggests *revelation to human beings*. One of the common dictionary definitions is "something revealed by God to man."[9] It is limited to human beings. But the word of God directing creation and providence is not so limited. God through his words of command governs the entire world, not just human beings. For example, the words "Let there be light" appear in Genesis 1:3. As part of Genesis 1:3, they are written down for Israel and for us. But Genesis 1:3 describes an earlier time, before human beings even existed, when God originally gave the command. At that time he did not address human beings— since there were none. So are those words *revelation*? If they are, to whom are they a revelation? The question is inappropriate, because our modern word *revelation* was not designed to illumine this case.

Second, the word *revelation* suggests to some only the narrow category of *miraculous* revelation, revelation of truths that would otherwise be totally unknowable. For example, by prophesying the coming of the Messiah, Isaiah 9:6-7 speaks of future events about which human beings could not otherwise know. Isaiah's prediction is "revelation" in the narrow sense. But the Bible also speaks about many facts that can be known through other sources. Second Kings 13:12 refers to records "written in the Book of the Chronicles of the Kings of Israel" (not to be confused with our books of 1–2 Chronicles, which focus on Judah). These "Chronicles" were probably semiofficial, noninspired records compiled by scribes who served under the kings in those times. One could learn from these "secular" sources some of the same information that one finds in 1–2 Kings. When such common information occurs in 1–2 Kings, do we call it *revelation*? I believe we should, in order to emphasize that *God* says it.

Or again, the Gospels record events that eyewitnesses observed through

---

[9] *Webster's Ninth New Collegiate Dictionary.*

ordinary means. So are the Gospels "revelation" at such points? Or does "revelation" cover only predictions about the second coming and other such humanly inaccessible information? The ambiguity about the word "revelation" is potentially troublesome. By contrast, if we talk about "God's speech," it is perfectly clear that God is free to speak either about the future, which is unknown, or about the past, which often can be known through other means. The authority of what God says remains the same. The Gospels are the word of God, and saying so clears up the potential ambiguity about their authority.

The word *revelation* also creates a problem when people build into it the idea that it must succeed in convincing its addressee. "Revelation," some people claim, "is genuinely revelation only if it reveals, that is, only if someone actually receives the truth that it is sent to convey." According to this reasoning, the Bible is not "revelation" while it sits on the bookshelf, but only when someone picks it up and reads it. And even when someone reads it, it is *still* not revelation until they understand it. If they misunderstand it, it is not revelation. And when they understand it, the real "revelation" is actually the personal process of coming to understand. So by this reasoning the Bible is simply, at some moments, a channel by which a process of revelation takes place. Even at the moment of coming to understand, the process is "revelation" but the message on the page is not. So might run some neo-orthodox thinking about revelation.

When we shift to talking about God speaking, we cut off this subterfuge. Jesus says, "The one who rejects me and does not receive my words has a judge; the word that I have spoken will judge him on the last day" (John 12:48). Jesus does not use here the terminology of "revelation," but the point is all the clearer. "The one who . . . does not receive my words" has not received the truth. The words of Jesus have not "got through" to him. He has not had something "revealed" to him by a proper, grateful reception. There is no "revelation" in that peculiar sense of the term. And yet, "The word that I have spoken will judge him on the last day." The word remains there, and remains as a standard by which he is judged, whether he received it or not. The obvious advantage of talking about God's speech, rather than "revelation," is that it becomes clear that God speaks even when no human being is listening properly. God's speaking does not become less than what it is just because a human being stops his ears. If fact, God's word retains power to judge the human being, for having stopped his ears and not received the words.

We cannot here engage in extensive interactions with neo-orthodox understandings of Scripture. Neo-orthodoxy appeals to the Bible in its support, but in the end fails to make its case.[10] Without unnecessarily repeating the arguments of those who go before me, I hold to the classical, orthodox understanding of the Bible, which asserts that the Bible is the word of God, while it is on the shelf as well as while it is being read. This assertion does not mean that the physical elements, the paper and the ink, are the word of God; rather the message recorded in paper and ink is the word of God.[11] Interpreting the Bible may present many challenges, and as human beings we may make mistakes, either innocently or (more often) through sinful biases. The word of God, as known by the Holy Spirit, remains to judge our failures.

THE WORD OF GOD

The Bible, then, is the word of God. It comes written in human language, and written with the primary purpose of instructing us, guiding us, rebuking and correcting us, in order that we may grow and serve God acceptably. "All Scripture is breathed out by God and profitable for teaching, for reproof, for correction, and for training in righteousness, that the man of God may be competent, equipped for every good work" (2 Tim. 3:16-17).

But, as we have seen, the Bible does not contain all the words that God has spoken or will speak. Jesus spoke many words while he was on earth. They were all the word of God, but they were not all recorded in the Bible (John 21:25). In addition, God speaks words that are not addressed primarily to human beings, such as the words directing the melting of snow and frost in Psalm 147:18. We may call these the words of God controlling the world.

All speech from God harmonizes with his character. God is righteous, holy, pure, and truthful. Consequently, his speech is righteous, holy, pure, and truthful (cf. Ps. 12:6; Prov. 30:5). These characteristics belong *both* to the words governing creation and providence *and* to the words spoken to human beings in the Bible. Because God is consistent with himself, there is no disharmony between the two kinds of words.

DEALING WITH APPARENT DISCREPANCIES

So where does that leave us? "That is all very well," someone may say, "but what about all the discrepancies between modern science and the Bible?" If

---

[10] For a fuller exposition of biblical teaching about God's speech, and critical interaction with neo-orthodox positions, see Frame, "God and Biblical Language"; and John M. Frame, "Scripture Speaks for Itself," in *God's Inerrant Word*, 178-200.

[11] For further explanation of my views, the reader may consult Vern S. Poythress, *God-Centered Biblical Interpretation* (Phillipsburg, N.J.: Presbyterian & Reformed, 1999).

God's words harmonize, these must be only *apparent* discrepancies. Trusting in God means trusting that he knows better than we do, even when there appear to be problems. God told Abraham to sacrifice his son Isaac, even though he earlier had promised Abraham that Isaac was the offspring through whom God would fulfill his purposes. It seemed like a contradiction, but Abraham did not give up his faith (Heb. 11:17-19).

Trusting in God does not mean denying that there are difficulties, or completely ignoring them. It means dealing with them from within the framework of guidance and truth that God has provided for us.

Some relief comes from reckoning with who we are as human beings. According to Genesis 1:26-28, we are made in the image of God. As such, we have hope of understanding at least in part the mind of God, and understanding what he says. We endeavor to understand what he says in the Bible. And we endeavor to understand what he says in governing the world in creation and providence. But both kinds of understanding are indeed partial and subject to correction. We are finite and sinful. Our finiteness implies that our grasp of God's ways is incomplete. Our sinfulness implies that we distort the truth in our favor. We corrupt the knowledge of God into idolatry; we make ourselves into tin gods who, like Adam and Eve, want to judge God and make up our own minds, independent of his instruction, as to whether he is true or whether we will do some forbidden thing (see Gen. 3:1-6).

Finiteness and sinfulness operate both in the interpretation of the Bible and in the interpretation of the world that scientists study. Within this life, interpretation of the Bible is always partial and incomplete, and sometimes plain wrong because of rebellious distortion. People's desires drive them to find in the Bible what they have decided must be there, or what they fervently hope will confirm their wishes.

The same is true in the work of science. Interpretation of the world, and exploration in scientific theory development, never comes to an end. Scientific theories are in principle subject to revision. And sometimes people's desires drive them to find explanations that harmonize with their desires and with a worldview that reinforces those desires. Scientists, like all of us, are sinners who hope to confirm their desires.

As we have seen, science is not a "neutral" endeavor but presupposes scientific law, which presupposes God. People either serve God or serve a counterfeit god. The kind of god that they serve influences their expectations concerning the kind of laws that they think they will find. Thus the entrance of bias is not merely an occasional, accidental error, but a pervasive problem. It is as pervasive as sin in the heart.

So when we find discrepancies between the Bible and science, we look for where we went astray. Somewhere someone has misinterpreted—whether misinterpreting Scripture, or misinterpreting the world of scientific study, or both! The task of dealing with discrepancies may not be easy, because we do not know beforehand where the mistakes entered. Does the mistake occur simply in ignoring counterevidence, or in ignoring alternative readings of the evidence, or in ignoring alternative explanations, or simply in drifting along within an atmosphere whose materialistic assumptions have excluded *a priori* some alternatives?

To some degree the same problems confront us even within a single narrower arena of research. In the Bible, the teachings of one verse sometimes appear to contradict the teachings of another. Such cases deserve patient, individual treatment, because we do not know at first what has gone wrong in our understanding. Likewise, sometimes theories in science do not completely harmonize with one another. Einstein realized that Maxwell's equations for electromagnetism did not harmonize with Newtonian mechanics. His examination of the discrepancy led to a revision of Newton's theory. Right now (as of 2006), quantum field theory does not harmonize with general relativity, because quantum field theory requires a fixed structure of space and time, whereas general relativity requires continuous changes in the structure of space and time influenced by matter and energy. No one yet knows for sure how to resolve the discrepancy in a thoroughly satisfactory way. But physicists do not give up believing that the laws of physics are self-consistent and harmonious in principle.

The key to an insightful resolution of discrepancies may crop up anywhere. It could lie in the details of evidence. It could lie in a subtle or radical revision of some unexamined assumption. It could lie in some new theory superseding the old. It could lie in a worldview that distorts one's understanding. It could lie in the joint effects of more than one area.

In the case of apparent discrepancies between the Bible and science, we must therefore be ready to reexamine both our thinking about the Bible and our thinking about science. We must not assume too quickly that the error lies in one particular direction. In the modern world, we find people who are always ready to assume that science is right and the Bible is wrong. Or, contrariwise, others assume that the Bible is always right and modern science is always wrong.

But the Bible *is* always right, and should be trusted on that account. Likewise, God's word concerning providence is always right and trustworthy. But modern science, as a *human* interpretation of God's providence, may make mistakes. Our *interpretation* of providence may need revision. And our *interpretation* of the Bible may need revision.

Galileo's opponents claimed that he must be wrong about the movement of the sun and the earth, because, they alleged, the Bible clearly taught that the earth was immovable. Actually, the opponents were quite concerned for preserving Aristotelian philosophy, and this as much as anything needed critical reexamination.[12] But it would also be appropriate to reexamine the verses in the Bible, to see whether they really teach what they are assumed to teach. In this case, a reexamination of biblical passages about the earth's immovability shows that they address us in terms of ordinary living, not esoteric scientific theory. In ordinary life and experience, the earth does remain fixed underfoot as we walk around on it![13] Reading the Bible as a technical claim about scientific theory was misreading it.

ONTOLOGICAL PRIORITY IN GOD'S WORD OF PROVIDENCE

Do we say, then, that in case of discrepancies we accord equal weight to the Bible and to science? No, not so fast. We ought not to treat the two areas as symmetrical.

In one sense the word of God governing creation and providence is more fundamental, in that it comes prior to the special words in the Bible and forms the indispensable environment in which the Bible makes sense. First God, through his word of command, creates the world and creates man in it. Only then does he address special verbal communication to Adam and his posterity. Moreover, if I am to read the Bible, I myself must first come into existence, by the power of God's providential word.

His providential word must sustain me, and must sustain my growth in learning the English language (or some other language). God also sustains the physical aspects of the book that I am reading, and the functioning of the eyes with which I am reading. We might say that in such ways God's word of providence forms the *ontological* and *epistemological* foundation for the coming of his word in Scripture.

---

[12] See the discussion in Charles Hummel, *The Galileo Connection: Resolving Conflicts Between Science and the Bible* (Downers Grove, Ill.: InterVarsity Press, 1986); and Richard J. Blackwell, *Galileo, Bellarmine, and the Bible* (Notre Dame, Ind.: University of Notre Dame Press, 1991).

[13] See Vern S. Poythress and Wayne A. Grudem, *The Gender-Neutral Bible Controversy* (Nashville: Broadman & Holman, 2000), 177-179; see also the larger discussion of "phenomenal language" in Bernard Ramm, *The Christian View of Science and Scripture* (Grand Rapids, Mich.: Eerdmans, 1954), 67-69.

LINGUISTIC PRIORITY IN THE BIBLE

On the other hand, the Scripture has a *linguistic* and *redemptive* priority. It has *linguistic* priority, because it comes to us in human language. By contrast, we do not have access to God's words of providence *in human language*. We know that God also speaks in creation, as when he said, "Let there be light" (Gen. 1:3). But we have no indication that such speech takes place in human language. In Genesis 1:3 God's speaking is represented in Hebrew—translated into human language, if you will. But God does not indicate whether he used Hebrew or English or an angelic language or his own unique divine language when he originally spoke, "Let there be light." In the case of Genesis 1:3, we at least have a representation in Hebrew. In the case of many other words used to govern the created world, we have no record in the Bible of the particular words. We simply do not know in detail what he said or what language he used to say it. Right now the wind is blowing the branches of a tree as I look outside my window. That wind is obeying God's word (Ps. 147:18) that commands it to blow. But what is God saying? I do not hear the words. I hear the wind. I hear and see only *effects* from the words. I do not have immediate access to the words of God, whereas with the Bible I do have such access. There the words are, recorded with paper and ink.

We thus have an *availability* of God's word in the Bible, unlike in the case of God's word about the wind. If I make a scientific study of the wind, I may try to *infer* God's word. I may, that is, infer some laws—perhaps the laws of aerodynamics—governing the wind. But it is an inference. It is an approximation. I am in part guessing, on the basis of the best particular evidence, and on the basis of the kind of laws I think most likely to explain the evidence. My judgments about the kind of laws are, of course, influenced by who I think God is. But if I am honest and humble, I will also admit that my description of the laws is mine. It is my human description, my human approximation. In this way, the Bible has a kind of *linguistic* ultimacy, in that it *is* the word of God, not merely a human approximation to the word, a guess at the word on the basis of an accumulation of observations about its effects. My linguistic formulation of the laws of aerodynamics is fallible; the Bible, as *linguistic* communication, is not fallible.

In this respect, the formulations by a human scientist are more like a commentary on the Bible than they are like the Bible itself. The commentary, as a human product, is fallible, whereas the Bible is infallible. But even this does not quite capture the differences. The human commentator on the Bible works from a starting message in the Bible that is already human language.

Other commentators and ordinary people can compare the commentary with the original text and judge for themselves the value of the commentary. By contrast, when we formulate the laws of aerodynamics, there is no linguistically available original to which to compare the human formulations.[14] It is as if we just had commentaries, with no known original text on which they are commenting. In fact, the analogy with commentaries breaks down completely, because commentaries depend in an essential way on interaction with an original text in human language.

We also should distinguish general revelation about God from information about the detailed ways in which God governs the world in his providence. Romans 1:18-23 indicates that the existence of God and aspects of his character are "plain" (1:19) and "clearly perceived" (1:20). It does not say that details about his ways of governance are plain. In fact, much knowledge about nature is not so immediately plain, but must be searched out with diligence and patience. Science has taken a long time to arrive at its present understanding, and even now we are not finished. Appropriately, God's address to Job in Job 38–41 reminds Job of how little he really knows about these details.

REDEMPTIVE PRIORITY IN THE BIBLE

The Bible also has a priority to God's word of providence in its *redemptive* function. God designed the Bible to help sinners turn back to him and grow in holiness. ". . . the sacred writings . . . are able to make you wise for salvation through faith in Christ Jesus. All Scripture is breathed out by God and profitable for teaching, for reproof, for correction, and for training in righteousness, that the man of God may be competent, equipped for every good work" (2 Tim. 3:15-17). Similarly Psalm 19:7-11 and Psalm 119, which focus on the inscripturated word of God, extol the role of the word in enlightening and cleansing. "The law of the LORD is perfect, reviving the soul" (Ps. 19:7). By contrast, Romans 1:18-31 indicates that general revelation brings a kind of knowledge of God that leaves people without excuse (1:20-21), but that they suppress the truth (verse 18) and corrupt their knowledge into idolatry (verse 23). General revelation typically brings sin out, making people *more guilty* ("without excuse," verse 20). By contrast, God designs the Bible

---

[14] The lack of preservation of autographic texts of biblical books continues to generate objections. On the unique role of the autograph, see Meredith G. Kline, *The Structure of Biblical Authority* (Grand Rapids, Mich.: Eerdmans, 1972). We cannot infallibly restore the autographic text at every point, but in practice the doctrines taught in the Bible are well established, because they are taught in more than one place. All of this still operates comfortably within the sphere of linguistic communication.

specifically with the function of overcoming sin, including intellectual sins in corrupting the truth.[15]

We are sinners and rebels by nature. We need the Bible. John Calvin rightly compares the Scriptures to spectacles, through which we are enabled to read the instruction of general revelation:

> Bright, however, as is the manifestation which God gives both of himself and his immortal kingdom in the mirror of his works, so great is our stupidity, so dull are we in regard to these bright manifestations, that we derive no benefit from them.[16]

> For as the aged, . . . when aided by glasses, begin to read distinctly, so Scripture, gathering together the impressions of Deity, which, till then, lay confused in their minds, dissipates the darkness, and shows us the true God clearly.[17]

The word of God in providence and his word in Scripture are both completely true and trustworthy. But we misunderstand the one word unless we have the other. We grow in understanding reliably only when the Bible has a central role in dissipating the cobwebs of sin. But because of the prestige of modern science, we experience a strong temptation to imagine either that we do not really need the Bible to understand the natural world, or that it plays at best a minor, incidental role. Thus we may devote some time to reflecting in greater detail on some of the ways in which sin corrupts human knowledge.

---

[15] We should also note that the word of God in the Bible can function to condemn as well as to enlighten: "Now we know that whatever the law says it speaks to those who are under the law, so that every mouth may be stopped, and the whole world may be held accountable to God" (Rom. 3:19).

[16] John Calvin, *Institutes of the Christian Religion*, trans. Henry Beveridge (reprint; Grand Rapids, Mich.: Eerdmans, 1970), 1.5.11 (p. 59).

[17] Ibid., 1.6.1 (p. 64).

3

Knowledge from Whose Authority?

How much should we pay attention to the common opinions of our culture?

In thinking about scientific law and about revelation, I have already arrived at conclusions distinctly at odds with most of the modern world. As a result, many people might lose patience with me. They think, "Those conclusions can't be right, because they are contrary to what virtually all of us believe." Most modern people assume that scientists operate independently of religious commitments. And in one sense they do. In their private lives scientists may hold a variety of religious views. They may be Christians, agnostics, atheists, Buddhists, Hindus, or what have you. Yet when they work on science, they seem to operate in harmony with one another.

The Reality of God

But we need to transform this picture with several kinds of observations. The most important of these concerns God himself. God really does exist, whether people think so or not.[1]

Moreover, God refuses to be confined to some private sphere, but is constantly present and active in everything public. He is constantly at work, in his providential government of the world. He judges people for both private and public acts. And God is not simply a blank page that we may fill with whatever ideas we have about him. He has specific character, as we have seen in looking at the divine attributes of scientific law: omnipresence, eternity,

---

[1] Note the insistence on "true truth" about God in Francis Schaeffer's popular treatment, *The God Who Is There: Speaking Historic Christianity into the Twentieth Century* (Chicago: InterVarsity Press, 1968).

immutability, omnipotence, and so on. God is the Trinitarian God of the Bible. The same God who reveals himself in the Bible in all his specificity also reveals himself in scientific law.

But not only does God reveal himself. Scientists must and do rely on who God is in their scientific practice. If scientific practice is inconsistent with scientists' private religious views, then we just have inconsistency. What we do *not* have is science that is neutral with respect to religious belief.

RELIGIOUS COMMITMENT IN POSTMODERN SECULARISM

Second, we need to look with suspicion on the modern secularist environment around us.[2] Modern life is diverse and complicated. So in what follows I must oversimplify and draw with broad strokes.

Modern secularism, as a social movement and a philosophy of life, has produced the kind of atmosphere in which it seems natural to confine religion to private opinion. In order for people of diverse religious views to live harmoniously together, it seems expedient for people to "keep their religion to themselves." People think, "Do not disrupt the smooth flow of science or business or education by bringing up religious questions that only divide." This atmosphere influences everyone, so that people no longer ask themselves whether there is a conflict between their private religion and their public practice. They live comfortably with their inconsistency, because everyone else does too.

But one has only to consider some hypothetical scenarios in which secularism is directly threatened by other belief systems to see the emptiness of its claim to religious neutrality. Consider animism. One form of animism says that various spirits, good or evil, dwell in specific places and in specific objects. There is a spirit in that antelope, and another in this tree. But if so, the antelope or the tree is in some respects sacred. Maybe we should leave the antelope strictly alone. Or maybe, with the right techniques for propitiating the spirits, one can kill an antelope for food but not use its hide, into which the spirit of the antelope retreats when we kill the animal. This kind of animism is obviously incompatible with experimental science. An animist cannot conduct scientific experiments because he cannot give himself permission to manipulate the world of nature at will. He does not think scientific practice is spiritually safe.

---

[2] On the social context of science, see Richard C. Lewontin, *Biology as Ideology: The Doctrine of DNA* (New York: HarperCollins, 1993). On the influence of worldviews, see Nancy Pearcey, *Total Truth: Liberating Christianity from Its Cultural Captivity* (Wheaton, Ill.: Crossway, 2004).

Now, the typical secularist presupposes that animism is wrong, not because he has himself checked it out but because everyone else in modern secular society behaves in a manner that assures him that animism is wrong. But the thesis that animism is wrong is itself a religious view. It makes a commitment concerning what things exist outside of the physical aspect, and what things are sacred. The secularist is not really secular, that is, independent of religion, but makes a religious commitment—although it is a negative commitment to the *non*existence of animistic spirits. He does so without having examined the facts dispassionately, but rather by "going along with the crowd."

Moreover, secularism conceals its own religious commitments by claiming that it is independent of religious commitment. It reinforces this half-truth by tolerating in its midst a small minority of "kooks" and eccentrics, including animists. The small minority of animists are welcome to practice their animistic views in private. As individuals they are welcome also to exercise their civic freedom by refraining from practicing science. By creating space for the kooks, secularism displays its alleged tolerance and religious neutrality and thereby confirms its claims and its plausibility for the modern person.

But suppose that the number of animists were to increase. Let us say that they became a majority and exerted their political will by denying federal funding for science. Would the secularist be happy? No. In fact, long before such a situation could develop, the secularists who control the media and public education would raise the alarm and take steps to mold the children of animists into "good citizens," that is, citizens who know how to keep their animism private. But to insist that animism be kept private is to deny in practice that the spirits are really there, at least in the way that the parents thought. Education and the media inculcate a belief system that is religious in nature by teaching that animism (at least in the old-fashioned sense) is mistaken.

Now consider Shankara's interpretation of Vedantic Hinduism. According to Shankara, Brahma, the supreme reality, is one, and is in some sense identical with the individual human soul. The material world is "maya," illusion, unreal in relation to Brahma, but "relatively real as a manifestation of the real Brahma."[3] The goal of human life is knowledge of Brahma. Within this view science is of little or no value, since it focuses wholly on the world of illusion.

Modern secularists have a relation to Shankara's Hinduism analogous to what we have seen with animism. To begin with, they implicitly reject Shankara by their practice of immersing themselves in the world of "illusion."

---

[3] *The Encyclopedia Americana*, 30 vols. (Danbury, Conn.: Americana, 1978), 14:213.

The commitment in practice shows that they have already decided in principle that Shankara is wrong. They have decided, not by looking at Shankara's claims and weighing them, but simply by going along with the crowd in their modern environment.

As with animism, so here secularists gladly tolerate in their society a small minority of adherents to Shankara's views. But those views are carefully "privatized,"[4] that is, confined to the privacy of individuals or families, and the modern secularist taboo against religion in the public sphere puts strong pressure on the minority to keep their views to themselves. But of course this pressure of moral disapproval can only arise from the prior religious commitment to the conviction that the material world is not illusion, but is the primary reality. Once again, "secularism" depends on a prior religious commitment.

Moreover, as with animism, so here, the secularists would go on the attack if Shankara's views spread widely and his adherents appeared to be gaining significant political control.

MORAL HYPOCRISY IN POSTMODERN SECULARISM

Secularism also shows its religious foundation in its moral pronouncements. A secularist worldview depends on a moral commitment to tolerance, to political pluralism, to continued government support of science, and to public education. But literal secularism, in and of itself, cannot produce any absolute basis for such morality. In fact, contemporary secular thinking typically undermines absolute moral claims: it equates morality with personal opinion,[5] in order to support a society in which people may differ in their moral opinions but still live together peaceably.

And yet secularity's own moral commitments secretly receive sacred status. The commitments to tolerance, political pluralism, and so on, are themselves moral commitments. Are they, too, merely opinion? In practice, no. If these are mere "opinion," the whole scheme collapses, because in that case the opinion that fascism or animism is right would have equal standing with the opinion that political pluralism is right. In practice, secularity requires trust and faith in its own moral commitments.

One sees the problem in dealing with fanatical forms of Islam in the Near

---

[4] The terms "privatize" and "privatization" I take from Os Guinness, *The Gravedigger File: Papers on the Subversion of the Modern Church* (Downers Grove, Ill.: InterVarsity Press, 1983), who in turn has learned from sociology of religion: Peter Berger, *The Sacred Canopy: Elements of a Sociological Theory of Religion* (Garden City, N.Y.: Doubleday, 1967). Note the critique of sociology as covert religion in John Milbank, *Theology and Social Theory: Beyond Secular Reason* (Oxford: Blackwell, 1993).

[5] See Pearcey, *Total Truth*, for a more thorough account of how this has come to be.

East. According to these fanatics, imposition of Islamic government is the morally and religiously right solution. Religious tolerance and political pluralism make no sense, but are part of the decadence of modernity. In the face of such claims, the postmodern pluralistic secularist must say with all the eloquence at his command that this religious intolerance is wrong. At the same time, he has no grounds for his moral denunciation, because, according to his own dogma, morality is a matter of personal opinion. Or, in one postmodern variation, morality is a matter of corporate social opinion. But what if in the Near East we find a differing social opinion? That too must be right "for them."

CHRISTIANITY IN THE MIDST OF A SECULARIST ENVIRONMENT

And how does Christianity fare in a secularist environment? The relations between Christian faith and modern secularism are complex, partly because secularism arose out of a Christian past and still clings to some of the moral foundations of that past.

The Bible teaches that man is made in the image of God, and as such is a morally responsible creature. It also makes clear that religious commitment and genuine allegiance to God spring from the heart, and ought not to be compelled by human pressure. Hence, a biblical worldview promotes religious and political tolerance.[6] Yes, the past history of Christianity shows many shameful instances of intolerance, but these are in conflict with the actual moral principles articulated in the Bible.

Christian tolerance does not mean that all views are equally right. Rather it means that one ought to put up with others' wrong views, out of respect for the image of God and out of respect for God's way of dealing with others in love. Secularism then twists biblically based tolerance into a rootless tolerance that attempts in practice to suppress the influence of religion on life.

Has secularism also twisted our conception of science? Modern science originated within societies that held a basically Christian worldview.[7] The

---

[6] The Old Testament laws prohibiting blasphemy and false prophecy are a special case, pertaining to Israel as a holy people and pointing forward to the holiness of the New Testament church (which must exclude from its membership those who will not repent of sin). The Old Testament laws do *not* apply to modern political arrangements. And the church exercises its discipline by spiritual means, not with physical punishments. I discuss the issue at length in Vern S. Poythress, *The Shadow of Christ in the Law of Moses* (Phillipsburg, N.J.: Presbyterian & Reformed, 1995), especially chapter 10.

[7] Nancy R. Pearcey and Charles B. Thaxton, *The Soul of Science: Christian Faith and Natural Philosophy* (Wheaton, Ill.: Crossway, 1994). There were, of course, intellectual and technological achievements in ancient Babylon, China, Egypt, and Greece. But the blossoming and multiplication of scientific knowledge belongs to the time since the Renaissance.

Christian doctrines of creation and providence guarantee that the world operates in accordance with divine rationality. Because man is made in the image of God, God's rationality is at least in part accessible to us and intelligible by us. Hence, there is hope for scientific discovery and progress. And because God has given man dominion over the world, the task of studying the world is both legitimate (contrary to animism) and fruitful (contrary to Shankara's monistic Hinduism).

Modern secularist thinking about science has taken over the ideas of divine rationality, human competence, and human dominion. But just as it does with the idea of tolerance, so here it uproots the original ideas from their religious origins and gives them its own twist. Divine rationality gets transformed into the rationality of scientific law, now conceived as impersonal. Human competence is no longer the gift of God but a brute fact of life to be pragmatically assumed.

As we saw in chapter 1, scientific practice continues to need the idea of God in its conception of scientific law. But secularism also twists the idea into an idolatrous substitute, in order to avoid painful spiritual consequences. Contrary to secularist myth, science in practice is innately and irrepressibly religious: it serves either God or idolatry. But one of the features of idolatry is deceit. In this case, idolatry conceals from itself that it is idolatry.

THE CORRUPTION AND REDEMPTION OF THE MIND

Do we now see that the modern environment offers a host of half-truths and deceits? Christians along with non-Christians have at least partially absorbed and believed the half-truths. Until one stands back and asks the right questions, one goes along with the crowd unawares. The commonplace assumptions of the great majority of people around us have a great influence.[8] And that influence is reinforced by the powerful influence of public education and mass media.

The myth of progress, which is one element within this environment, whispers to us that since we are seeing technological progress, we must be progressing in knowledge and social wisdom across the board, making it unnecessary to ask whether our present society may along the way have lost or twisted truth. On top of the social forces inviting us to conform, we have personal forces: my own pride says that all is well and that I am not guilty of idolatry.

---

[8] That is, there is communal influence on what counts as knowledge. The story of that influence has been told by the sociology of knowledge: Peter L. Berger and Thomas Luckmann, *The Social Construction of Reality: A Treatise in the Sociology of Knowledge* (New York: Doubleday, 1966).

We are dealing with what theologians have called "the noetic effects of sin," the effects of sin on the mind and on human knowledge.[9] To cite some familiar passages from Scripture,

> Now this I say and testify in the Lord, that you must no longer walk as the Gentiles do, in the futility of their minds. They are darkened in their understanding, alienated from the life of God because of the ignorance that is in them, due to their hardness of heart (Eph. 4:17-18).

> For although they knew God, they did not honor him as God or give thanks to him, but they became futile in their thinking, and their foolish hearts were darkened. Claiming to be wise, they became fools, and exchanged the glory of the immortal God for images resembling mortal man and birds and animals and creeping things (Rom. 1:21-23).

> And this is the judgment: the light has come into the world, and people loved the darkness rather than the light because their works were evil. For everyone who does wicked things hates the light and does not come to the light, lest his works should be exposed (John 3:19-20).

Even when one is partly aware of this desperate problem, human pride tempts one to try to come up with a merely human remedy. If we are deceived, we will think our way out of the problem. With sufficient mental power we may triumph over deceit and come into the light (as the Enlightenment wished). But this kind of human pride is only another form of idolatry.[10] We are worshiping our own minds and our own rational powers. We may walk out of one idolatry only to fall into a deeper and more concealed form. To move beyond the deceits within a given social environment is hard enough. To move beyond the deceits of one's own heart is impossible for unaided humanity:

> "Then who can be saved?" But he said, "What is impossible with men is possible with God" (Luke 18:26-27).

In preparing to write this book, I have read quite a few books on science, the philosophy of science, and the Bible and science. As might be

---

[9] Cornelius Van Til makes the point over and over again, that a non-Christian worldview fundamentally presupposes that the human mind as we now observe it is normal. The Christian worldview, believing in the fall of man, holds that the human mind at present is abnormal, disfigured by sin. See, for example, Cornelius Van Til, *A Survey of Christian Epistemology* (n.l.: den Dulk Christian Foundation, 1969).

[10] See Vern S. Poythress, "Christ the Only Savior of Interpretation," *Westminster Theological Journal* 50/2 (1988): 305-321.

expected, I found much good. But, even from books written by Christians, I have too seldom found a pointed expression of the depth of our problem with knowledge.

The truth is that our minds are corrupted by sin. Not just a little bit, but deeply, down to the depths as far as we can perceive, and beyond. And not just grossly, so that it is easy to figure out where we went wrong, but subtly, delicately, invisibly. If we think we know and appreciate how far we have gone wrong, we are still deceiving ourselves at this point also.

We *desperately* need God to save us from a pit from which we cannot climb out. And God has acted. He has sent Christ with his wisdom. He has called us to come to Christ for mercy. Christ has taken the punishment for our sins on the cross. God raised him from the dead, and he appeared to many people, confirming the truth of his claims (1 Cor. 15:3-8). He lives to this day and reigns in heaven (Rev. 1:18). When we cry out to God for mercy, on the basis of Christ's work for us, he gives us the Spirit and teaches us (1 Cor. 2:12). He gives us the Bible as his own word to tell us the truth. And so, wonderfully, as a result of God's gift to those who come to him for help, "we have the mind of Christ" (1 Cor. 2:16). Yes, we are still beset by corruption, in mind and in action, but in a fundamental way we have been rescued from the "domain of darkness and transferred . . . to the kingdom of his beloved Son, in whom we have redemption, the forgiveness of sins" (Col. 1:13-14).

"But," I hear someone say, "this concerns our spiritual life, not the life of science." Ah, the very dichotomy between "spiritual life" and "life of science" shows the continuing influence of secularist deceit. Modern science, as typically practiced, is idolatry. Science *is* a form of "spiritual life," and a corrupted and guilty form at that. The entirety of our life is in bondage to sin and deceit, until Christ delivers us. And the deliverance is incomplete within this life, so that we must continue to grow and work at it (Phil. 2:12-13; 1:6).

We do not really appreciate the gifts that God has given us until we appreciate more deeply just how desperate is our situation as sinners and rebels against God. When we appreciate our desperation, we appreciate also the goodness of God in the rescue. In particular, we appreciate the Bible.

I have argued elsewhere that the Bible is fully the word of God, in spite of the objections that continue to be raised by unbelief.[11] I will not repeat the

---

[11] Vern S. Poythress, *God-Centered Biblical Interpretation* (Phillipsburg, N.J.: Presbyterian & Reformed, 1999), especially chapter 2 and p. 47n1; John M. Frame, "God and Biblical Language," in John Warwick Montgomery, ed., *God's Inerrant Word* (Minneapolis: Bethany, 1974), 159-177; and Frame, "Scripture Speaks for Itself," in *God's Inerrant Word,* 178-200.

discussion here. I would also affirm that the Holy Spirit must interpret the Bible to us if we are genuinely to understand.

Now we need to take account of two additional facts.

First, as fallen and sinful human beings we are in no position to make an accurate independent judgment about the character of the Bible and its truthfulness. We are not neutral judges, but judges who will inevitably misconstrue the truth. Those who attempt an independent judgment only show their own lack of self-knowledge.

Second, we *desperately need* the Bible as part of the remedy for our mental and spiritual corruption. We need instruction from God, not only instruction that is pure and free of our personal and social corruption, but instruction that will serve as a means for our personal and social and political purification. The Bible has both properties: purity (Ps. 12:6; 19:8-9) and purifying power (Ps. 19:7-14; 2 Tim. 3:16-17). After extolling the character of God's law in both of these respects, Psalm 19 also confesses the need for personal application:

> Moreover, by them [the rules of the LORD] is your servant warned;
>   in keeping them there is great reward.
> Who can discern his errors?
>   Declare me innocent from hidden faults.
> Keep back your servant also from presumptuous sins;
>   let them not have dominion over me!
> Then I shall be blameless,
>   and innocent of great transgression.
> Let the words of my mouth and the meditation of my heart
>   be acceptable in your sight,
> O LORD, my rock and my redeemer (Ps. 19:11-14).

For the sake of our need, we must respond to what God says in the Bible with submission. Years ago Gerhard Maier argued that a critical mentality in approaching the Bible was incompatible with the character of the Bible as revelation from God.[12] Equally, a critical mentality is incompatible with human need. A person cannot receive the depth of purification that he needs if he retains an independent spirit, because the independence itself represents a crucial stronghold for sin.

Since I do not accept the secularist dichotomy between public science and

---

[12] Gerhard Maier, *The End of the Historical-Critical Method* (St. Louis: Concordia, 1977).

private spirituality, it goes without saying that I believe that the Bible must reform the life of science along with every other area of life. We must not allow any area of life to become a stronghold for sin, which we secretly and invisibly fence off from God's scrutiny and purification.

But now fear arises. Someone says, "Submission to the Bible, with its outmoded worldview, will destroy science." This fear invites several kinds of reply.

First, it remains to be seen what the Bible actually has within it, and what sort of worldview we are actually dealing with, which may be quite different from claims made about it and naive impressions of it.

Second, suppose for the sake of argument that the Bible does destroy science as we know it. In principle the result might be an alternative form of science, or a redeemed form of science, or a return to a prescientific era. The third of these alternatives, a prescientific era, stirs people's fears the most, but using it to frighten people artificially forecloses the other alternatives.

Third, let us face the fact: we fear what the Bible will do to us if we take it with utter seriousness. This fear toward the Bible is a form of fearing God's way. We fear that God will not be good to us—not as good as if we retain control for ourselves. If we retain control, at least in some fundamental areas, we can assure ourselves of a good result, whereas there is no assurance if we simply abandon ourselves wholly to God.

This fear is simply unbelief. It is refusing to trust in God, and trusting in ourselves instead. It is a mirror of the fall, in which Adam and Eve refused to trust God but thought that they knew better (Gen. 3:1-6). This too is idolatry, an idolatry in which man becomes his own god and worships himself.

Now, many will dispute my view. They would want to distinguish between trusting in God and trusting in the Bible. Trusting in God is good, they would say, but trusting in the Bible is not so good when you do it completely.

To me, this kind of talk implies that the Bible is not really the word of God—at least, not without qualification. Perhaps it contains the word of God. Perhaps it becomes the word of God for some people on some occasions, as they experience God when they read it. Perhaps it witnesses to Christ, who is the word of God. And so on. There are varieties of neo-orthodoxy and other positions. The discussions continue among theologians, with no signs of increasing agreement.

I do not propose to repeat here the defense of the orthodox understanding of Scriptural inspiration and authority. Rather, I want to observe the practical dilemma created by not trusting the Bible completely.

Someone says that he wants to trust in God. But who is God? Our hearts deceive us and construct idols. How shall we know specifically what to trust, unless we have some specific words of promise, instruction, and rebuke from this God? "Trust in God" turns out to be empty unless there are specific ways in which we trust. Are those ways determined by us, independent of special revelation? Then we can make them suit the desires of our own darkened hearts. Or if the ways are determined outside of us, from specific special revelation, what is this special revelation? The Bible, you say? But then either we are accepting the Bible with trust, or we are picking and choosing among its contents, in which case it is *we* who are still covertly in control of every requirement that the Bible threatens to impose on us. Such control over revelation is not yet discipleship, but is still the autonomous independence that Adam fell into in his rebellion.

Some theologians defend deviant views of biblical authority with great cleverness and acuity. The cleverness may be impressive. But it gives no signs yet of having understood the problem. The problem is that we are in desperate need of guidance, guidance from God that is pure and enlightening. In the deficient views, where is there an appreciation of the noetic effects of sin? And where is there a concrete proposal as to what practical means God offers for redeeming our minds out of this mess? If I do not trust the Bible "completely," by what standard am I to subject modern culture to criticism? Deficient views of the Bible leave me at the mercy of modern culture. The only conclusion must be that modern culture is not so idolatrous, or that idolatry is not so bad, or that we do not really need to be rescued in the mind, or that God has not seen fit to provide a remedy. One must think one knows a lot to make claims like these. And, I think, one must be credulous to believe them.

Fear of Fundamentalism

We may look briefly at one more fear that draws people back from trusting in the Bible. They fear that they will become "fundamentalists" or will be labeled as fundamentalists.

But what is fundamentalism, and why do people think it is so bad? We are actually talking about a variety of kinds of people, and a variety of possible definitions of the term "fundamentalism." It is not easy to pin down. But let us begin with the obvious. In this life, Christian people continue to fall into sins. Sin is subtle, deep, and difficult to root out. Becoming a Christian changes a person in the heart, and it removes the penalty of sin, but it does not totally remove the power of sin either in its subtlety or in its depth.

Some of these sins belong to a whole culture, when the culture endorses a particular sinful practice and refuses to call it sin. We have a particular instance of this in the scientific practice of converting scientific law into an impersonal substitute for God.

Some sins belong more exclusively to various Christian subcultures. The nature of sin makes this unsurprising. But then a non-Christian, standing outside the Christian subculture, can frequently see the sin more clearly than does the insider. Non-Christians see many sinning Christians. Christians are then labeled hypocrites, and it becomes a black mark against the Christian faith.

So what is so bad about fundamentalists? I hear a chorus of objections: "they are ignorant, they are judgmental, they are intolerant, . . ." Let us suppose for the sake of argument that they are. Are they any worse than many other people who are ignorant, judgmental, and so on? The answer may come, "Yes, they are, because they think that they are better." Let us then add the charge of self-righteousness and hypocrisy. In addition, let us specify that the ignorance of which the objector speaks is not innocent ignorance—ignorance from mere lack of information—but a culpable ignorance, an ignorance that refuses opportunities to learn.

Sin is sin, whether among Christians or non-Christians. So what does this prove? It proves little unless it comes with the suspicion that the Bible has had a part in producing the problem. And there is a grain of truth here. Knowing the truth that God has given to us in Scripture tempts us to take pride in it, or to overestimate our grasp of it, or to make quick judgments without knowing enough. (Sometimes, however, the effects are magnified by outsiders, who in their evaluation of Christians bring to bear their own faulty standards for what is dogmatic and intolerant and so on.) The Bible can become an occasion for sin, sin that is subtle, deep, and dangerous. But that simply confirms the Bible's teaching about the seriousness of sin. As Romans 7:11-13 observes,

> For sin, seizing an opportunity through the commandment, deceived me and through it killed me. So the law is holy, and the commandment is holy and righteous and good. Did that which is good, then, bring death to me? By no means! It was sin, producing death in me through what is good, in order that sin might be shown to be sin, and through the commandment might become sinful beyond measure.

What Romans 7 says about the role of the law can be generalized into a principle applying also to the use of the word of God in general. Even though it is good itself, the word of God can become an occasion for multiplying sin, when people twist it or take pride in their understanding of it.

The objection to the sins of fundamentalists also shows that objectors have a standard for sin. But do they have any ground to stand on, to justify the standard? Maybe their standard is just their personal preference. And if it is not, if it is absolute, they are in the same danger as Bible-believing Christians of taking pride in it, making quick judgments, and so on. Hypocrisy is not the exclusive property of Bible-believing Christians.

The objection also shows how subtle and serious sin is, by showing that it can capture in a deadly way those who are most sure that they have escaped it. But if so, what will be the remedy for this deadly peril? Magnify the peril all you will, as the objector does, and you only provide that much more evidence for the necessity of using the Bible to root out the peril.

Can We Eradicate Pride?

Can the objector provide an alternative remedy? Will the sweet reasonableness of Enlightenment secularism do it? Some people think so. More often, people have in mind a long-range educational answer. Educate the children in tolerance and steer them clear of fundamentalism, so that the next generation may be freed from this oppressive and dangerous mode of thinking.

But difficulties arise. First, though education may steer children away from allegedly dangerous styles of thought and living, will it root out the underlying human tendency in the heart toward pride, self-centeredness, and over-confidence in one's own views? If the problems of fundamentalists open a window onto the human heart, they reveal depths of perversity not so easily eradicated.

Second, though this secularist educational approach looks patient and civil, it has a darker underbelly. It proposes to suppress the fundamentalist opponent not by a friendly discussion searching for truth but by the use of state power and state money to smother a generation of vulnerable children with propaganda. Propaganda in the schools will preach tolerance and, by implication, the errors of fundamentalism. Power and money will take away from fundamentalists the opportunity for equal means to educate their own children or to spread their particular views. This procedure appears to mean, "We will tolerate you temporarily, but we will make sure by political power that we seize the minds of your children and educate them against your views." Tolerance has apparently become intolerance. People who abhor oppression nevertheless oppress. People who abhor dogmatism turn dogmatic. People who may say that all their knowledge is tentative, and who may even say that there is no absolute truth, have remarkable confidence in their ability to use political power. They craft a compulsory educational system that they allege will solve our moral problems. (See, at the end of this chapter, the excursus on public education.) Implicitly, they have supposed that they can diagnose the deepest ills behind human moral failures. They are really proposing an alternative means of salvation, a means of rescue from the evils of the human heart. That amounts to an alternative religion.

Human nature is strange. It is not only strange, but also deeper and more deceitful than what people imagine. "The heart is deceitful above all things, and desperately sick; who can understand it?" (Jer. 17:9).

Scorn

Other reasons, less worthy, rear their heads, as suggestions for why people fear becoming fundamentalists. Perhaps they fear that they will suffer the humiliation and scorn of intellectuals, who nowadays make a sport out of mocking fundamentalists. "Fundamentalism" in popular culture has become a term of derision, condemnation, and moral disapproval thrown on any Christian who believes the Bible.

They fear also because they want it understood that they believe in the life of the mind, not the life of submission to a book. Adherents to the historical-critical approach to Scripture likewise argued that they believed in the life of the mind, and that the alternative of submission involved a "sacrifice of the intellect" or sacrifice of the mind. Gerhard Maier replied that revelation demanded not the sacrifice of the mind but the sacrifice of pride.[13] There is plenty of pride around for all of us to repent of, including both the pride of intellectuals and the pride in ignorance among some Bible believers.

Amid all the prevailing negative views about Bible believers, I want to propound this unpalatable thesis: whatever else may be their faults (and they may be many), the Bible believers have it right and everyone else has it wrong about a most crucial point: trusting the Bible as the word of God, as an aspect of an even more fundamental trust in Christ, is the right way to find relief from sin. Alvin Plantinga, though disagreeing with young-earth creationists, stresses the areas of agreement:

---

[13] Ibid., 54.

Creation scientists are wrong (so I think), but some of them are nonetheless admirable. Their aim is to be faithful to the Christian faith and to the Lord; they do their best to do so, often at considerable personal cost. (They don't, after all, *enjoy* being called fundamentalist ignoramuses; nor do they take delight in the rest of the ridicule and disapprobation heaped upon them by the scientific establishment.) I happen to think they are mistaken; but their errors, to my mind, are enormously less important than the errors of many of those—the Dawkins and Provines and Sagans of this world, for example—who load abuse upon them. It is vastly more important to be clear that the Lord created the heavens, the earth, and all that they contain, than to know that he didn't do it 10,000 years ago. I disagree with the creation scientists, and, like most other academics, I don't relish the scorn and obloquy that goes with being associated with them; but at a deep level I feel much closer to them, both spiritually and intellectually, than to their cultured despisers. Christians who disagree with them should treat them as Christian brothers and sisters who, perhaps through an excess of zeal, err on a point of some importance; but Christians should *not* treat them as intellectual pariahs, or join in the cultural chorus expressing scorn, contempt, and disdain for them.[14]

Our intellectual environment throws up a host of objections to the fundamentalist's unwavering trust in the Bible. "We have shown that this kind of trust involves a false worship or devotion to the Bible." "We have shown that only Christ deserves trust, and the Bible gets it only insofar as it witnesses to Christ." "We have shown that this means intellectual suicide." "We have shown that hermeneutical problems make this approach unworkable." To all these objections extensive answers are possible.

Faith

But there is a more fundamental problem. All of these objections fail to engage the point. They fail to understand that I am proposing not the abolition of intellect but the historically tested and biblically endorsed method of believing in order that I may understand. We reform modern ideas on the basis of scriptural teaching. We reform even our ideas of scriptural teaching, which are themselves partial and subject to reform, in the same way.

We trust that God knows better than we do how to guide us, and we come to the Bible not with all kinds of objections and resistances to it, but

---

[14] Alvin Plantinga, "Evolution, Neutrality, and Antecedent Probability: A Reply to McMullin and Van Till," *Christian Scholars Review* 21 (1991/1992): 90.

with the expectation that God will teach us. We come in faith. Such faith, of course, does not come in a vacuum. Faith comes from God (Eph. 2:8-9). He gives us faith as he opens our eyes to who Christ is and what he has done in mercy to rescue us. Out of that fundamental, heartfelt trust, we grow in trusting what he says in the Bible.[15]

Modern thinking, by contrast, supposes that something else is more reliable than the Bible, whether it be the pronouncements of modern science, or an insight into an alleged idolatry that occurs in trusting the Bible, or a dichotomy between Christ and the Bible, or an alleged hermeneutical principle that makes the Bible an uncertain voice. All such claims coming out of the modern environment, as many now know well, are historically conditioned by our culture and its history. So according to modernist and postmodernist principles, we need to subject them to critical scrutiny.

THE BIBLE AS A SOURCE FOR INTELLECTUAL REDEMPTION

I only propose that we shall never escape the circle of sin unless we have a pure word of God as the standard for criticism, rather than autonomous reason or values and insights that themselves come merely from our human environment. All other proposals represent alternative religious commitments, even alternative religions.[16] When once we listen to the pure word of God, we find that the modern world is full of subtle idolatries in the form of these religious alternatives; among them is the alternative of trying to receive the most fundamental guidance from science in order to find out the meaning of the world.

Now science in many respects is a good thing, as I have hinted already and will continue to show later in this book. But, as the idolatry in modern science shows, it is not perfectly pure. Nor, because of its limited focus on the

---

[15] See, for example, Westminster Theological Seminary, *The Infallible Word: A Symposium* (Philadelphia: Presbyterian & Reformed, 1946); Benjamin Breckinridge Warfield, *The Inspiration and Authority of the Bible* (Philadelphia: Presbyterian & Reformed, 1967).

[16] Herman Bavinck's remarks about hopes of transcending religious differences are still pertinent:

Although we cannot endorse Lessing's views, it is certainly understandable that many theorists join him in retreating to the position of indifferentism [in religion] and try to console themselves with the idea that it does not matter what one believes provided one lives a good life. But this consolation soon evaporates. Aside from the fact that religion does not simply allow itself to be shouldered aside, the study of ethnology shows that humanity is as divided over morality and justice as it is over religion. . . . No science, however "presuppositionless," is or will ever be able to undo this division and bring about, in the life of all nations and people, unity in the most basic convictions of the heart. If there is ever to be unity, it will have to be achieved in the way of mission; only religious unity will be able to bring about the spiritual and intellectual unity of humankind. As long as disagreement prevails in religion, science too will be unable to achieve the ideal of unity (Bavinck, *Reformed Dogmatics,* 2 vols. [Grand Rapids, Mich.: Baker, 2003], 1:298-299).

physical world, does it really provide the resources for answering definitively the big questions about morality, the meaning of life, and so on. Some people may daringly extend their reach from science into a philosophy of life, but the daring extension makes the conclusions even more subject to distorting influences from hidden agenda.

Or, in the fashion of postmodernism, one may try to save oneself by hermeneutical acuity.[17] Some postmodernists advise us just to live in peace, by having us admit that each person or group just represents one more opinion and that no one really knows—no human being has a God's-eye view of truth. But there is really no way to negotiate middle ground between alternative proposals for the way of salvation. The postmodernist offers just one more proposal, and it is just as religious and just as exclusivist as any other, in that it implicitly *rejects* the exclusivism of the biblical claim. The Bible claims to be the word of God, and therefore to offer a God's-eye view. The Bible also promises that the Holy Spirit comes to interpret the Bible for us, thereby overcoming interpretive problems. Interpretation does not succeed primarily by intellectual acuity, but by the work of saving us from our sin so that we see what the Bible says. Without overcoming human finiteness, we come to know God and to know the truth about God. We do not know the truth exhaustively, nor is our knowledge free from the contamination of sin. But we know enough to take the next step in conducting our lives, including our intellectual and hermeneutical lives. Much of postmodernist hermeneutics, on the other hand, proposes that we rely primarily on hermeneutical sophistication—and then *we* rather than God become the source of our salvation.

I therefore intend to examine what the world looks like, and what science looks like, when we take the contents of the Bible seriously, and when we listen obediently with the conviction that this is God's instruction. I will describe this approach as building on or following *a Christian worldview*.[18] Many who call themselves Christians might differ. ("Christians" are in great disarray nowadays.) But, granted that the Bible is what it is, this approach alone harmonizes with a whole-souled commitment to be a follower of Christ.

It should be evident, however, that I am merely "on the way," as all fallible human beings are on the way. We progress by fits and starts, and we make mistakes, some innocent, but many due to our sin. Non-Christians are

---

[17] The point is made at some length in Poythress, "Christ the Only Savior of Interpretation."
[18] For more on worldviews, see Pearcey, *Total Truth*.

sometimes right to complain about the high-handedness and arrogant dog-matism that stains the past history of Christianity. I do not offer my reflec-tions as a final answer, but as steps toward the light, which others may not only build on but may also find it necessary sometimes to correct in the light of Scripture. I might preface all my statements with the qualification, "Right now I think that . . . ," to remind readers of fallibility. But that would be tedious, and, I think, redundant.

EXCURSUS: THE PROBLEM OF PUBLIC EDUCATION

Earlier in this chapter I raised a problem about public, state-controlled edu-cation. State-controlled education in its present form in the United States tends to impose secularism. Secularism is a whole worldview, and in its approach to the nature of scientific law, it is intrinsically religious, in that it exchanges God for an idolatrous view of scientific law. Moreover, as we have seen, it excludes minority views like animism and Shankara's interpretation of Vedantic Hinduism. It is oppressive toward those who radically disagree with its worldview.

But is this unique to secularism? Does not everyone have the same prob-lem when it comes to state-controlled education? Parents naturally want their children to be taught in conformity with their own beliefs. But state-controlled education cannot possibly please all parents at the same time. It cannot please both those who believe in absolute moral standards and those who believe that morality is merely the product of personal choices and opin-ions. It cannot please both those who believe that scientific law is impersonal and those who believe that it is the personal word of God. It cannot please those who believe that the universe is a product of chance and mindless evo-lution and those who believe that it is the creation of God. In political science courses, it cannot please both political conservatives and political liberals.

At an earlier point in the history of the United States, state-controlled education tended to draw on a broad Protestant consensus as its main reli-gious background. In Europe, education was influenced by state churches. These approaches oppressed all kinds of religious minorities, as well as athe-ists and agnostics. Nowadays, in the United States and to some extent in Europe, state-controlled education is controlled by secularist ideology and opposes religious "interference" and minority views that would take a dif-ferent approach to issues like scientific law and moral standards. The victims of oppression have shifted, but the general problem has not disappeared.

I cannot pursue the issue here, but it seems to me the morally proper remedy is not, as many Christians might wish, the reintroduction of less hostility toward the Bible and Christianity in state-controlled schools, but the introduction of real parental control and choice in education. As it is now, because of the tax system for supporting education, only the very rich can afford to send their children to schools of their choice.[19] School vouchers—or better, tax credits for education of the parents' choice—can provide relief that gives the average parent real choice. And with choice comes control of what kind of worldview and educational approach the child receives. But there is a political price: we must then give up the hope of using state power to impose our own views on others' children.

---

[19] Or the very determined can undertake to homeschool their children. I am grateful that homeschooling is allowed in the United States. But it is a great injustice that homeschoolers still see their tax money go to support public schools, while they pay out of their own pockets in time and money for their homeschooling activities.

4

CREATION

We may now consider biblical teaching about creation. Genesis 1,[1] taken together with other biblical texts that build on it, provides the overall doctrine of creation. We need an understanding of creation in order to understand the character of the world and then the nature of modern science. In addition, alleged discrepancies between Genesis 1 and scientific accounts of origins make Genesis 1 an important test case for how we go about treating the relation between science and the Bible.

For these purposes we need a careful, in fact a minute examination of Genesis 1. Fortunately, a number of good scholarly commentaries come to our aid. Naturally minor points of disagreement still exist, but I can in general recommend the commentaries by Kidner, Wenham, Hamilton, and Collins.[2] All four commentators are evangelicals, who approach Genesis with the conviction that it is the word of God given through human writers. Through a human agent whom God inspired, God wrote a book with divine authority for our instruction. He also wrote to the people of the ancient Near East, and Genesis speaks fluently to the people of that time. Other commentaries, coming from within the mainstream "historical-critical" tradition, may provide individual insights and helpful comments here and there. But because they have abandoned the conviction that Genesis is the word of God, their approach to Genesis misjudges its author and its character at a fundamental level.

---

[1] Actually, the opening creation narrative goes from Genesis 1:1 to 2:3. Genesis 2:4-25 then focuses on the creation of man and the garden of Eden.

[2] Derek Kidner, *Genesis: An Introduction and Commentary,* Tyndale Old Testament Commentary (Downers Grove, Ill.: InterVarsity Press, 1967); Gordon Wenham, *Genesis 1–15,* Word Biblical Commentary, vol. 1 (Waco, Tex.: Word, 1987); Victor P. Hamilton, *The Book of Genesis: Chapters 1–17,* New International Commentary on the Old Testament (Grand Rapids, Mich.: Eerdmans, 1990); C. John Collins, *Genesis 1–4: A Linguistic, Literary, and Theological Commentary* (Phillipsburg, N.J.: Presbyterian & Reformed, 2006). One may also consult with profit C. John Collins, *Science and Faith: Friends or Foes?* (Wheaton, Ill.: Crossway, 2003), which offers less technical exegetical detail, but in return devotes more space to hermeneutical, theological, and scientific issues. Collins's book forms a useful complement to this book in many areas.

It would be tiresome and unnecessary for me to repeat here what the commentaries have already achieved. I shall therefore summarize in this chapter some of the main points and then in subsequent chapters take up where they leave off, by considering the larger theological and scientific questions to which commentaries devote less space.

ONE GOD

What does Genesis 1 teach? First, there is only one God. This God comprehensively rules and controls the world. He has no "competition" or "interference" from other gods. The created world offers no resistance to his will, but does what he says.

Many modern Christian readers of the Bible tend to take these points for granted. But within the context of the ancient Near East, Genesis 1 presented a radical and startling message. In the ancient Near East, polytheism abounded. The Old Testament repeatedly warned Israel not to pursue "other gods, the gods of the peoples who are around you" (Deut. 6:14). Joshua posed the challenge: "And if it is evil in your eyes to serve the LORD, choose this day whom you will serve, whether the gods your fathers served in the region beyond the River, or the gods of the Amorites in whose land you dwell. But as for me and my house, we will serve the LORD" (Josh. 24:15).

ANCIENT NEAR EASTERN STORIES OF ORIGINS

Ancient Near Eastern literature included stories and traditions about creation (e.g., *Enuma Elish; Atrahasis Epic*) and the flood (e.g., the *Gilgamesh Epic; the Atrahasis Epic* also includes the flood).[3] These stories existed in an atmosphere very different from modern thinking. Most of the people in the ancient Near East believed in many gods and worshiped many gods. The stories that they wrote described the interaction of many gods. The reader may skip over this section if polytheistic myths are distasteful to him. They are distasteful and abhorrent to me as well, but I include here a summary of parts of their plots in order to show something about the atmosphere that surrounded the Israelites in Old Testament times.

In the *Atrahasis Epic*[4] the subordinate gods complain because of the heavy toil assigned by the principal god, Enlil. Because of this problem, the

---

[3] Egyptian material is complex; see "Report of the Committee to Study the Views of Creation," *Minutes of the Seventy-First General Assembly . . . of the Orthodox Presbyterian Church* (Willow Grove, Pa.: Orthodox Presbyterian Church, 2004), 276-277, 292-294.

[4] See W. G. Lambert and A. R. Millard, *Atra-hasis: The Babylonian Story of the Flood* (Oxford: Oxford University Press, 1969). In my summary I have smoothed over some of the obscurities.

council of gods proposes that Beletili/Mami, the birth-goddess, should make man to "bear the toil of the gods" (I.191). She says that she needs the help of another god, Enki, who then undertakes to make purifying baths for the first, seventh, and fifteenth day of the month (I.206). Weila, a god with personality, is slaughtered, so that "all the gods may be cleansed in a dipping" (I.209). From Weila's flesh and blood Nintu mixes "clay," on which the gods spit (I.234). The account also mentions "spirit" (I.230), apparently derived from the slain god, which becomes an aspect of man, who is the product of the clay.

In the *Enuma Elish*,[5] Apsu and Tiamat (the water goddess) are the original father and mother gods. They give birth to a series of gods. When the gods become too noisy, they take counsel, and Apsu decides to destroy the gods. However, his plot becomes known to another god, Ea. Using a spell, Ea gets Apsu asleep and kills him. Ea and his consort Damkina give birth to Marduk, the patron god of Babylon.

Tiamat, enraged by the death of Apsu, gathers other gods, appoints Kingu as the chief, using a spell, and goes to war. She produces demon-like beings, the viper, the dragon, and the sphinx, to aid her in battle. No god can stand up to her until Marduk undertakes to go to meet her. But as a condition, he asks the gods to grant him supreme rule, to which they agree. Marduk prepares bow, arrow, and mace, plus winds and flood. He meets Tiamat, drives in the wind when she opens her mouth, and sends in the arrow, which tears her belly and splits her heart. He imprisons her followers and her demon assistants. Marduk crushes the skull of Tiamat with his mace. He splits her in two and one half becomes the sky. Her belly becomes the zenith (the point of the sky directly overhead). He sets guardians in place so that her waters will not escape. Orders from Marduk establish the constellations and the phases of the moon.

Marduk then proposes to the assembly of gods that he should make man to relieve the gods of labor. For this purpose one of the gods must be killed. It is Kingu, who organized the rebellion. They sever Kingu's blood vessels, and from his blood they fashion mankind. Marduk divides the assembly of gods in two, and appoints one half to have charge of heaven, the other half of earth. The gods propose to honor Marduk by building a shrine for him. They mold bricks for a whole year and build Babylon as his sanctuary.

---

[5] James B. Pritchard, ed., *Ancient Near Eastern Texts Relating to the Old Testament* (Princeton, N.J.: Princeton University Press, 1950), 60-72.

GENESIS 1–3 IN ITS CULTURAL CONTEXT

The biblical account in Genesis 1–3 shows some points of contact with these two ancient Near Eastern stories. But the differences stand out. In contrast to the crass, immoral, quarreling gods of polytheism stands the majestic, ordered, unopposed work of the one true God. Instead of creating man to serve the needs of complaining gods, God creates man out of his sheer bounty, blessing him and caring for him. Disorder and suffering come from the human fall and apostasy, not from the disorder of gods in conflict. Man does not spring from parts of a slain god but from dust, to which God imparts form and life. Gordon Wenham concludes, "It [Genesis 1] is not merely a demythologization of oriental creations myths, whether Babylonian or Egyptian; rather it is a polemical repudiation of such myths."[6]

Wenham summarizes the force of the contrasts in Genesis:

> [If Genesis 1–11 presents] the nature of the true God as one, omnipotent, omniscient, and good, as opposed to the fallible capricious, weak deities who populated the rest of the ancient world; if further it is concerned to show that humanity is central in the divine plan, not an afterthought; if finally it wants to show that man's plight is the product of his own dis-obedience and indeed is bound to worsen without divine intervention, Gen 1-11 is setting out a picture of the world that is at odds both with the poly-theistic optimism of ancient Mesopotamia and the humanistic secularism of the modern world.
>
> Genesis is thus a fundamental challenge to the ideologies of civilized men and women, past and present, who like to suppose their own efforts will ultimately suffice to save them. Gen 1-11 declares that mankind is without hope if individuals are without God. Human society will disinte-grate where divine law is not respected and divine mercy not implored. Yet Genesis, so pessimistic about mankind without God, is fundamentally opti-mistic, precisely because God created men and women in his own image and disclosed his ideal for humanity at the beginning of time. And through Noah's obedience and his sacrifice mankind's future was secured. And in the promise to the patriarchs the ultimate fulfillment of the creator's ideals for humanity is guaranteed.
>
> These then are the overriding concerns of Genesis. It is important to bear them in mind in studying its details. Though historical and scientific questions may be uppermost in our minds as we approach the text, it is

---

[6] Wenham, *Genesis*, 9. But Collins, *Genesis 1–4*, chapter 9, and Umberto Cassuto, *A Commentary on the Book of Genesis* (Jerusalem: Magnes, n.d.), 1:7, rightly point out that the polemical effect is indirect. Genesis 1 is first of all a positive account of God's acts of creation.

doubtful whether they were in the writer's mind, and we should therefore be cautious about looking for answers to questions he was not concerned with. Genesis is primarily about God's character and his purposes for sinful mankind. Let us beware of allowing our interests to divert us from the central thrust of the book, so that we miss what the LORD, our creator and redeemer, is saying to us.[7]

From a purely literary point of view, it does not look as if Genesis 1 directly uses or interacts with one specific polytheistic story. Rather, it interacts with the broader polytheistic atmosphere that all the pagan stories embody. By teaching strict monotheism it repudiates the entire atmosphere of the ancient Near East.[8]

CREATION WITHOUT PREEXISTING MATTER

The complete subjection of creation to God leaves no place for anything coeternal with God. There is no uncreated "prime matter" that was there from the beginning. The beginning in Genesis 1:1 is an absolute beginning.

Genesis 1 naturally focuses on theological issues prominent in the ancient Near East; it does not directly address philosophical speculations about the ultimacy of matter. But the thrust of Genesis 1 clearly does declare the supremacy and control of God over all. Theologically speaking, then, it invites the conclusion that God controls the very being and origin of everything, as well as more mundane developments that bring order into previously unordered situations.

I mention this point because considerable discussion has arisen about Genesis 1:1-2, concerning this very issue.[9] Some interpreters suggest that Genesis 1:1-2 should be translated, "When God began to create the heavens and the earth, the earth was without form . . ."[10] This interpretation then leaves open the question of where the earth came from originally. Was the earth already there when God began to create? Maybe it was just there, eternally, and then God began to create using this preexisting material. But the grammatical structure of the sequence of clauses in Hebrew indicates that

---

[7] Wenham, *Genesis,* liii.
[8] "This is not to say that the writer of Genesis had ever heard or read the Gilgamesh epic: these traditions were part of the intellectual furniture of that time in the Near East, just as most people today have some idea of Darwin's *Origin of Species* though they have never read it" (ibid., xlviii).
[9] See ibid., 11-15; Collins, *Genesis 1–4,* chapter 4.
[10] See RSV marginal note.

Genesis 1:1 is not subordinate, as this interpretation would require.[11] So we must reject this interpretation.

Others think that Genesis 1:1 is a title for the whole of Genesis 1. It states in a general way that God created the heavens and the earth; then Genesis 1:2–3:31 explains the creation more expansively. But this interpretation again leaves open the question of where the "earth" and the "deep" came from. They are just there, with no further explanation. This understanding in turn leaves open the question of whether the earth and the deep represent a "prime matter" that is itself uncreated, but that undergoes a process of formation and structuring during the six days of the creation week.

Other interpreters, however, think that Genesis 1:1 is not a title but is the first step in the entire process. Verse 1 announces the first, initial act of creating the whole world. But the result is initially unformed. It then undergoes development and ordering in verses 2-31. This interpretation seems best to me, partly because otherwise the "earth" that appears in verse 2 has no explanation.

Some interpreters point out that elsewhere in the Old Testament "the heavens and the earth" designate heavens and earth that have already undergone structuring and are already formed (see, for example, 2:1). So they conclude that the same is true in 1:1. "The heavens and the earth" must then represent the cosmos in its formed state, and so 1:1 is a general statement or a title for the whole of Genesis 1. Over against this view, one must allow for some flexibility in use of language. The beginning of creation involves a unique, unformed situation. What else would one call the world in the unformed state? Hebrew does not have a single word that is equivalent to "universe." Rather, one designates the whole by means of the pairing, "heaven(s) and earth."[12] It asserts thereby that God created everything that there is. I conclude, then, that Genesis 1:1 describes the original act of creating out of nothing.[13]

But even if this interpretation is not correct, the rest of Genesis 1 shows God's comprehensive control. We then infer that such control extends to the very being of the things that are controlled. Other biblical passages clearly exclude the idea of eternal prime matter by declaring the comprehensiveness of the act of creation: "For by him [the second person of the Trinity] all things

---

[11] Collins, *Science and Faith*, 67; Edward J. Young, "The Relation of the First Verse of Genesis One to Verses Two and Three," *Westminster Theological Journal* 21 (1959): 138-139.

[12] "It is characteristic of many languages to describe the totality of something in terms of its extremes, e.g., 'good and bad,' . . . . Here we have an example of this usage to define the universe" (Wenham, *Genesis*, 15).

[13] See the further discussion in Collins, *Science and Faith*, 66-68.

were created, in heaven and on earth, visible and invisible, whether thrones or dominions or rulers or authorities—all things were created through him and for him" (Col. 1:16; compare 1 Cor. 8:6).[14]

In the light of the New Testament, we know that God is one God in three persons. Genesis 1:2 already mentions the "Spirit of God" hovering over the face of the waters. And God brings about creation through his word. In John 1:1 the Word is identified as a distinct person ("with God"), and as the One who became flesh (1:14). All three persons participate in the creation of the world, though this mystery is only gradually revealed through the progress of revelation, ending with the New Testament.

IMPLICATIONS OF THE DOCTRINE OF CREATION

We are now ready to lay out some of the implications of the basic doctrine of creation.

1. The unity of God implies unity, order, and harmony in the world he has made. In polytheism, the gods interact with one another in a semi-chaotic manner, and threaten to make chaos a permanent aspect of practical experience. If one god intervenes at one point, the effects will depend on that particular god's "law" or agenda. Later, another god with another agenda comes. The laws shift accordingly. The course of the world is fundamentally unpredictable. Polytheism offers no basis for stable and permanent laws that science can explore. By contrast, biblical monotheism offers a foundation for the dependability and constancy of law. One self-consistent God with one self-consistent purpose governs the whole world. Scientists can investigate the world in the hope that they can uncover the consistency in God's governance.

2. Second, within polytheism the limitations in the power of any one god, or even all the gods taken together, give to the world a certain independence. Polytheists picture the gods as intervening from time to time, here and there, but also conceive of the world as going on its way with some independence when the gods are engaged in other affairs. By contrast, in the biblical worldview God is constantly and intimately involved with the world, and the world is absolutely under his control. The world is not semi-independent. Once again, this has implications for science. An independent world might show signs of irrationality at many points; but a world governed by the rational, personal, omnipotent God of Scripture will display the rationality of his pur-

---

[14] For further discussion of creation from nothing (*ex nihilo*), see John M. Frame, *The Doctrine of God* (Phillipsburg, N.J.: Presbyterian & Reformed, 2002), 298-302; and Paul Copan and William Lane Craig, *Creation Out of Nothing: A Biblical, Philosophical, and Scientific Exploration* (Grand Rapids, Mich.: Baker, 2004).

pose. A scientist can hope to understand something about God's purposes, rather than having to give up that possibility because the world is fundamentally irrational.

3. There is no eternal prime matter. The complete subjection of the world to God implies God's complete lordship. In conformity with this lordship, we as human beings are called on to submit to him. We need not fear alleged rival lords, which we would otherwise be tempted to propitiate.

Eliminating prime matter also eliminates irrationality that is beyond the scope of God's plan. The elimination of irrationality gives a firm basis for science.

4. Because the world is wholly created and is subjected to God, it is not semidivine. It is not an "emanation" from God that participates in the divine Being. It is not to be worshiped. Genesis 1 pointedly proclaims that the sun, the moon, and the stars were created by God, which contradicts the surrounding cultural thinking that these were divine. In this way the doctrine of creation "desacralizes" the creature. The creature is creature, not divine, though it proclaims the deity of the One who made it. Thus, unlike animists who fear that they will upset the spirits in the trees, Christians investigate the created world without fear.

5. Creation is a free act of God. That is, God did not have to create any world. Having decided to create, he made the world in a manner consistent with his own character. Yet he also made choices about the world that he was not compelled to make. Genesis 1 does not say all this in so many words, but implies it by the overall assertion of God's sovereignty and control. God spoke words of command that brought into existence light and plants and so forth. By implication, he spoke these words rather than many others that he could have spoken. He made choices to create exactly what he did.

This freedom of God again asserts his lordship over creation. But it also has implications for science. Scientists cannot hope to deduce the character of the world in detail, just from first principles. They cannot do so even if those first principles involve what they know of God. Because God created freely, in this way and not that way, we must go out and see what he decided to create, rather than deducing what he allegedly *must* have created.

Here we find the foundation for and encouragement of experimental science, and the necessity for testing theories against experiment. At the same time, of course, because God is rational and knowable, theories, as rational speculations about what God may have done, are as pertinent as experiment. God is both free (thus demanding experiment) and unchangeable is his character (demanding rational reflection on our part).

6. The acts of creation took place in time, long ago, and are now finished. God rested on the seventh day (Gen. 2:2). We know from other parts of Scripture that God continues to act in providence (Ps. 147:13-18), in miracle, and in redeeming acts (John 5:17). But the acts of creation in Genesis 1 do not continue to occur. God created light on the first day. He does not have to do it again (though he sustains the world and brings us light through his providence). He created man, and does not have to do that again—though in a subordinate sense he makes every new baby that comes into the world (Ps. 139:14-16).

The finishing of creation has an important bearing on science. If God were continually making new kinds of creatures, or perhaps even promulgating new laws, science would become difficult to maintain over the course of time. God's laws would seem to be shifting around, and correspondingly the scientist would find himself shifting to keep up. The permanency of the present order of things is important if science is not to be frustrated by having the rules changed.

7. Creation is the foundation for God's continual providential governance of the world. The six days are now past. But God's work of ruling the world takes place in the present as well. And the acts of creation enjoy a continued relation to the present acts of governing. For example, God created plants on the third day. "The earth brought forth vegetation, plants yielding seed according to their own kinds" (Gen. 1:12). The plants came into being in response to the word of God. But a careful reading of that word of God shows that the word has two aspects. First, God's word caused the first springing up of plants. Second, God's word describes and governs the *continued* springing up of plants. The explicit reference to seed indicates that God is laying down a permanent pattern for plants, by which they will reproduce, producing more plants "according to their own kinds." On the fifth day God gives the command, "Be fruitful and multiply" to the sea creatures (1:22). That command clearly governs sea creatures up to this day. God created them in the beginning and laid down permanent orders for their propagation through many generations. Sea creatures are still obeying those orders.

The harmony between creation and providence shows in one more way the harmony in God's plan and government. For the purposes of science, it says that the way things function now is in harmony with what they really are. God's law that governs them now is not an afterthought, imposed on things that were originally made for some radically different purpose. Rather, the law is an expression of that original purpose of God.

5

ISSUES WITH GENESIS 1
AND SCIENCE

Now we consider specific areas of potential conflict between Genesis 1 and modern science. We find at least three main issues: (1) worldview; (2) the age of the earth; and (3) the origin of living things. The first of these, worldview, concerns the difference between a Christian view of the world, with God as Creator, and a host of modern views that alter the doctrine of God, or deny that he exists, or deny that he is relevant. Some alternate views, like Islam, claim to rely on a divine revelation. But we cannot enter into this kind of debate in any detail in a book that focuses on science. Suffice it to say that the Bible is the word of God, and that competing claims for revelatory authority are counterfeit.

THE WORLDVIEW OF EVOLUTIONARY NATURALISM

More to the point in our discussion are counterclaims that partly depend on the prestige of science. One in particular deserves attention. *Evolutionary naturalism* expands the biological theory of evolution into a complete worldview that offers answers for the big questions about meaning and destiny.

- Who rules? God does not exist or is irrelevant.
- From where do we come? Purposeless evolution has cast up the human race alongside other living species.
- Where are we going? To dust and death. Eventually the human race will evolve into something else nonhuman, or superhuman, or else it will die out. In the end, the increase of entropy and decrease in useful energy available for work seem to imply the extinction of every form of life.

- Why are we here? To propagate the species. But ultimately the universe as a whole is purposeless, and hence human life in its cosmic setting is purposeless.

These views go far beyond biological investigations of the fossil record, embryology, and genetics. In fact, they involve sweeping metaphysical and religious assumptions. The assumptions are religious because they make a decision about the existence and nature of God. Yet, because of various features in contemporary society, evolutionary naturalism tends to enjoy the prestige of science, and its metaphysical underpinnings tend to go unquestioned. We also see a tendency to use the same word, "evolution," in several distinct ways.

(1) *Microevolution* describes the observable changes that take place within a living genus or species as it reproduces over a number of generations, particularly when survival pressures from the environment drive the changes. Animal and plant breeding and the acquisition of antibiotic resistance by bacteria offer clear examples of such changes. Scientists frequently call these changes "evolution," but we could also call them "adaptation" if we do not want to confuse these changes with the other meanings of the word "evolution."

(2) *Macroevolution* describes the hypothesis that shifts from one type of living thing to a quite different type (with, for example, a different ground-plan for bodily organization) can take place by the accumulation of microevolutionary changes over a huge number of generations. Under the influence of a materialist worldview, it is commonly assumed that these changes over time are not directed by intelligence or long-range purpose.

(3) *Evolutionary origin of life* describes the hypothesis that the first living thing arose through a gradual series of steps, each of which had a reasonable probability according to physical and chemical laws. The sudden assembly of a whole cell, either from its constituent atoms or from available organic molecules, is ruled out.

(4) *Evolutionary naturalism* describes the materialistic worldview already defined above.

Evolutionary naturalism represents a full-blown worldview, with answers to the big questions about the meaning of the world. Its answers directly contradict the view set forth in the Bible, and compete with it. As a worldview, evolutionary naturalism has no evidence to support it, but only an enormous leap from the observation that natural laws can explain some things to the conclusion that the material world is all there is to explain. Moreover, by appealing to science and scientific law, it relies on law, which, as we have seen (chapter 1), amounts to relying on God. This position is incoherent, but it enjoys prestige from its association with the successes of science, and also from the sheer number of prominent people who hold to it.

The three other uses of the word *evolution* need separate evaluation. *Microevolution* takes place all the time in the present, and is not in dispute. *Macroevolution* is more problematic, because it represents a daring extrapolation of microevolution. Its plausibility depends on many cultural as well as scientific factors, including the presence or absence of various alternative explanations. And a great deal of difference remains between a view that says that alleged steps in evolution are guided by divine intelligence and a view that excludes any such guidance.[1]

The discussions about the *evolutionary origin of life* have generated a number of hypotheses, but going from a lifeless earth environment to the high organization characterizing even the simplest bacterium presents a tremendous gap.[2]

Whole books discuss macroevolution and the evolutionary origin of life. We do not propose to duplicate ground already well covered elsewhere. But later on we will look at the assumptions and frameworks that surround evolutionary theory.

THE AGE OF THE EARTH

The age of the earth presents an important test case in dealing with the relation of the Bible to science. Mainstream science currently estimates the age of the earth at about 4.5 billion years, and the age of the universe at about 14 billion years. But Genesis 1 describes God as creating the world in six days.

Bernard Ramm's book *The Christian View of Science and Scripture,* published in 1954, surveyed this and other problems with the relation of the Bible to modern science.[3] In the fifty years since Ramm wrote, science has continued to advance and change. But, interestingly, the shape of the basic alterna-

---

[1] For a survey of the difficulties with undirected macroevolution, see Philip E. Johnson, *Darwin on Trial* (Downers Grove, Ill.: InterVarsity Press, 1991); Michael Denton, *Evolution: A Theory in Crisis* (Bethesda, Md.: Adler & Adler, 1985); Michael Behe, *Darwin's Black Box: The Biochemical Challenge to Evolution* (New York: Free Press, 1996); updated by information-theoretic considerations in William A. Dembski, *No Free Lunch: Why Specified Complexity Cannot Be Purchased Without Intelligence* (Lanham/Boulder/New York/Oxford: Rowman & Littlefield, 2002). The defenders of evolution are many. We may cite as examples Robert T. Pennock, *Tower of Babel: The Evidence Against the New Creationism* (Cambridge, Mass.: MIT Press, 1999); Kenneth R. Miller, *Finding Darwin's God* (New York: Cliff Street, 1999); Stephen J. Gould, *The Structure of Evolutionary Theory* (Cambridge, Mass.: Harvard University Press, 2002).

[2] Charles Thaxton, Walter Bradley, and Roger Olsen, *The Mystery of Life's Origin: Reassessing Current Theories* (New York: Philosophical Library, 1984); Denton, *Evolution,* 249-273; Dembski, *No Free Lunch,* 179-180; Fazale Rana and Hugh Ross, *Origins of Life: Biblical and Evolutionary Models Face Off* (Colorado Springs: NavPress, 2004).

[3] Bernard Ramm, *The Christian View of Science and Scripture* (Grand Rapids, Mich.: Eerdmans, 1954). The discussion of the age of the earth is found on 173-229.

tives for explaining the relation of science to the Bible has changed very little. We shall list these alternatives one by one, and then proceed to evaluate them.[4]

24-Hour-Day View

The *24-hour-day* view[5] says that the six days of creation in Genesis 1 are all 24 hours long. By itself, this view offers an interpretation of Genesis 1 but not an interpretation of modern science. Hence, in order to address modern science, it needs to be combined with an explanation of scientific results. The usual way offered is *flood geology.*

Flood Geology

Flood geology says that the great majority of geologic strata, including virtually all fossil-bearing strata, derive from the flood of Noah. It thus maintains that mainstream geology is radically mistaken in attaching dates of millions of years to many of the strata.

Religious-Only Theory

The *religious-only* theory says that the Bible *only* addresses matters of "religion," not matters of scientific fact. Alleged discrepancies arise only because people have misjudged the purpose of the Bible.

Local Creation Theory

The theory of *local creation,* in its common form, says that Genesis 1:1 describes God's original act of creation. Then in Genesis 1:2 we shift to a limited territory in the Near East, which was devastated. Genesis 1:3-31 describes God's acts of restoration and re-creation within this limited local area. Genesis 1 harmonizes with modern science mainly through interpreting it as referring only to this local area.

Mature Creation Theory

Mature creation[6] says that the universe was created over a short span of time (probably six 24-hour days), with the endpoint of creation being a situation

---

[4] For convenience, I have usually followed the order in Ramm's list (ibid., 173-229). But I have moved flood geology forward in the list in order to put it next to the 24-hour-day view, with which it is usually associated. I have dropped Ramm's theory of *successive catastrophes,* because it is no longer widely held.

[5] Ramm labels this view the "naive-literal view" (ibid., 173). But "naive" is an inappropriate label, since not all the adherents are naive.

[6] Ramm labels this view the "pro-chronic or ideal time view" (ibid., 192).

that would have a consistent appearance of age. It was created *mature*. This theory points to Adam as a key example. God created Adam already an adult, already *mature*. But a scientific investigator who examined Adam's body—not knowing his actual origin—might guess that Adam was (say) 23 years old. Adam had a navel, just as later human beings would whose actual origin included gestation in the womb.[7] The trees in the garden of Eden looked mature, and would have had rings in their trunks from which a scientist could have inferred their age in years. But it would have been an age in "ideal time," an unreal time projected backward in the scientist's mind when he examined the mature result.

Gap Theory

The *gap* theory says that God's original act of creation described in Genesis 1:1 was followed by a catastrophe in 1:2 and a re-creation in 1:3-31. Verse 2 is to be read, "And the earth *became* without form and void." A large amount of time passed in verses 1-2, into which the data of geology can be fit.

Day-Age Theory

The *day-age* theory, or "day-age concordism"[8] says that the "days" in Genesis 1 are not 24-hour days but are long periods of time, corresponding in many cases to millions of years on the geological time-scale. It typically appeals to the fact that in some contexts the word "day" can designate a longer period, as in the expression "the day of the LORD."

Intermittent Day Theory

The *intermittent day* theory[9] says that each day described in Genesis 1 is 24 hours long, but that there are large gaps in time between the days. The creative activity described in Genesis 1 takes place largely in the gaps between the days. For example, the day described in verse 13 (the "third day") falls after the creation of dry land and plants, and before the creation of the heavenly bodies.

---

[7] Hence this theory is also called the *omphalos* theory, from the Greek word for navel.

[8] Ramm labels this view "Age-day or Divine-day, or concordism" (Ramm, *Christian View of Science and Scripture*, 211). It has also been called the *geologic-day* theory (ibid.).

[9] This approach is not included in Ramm's list. For more discussion of this approach, see Robert C. Newman, *Genesis One and the Origin of the Earth* (Downers Grove, Ill.: InterVarsity Press, 1977).

Revelatory Day Theory

The *revelatory day* theory[10] says that God revealed to Moses (or to whoever authored Genesis) the truths about creation in a period of six days in Moses' life. The days are thus literal 24-hour days, but they are days in Moses' life, not the times within which God acted to create.

Framework View

The *framework* view[11] (also called the *framework hypothesis*) says that the six days provide a literary framework for displaying the acts of creation. The acts are real acts in space and time, but the framework of days does not offer information either about the length of time or about the relative sequence of events.

Analogical Day Theory

The *analogical day* theory[12] says that Genesis 1 sets up an *analogy* between God's work and human work. God works six days and then rests on the seventh day. Man is to imitate this pattern by his Sabbath observance (Ex. 20:11). God's works are real (historical) acts of God in time and space. But God's work is analogous to man's work, rather than being on the same level.

Consistent with this analogy, the use of the word *day* for both God and man establishes an analogy, not an identity. The days of creation thus have unspecified length, and form the basis for analogical imitation on the part

---

[10] The last of the approaches on Ramm's list is entitled "Pictorial Day and Moderate Concordism." Because this heading encompasses a number of distinct approaches, we have chosen to subdivide it.

[11] See Arie Noordtzij, *Gods Woord en der Eeuwen Getuigenis* (Kampen, Netherlands: 1924); Nicolaas H. Ridderbos, *Is There a Conflict Between Genesis 1 and Natural Science?* (Grand Rapids, Mich.: Eerdmans, 1957); Meredith G. Kline, "Space and Time in the Genesis Cosmogony," *Perspectives on Science and Christian Faith* 48/1 (1996): 2-15. See also Meredith G. Kline, "Because It Had Not Rained," *Westminster Theological Journal* 20 (1958): 146-157; Mark D. Futato, "Because It Had Rained: A Study of Gen 2:5-7 with Implications for Gen 2:4-25 and Gen 1:1–2:3," *Westminster Theological Journal* 60/1 (1998): 1-21. W. Robert Godfrey's covenantal exposition of Genesis 1 shows affinity to the framework hypothesis but has questions about some of the detailed exegetical claims in Kline (Godfrey, *God's Pattern for Creation: A Covenantal Reading of Genesis 1* [Phillipsburg, N.J.: Presbyterian & Reformed, 2003]). The "Report of the Committee to Study the Views of Creation," *Minutes of the Seventy-First General Assembly . . . of the Orthodox Presbyterian Church* (Willow Grove, Pa.: Orthodox Presbyterian Church, 2004), 251, classifies Godfrey with the analogical day theory, discussed below.

[12] This theory is represented most adequately by C. John Collins, "Reading Genesis 1:1–2:3 as an Act of Communication: Discourse Analysis and Literal Interpretation," in Joseph Pipa, Jr., and David Hall, eds., *Did God Create in Six Days?* (Taylors, S.C.: Southern Presbyterian Press, 1999), 131-151; see also C. John Collins, *Science and Faith: Friends or Foes?* (Wheaton, Ill.: Crossway, 2003), especially chapter 5. Something like it seems to have been anticipated by Herman Bavinck: "The creation days are the work-days of God. By a labor, resumed and renewed six times, he prepared the whole earth and transformed the chaos into a cosmos. In the Sabbath command this pattern is prescribed to us as well. As they did for God, so for man too six days of labor are followed by a day of rest" (Bavinck, *In the Beginning: Foundations of Creation Theology* [Grand Rapids, Mich.: Baker, 1999], 126). Edward J. Young also held a similar view:

of man. This view differs from the day-age view mainly in that it does not appeal to other lexical meanings of the word *day* (Hebrew *yom*) as an isolated word but claims that the *whole* passage involves an analogy. The analogy, if present, does not pertain narrowly to the word *day* but to the passage as a whole.

One matter that Christians like to talk about is the length of these days. It is not too profitable to do so, for the simple reason that God has not revealed sufficient for us to say very much about it. . . . The first three days are not solar days such as we now know. . . . And the work of the third day seems to suggest that there was some process, and that what took place occurred in a period longer than twenty-four hours (Young, *In the Beginning: Genesis Chapters 1 to 3 and the Authority of Scripture* [Edinburgh/Carlisle: Banner of Truth, 1976], 43).

The "Report of the Committee to Study the Views of Creation" classifies Herman Bavinck and E. J. Young as holding to "the day of unspecified length view," which is not very different from the analogical day view.

6

THE TEACHING IN
GENESIS 1

Now we need to undertake an evaluation of the various interpretations of Genesis 1. But how do we go about it? We do so as finite, sinful creatures. God calls us to trust what he says in the Bible. But our interpretation of the Bible is fallible, modern science is fallible, and our interpretation of science is fallible. We must submit to God and at the same time exercise humility about our own understanding. If we see an apparent discrepancy, we do not know right away where the problem has arisen. Does the fault lie with misinterpreting the Bible or with misinterpretations within science or with both? Moreover, our knowledge is partial. We believe that God has the answers. But in some circumstances we do not have the answers ourselves.

In a situation like this, one possible answer may stand out as clearly right. Or it may be that no satisfactory answer presents itself, and we just have to wait for something better. Or several answers may be attractive, while others can be excluded with some confidence. The persistence of several alternative views, even among those with a high regard for biblical authority, suggests that we exercise caution and admit our own limitations as well as the limitations of the scientific enterprise as a whole.

But we can make a beginning, and try to exclude the less plausible alternatives. To do so, we have to give attention both to the teaching of the Bible and to possible sources of problems in the scientific enterprise.

DISCERNING THE TEACHING OF THE BIBLE

What sort of teaching is God giving us in Genesis 1? What type of communication do we have here? Two extremes present themselves. On the one hand, some people see Genesis 1 as hopelessly primitive, and therefore of little value, except perhaps in some narrow "religious" area. On the other hand, others read Genesis 1 almost as if it were a scientific description of the events, albeit a short and abbreviated description. Both of these views fail to treat Genesis 1 with care within its actual context in the Bible.[1]

Genesis 1 ends with a description of the sixth day of creation, but that is not the end of its account. A seventh day in 2:1-3 ends the cycle. Then begins a series of sections of genealogical history, each of which opens with an expression like "These are the generations of . . .":

These are the generations of the heavens and the earth . . . (2:4).

This is the book of the generations of Adam (5:1).

These are the generations of Noah (6:9).

These are the generations of the sons of Noah (10:1).

These are the generations of Shem (11:10).

Now these are the generations of Terah (11:27).

These are the generations of Ishmael (25:12).

These are the generations of Isaac (25:19).

These are the generations of Esau (36:1).

These are the generations of Jacob (37:2).

The first two sections, Genesis 1:1–2:3 and 2:4–4:26, overlap in the events that they mention. Some people have seen discrepancies here, and have spoken of two distinct accounts of creation.[2] But when read as a literary whole, Genesis does not really show discrepancy. The first account is orga-

---

[1] On the history of interpretation of the days of creation, see Robert Letham, "'In the Space of Six Days': The Days of Creation from Origen to the Westminster Assembly," *Westminster Theological Journal* 61/2 (1999): 147-174. Further discussion from the standpoint of the 24-hour-day view can be found in J. Ligon Duncan III and David W. Hall, "The 24-Hour View," in David G. Hagopian, ed., *The Genesis Debate: Three Views on the Days of Creation* (Mission Viejo, Calif.: Crux, 2001), 47-52 (with responses on 68-70, 89-90, and 99-106); and from the standpoint of the day-age view in Hugh Ross, *Creation and Time: A Biblical and Scientific Perspective on the Creation-Date Controversy* (Colorado Springs: NavPress, 1994), 16-24.

[2] We cannot enter into a discussion of the documentary hypothesis. I refer readers to the commentaries on Genesis by Wenham, Hamilton, and Kidner.

nized more taxonomically, in terms of the various types of creatures that God made. The second account focuses on the creation of man, and is organized primarily *teleologically*, that is, from the standpoint of purposes. The creation of man comes near the beginning of the account, and then we hear about various other aspects primarily in terms of their purposes in relation to man, and the ways in which they may serve human needs. God makes the garden and its trees for human food and enjoyment; the gold in Havilah is for his use; the animals are subordinate creatures, while the woman is created as one like him, so that he will not be alone.

The second account opens, as we observed, with the first notice of genealogical history, "These are the generations of . . ." (2:4). This structuring of Genesis holds it together as a literary whole. Now, the later part of Genesis records incidents in the lives of Abraham, Isaac, Jacob, and Joseph, incidents that sound like real-life events. The later parts of the Bible confirm that ancient readers understood that the patriarchs were real people, and that the recorded incidents actually took place.

Modern skeptics have said that these descriptions are perhaps legends or inventions, with little or no historical core. They have argued that probably the events were recorded in written form only long after the time when they happened. But we do not know when the events were first recorded. It is quite possible that written records were made at a very early period, even before the whole of Genesis was written. In fact, the contents of almost the whole of the book of Genesis could have been recorded by Joseph the son of Jacob. As a ruler in Egypt and as a recipient of divine revelation, he had the resources to be able to produce such a work. Earlier records like his could have been used by Moses. As long as we recognize the divine authority of Genesis, it does not matter much what human sources were involved in its composition.

In addition, the passage of time poses no obstacle to God's memory. The God of the Bible, who is all powerful, can preserve the memories of events through generations, if he so wishes, or he can reveal the truths afresh to a new generation, if he so wishes. Skepticism concerning the patriarchs presupposes skepticism about the God of the Bible.

USE OF THE TERM "MYTH"

Skeptics have also labeled parts of the Bible as "myth." But "myth" is a very slippery word. It could mean any nonscientific account of how the world came to be. It could mean any story involving the action of gods or superhuman characters. In ordinary English it connotes something made up or untrue. And it is convenient for skeptics to slip into this meaning when they want.

It is better, then, not to use such a slippery word. Or if we do, use it consistently. (Below I will use it in its popular sense, a made-up story that includes superhuman characters.) Perhaps we want to consider stories that involve the actions of superhuman beings, either gods or superhuman heroes. These stories occurred in the ancient world, and typically they were fanciful and polytheistic. But the central question remains, "How do we know whether the gods or superhuman heroes actually existed?" Those who listened to the stories may possibly have had a number of attitudes. Greek philosophers questioned the validity of some of the ancient stories about the Greek gods. Perhaps, centuries earlier, some skeptically minded people questioned the Mesopotamian and Canaanite and Egyptian stories too. We do not know for sure. But typically the people of the Near East accepted the real existence of the gods, as is proved by their willingness in times of desperation even to offer a child in sacrifice to a god (Lev. 18:21; 2 Kings 16:3; Ps. 106:38). In calling the stories about ancient gods "myths," we modern people agree that these gods were illusory. The stories were counterfeits. But they were counterfeits of something true. False gods counterfeit the true God, and replace worship of the true God with a substitute, corrupt worship. But they are close enough to the truth to entice people into the falsehood.

Thus, in pagan stories about the gods we find idolatrous deformations of the knowledge of God, which all human beings confront through general revelation (Rom. 1:18-23). God gives us the true story, which frees us from the counterfeit. Modern people have noticed some similarities between the Bible and the ancient Near East, and some have concluded that the biblical story is also made up, "mythical." But the similarities in the accounts come from the natural resemblances between truth and its counterfeits. The skeptics overlook this possibility in concluding that everything in the ancient Near East is necessarily counterfeit.

So I conclude that we are dealing with real events in Genesis, not made-up stories. The presence of divine action in a story does not change its character into "myth," but instructs us appropriately about God's involvement in the world. Modern skepticism about biblical description of divine action actually rests on the assumption that the God of the Bible does not exist.

FOCUS AND SELECTIVITY IN GENESIS

Genesis tells us, then, about real events. But it shows great selectivity and restraint in the subjects that it covers. The later parts of Genesis focus almost wholly on the lives of the patriarchs, Abraham, Isaac, Jacob, and the sons of Jacob. Genesis 10–11 describes the multiplication and dispersal of human beings after the flood, but then Genesis zeros in on the line of Terah and Abraham, which numerically constituted only a tiny part of the whole. The genealogical organization in Genesis clearly focuses much more on Isaac and Jacob than on the collateral lines of Ishmael and Esau. We find here, not a general history of the ancient Near East, but a *theological* history concentrating on God's special covenantal commitment to Abraham and his descendants. Even the history of Abraham, Isaac, and Jacob does not offer a full biography but concentrates on a small number of events that represent key turning points.

Moreover, Genesis does not always offer a purely linear, chronologically arranged account. For example, it takes care of the line of Ishmael all at once, up to his death (Gen. 25:17), and then two verses later (25:19) picks up the line of Isaac from its beginning by mentioning his birth, which Genesis already described earlier (21:2-3). Clearly we have some degree of topical arrangement.

As we already noted, Genesis 2:4-24 describes some of the same events as Genesis 1. Genesis 2:4-24 does not give all the events in chronological order. For example, Genesis 2:8 and 2:15 both say that God "put" the man in the garden of Eden. These two verses appear to be descriptions of the same event. In between come the description of growth of trees (2:9) and information about the broader setting (2:10-14). In addition, both Genesis 2:4-24 and Genesis 1:1–2:3 are selective, each including some details that their companion account does not mention explicitly. Genesis 1:27 proclaims that God made man, male and female. But it does not describe *how* he did it. Only in Genesis 2 do we learn that God made man from dust (2:7), and that he used a rib from Adam to make Eve (2:22).

GENESIS 1–2 IN RELATION TO THE ANCIENT NEAR EAST

We also need to reckon with the fact that God originally caused Genesis to be written within the ancient Near Eastern environment. As we saw in chapter 4, that environment included people who told and wrote fanciful stories about the origins of the world, stories that included the polytheistic distortions of polytheistic cultures. Ancient Israelite readers would have recognized immediately that Genesis 1–2 was contradicting widespread polytheism and its distortions of the idea of creation.

We need then to take seriously the character of Genesis 1–2. It is not *directly* addressing questions that we bring to it out of a modern scientific environment. It addresses the ancient world, with its questions about what the gods are like, and what role they had in bringing the world into its present state.

ORDINARY LANGUAGE

So we should not be surprised to find that Genesis 1–2 does not employ modern scientific language. If it had done so, the original ancient recipients would not have understood it. And that is not its purpose, anyway. It addresses us using "phenomenal language," the language of appearances, the ordinary language that one would use to describe how things look to an average human being.[3] What do we see? The ground is underneath, the sky is overhead, the sun rises and sets. To this day we still talk about the sun rising and setting, even though the astronomers have told us that the earth is spinning while the sun stays still.

Do we speak erroneously in saying that the sun sets? No, we are speaking truly. We are not claiming to offer a new astronomical theory but are speaking in the context of ordinary, "phenomenal" experience. In fact, the use of this ordinary language gives Genesis great communicative power and universal relevance. People in every culture, in every location, in every century, see the ground underneath and the sky above. But not all cultures know of modern science, with its heavy use of technical, experimental, and mathematical tools.

By using ordinary language, God speaks through Genesis to every culture. All cultures can come to understand what Genesis says, and what it says is completely true. It is true not just in the way in which it addresses the immediate needs in the ancient Near East, but true for all times and all places. Moreover, because Genesis focuses on the level of ordinary experience, it has direct relevance for people in their everyday experiences in all cultures and situations, not just for people engaged in science or heavily influenced by sci-

---

[3] On "phenomenal" language, see Bernard Ramm, *The Christian View of Science and Scripture* (Grand Rapids, Mich.: Eerdmans, 1954), 67-69; John Calvin, *Commentaries on the First Book of Moses, Called Genesis*, trans. John King, 2 vols. (reprint; Grand Rapids, Mich.: Eerdmans, 1948), 1:79-80. Thomas Aquinas says, "Moses, accommodating himself to uneducated people, followed the things which appear to the senses" (Herman Bavinck, *In the Beginning: Foundations of Creation Theology* [Grand Rapids, Mich.: Baker, 1999], 120; quoting from Thomas Aquinas, *Summa Theologica*, 1.70.4).

ence. It is important to see that in Genesis God does not propound *any* specific technical scientific theory, so that we may appreciate what God *does* do, namely set forth the truth for all people everywhere. God showed profound wisdom in giving us what all of us as fallen human beings really *need* to know.

John Calvin makes a similar observation about Genesis 1:

> For, to my mind, this is a certain principle, that nothing is here [in Genesis 1] treated of but the visible form of the world. He who would learn astronomy, and other recondite arts, let him go elsewhere. Here the Spirit of God would teach all men without exception; and therefore what Gregory declares falsely and in vain respecting statues and pictures is truly applicable to the history of the creation, namely, that it is the book of the unlearned.[4]

Thus the Bible is not at all giving a technical, scientific theory about the solar system. It is not offering either a modern theory or an ancient theory. It is offering us ordinary language as a way of talking that is neither a "theory," nor "scientific," but just plain ordinary. "Theory" and "science" imply the use of technical, experimental, and mathematical tools, and that sets us up to have mistaken expectations.

IMPOSING A TECHNICAL READING

We may find a tendency to read the Bible with technical expectations in some of the discussions about the "waters that were above the expanse" in Genesis 1:7. John C. Whitcomb, Jr., and the late Henry M. Morris propose that these

---

[4] Calvin, *Genesis,* 1:79-80. See also Calvin's later remarks commenting on Genesis 1:16:

Moses makes two great luminaries; but astronomers prove, by conclusive reasons, that the star of Saturn, which, on account of its great distance, appears the least of all, is greater than the moon. Here lies the difference; Moses wrote in a popular style things which, without instruction, all ordinary persons, endued with common sense, are able to understand; but astronomers investigate with great labour whatever the sagacity of the human mind can comprehend. Nevertheless, this study is not to be reprobated, nor this science to be condemned, because some frantic persons are wont boldly to reject whatever is unknown to them. For astronomy is not only pleasant, but also very useful to be known: it cannot be denied that this art unfolds the admirable wisdom of God. Wherefore, as ingenious men are to be honoured who have expended useful labour on this subject, so they who have leisure and capacity ought not to neglect this kind of exercise. Nor did Moses truly wish to withdraw us from this pursuit in omitting such things as are peculiar to the art; but because he was ordained a teacher as well of the unlearned and rude as of the learned, he could not otherwise fulfil his office than by descending to this grosser method of instruction. Had he spoken of things generally unknown, the uneducated might have pleaded in excuse that such subjects were beyond their capacity. Lastly, since the Spirit of God here opens a common school for all, it is not surprising that he should chiefly choose those subjects which would be intelligible to all. If the astronomer inquires respecting the actual dimensions of the stars, he will find the moon to be less than Saturn; but this is something abstruse, for to the sight it appears differently. Moses, therefore, rather adapts his discourse to common usage (86-87).

waters formed "a great vapor canopy around the earth," which afterward provided some of the water in Noah's flood.[5] Others think it was an ice canopy that melted to provide the flood. But Psalm 148:4 speaks of the "waters above the heavens" as something still existing when the psalmist wrote, long after the flood. Moreover, Genesis 1, addressed to people who lived long after the flood, needs to be interpreted in a way that makes sense to these people. They did not have an elaborate scientific theory about the pre-flood world. When they read Genesis 1, they needed to have it describe things that they could identify. Psalm 148:4 confirms that the "waters above the heavens" were something familiar to them.

Calvin thinks it refers to the clouds.[6] Or it may be a reference to the experience of rain coming down from above.[7] The rainwater was up there before it came down. But an ordinary person in the ancient world might not know the scientific details, such as the fact that water vapor exists in invisible form before it condenses into clouds or rain. These details are irrelevant to the purpose in Genesis 1.

In addition, skeptical readers of the Bible have sometimes tried to force a technical meaning onto Genesis 1. They have ascribed to the Bible an erroneous, primitive "science." For example, some have claimed that the Bible teaches that rainwater is held in check by a solid barrier of sky. The water comes down from heaven when God opens "the windows of the heavens," which are conceived of as solid plates that he moves aside. But the ancients knew well enough that rain came from clouds:

> . . . the heavens dropped,
> yes, the clouds dropped water (Judg. 5:4).

> The clouds poured out water; . . . (Ps. 77:17).
> . . . the clouds that bring the spring rain (Prov. 16:15).

> If the clouds are full of rain,
>   they empty themselves on the earth, . . . (Eccles. 11:3).

---

[5] John C. Whitcomb, Jr., and Henry M. Morris, *The Genesis Flood: The Biblical Record and Its Scientific Implications* (Philadelphia: Presbyterian & Reformed, 1961), 229, 240.

[6] Calvin, *Genesis*, 1:80-81; similarly Augustine, *The Literal Meaning of Genesis (De Genesi ad litteram)* 2.7; St. Basil, *Hexaemeron* 3.8.

[7] Thomas Aquinas seems to favor a view similar to this when he says that the "firmament" or "expanse" may be "that part of the atmosphere where clouds undergo condensation," and "the waters that are above the firmament are the same so that, when evaporated and taken up in to the atmosphere, are the source of rain" (Aquinas, *Summa theologiae* [Latin text and English translation; New York: Blackfriars & McGraw-Hill; London: Eyre & Spottiswoode, 1964], 1a. q. 68, 1, p. 75; and 1a. q. 68, 2, p. 79).

I will also command the clouds
    that they rain no rain upon it (Isa. 5:6).

In 1 Kings 18:44 Elijah's servant sees "a little cloud like a man's hand," indicating the coming of rain.

The whole language about windows (Gen. 7:11; 8:2) is a colorful metaphor, as one sees from the fact that in Malachi 3:10 God opens "the windows of heaven" to pour down a blessing. In 2 Kings 7:2 the captain postulates that the Lord would "make windows in heaven" to supply grain. Literally understood, this is inconsistent with the windows already being there to provide rain! Such language does not provide a quasi-scientific theory but a colorful picture. Some time ago I myself heard an acquaintance (not a Bible scholar) describing an experience in which, as he said, "the heavens were opened" and a strong downpour descended.

With this in mind, we may go back to the account of Noah's flood in Genesis 7–8. At the start of Noah's flood, Genesis 7:11-12 says that "the windows of the heavens were opened. And rain fell upon the earth forty days and forty nights." Even though people knew that rain came from clouds, they did not necessarily know what supplied the clouds with water. And the amount of water that fell during Noah's flood was truly remarkable. It is therefore pictured as being like someone who opens a hole in a ceiling and pours down bucketfuls. Later on, in Genesis 8:2, "the windows of the heavens were closed," terminating the downpour. The second part of the verse explains the same thing without using the picture of windows: "the rain from the heavens was restrained."

We can receive further illumination by asking what are these "heavens" to which Genesis refers? In Genesis 1:6 God made "an expanse" (KJV "firmament") and then called it "Heaven" (1:8). (The words *heavens* and *heaven* in English translate the same Hebrew word, *shamayim*.) Later on, in verse 15, the heavenly lights are "in the expanse of the heavens" (Hebrew *shamayim*). That is, they are in the sky. The word for "heaven" in Hebrew can denote the sky (as it does in Gen. 1:15; see also Gen. 15:5). It is the location from which rain comes (as in Gen. 8:2). The land of Canaan "drinks water by the rain from *heaven*" (Deut. 11:11). If God is angry, he will "*shut up the heavens, so that there will be no rain*" (Deut. 11:17). In blessing, "The LORD will open to you his good treasury, *the heavens,* to give the rain to your land in its season . . ." (Deut. 28:12). See also 2 Samuel 21:10; 1 Kings 8:35; Psalm 104:13; Isaiah 55:10; and Jeremiah 10:13.

The same word for "heaven" can also denote the invisible heaven where

God is surrounded by angels: "Look down from your holy habitation, from *heaven,* and bless your people Israel . . ." (Deut. 26:15). "Listen in *heaven* your dwelling place" (1 Kings 8:30). But in Genesis 1:15 it refers to the sky, and it is natural to take the earlier reference in Genesis 1:8 the same way. The waters below eventually come together to form "Seas" (Gen. 1:10). The "waters above the heavens" are then the source of rain, as they are in Noah's flood and in the passages in Deuteronomy and elsewhere. No technical scientific explanation is being provided.

In fact, in God's speech to Job he points out that Job does not know the mysteries about rain, snow, and hail (Job 38:22, 25-30). Making "the waters above the heavens" into technical language flies in the face of God's own statements about the limitations in ancient knowledge. The Bible is describing what an ordinary person could observe about the sky overhead and the rain coming down.[8]

PROTO-SCIENCE AMONG THE BABYLONIANS

The Babylonians from a fairly early period had experts who devoted attention to the sky. They built up a technical expertise that enabled them to calculate the periods of the moon, and eventually to predict eclipses of the sun and the moon.[9] Predicting eclipses is not easy, and represents a most impressive achievement within the ancient world. This technical expertise was not quite like modern science. Its knowledge did not "take off" and grow expo-

---

[8] Sometimes it is said that the language in the Bible arises against the background of ancient "cosmology" that postulated underlying waters, then solid earth, then a solid "firmament" dome for the sky, then the sea above the firmament (Paul H. Seely, "The Firmament and the Water Above. Part I: The Meaning of *raqia'* in Gen 1:6-8," *Westminster Theological Journal* 53 [1991]: 227-240; Seely, "The Firmament and the Water Above. Part II: The Meaning of 'The Water Above the Firmament' in Gen 1:6-8," *Westminster Theological Journal* 54/1 [1992]: 31-46; Seely, "The Geographical Meaning of 'Earth' and 'Seas' in Genesis 1:10," *Westminster Theological Journal* 59 [1997]: 231-255; Seely, "Noah's Flood: Its Date, Extent, and Divine Accommodation," *Westminster Theological Journal* 66 [2004]: 291-311).

For one thing, the ancient Near East did not have one unified "ancient cosmology" but several accounts—Sumerian, Babylonian, Egyptian, and Hittite—contradicting one another at points but nevertheless with some similarities. Genesis 1, as we have observed, does show some similarities to these accounts, but it repudiates the pagan accounts in favor of a monotheistic alternative.

Now, for the sake of argument, let us suppose that from these mixed pagan accounts we can distill a core of assumptions that were also shared by ancient Hebrews. The Bible nevertheless describes things that Hebrews (and eventually other readers) could see for themselves. To suppose that the text teaches detailed technical cosmological views is to confuse the text with the totality of what its readers may have believed.

Moreover, a modern cosmological interpretation of the ancient accounts may sometimes impose on the texts a preoccupation with physicalism that does not belong to this kind of literature within the ancient cultural milieu. For example, the idea that the firmament is literally solid is disconfirmed by the statement in Genesis 1:17 that God set the lights "in the expanse [firmament] of the heavens." If the lights in heaven were literally embedded in a solid, they could not move in the way that they obviously do. Perhaps some ancient people could see the obvious, as well as be skeptical about alleged physicalistic implications of pagan cosmogonic stories.

[9] *The Encyclopaedia Britannica,* 11th ed. (Cambridge/New York: The University Press, 1910) 2:809c.

nentially, expanding to include more and more within its scope. But it still had affinities with the technical directions of modern science. Like modern science, it focused on the phenomena, including their quantitative details, and did not stop merely with very general metaphysical or teleological explanations. It was a kind of proto-science.

In ancient Mesopotamia the astronomical calculations, the nearest thing to "science," belonged to a different subculture from the ancient creation stories. The creation stories from Mesopotamia show no interest in calculation, or technical precision, or technical accounts of the mechanisms of astronomic phenomena. Rather, the *Enuma Elish* tells us that the zenith is made from the navel of the goddess Tiamat, though the zenith now looks no different from any other part of the sky. And *Enuma Elish* implies that the earth was made from half of Tiamat's corpse. But no Babylonian farmer expected to discover the remains of Tiamat's liver or her finger bone in his field, and then to alter his farming techniques accordingly! The Babylonian and Sumerian creation stories do not give us "science," not even ancient proto-science. Nor do they give us a substitute for science in order to fill the gap, because Babylon already had proto-science of a sort. Babylon already had its experts in astronomical calculations.

The *Enuma Elish* has a different type of direction, namely to give a broad, sweeping account of how gods, humans, and the world came long ago into the kind of mutual relations that they now enjoy. But a person would have looked elsewhere for technical information about the present course of the workings of the world.

Genesis 1–3, as we have indicated, does not build on the polytheistic stories but rather repudiates them. But in so doing, it does not repudiate Babylonian astronomical calculations. Neither does it directly endorse them. It is not speaking within the genre of astronomy. Like the competing polytheistic stories, it is describing "the big picture." It is answering the big questions about the world, the questions that a person asks in order to get his bearings about the meaning of his life, the meaning of the world around him, the character of God or of idols, and their relation to mankind. The proto-scientific calculations lie to one side, as part of a small expert subculture within this big picture.

Indirectly, Genesis 1 does give some hint about the role that astronomic calculation might take. On the fourth day, when God made the heavenly bodies, he specified, "Let them be for signs and for seasons, and for days and years" (1:14). God's word of command specifies that the heavenly bodies will serve as timekeepers. In particular, the sun controls the alterations between light and darkness, day and night, that form a single day. The sun and stars together indicate the course of a year. So, indirectly, the student of astronomy is invited to come along and observe the movements of the heavenly bodies, and to try to discern ever more accurately how God commands them to move, and how they mark out time. Indirectly, Genesis 1 leads to opening up and affirming the calculating role of ancient proto-science. Proto-science takes a subordinate role *within* the "big picture," the relation between God and man and world that Genesis 1–3 expounds.

THE CONTRIBUTION OF GENESIS I

But now we should stress again that the big picture of Genesis 1 is not science or a substitute for science, and critics make a mistake about literary genre when they treat it as such. In particular, Genesis 1:7 does not provide scientific, technical detail about the nature of the "waters that were above the expanse." John Calvin shows the way to deal with this kind of language when he considers Psalm 148:4:

> There is no foundation for the conjecture which some have made, that there are waters deposited above the four elements; and when the Psalmist speaks of these waters as being above, he clearly points at the descent of the rain. It is adhering too strictly to the letter of the words employed, to conceive as if there were some sea up in the heavens, where the waters were permanently deposited; for we know that Moses and the Prophets ordinarily speak in a popular style, suited to the lowest apprehension. It would be absurd, then, to seek to reduce what they say to the rules of philosophy; . . . [10]

Calvin's reference to "the rules of philosophy" is close to the "natural philosophy" that later developed into modern science. Calvin perceives the difference between speaking "in a popular style," in order to address common people, and speaking to address technical issues within "philosophy" or science.

---

[10] John Calvin, *Commentary on the Book of Psalms*, 5 vols. (reprint; Grand Rapids, Mich.: Eerdmans, 1949), 5.305.

7

Evaluating Modern Science on the Age of the Earth

We also need to look critically at modern science. Fallible human beings, corrupted by sin, populate this world. When they do science, they do not cease to be fallible and sinful. Moreover, as we saw from chapter 1, one's assumptions about scientific law always lie in the background of the practice of science. These assumptions basically presuppose that law is a product of God. And yet idolatry corrupts people's view of God and hence their view of law. We cannot assume that the products of science are all thoroughly invalid, because scientists are still working within God's world, with a conception of scientific law that depends on God. Conversely, we cannot assume that the products of science are thoroughly valid. Not only are scientists fallible, but idolatry corrupts the practice of science through distortion of the conception of scientific law.

So we will find a mixture of good and bad. No simple recipe enables us to sort it out. We ourselves, the would-be sorters, remain fallible and sinful. Sometimes science may yield very good products in spite of the flawed assumptions of the practitioners. Sometimes not. We just have to look, and do the best we can.

Scientific Evidence for an Old Earth

Mainstream science claims that the earth is about 4.5 billion years old, and the universe as a whole is about 14 billion years old. I call it "mainstream science" because some Christians have endeavored to produce an alternative, "creation science," that maintains that the earth and the universe both came into existence only thousands of years ago.[1] I shall call these people "young-earth creationists."[2]

Let us focus first on mainstream science. To what evidence does it appeal? The evidence comes primarily from geology and astronomy. The mainstream claims that the geologic formations contain rocks that were formed millions of years ago. And astronomers claim that by extrapolating backward from the present motions of distant galaxies, we arrive at a time about 14 billion years ago, when the matter and energy of the present visible universe were concentrated in a very small region of space, from which they moved outward explosively in a "Big Bang." The universe then gradually expanded outward to its present size.

A lengthy discussion of the geologic evidence may be found in Davis A. Young, *Creation and the Flood*.[3] The evidence is complex, and its interpretation complex. We can only summarize here, and direct interested readers to Young's discussion.

For a long time advocates of a young-earth approach claimed that mainstream scientists dated the rocks by the fossils, and dated the fossils by the rocks, so that the whole system was circular. That claim lost some of its plausibility with the development of radiometric dating.

Radiometric dating uses measurements of minute quantities of various radioactive isotopes and their decay products, together with the known rate of decay of the isotopes, to estimate the age of rocks in which the isotopes are found. Carbon-14 dating is one of the more famous methods, but it sometimes leads to demonstrably incorrect dates, and in any case it cannot be effectively used to estimate dates beyond tens of thousands of years, because the half-life of carbon-14 is only 5,700 years.[4] By contrast, uranium-lead dating promises to reach into the far past, because the two main isotopes of uranium, U^{235} and U^{238}, have half-lives of 700 million years and 4.5 billion years, respectively. Young-earth advocates

---

[1] John C. Whitcomb, Jr., and Henry M. Morris, *The Genesis Flood: The Biblical Record and Its Scientific Implications* (Philadelphia: Presbyterian & Reformed, 1961) offers a kind of foundational document. Ongoing research centers on the Institute for Creation Research, which publishes the periodical *The Creation Research Society Quarterly*.

[2] This terminology is not to be confused with the more general term "creationist," which can be used to describe someone who believes that God had a decisive role in the origin of living things, as opposed to the view that living things arose through purely chance processes without purpose.

[3] Davis A. Young, *Creation and the Flood: An Alternative to Flood Geology and Theistic Evolution* (Grand Rapids, Mich.: Baker, 1977). See also Brent Dalrymple, *The Age of the Earth* (Stanford, Calif.: Stanford University Press, 1991); and the literature cited in C. John Collins, *Science and Faith: Friends or Foes?* (Wheaton, Ill.: Crossway, 2003), 249-250, 397-398.

[4] The *half-life* of a radioactive isotope is the amount of time it takes for exactly half of the isotope to decay. After two half-lives (11,400 years for carbon-14), only 1/4 of the original will be left, and after three half-lives, 1/8 will be left. After many half-lives, the amount left eventually becomes too small to provide an accurate measurement.

have pointed to problems with this and other radioactive dating methods, but they have great difficulty discrediting the rubidium-strontium method.[5]

The astronomic evidence comes from several directions. The most well-known argument involves extrapolating backwards from observations that indicate that more distant galaxies are moving away from us at a rate roughly proportional to their distance away from us. Extrapolation backwards leads to an origin about 14 billion years ago in an explosion from a very condensed source (the Big Bang).

A lot of assumptions, and a lot of sifting of evidence, go into the Big Bang theory of cosmology. So we may choose something simpler. Distant galaxies observable through telescopes lie up to several billion light-years away. That means that it takes light from those galaxies billions of years to travel from there to here. For us to be observing it now, it must have started on its way billions of years ago. Hence, according to the mainstream viewpoint, the universe is billions of years old.

One might question whether the estimates of distance to faraway galaxies are accurate. So consider the Andromeda galaxy (also called the Great Nebula in Andromeda), a neighboring galaxy about 2 million light-years away (a light-year, the distance that light travels in one year, is about 6 trillion miles [6,000,000,000,000 miles] or 9 trillion kilometers).[6] Even this distance is too much for a young-earth theory of origins, because it suggests that the Andromeda galaxy as we now observe it is over two million years old. Even within the Milky Way galaxy, we deal with distances up to 100,000 light-years, which is still too much for young-earth creationists, who usually maintain an origin less than 20,000 years ago.

Whitcomb and Morris claim that "all cosmological theory is still highly speculative."[7] But the distance to the Andromeda galaxy is not so speculative. Yes, many inferences contribute to distance estimates, but the same is true of estimates of the distance to the moon.[8] Science, in the nature of the

---

[5] Young, *Creation and the Flood*, 185-193, 215-217. See also the more recent discussion in Collins, *Science and Faith*, 247-253.

[6] The Andromeda galaxy is officially labeled M31 (Messier number) and NGC 224. An Internet search will easily turn up much information and beautiful photographs.

[7] Whitcomb and Morris, *Genesis Flood*, 370. But in the years since Whitcomb and Morris wrote *Genesis Flood* (1970), quite a few aspects of cosmological theory have received support from detailed empirical data. The language in *Genesis Flood* may therefore need reassessment.

[8] The simplest way to estimate the distance to the moon is by "triangulation." Two people simultaneously measure the exact angle between a star and a fixed feature on the moon, using two widely separated viewing points, A and B, on the globe. The difference between the two measurements, combined with an estimate of the distance between the two points A and B on earth, allows a calculation of the length of all three sides of the triangle composed of A, B, and the fixed feature on the moon. Similarly, measurements of the angle to a nearby star at two opposite points in the earth's orbit around the sun allow a triangulation to calculate the distance to the star.

case, is always tentative, always subject to revision. But that general truism gives us no concrete help in interpreting the meaning of star light from Andromeda, or from the more distant stars within the Milky Way galaxy.

YOUNG-EARTH RESPONSE

The young-earth creationists have devoted a little attention to these astronomical problems, but up to this point things are sketchy, to say the least. We may consider four different "radical" proposals for dealing with the problems.

First, Whitcomb and Morris cite an article by Parry Moon and Domina Eberle Spencer, which proposes special rules for light traveling over large distances.[9] But the article does not offer anything like a complete alternative astronomy; it succeeds only in proposing a highly speculative theory that deals with one slice of data concerning binary stars.

Second, Barry Setterfield and Walter T. Brown argue that the speed of light is decreasing with time.[10] Based on records of measurements going back to 1675, Setterfield argues for a decrease of 5.7 kilometers per second from 1675 to 1728, 2.5 kilometers per second from 1880 to 1924, and so on.[11] But there are many problems with this proposal.[12] First, measurements made before 1900 were less accurate, so it is unclear that we have good data from that early period. Second, Setterfield's extrapolations for before 1675 are extremely speculative, unless we know why the speed of light is changing (what "drives it"?). Third, the changes are too small to serve to explain the Andromeda galaxy, unless one postulates enormous changes in the more distant past. In fact, Setterfield "postulates that at the time of creation the speed of light was 5×10^{11} (500 billion times) faster than now,"[13] a most audacious speculation. Fourth, according to current physical theory, the speed of light is bound up with so many physical processes that even small changes in its value can have huge disruptive physical effects, unless they are precisely balanced by exactly matching changes in other fundamental physical constants and physical processes. So far, this postulated change in the speed of light does

---

[9] Whitcomb and Morris, Genesis Flood, 370, citing Parry Moon and Domina Eberle Spencer, "Binary Stars and the Velocity of Light," Journal of the Optical Society of America 43 (August 1953): 639.

[10] Barry Setterfield, The Velocity of Light and the Age of the Universe (Adelaide: Creation Science Association, 1983); Walter T. Brown, In the Beginning: Compelling Evidence for Creation and the Flood, 6th ed. (Phoenix: Center for Scientific Creation, 1995). See discussion in Douglas F. Kelly, Creation and Change: Genesis 1.1–2.4 in the Light of Changing Scientific Paradigms (Fearn, Ross-shire, UK: Christian Focus, 1997), 144-155.

[11] Barry Setterfield, cited in Kelly, Creation and Change, 145.

[12] For one critical evaluation, see ibid., 153-155.

[13] Ibid., 146.

not offer us a new physical theory but only a vague hope that eventually some theory might be forthcoming.

Third, D. Russell Humphreys employs the general theory of relativity in order to try to "rescale" the time back to the Big Bang.[14] But he misapplies the mathematics of general relativity, and does not realize that in any case general relativity would not significantly affect the time estimates to nearby galaxies like the Andromeda galaxy.[15]

Fourth, James Jordan suggests that the speed of light may be much greater beyond the neighborhood of the earth and the sun, but does not back up his suggestion.[16]

We need to exercise circumspection in evaluating approaches like those above. The last two approaches, proposed respectively by D. Russell Humphreys and James Jordan, do not really help. The other two are highly speculative, and at present they do not really explain more than a few pieces of data. As finite human beings, we should admit that in principle a radical revision or transformation of present-day science is possible. But we should

---

[14] D. Russell Humphreys, *Starlight and Time: Solving the Puzzle of Distant Starlight in a Young Universe* (Colorado Springs: Master, 1994).

[15] Because the relative velocities of our solar system and of the Andromeda galaxy are small compared with the velocity of light, and because there are no gargantuan gravitational fields in the line of sight to Andromeda, neither special relativity nor general relativity significantly affects time estimates for light coming from the Andromeda galaxy. For further discussion on Humphreys, see http://www.reasons.org/resources/apologetics/unravelling.shtml?main, and the more technical http://www.trueorigins.org/rh_fackmcin1.pdf.

[16] James B. Jordan, *Creation in Six Days: A Defense of the Traditional Reading of Genesis One* (Moscow, Idaho: Canon, 1999), 193, writes, "There is no good reason to think that the speed of light is the same everywhere in the universe. Light may travel much faster between stars, and still faster between galaxies; that is, light may travel much faster away from 'gravity wells' like the sun and the earth." He does not provide footnotes or indicate sources.

A reader with little knowledge of physics and astronomy may wonder, "How could the scientists have good reasons for their views, since they have not traveled out themselves into interstellar space to check it out?" Scientists do it by inference. Astronomers have massive collections of inferential reasons of which the reader may be unaware. To name one: in 1977 NASA launched two scientific spacecraft, Voyager I and Voyager II, into orbits that would take them past the planet Neptune and into deep space. As of 2004 Voyager I was more than twice as far away from the earth as Pluto. Both Voyager I and Voyager II were still transmitting scientific data back to earth, and during the earlier parts of their journey they transmitted photos of Jupiter, Saturn, Uranus, and Neptune (see http://voyager.jpl.nasa.gov/mission/mission.html and http://voyager.jpl.nasa.gov/neptune.html). The gravitational field of the sun is much weaker at Neptune than it is in earth's orbit, and the sun's field in earth's orbit is in turn much weaker than the field at the surface of the earth. Any change in the speed of light would be immediately detected in the amount of time it takes for the signals (which are carried by electromagnetic radiation traveling at the speed of light) to go from earth to a satellite and back to earth.

In fact, the theory of general relativity, which depends on the speed of light, has proved to be the most numerically accurate physical theory ever known. The binary pulsar system PSR 1913+16, located in the constellation Aquila, is about 20,000 light-years from the earth. Predictions from general relativity concerning this system match experimental data to 1 part in 100 trillion (1 in 100,000,000,000,000), and the data derive from extremely high gravitational fields (the "bottom" of deep gravitational wells; see Roger Penrose, *Shadows of the Mind: A Search for the Missing Science of Consciousness* [Oxford: Oxford University Press, 1994], 227-230; see also http://astrosun2.astro.cornell.edu/academics/courses//astro201/psr1913.htm). Of course, it is always theoretically possible that the theory is radically wrong, and that there is some other, entirely different explanation for the data. But there is no other explanation currently on the horizon that will deal with the data with this kind of accuracy.

These are among the many reasons why physicists think that the speed of light is constant.

also be honest about the existing state of things. For example, Paul Nelson and John Mark Reynolds, representing the young-earth approach, state frankly:

> Recent creationists should humbly agree that their view is, at the moment, implausible on purely scientific grounds . . . [17]

In contrast to this humble approach, *some* young-earth creationists have a tendency to give speculative approaches more weight or attention than they deserve; worse, some keep repeating lines of argument that have been discredited.[18] Those who have expertise in the areas concerned must evaluate the situation fairly; and those who do not have expertise must not overestimate their own competence, or rely on the judgment only of those who give them the most favorable report. Yes, Christians want to encourage the faith of believers and challenge the lack of faith among unbelievers. But using less than honest means does not honor God, nor does it work well in practice, because inquiring people sooner or later find out that the earlier rosy report was a distortion.

One might throw up one's hands and resort to a general distrust of astronomy or physics. One thinks, *"Something* is wrong in modern astronomy, but we do not know what." Maybe so. Science, as we have said, is subject to revision. But we must be careful. We ought not simply to write off science as worthless. It is interacting with God's law, and God's law rules the world. Science at its best discovers the wonders and beauties of God's law, and leads to praising God. We ought not hastily to take action that would blind us to some of the display of God's wisdom and beauty.

In fact, the young-earth creationists do not reject science as a whole. They use scientific methods, scientific assumptions, and scientific theories in many cases where they hope that it will help them fit things into the picture of a young earth. The question then arises, "On what grounds do you exercise suspicion toward one area, galactic astronomy, even though you can find no serious flaws in it, and not toward another area?"

In fact, the young-earth creationists have a possible solution lying close

---

[17] Paul Nelson and John Mark Reynolds, "Young Earth Creationism," in J. P. Moreland and John Mark Reynolds, eds., *Three Views on Creation and Evolution* (Grand Rapids, Mich.: Zondervan, 1999), 51; quoted by Collins in *Science and Faith,* 239 (see also 395). Collins points out that "Not all young earth creationists agree with this assessment," but also points to others who show similar caution (239).

[18] Collins points to the webpage http://www.answersingenesis.org/Home/Area/faq/dont_use.asp, "Arguments We Think Creationists Should NOT Use," which counsels people not to use any of the arguments in a specific list (Collins, *Science and Faith,* 395).

at hand, within their own writings. Whitcomb and Morris postulate that on the third day soil was created with the "appearance" of age for the nourishment of the first plants, and the plants themselves were created with the appearance of age.[19] All right. Then the same principle, if true, may easily apply to astronomy. The present state of the stars gives the appearance of age. So let us suppose that it is precisely that—appearance. Starlight from the Andromeda galaxy was created in progress, just as if it were a million years old. Why not? It is mysterious why Whitcomb and Morris freely allow this option when God creates plants and fishes, but then suddenly turn to search for wild, unlikely explanations when they come to astronomy.

In conclusion, the light from the Andromeda galaxy and light from other distant galaxies shows that the universe has the appearance of age. Either this appearance is mere appearance, like the mature creation of Adam's body, or the universe really is old, in which case the astronomers are probably right in giving us a dating of about 14 billion years.

How does this information affect our evaluation of the different theories about the age of the earth?

---

[19] Whitcomb and Morris, *Genesis Flood,* 232-233.

8

Evaluating Theories on the
Age of the Earth

Having first looked broadly at Genesis 1 and the scientific evidence, we now turn to evaluating specific theories for harmonizing them. We have briefly described the theories in chapter 5, without giving much evidence either in favor of or against them. We now proceed to look at the more specific evidence and to evaluate the theories. For convenience, we will not take the theories in the order in which they appear in chapter 5 and in Bernard Ramm's book, but will first of all dispose of the less plausible theories.[1] We will then, in chapters 9 and 10, consider the more attractive theories at greater length.

Religious-Only Theory

The *religious-only* theory says that the Bible *only* addresses matters of "religion," not matters of scientific fact. The religious-only theory gains some plausibility from the fact that the biblical account in Genesis 1–3 *does* focus on the big picture. It offers an alternative to polytheism rather than occupying itself primarily with technical details. But the religious-only theory too quickly compartmentalizes religion and science. It is too neat, too simple, and too hasty. As we have seen, the worldview of evolutionary naturalism cloaks itself in the prestige of science, but constitutes an alternative "religion," in the sense that it gives answers to the big questions, answers that contradict the biblical answers. Moreover, the Bible over and over again shows its concern for events in space and time. Christ became incarnate and walked the hills of Palestine. The crucifixion and the resurrection took place in space and time.

---

[1] Readers who wish to explore the less plausible theories in greater detail may consult Bernard Ramm, *The Christian View of Science and Scripture* (Grand Rapids, Mich.: Eerdmans, 1954), 173-232.

So-called "science" may claim that a resurrection is impossible. But in doing so, it has secretly brought in unfounded philosophical assumptions about the nature of the world, causation, and miracle. The Bible calls on Christians to develop a conceptualization of science that does not automatically eliminate miracles from the outset.

LOCAL CREATION

The theory of *local creation* says that, although Genesis 1:1 may be a general statement about the creation of the universe, Genesis 1:3-31 describes God's creative work within a small territory, focused on the garden of Eden.

But the language in Genesis 1:1-3 provides no hint of a major shift from general creation to a specific area. It is true the Hebrew word for "earth" (*'erets*) can also mean "land" and refer to a smaller area. But Genesis as a whole fits the history of Abraham and the patriarchs into a larger setting, a setting that includes other nations (Gen. 10:1–11:9; 12:3). Genesis 1 provides the most general setting of all. Hence, Genesis as a literary whole indicates that Genesis 1 is universal in scope. The later passages in Psalms and in the New Testament that build on Genesis appear to assume this universality.

But we have also seen that Genesis 1 addresses ancient hearers, who had no modern astronomical information about the size of the universe. Genesis 1 addresses them in ordinary language, the language of appearances, and talks about things that they can see around them. This focus in its address leads naturally to a focus in space, a focus on surroundings with which the ordinary person is familiar. We will not find a discussion of black holes or distant galaxies or the earth's iron core or single-celled organisms. Genesis 1 involves a kind of "localization" to the experience of ancient Israelites. But it still includes the universal thrust. God is creator and sovereign over all—all that is visible to Israelite eyes, but also whatever lies beyond, "all things . . . visible and invisible," as Paul rightly says in expanding on Genesis 1 (Col. 1:16).

I conclude that local creation fails as a complete theory, but does contain a grain of truth about Genesis's focus on Israelite readers.

THE GAP THEORY

The *gap* theory postulates that a large gap in time lies between Genesis 1:1 and 1:2. Genesis 1:1 describes the initial creation, and includes most of the geologic ages. But then God destroyed the order of the old world, perhaps because of the fall of Satan, and re-created it beginning in 1:3. Or perhaps

God's destruction of the earth was confined to a smaller region around Eden, which brings us back to the theory of local creation.[2]

We have already eliminated the theory of local creation. The gap theory also suffers from the fact that it wants to read 1:2 with the meaning, "And the earth *became* without form and void." The construction in Hebrew begins with *and* (Hebrew *waw*), followed by the noun for "earth," followed by a perfect tense of the verb *to be* (Hebrew root *hyh*). This Hebrew construction usually indicates an accompanying circumstance rather than the main line of action of a story. The translation "The earth was without form . . ." is appropriate.

The gap theory also suffers from the implausibility of having to claim that the writer of Genesis devoted only one verse to the all-important work of original creation, and then a whole chapter to the work of restoration. Given the centrality of the doctrine of creation in the Bible as a whole, this is highly unlikely.

But the gap theory also has a grain of truth in it. Genesis 1:1-2 describes a situation *before* the beginning of the first day. It does not indicate how much time elapsed before the creation of light on the first day. Conceivably a very long period of time might have been involved. This lack of information about time does not, however, resolve all the discrepancies between science and the Bible, since scientific accounts of the past appear to describe some of the same events as those mentioned in Genesis 1:3-31.

INTERMITTENT DAY THEORY

The *intermittent day* theory says that most of God's creative activity took place in long periods in between the six days, which are 24-hour days. It is true that Genesis 1 does not explicitly state that the days follow one another without gaps. Each new section opens with the words, "And God said," which theoretically might describe events much later than the ones preceding. Moreover, the final verse in each section has the form, "And there was evening and there was morning, the . . . day." We find no explicit indication whether the "day" is the time during which God acted, or a time at the end of the period of his action.

Thus a purely grammatical and mechanical analysis of Genesis 1 cannot exclude the theoretical possibility of this interpretation. But when we think

[2] For further discussion of the gap theory, see John S. Feinberg, *No One Like Him* (Wheaton, Ill.: Crossway, 2001), 584-587; Feinberg also discusses another related but distinct theory, "Pre-Genesis 1 Creation Theory" (ibid., 582-584).

of the larger significance of what Genesis 1 as a whole is saying, this view loses plausibility.

First, consider the entire pattern. God accomplishes works of creation during six days. At the end of six days, he is finished, and he rests on the seventh day and makes it holy (2:3). Israelite readers would clearly see here a pattern of six days of work, followed by one of rest, and would think of their own Sabbath celebration. Exodus 20:8-11 makes the connection explicit:

> Remember the Sabbath day, to keep it holy. Six days you shall labor, and do all your work, but the seventh day is a Sabbath to the LORD your God. On it you shall not do any work, you, or your son, or your daughter, your male servant, or your female servant, or your livestock, or the sojourner who is within your gates. For in six days the LORD made heaven and earth, the sea, and all that is in them, and rested on the seventh day. Therefore the LORD blessed the Sabbath day and made it holy.

The analogy between the Lord's work and Israelite work holds together only if the Lord worked for six days, just as Israelites work for six days. In both cases, the work takes place *during* the days, not in long gaps between the days. This observation already results in a monumental difficulty for the intermittent day theory.

But we also find some subordinate difficulties. According to the theory, God actually works primarily during the gaps between labeled days. Each gap may contain a very large number of ordinary days. And according to this view, once the sun and moon are created to mark the times, these days will be fairly normal in appearance. There are many days between day 4 and day 5. Then how can day 5 be called day 5 and not day 72,510,338? What is distinctive about day 72,510,338, that causes it to be singled out for special mention? Because these specially marked "days" no longer include the principal work of creation, we find it difficult to know why they are singled out at all. They are superfluous. The only reason we can find for their mention is to produce a pattern for man to imitate on the Sabbath. But then Sabbath celebration builds on an artificiality, and threatens to become artificial itself.

Consider also the analogy between divine work and human work. If God works during the gaps, then by analogy an Israelite may work during the days that are gaps between specially labeled days. It is just a question of whether they are especially labeled or not. This kind of reasoning undermines the Sabbath commandment.

Thus the intermittent day theory will not work.

THE REVELATORY DAY THEORY

The *revelatory day* theory says that God revealed the story of creation to Moses in six distinct days of Moses' life. This theory offers an ingenious way of harmonizing, but nothing in the text of Genesis 1 indicates that the days belong to Moses' life. This theory also has the effect of weakening the force of the Sabbath commandment, which is about imitating God, not imitating Moses. No, the six days in Genesis 1 are six days during which God works. The revelatory day theory fails.

MORE ATTRACTIVE VIEWS

The remaining views, the day-age theory, the 24-hour-day view, the mature creation view, the analogical day theory, and the framework view, have greater strengths, and we must discuss them at somewhat greater length.

THE DAY-AGE THEORY

The *day-age* theory proposes that each "day" in Genesis 1 represents a long period, maybe millions of years. Many advocates of the day-age view have pointed out that the underlying Hebrew word *yom* has more than one meaning. It can designate a 24-hour day: "on the eighth *day* the flesh of his foreskin shall be circumcised" (Lev. 12:3). It can also designate the period of light within one 24-hour day, that is, day as opposed to night: "God called the light *Day*" (Gen. 1:5). It can designate a period of time with a special character: "the great day of the LORD" (Zeph. 1:14), "a day of wrath" (Zeph. 1:15), "a day of the trumpet" (1:16). Expressions like "on that day" (Zeph. 3:11) and "to this day" (Gen. 19:37) probably convey a similar idea of a period of time of unspecified length. "In that day" means "in that time," where the time may be fairly short but is not limited to one 24-hour day. Genesis 2:4 also speaks of what happened "in the *day* that the LORD God made the earth and the heavens," where "day" covers the entire period of the six days! The day-age view uses this evidence in its favor.

The day-age view is right that Genesis 1:5 and 2:4 use the word "day" in distinct senses. But each of the six days has a *number* attached, and each goes together with the statement, "And there was evening and there was morning, the second [or third, etc.] day." The mention of "evening" and "morning" results in an association with the evening and morning of ordinary Israelite days. In addition, the fact that there are exactly six days, followed by a seventh on which God rests, would undoubtedly remind Israelite readers of the Sabbath pattern of six days of work and one of rest. God confirms this impression explicitly in Exodus 20:11, "For in six days the LORD made heaven and earth, the sea, and all that is in them, and rested on the seventh day. Therefore the LORD blessed the Sabbath day and made it holy."

The context of Genesis 1 connects the word "day" (Hebrew *yom*) to the ordinary experience of Israelites, who experience an evening and a morning, and who work during the day and rest at night. By contrast, in its usual form, the day-age theory relies on the claim that in Genesis 1 the word *day* literally *means* "a long period."[3] This claim is invalid, and the day-age theory (in its usual form) is therefore to be rejected. But the framework view and the analogical day theory cannot be so easily dismissed. Both of these latter two approaches acknowledge the relationship of the days of the creation account to man's work week. But they think that the relation is one of analogy rather than identity.

---

[3] Henri Blocher makes the same observation when he rejects the day-age theory (which he calls the "concordist theory"):

> The metaphorical use of a word like 'day' is a function of style which must not be confused with the presence of a broad meaning [like "long period"] amongst the usual meanings of the word (Henri Blocher, *In the Beginning: The Opening Chapters of Genesis* [Downers Grove, Ill.: InterVarsity Press, 1984], 44).

9

THE 24-HOUR-DAY AND
MATURE CREATION VIEWS

In contrast to the day-age view, the 24-hour-day view has in its favor the fact that it takes the word *day* in a sense that harmonizes with the context of a sabbatical pattern. According to this view, the days of Genesis last 24 hours, just as human days of work and rest last 24 hours.

The 24-hour-day view gives us a clear position with respect to Genesis 1. But by itself it does not yet tell us how to interact with modern science. Accordingly, it needs to be supplemented by advice concerning science.

ADEQUATE KNOWLEDGE FOR ORDINARY LIFE

Of course, some people may decide that they do not need any supplementation at all. They do not worry about any of the views put forward by modern science. In practice they can get along quite well. They believe that they have understood Genesis 1 correctly, and so they conclude that something has gone wrong in mainstream scientific treatment of the distant past. But what exactly has gone wrong does not concern them. They can still live ordinary lives.

This approach is in many respects reasonable. According to a Christian worldview, human beings are finite and fallible. They cannot know everything, and as a matter of fact they do not need to know everything. God assures us in the Bible that he knows everything. And he rules the world in a way that has compassion on human beings, especially those who trust in him (Ps. 37:3; 115:9; 125:1). He takes care of them, so that they can serve him without knowing everything.

In fact, for ordinary purposes we do not need to know technical details about the origin of the world. We need to have the big picture of who God is, who we are, what has gone wrong with the world (sin), how to remedy the wrong (redemption), how to serve God, and what we can hope for. Also, in a world heavily influenced by science and technology, we need to have some idea how to use science and technology. But in its practical uses, the vast bulk of modern science and technology concerns what happens now, not what happened in the distant past. It matters little whether the universe originated 6,000 years ago or 14 billion years ago. Most science and technology focus on how the universe functions now. What matters is how I use my car or my telephone.

Genesis 1–3 furnishes important direction, precisely because it provides an important framework; it gives us the means for grasping the big picture. It puts the all-powerful God at the sovereign origin of all. It provides a substantial beginning for a doctrine of God, of nature, of man, of sin, and of the Sabbath. It gives a clear basis for the weekly Sabbath pattern. But besides the issue of the Sabbath, what else do we gain from thinking that God created the world in the space of 144 hours, instead of 24 hours, or one hour, or 48 hours, or 3 years—or a billion years? Not much, really. The exact amount of time makes no difference theologically.[1]

In terms of basic theology, many of the principal approaches to Genesis have the same outcome. Along with the 24-hour-day view, the mature creation view, the framework view, and the analogical day theory all affirm the same theological truths about God, nature, man, and the Sabbath.

But some issues of moment do remain. How do we address those who have imbibed the ideas of origins associated with mainstream science? A strong cultural atmosphere feeds the impression that the Bible is "primitive" and "outmoded," and that "modern science has proved that the Bible is not

---

[1] Of course as we consider the implications of a particular passage or a particular doctrine in the Bible, there is always one additional theological issue, as to whether the Bible is completely true and whether it can be trusted completely. Yes, it is trustworthy. That is one reason why it is worthwhile to understand with care what it says. In addition to giving us a trustworthy Bible, God has made provision even for those who may misunderstand some details. In particular, if someone misunderstands the length or character of the days in Genesis, that by itself does not necessarily lead to disasters in major theological areas.

Some people are attracted to the idea of God creating the world within a relatively short period of time because it seems to magnify the power of God more dramatically, and because it would be potentially useful in apologetics for confronting unbelievers with clear evidence for God's power. I sympathize with these attractions. But, first, it is up to God, not us, to decide how he will create, and how much time he will take. He may have his reasons beyond what we can understand. Second, if a shorter time period is preferable to a longer one, would not a single period of 24 hours, or even less, magnify the power of God even more than a six-day period? An argument for the superiority of a short time for creation seems to prove too much. Third, with respect to apologetics, unbelievers already have plenty of evidence from God's ordinary providence (Acts 14:17). They have no excuse for their rebellion (Rom. 1:19-21). God may, if he wishes, provide still more evidence of a most dramatic kind (Luke 16:30-31). But that is up to him.

My basic point remains: the theology of creation, and the theology of God's control and goodness displayed in creation, remain fundamentally the same, however short or long the timing for the various acts of creation.

trustworthy." How do we address Christian believers who begin to doubt, and how do we address non-Christians who use modern science as one excuse for staying away from Bible-believing, orthodox Christianity?

Coupled with these practical questions are more long-range issues. Do we feel pressure from modern science and from the surrounding culture to compromise our understanding of Genesis? Do we force on Genesis an interpretation that gives way to whatever is modern? Then we are on a slippery slope down which we may slide into compromising the reality of the virgin birth, the resurrection of Christ, and his bodily second coming. Or does some highly metaphorical interpretation of Genesis 1–3 move it away from the central role that God intended it to have in giving us the big picture?

Some people feel strongly the temptation to compromise with the world, in order to have the world's approval, and to avoid being looked down on and laughed at for being "fundamentalists." Or maybe they compromise just because they do not know of other options for the interpretation of Genesis and of science.

But temptations arise in other directions as well. Other people may congratulate themselves on their purity for having rejected the compromises. The 24-hour-day view becomes a badge of honor, proving that they are pure. And it becomes a means of rejecting evolutionary naturalism in the most obvious and vigorous way. We are tired of being knocked around and beaten down by the surrounding culture, and here is a place where we are going to stand and show how thoroughly wrong the world is. A good determination to remain faithful to God whatever the cost can be combined with a sinful pride and self-congratulation on how well we are doing that!

Or for some people, choosing what seems to be an "obvious" interpretation is an easy way out. They do not want to wrestle with any hard questions.

So let us exercise some caution about our own motives. All of us undergo temptation, sometimes from unexpected quarters. On the other hand, let us remember that a theory does not become untrue because of moral or spiritual failures among its defenders. We must still assess each theory on its own merits.

So what about the 24-hour-day view? When we interact with scientific accounts of origins, we do need something more. The standard supplement is flood geology, which, contrary to mainstream geology, says that most of the geologic strata derive from Noah's flood. We discussed it briefly in the previous chapter. But this approach still does not give us an answer for astronomical arguments. Mainstream astronomy says that starlight from distant galaxies takes millions of years to get here. We could just say that we do not know, but that somewhere astronomy is making major mistakes. Because of the tentative character of science, this remains theoretically possible. But the mature creation approach becomes much more attractive. Young-earth creationists already employ the idea of mature creation on some occasions. So why not here?

THE MATURE CREATION VIEW

I suggest, then, that the mature creation view offers an attractive supplement to the 24-hour-day view. It retains all the main advantages of the 24-hour-day view, by maintaining that God created the universe within six 24-hour days. It supplements this view with a clear and simple explanation for the conclusions of modern astronomy. The universe *appears* to be 14 billion years old because God created it mature. Moreover, the universe is *coherently* mature, in the sense that estimates of age deriving from different methods arrive at similar results. This coherence makes some sense. God created Adam mature. Why should we not think that Adam was *coherently* mature? It seems a little monstrous to think that Adam might have a heart that tested as twenty years old, and a hand with wrinkles that made it look a hundred years old.

But now the same approach can apply to geology. If rocks look millions of years old according to rubidium-strontium dating, we can say that they appear mature. Perhaps the whole geological structure of the earth is coherently mature. When fossils lie in older strata, the associated age is coherent apparent age. But then the fossils do not represent the remains of animals or plants that were actually alive millions of years ago. They represent a coherent mature structure that shows how God would have worked, millions of years ago, if he had started back then creating and extinguishing various kinds of animals over long periods of time. If we believe in the mature creation view, we can believe that such creation is utterly consistent and coherent. Of course, God as the sovereign has the right to leave inconsistent signs of age and of youth. But he also has the right to make the world coherent, and in some respects the coherence makes more sense. If one is going to produce some creatures in mature state, like Adam, why not do the whole thing the same way?

But not everyone likes the idea of mature creation. People have raised objections of several different kinds.

Objection 1: The Mature Creation View Implies That
God Has Deceived Us

First, would God be "playing fair" with us by making the creation mature? Would he be deceiving us by "faking" an artificial universe, which makes us think that things are old? We do not have the right or the wisdom to question God. God decides what he wants to do. So we must beware of imposing on God our standards of what we think he ought to do. Instead, we are to accept what he does by *his* standards.

But still people may find a problem here. They do not want to challenge the fact that God himself is the ultimate standard for what is right. Nor do they challenge his right to do as he sees fit. But the idea of mature creation threatens to produce doubts in their mind. If God would do something like this, which appears to be deceptive, how can we trust him in other areas?

Looking closely at the example of Adam helps to solve such questions. Suppose that God created Adam with a body that had the appearance of being about 22 years old. What is the matter with that? If Eve examined Adam's body, or if Adam examined Eve, would God be "deceiving" them by the apparent evidence of age? No. Why should we think so? In the case of Eve, God apparently indicated to Adam, either by direct words or by some other means, that he had newly created Eve from Adam's rib. Adam said, ". . . she shall be called Woman, because she was taken out of Man" (Gen. 2:23b). Adam saw a mature woman in front of him, but he did not mistakenly think that she had already actually lived for 20 some years.

Why did Adam not make a mistake about Eve's actual age? Somehow he already had a doctrine of mature creation. Perhaps God directly explained it to him. But Adam had indirect evidence as well. He had previously named the animals (Gen. 2:19-20). Adam must have had some sense that his experiences with the animals were part of the beginnings of the world. And he did not see an animal like Eve until after the deep sleep. So Eve, he might conclude, was newly created.

If Adam sensed that the animals were new, he would have had a doctrine of mature creation with respect to the animals. He saw adult animals, but understood that they were freshly created.

In fact, Adam or other, later human beings would make a mistake about age only if they assumed that the apparent age was real. And this assumption is not necessary, as Adam's initial response to Eve shows. The assumption comes in only if we first *deny* the possibility of mature creation. And this denial presumes more than we know. We were not around when God created the plants and animals. So how do we know whether he created them mature or not? We do not know. In fact, if the 24-hour-day reading of Genesis 1 is correct, God has undertaken in Genesis to inform us that the earth is actually young. Only those who reject that teaching get deceived about the actual age.

Consider another example of apparent age. Since the garden of Eden was a healthy garden, it seems logical to infer that it had a normal, healthy soil. Soil, as we now know it, contains decaying organic matter from dead plants. Bacteria and soil-dwelling creatures like earthworms work over this matter and contribute to making a healthy soil in which new plants grow. So the soil in the garden would have the necessary organic matter and the bacteria, even if God in fact prepared the garden and its soil over a period of seconds or hours rather than the many years that it takes to generate soil by gradual processes.[2]

But now a more nuanced objection arises: mature structures are not a problem, but records or traces of earlier apparent events from an unreal (ideal) past *are* a problem. This kind of objection acknowledges that Adam and Eve were created mature, and that other items, like the soil in the Garden of Eden, or the trees in the garden, may have been created mature. A mature structure is not innately deceitful. But for the objector it still seems deceitful for a mature structure to contain within it evidence that appears to point to specific past *events*. For instance, if Adam had a belly button, it would point to a specific event in which as a newly born baby his umbilical cord had been cut.[3] The presence of a belly button would therefore be deceitful, like a road sign pointing to a detour that was really just a dead-end street. Likewise, decaying organic matter in the soil, such as a piece of a decaying oak leaf, would be deceitful because it would falsely point to earlier events involving the growth of the leaf on an oak tree and the dropping of the leaf to the ground. The trees in the garden of Eden could be full-sized. But the objector would not accept rings within the trunk indicating a succession of seasons, or a knot indicating where a branch had fallen off, because such things would deceitfully point to unreal events in an unreal past.

In reply, let us first observe that the analogy with a detour sign glosses over an important distinction. A detour sign, as a kind of symbolic extension of human language, involves a human commitment to express a symbolic

---

[2] The young-earth creationists John C. Whitcomb, Jr., and Henry M. Morris make this point about soil in *The Genesis Flood: The Biblical Record and Its Scientific Implications* (Philadelphia: Presbyterian & Reformed, 1961), 233.

[3] As indicated earlier, one of the labels for the theory of mature creation, namely the *omphalos* theory (from the Greek word for navel), specifically affirms that Adam would have had a belly button.

meaning. We know what it means. But a ring on a tree or a decaying leaf is not part of a human symbol system. It has meaning within the plan of God, but that meaning remains hidden in God until some human being discerns meaning and truth on the basis of the tree ring. Meaning and truth, as symbol-laden realities, must be inferred, and the inferences always depend on a host of assumptions and a framework for interpretation. Precisely these assumptions and frameworks are in question when the theory of mature creation postulates a newly born mature world. Mature creation says that, given the doctrine of creation, we must not invoke our usual assumptions when examining alleged evidence for a remote past.

Second, given what we know of God's ways in his present providential rule of the world, it is not so easy to separate cleanly between mature structures and specific past events leading to those structures. Within our present world, mature structures like trees typically derive from earlier stages of less maturity: the oak tree comes from a younger tree, which comes from a sapling, which comes from a first shoot, which comes from an acorn. The transitions between different stages take place through a multitude of specific events: germination of the acorn, growth of roots, movement of water and nutrients into the roots, and so forth. Given virtually any mature structure, we infer *both* earlier stages of the structure *and* earlier specific events. Maturity *means* maturity such as normally arises from a series of preceding stages and events.

It sounds as if the objector, by contrast, cannot really accept *mature* creation, but rather only creation of a complex structure. And this structure would then have no record within it of a past history. According to this model, God created Adam or a tree *but without coherent apparent age.* Coherent age would point both to earlier structures and to earlier events—and the latter the objector cannot accept. Hence, if the soil in the garden of Eden were newly created, it could not really have been like normal soil today, containing bits of decaying organic matter, some of which can clearly be identified as deriving from specific living things from the past. If a tree in Eden were cut down, it would not have had rings in the trunk.

When Jesus turned water into wine at Cana in Galilee (John 2:1-11), the wine would have tasted like the product from grapes. Presumably, it would be a complex structure. But could it have contained any grape plant cells or yeast cells or fragments from cells? Such cells would contain DNA, and the DNA would by its distinctive signature enable a scientist to infer from what grapevine stock the wine derived. He would then infer past events like the picking of the grapes, the pressing in a wine press, the operation of yeast in aging, and so on.

The objector now seems to be on the horns of a dilemma. He might claim that the drink at Cana in Galilee only tasted like wine, but did not have the complex inner structure that would include the remains of yeast cells. But that would mean a denial that God could have freshly created complex structures in a moment. (But then what about the creation of Adam?) So suppose that he allows that the wine might actually contain yeast cell DNA. In that case, he seems to allow both mature structures (yeast cells) and apparent past events that one can infer from them (cell growth and division). I conclude, then, that a hard-and-fast distinction between complex structures and mature structures with an ideal past is implausible.

Modern scientists often research the past using the assumptions that all apparent ages must be real. But that is their assumption. They assume that God (or their idolatrous substitute for God) must have acted in the past in exactly the same way as they see him operating now. But again, that assumes more than they know. The "deceit" arises *not* because God has deceived perfectly innocent people, but because people have ignored Genesis and have deceived *themselves* about how much they know about God and how much they know about his ways in the past. They have assumed *from the beginning* that mature creation is untrue.[4] A little humility would help.

Objection 2: Mature Creation Would Falsely Imply That Death Preceded the Fall

A second objection to the mature creation view concerns the presence of death *before the fall*. The mature creation view in its consistent form says that older fossils belong to the projected past. They are one effect of a creation with coherent maturity. But fossils indicate that death occurred in this projected past. This presence of death seems in disharmony with the pronouncement that the creation was "very good" (Gen. 1:31), and with the later scriptural statements that death came through one man, Adam (Rom. 5:12; 1 Cor. 15:21; Gen. 3:19).

Of course, one possible answer might be that the deaths of animals seen

---

[4] One also hears the objection that if we cannot trust inferences about age, how do we know that the universe did not come into being one minute ago, together with our memories? Actually, this is a problem for unbelievers, not for Christians. The unbeliever truly cannot know, without covertly relying on the faithfulness of God. By contrast, Christians know from the Bible that God intended general revelation and special revelation to act in concert. We hear the word of God in Scripture, and know from it that this world has had a long past and that God faithfully governs the world. This assurance guarantees both the reality of the past (back to the time of creation) and the integrity of our memories.

in older fossils were not real, but only part of the projected past. According to the mature creation view, there was no real suffering or death before the time of Adam and Eve, since the projected past is merely projected (ideal), not real. But there is still a potential problem. The projected past does still seem to indicate the kind of world that would have been, if God had brought it into genuine existence at an earlier point. And it indicates the kind of world into which Adam and Eve were introduced. It seems reasonable to infer that, if Adam and Eve had not fallen, they would still have eventually witnessed animal deaths, because the kind of world where they lived was consistent with its own projected past. So the potential for animal death still produces a problem.

What do we say about animal death? The later scriptural statements are talking about human death. God created man to have fellowship with him and to enjoy life in the presence of God forever, as the tree of life reminds us (Gen. 2:9; 3:22). For *man,* death broke up this original purpose. Human death came in as a horror and a curse. Spiritual death in the form of separation and alienation from God is at the heart of our present human condition. And spiritual death entrains physical death as well.

The animals and plants, however, did not enjoy the same exalted status as man. In fact, later on God explicitly gives to man the authority to kill animals for food, but not to kill a fellow human being (Gen. 9:3, 6). Some people think that this right to kill animals is appropriate only in a fallen world. But we do not know. God created man in his image, in distinction from the animals. The animals clearly belong to a lower category. Moreover, God's pre-fall gift to man of plant foods (Gen. 1:29) implies in some cases the death of plant products.

Psalm 104, a psalm that repeatedly alludes to the creation in Genesis 1, includes details that imply animal death:

The young lions roar for *their prey,* seeking their food from God (Ps. 104:21).

These all [all sea creatures, and probably all land creatures as well] look to you, to give them their food in due season (Ps. 104:27) ["food" here must include large fish eating small fish; this verse describes God's continuing providential control over the present order, not a vegetarian past].

When you hide your face, they [animals] are dismayed; when you take away their breath, they *die* and return to their dust (Ps. 104:29).

The verses from Psalm 104 are not decisive, since the human writer is describing God's providential provision for animals in the *post-fall* world. One can still hypothesize that the situation differed radically before the fall. But Psalm 104 weaves together thoughts about creation and providence, and does not indicate a radical discontinuity between the created order and continuing providence (except in the matter of human sin, verse 35!). The psalmist shows his positive evaluation of God's providence in verse 33: "I will sing to the LORD as long as I live; I will sing praise to my God while I have being." He praises God for supplying the lions with their prey. This psalm does not at all suggest that lions' carnivorous eating habits are a "bad" thing.[5]

I conclude that we do not have any firm basis for saying that animal death started only after the fall of man. Again, we must beware of presuming to dictate to God what kind of world he had to create. It had to be "very good" in his sight; but that is not the same as saying that it must match what some of *us* may think ideal.[6]

Objection 3: The Mature Creation View Makes Scientific Investigation Illegitimate

Davis Young raises a third objection, namely that the mature creation approach would make illegitimate the scientific investigation of the distant past. According to the theory of mature creation, projected dates before the time of creation are only apparent; they are "ideal time," because the time never really existed. Young claims that it is illegitimate to probe scientifically into this ideal time.[7] He points out that in mature creation, "the laws of nature were essentially different during the creation week than they are now."[8]

First, it would be better for Young to have said that the words of God governed the world in a different manner during the creation week. Such a formulation helps us to maintain more consistently the biblical view of God's governance of the world. God did act differently at times during the creation week, as the creation of Eve from the rib of Adam shows. The word of God governs both the regularities that we now see and the extraordinary works of creation.

---

[5] C. John Collins points out this significance of Psalm 104:21 in *Science and Faith: Friends or Foes?* (Wheaton, Ill.: Crossway, 2003), 154.

[6] See the further discussion about animal death in Collins, *Science and Faith*, 152-160. One must also remember that, though the creation is "very good," it is heading for a consummation that will be even better.

[7] Davis A. Young, *Creation and the Flood: An Alternative to Flood Geology and Theistic Evolution* (Grand Rapids, Mich.: Baker, 1977), 53-55. The title of the first of two sections on this point runs, "The Impossibility and Illegitimacy of Scientific Investigation on the Mature Creation Doctrine."

[8] Ibid., 53.

At a fundamental level Young wants everything to be the same during the creation week as it is later on. This sameness or continuity would guarantee that scientific investigation back into that time period could proceed according to essentially the same principles that scientists use now, as they observe the providential rule of God now.

One may sympathize with this desire. But the creation of Eve frustrates it. In fact, any supernatural act of God, which we find inexplicable by appeal to his ordinary ways of governing, frustrates it. Nowhere in Scripture does God promise that he has worked in the past in a way that will perfectly accommodate the desires of scientists! The resurrection of Christ and the promise of his second coming frustrate the desires of some scientists to have everything everywhere "the same." What we have at stake here includes conceptions of science, conceptions of miracle, and conceptions of what God may or may not do in order to allow for the formation of science. We have here a large topic, to which we will devote attention later on in this book. For the moment, suffice it to say that Young cannot validate the assumptions that "natural laws" were always the same during the creation week.[9] He cannot therefore provide a sound foundation for scientific investigation of the past in this way.

Ironically, the mature creation theory itself provides the foundation that Young cannot provide. Suppose, at the end of the six days of creation, the world is coherently mature. Because we cannot find out the details of how God worked during the six days, and because we know that his working then was different from his working now, we cannot reconstruct the actual detailed course of events (beyond the summary that Genesis 1 gives us). But this limitation *does not concern the scientist.* The scientist studies the completed product. Because this product is *coherently* mature, the scientist can happily study this coherence with confidence. Adam could infer the "ideal time" age of Eve coherently by examining her fingernails and her skin. All sources would add up to a coherent picture. Likewise, the scientist may find a coherent astronomical picture in which the universe is 14 billion years old *in ideal time.*

Consider a further illustration. Davis Young tells us that he has been studying "one-billion-year-old rocks of northern New Jersey . . . for the past several years."[10] He complains that according to mature creation, "I am wasting my time talking about magmas and metamorphism inasmuch as these rocks were created instantaneously in place."[11] But he is not wasting his time.

---

[9] But see the discussion below of the framework theory, which attempts to use Genesis 2:5-6 to establish a measure of uniformity in law during the days of creation.

[10] Young, *Creation and the Flood,* 54.

[11] Ibid.

All his effort is quite meaningful as an investigation of the processes that he is seeing *in ideal time*. The coherence of processes in ideal time is also an aspect of the display of God's wisdom, and Young makes a genuine contribution by studying this wisdom.

Objection 4: The Mature Creation View Undermines Noah's Flood

A fourth and final objection says that the theory of mature creation, when applied to geology, undermines the biblical teaching about Noah's flood. Recall that mainstream geology and astronomy both offer arguments in favor of great age. Geology postulates an age of about 4.5 billion years for the earth, while astronomy postulates about 14 billion years for the universe as a whole. In astronomy, the mature creation theory works well, because it explains the coherent astronomical results. Can the mature creation view also work in explaining the apparent great ages of rocks?

The most straightforward explanation would be to say that these geologic ages, like astronomical ages, are all *apparent* ages, that is, ages in a projected past that never really existed. This explanation works for coherently explaining the findings of mainstream geology. But does it account for Noah's flood? A flood that covered the whole globe would presumably leave many notable deposits in the rocks, and these deposits would have come about in *real* time, the time of Noah, not the ideal time of a merely "projected" past. So where are these deposits, if what the geologists are seeing is mostly in "ideal time"?

When we try to relate the flood of Noah to science, we confront two main issues in interpretation, namely the extent of the flood and the mechanics of the flood. Nearly all young-earth creationists think that the flood in the Bible covered the entire earth ("universal flood"). Old earth creationists, on the other hand, usually think that the flood covered only a more limited area in the ancient Near East ("local flood"). We also confront questions about the mechanics of the flood. Did God act in a spectacularly miraculous way, quite out of the ordinary? Or did he use ordinary processes, which came together at just the right time and in just the right way to produce the flood?

Depending on our answers to these questions, we may or may not decide that the flood of Noah can be expected to have left concrete, specific results in today's geologic strata.

Let us take the second question first, the question about the mechanics of the flood. Did God act in a highly miraculous way in the whole course of the flood, or perhaps just at its beginning?

What counts as miraculous? As we saw in chapter 1, the word of God governs everything that happens, both the ordinary and the extraordinary. After the flood, God promises Noah that seedtime and harvest shall not cease (Gen. 8:22). The seasons are ordinary, repeated, regular. God also promises the resurrection of Christ, which is not ordinary and not repeated (Luke 9:22). His word controls both kinds of events. Miracle is not a violation of a so-called "natural law" that exists independently of God. Rather miracle conforms exactly to the real "law," the law laid down by God's word. So how do miracle and ordinary providence differ? The difference is partly one of degree, in that miracles are extraordinary and other events ("providence") are ordinary. In many cases miracles also play a key role in accomplishing redemption and in confirming the authority of God's special messengers, the prophets and apostles.

Miracles are truly extraordinary exhibitions of God's power. But God may sometimes use some quite ordinary means in accomplishing them. In the crossing of the Red Sea, "the LORD drove the sea back *by a strong east wind all night* and made the sea dry land, and the waters were divided" (Ex. 14:21). God fulfilled his prophecy about the death of Ahab in a striking way when someone *"drew his bow at random"* and shot an arrow that found its way through a crack between the pieces of Ahab's armor (1 Kings 22:34). God may choose to act apart from humanly discernible means, if he so wishes. But his action is just as much his when he uses the means of the strong east wind or the person who shot at random.

What about the flood? It is clearly a major redemptive and judgmental event. Noah and his family are saved, while the surrounding godless world is condemned to death. Later Scripture indicates that Noah and the flood are a type or preliminary picture of final judgment. "Just as it was in the days of Noah, so will it be in the days of the Son of Man" (Luke 17:26; see 2 Pet. 3:6). This language implies that Noah's flood was a "miracle," in the broad sense of the term. But did God do it through ordinary means, or in a completely extraordinary, unfathomable way that we can never reconstruct? We do not know. Genesis does not say. After the flood, the promise given to Noah about seedtime and harvest guarantees a general regularity, "While the earth remains" (Gen. 8:22). The guaranteed regularity offers a basis for science, which studies the regularities. But the promise in Genesis 8:22 covers the period from the flood onward. It does not say anything about the flood itself, nor the time before the flood.

If the mechanics of the flood are completely unfathomable, no scientific theory can hope to capture them. The flood remains permanently beyond the reach of science. What, then, would scientists find when they examine rocks left behind by the flood? They might find pure chaos, such that no one could make sense of it. But both flood geologists and mainstream geologists think that they find order, and that a great deal can be explained. Evidently, God did not choose to act in a way that just left behind a complete chaos.

Second, one might find that the flood left behind a mature creation, after the manner of the mature creation at the end of the six days of creation. This alternative is less far-fetched than one might think, because the Bible gives clear hints that the flood of Noah represents a pattern of destruction and re-creation. In a manner of speaking, the flood returns the world to the watery, empty situation of Genesis 1:2. The Lord then proceeds to "re-create" an ordered world. For this new world, God repeats in Genesis 9:1-4, 7 some of the commands from the first creation. Peter picks up this theme in a New Testament context, when he describes the "old" world, before the flood:

> . . . that the heavens existed long ago, and the earth was formed out of water and through water by the word of God, and that by means of these the world that then existed was deluged with water and perished. But by the same word the heavens and earth that now exist are stored up for fire, . . . (2 Pet. 3:5-7).

The first, pre-flood world was "formed out of water," and then returned to water ("deluged with water"), and that process parallels the present heavens and earth, though they will perish with fire.

If, then, the situation after the flood is a "new world," it may be a mature world and may again contain the appearance of age. The same reasoning that supported mature creation will support the possibility of a mature "new world" after the flood.

In practice, Christians do not agree on how to approach the evidence from rocks. They find themselves mostly in two camps. Flood geologists think that much of the existing rock formations derive from the flood, while old-earth geologists think that the rock formations are millions of years old. Both assume that the flood resulted from ordinary means. I am saying that this last assumption need not be valid.

On the other hand, it may be valid, or partially valid. God can use ordinary means, even when he accomplishes quite extraordinary redemptive results. We need to go and look.

Universal or Local Flood?

We come then to the second issue with the flood. Was it universal (covering the whole face of the globe) or local (covering a limited area in the ancient Near East)? If it was universal, *and if God used ordinary means,* such a huge catastrophe should have left many marks of its passage. It would suggest that flood geologists are on the right track, even if at present they have difficulties in explaining some areas.

The language in Genesis 6–9 repeatedly uses the sweeping word *all:*

All flesh had corrupted their way on the earth (6:12).

"For behold, I will bring a flood of waters upon the earth to destroy *all* flesh in which is the breath of life under heaven. *Everything* that is on the earth shall die" (6:17).

"And of every living thing of *all* flesh . . ." (6:19).

And even more strikingly,

And the waters prevailed so mightily on the earth that *all* the high mountains under the *whole* heaven were covered (7:19).

And *all* flesh died that moved on the earth, . . . (7:21).

Many modern readers see this language as decisively affirming a universal flood. We can see why. But let us stand back and consider the differences between modern readers and ancient readers. We as modern readers come to the passage already carrying some modern baggage. We may have seen pictures of the earth taken from satellites. We have seen models where the earth is a sphere with continents drawn on it. To us the word *earth* means "the globe," the round ball sitting in space.

This picture actually produces tension with Genesis 6–8. In 7:19 "all the high mountains *under* the whole heaven were covered," and 6:17 mentions "the breath of life *under* heaven." If "heaven" means outer space or even the earth's atmosphere, it would be odd to say that the solid ball of the earth is "under" outer space. Rather, it is surrounded by it on all sides.

Then what does Genesis 7:19 mean? We must apply the same reasoning that we used with Genesis 1. Genesis 1, as John Calvin pointed out, addresses the ordinary person, the "unlearned." It does not propose to teach astronomy to the expert but teaches the theology of creation to the ordinary person. Similarly, Genesis 6–9 addresses the ordinary person—in particular, the ordinary person in the ancient Near East. The ordinary person does not think in terms of "the globe." That is a foreign concept.[12] The "earth," in Hebrew *'erets,* means the land underfoot. In fact, in some contexts it designates a limited expanse of land: "the whole *land* [*'erets*] of Havilah" (Gen. 2:11); "the whole *land* [*'erets*] of Cush" (Gen. 2:13); "At that time the Canaanites were in the *land* [*'erets*]" (that is, in the land of Palestine where Abraham was sojourning, Gen. 12:6). When Genesis speaks of earth in contrast to heaven, the "earth" clearly extends farther than any one "land." But "heaven" is not to be equated with outer space in which the globe is embedded. Rather, the language is still thoroughly ordinary, thoroughly "phenomenal." "Heaven" is what you see overhead, the sky (and sometimes one includes the invisible throne of God, which is totally inaccessible to human travel). The mountains really are *under* heaven, that is, beneath the sky. "Everything on the earth" means everything that exists on the surface of the ground. And the context qualifies it still more, because the concern is for animals, not for plants, which recover from the flood without Noah's aid (Gen. 8:11; 9:3b). "Everything" may not be literally everything, but "everything pertinent to this discussion." In short, the whole biblical description of the flood addresses the ordinary person, in order to show that person what he would see and experience if he were there back in Noah's time.

God first of all addressed the people who lived in the ancient Near East. But he also designed the Bible to address people in all the cultures of the world, since he planned that the gospel would spread through all nations and that people from these nations would come to be disciples (Matt. 28:18-20). People in all these cultures need to hear Genesis. It is merely a modern prejudice to think that God would have to adopt the technical viewpoint of modern science. No, he can speak in an ordinary manner, and this manner of

---

[12] Does the concept of the earth as a globe occur in Job 26:7, "He stretches out the north over the void and *hangs* the earth on nothing"? Or does it perhaps occur in Isaiah 40:22: "It is he who sits above the *circle* of the earth"? Remember that the Bible is designed to address ordinary people in the ancient Near East and ultimately people in all other cultures, not merely modern technological cultures. To do so it uses ordinary descriptive language. "The earth" is what a person sees underneath him, stretching to the horizon. When Job 26:7 says that God "hangs the earth on nothing," it means that the earth needs no support from above. Job 26:7 does not specify whether the earth in its widest possible extent is shaped like a sphere or like a block or like a plain. Only if we as modern people *already* have in our minds the picture of a spherical globe, do we then read it into the text. Similarly, in Isaiah 40:22 the "circle" of earth is the horizon, which extends around on every side in the shape of a circle. Modern people almost automatically equate the word *circle* with the circular shape of the globe. But that is because they already have in their minds a picture of the globe. These two instances only show how easy it is for a modern person to import a modern conception of the planet earth as a globe, and to read it into a text that is not really talking that way but is talking to ordinary people living in many different cultures.

speaking is not only completely true but is better designed to speak to all people, since it does not demand that they first learn modern science.

The ground is underfoot, and the sky is above. Within that situation, the flood comes. The water covers the "earth"—the land as far out as one can see. Genesis is not talking about "the globe." It is talking about the land. How far out does this "land" extend, and how far out did the waters go? Far enough to cover "everything," that is, everything within the scope of an ordinary person's experience. The Bible does not say one way or the other whether the waters covered the whole globe or only an extensive area in the ancient Near East—enough to wipe out all the human beings, who in Noah's time had not yet spread out over all the earth (Gen. 11:8-9).

But what about the covering of "all the high mountains" (Gen. 7:19)? This would include the mountains of Ararat (8:4), which in today's geography are quite high. The waters covered the mountains for a considerable period. And water "seeks its level," so that it does not remain heaped up in one place, but spreads out as far as it can. One then infers that the water must have covered the globe, even though Genesis does not directly say so.

But two assumptions have crept in. First, one has assumed that ordinary mechanical processes are operative during the flood, so that water would continue, according to its ordinary behavior, to "seek its level" and to spread out evenly. One has assumed that water retains the same physical properties that it exhibits today. This is a natural assumption, but if God acted supernaturally, we cannot say for sure to what extent he might have suspended normal regularities. Second, one has assumed that the "water" in question all has liquid form. But how does one know this? Is it not possible that, on the mountains, we might find snow, sleet, and ice? The water might cover this area, and snuff out the life of animals, whether it took liquid or solid form. The later receding of the waters (Gen. 8:3) might include melting.

Genesis 6–9 gives us the large-scale picture of the flood and its effects. But it keeps to the main point, focusing on Noah. It makes the point that the human beings and animals outside the ark died. It does not provide clear information about the exact form that the waters took on top of the mountains.

I conclude therefore that Genesis 6–9 by itself does not clearly indicate exactly how extensive the flood was. It covered an extensive area—the ordinary "world" of the ordinary person in the ancient Near East. Possibly it covered the entire globe, but Genesis does not turn this possibility into a certainty. Consequently, we must go out and look at other parts of the world, alert to what further information may appear there.

Genesis 6–9 thus leaves open the question whether flood geologists or mainstream geologists are right. Let them each work at their theories, trying to understand more and more, and see which does better over the long run.[13] To most people knowledgeable about the technical details, it currently looks as if the mainstream geologists are doing better in technical explanation, partly because the key area of radiometric dating supports them (chapter 7).

Flood geologists themselves might be disposed to admit this, if it were not for the fact that they think they *must* hold to some form of flood geology in order to maintain the truth of the Bible. Given their interpretation of the Bible, and given their assumption that God used ordinary means to bring about the flood, I think they are right to maintain their approach. But when an approach runs into difficulties, it may be wiser to stand back and reexamine the initial assumptions. The initial assumptions, both the assumption that the Bible unequivocally teaches a flood of global extent, and the assumption that God used ordinary means, might be suspect.

In fact, we adopt these assumptions so easily because we have absorbed too much of a modern worldview. Living within this view, we think that it is natural for everyone to picture the "earth" as a globe, and we think that the existing regularities of science are absolutely permanent and therefore apply to the time of the flood. But when we return to the Bible and let it free us from some of the limitations of the modern worldview, we may recognize that both of these assumptions are just that—assumptions. The assumptions are natural and plausible, but need not necessarily be true.

---

[13] They have already been working on this question for centuries. Davis Young provides a useful history of people's attempts to harmonize the flood account in the Bible with geological evidence (Young, *The Biblical Flood: A Case Study of the Church's Response to Extrabiblical Evidence* [Grand Rapids, Mich.: Eerdmans, 1995]). Paul H. Seely mentions more recent evidence that produces still more problems for flood geology (Seely, "Noah's Flood: Its Date, Extent, and Divine Accommodation," *Westminster Theological Journal* 66 [2004]: 291-311, especially pp. 298-303).

10

THE ANALOGICAL DAY THEORY
AND THE FRAMEWORK VIEW

We now need to consider the analogical day theory.[1] This theory says that God created the world in six days of work, followed by one of rest, but that these days of divine work offer an *analogy* to days of human work rather than an *identity*.

Clearly we do have an analogy between God's work and human work, as the pattern of six days indicates, and as the Sabbath commandment in Exodus 20:8-11 confirms. God's work falls into six days, and each day has associated with it the refrain, "and there was evening, and there was morning, the third [or second, or fourth, etc.] day." Of course the 24-hour-day view would say, why should we not think of this analogy as essentially an identity, at least as far as the length of days is concerned? Is not that the "obvious" interpretation?

First, even if some people think that a length of 24 hours is "obvious," the text does not directly state how long the days were in terms of ordinary human measurement. It uses the word *day* (Hebrew *yom*), and includes the associated words "evening" and "morning." This all contributes to pointing out the analogy between God's work and the human sabbatical pattern, but it does not prove that the analogy is an identity.

THE SEVENTH DAY IN GENESIS 2:2-3

Next, the text gives some information that actually introduces problems for the 24-hour-day approach. Genesis 1:1–2:3 includes not merely six days, but seven. The seventh day does not include further work by God, but is described

---

[1] This approach is expounded by C. John Collins, "Reading Genesis 1:1–2:3 as an Act of Communication: Discourse Analysis and Literal Interpretation," in Joseph Pipa, Jr., and David Hall, eds., *Did God Create in Six Days?* (Taylors, S.C.: Southern Presbyterian Press, 1999), 131-151; Collins, *Science and Faith: Friends or Foes?* (Wheaton, Ill.: Crossway, 2003), 77-96; and Collins, *Genesis 1–4: A Linguistic, Literary, and Theological Commentary* (Phillipsburg, N.J.: Presbyterian & Reformed, 2006). My own explanation does not agree with Collins at every point but still belongs to the same broad category.

as the day on which God "rested . . . from all his work that he had done" (2:2). Accordingly, God "blessed the seventh day and made it holy" (2:3).

What kind of rest does Genesis 2:2 describe? Does it mean that God ceased governing the universe? By no means. The second person of the Trinity "upholds the universe by the word of his power" (Heb. 1:3), which describes a continual governance of the world, day by day, even minute by minute. God is not a deistic god who creates and then walks away. He continues to govern the universe. Then what does cease? He ceases his acts of *creation*. Genesis 2:3 says this, in noting that God *"rested* from all his work that he had done *in creation."* It does not say, "all his work," with perfect universality, but work *in creation.*

God made man, and he never needs to do it a second time. God does bring into existence every individual human being who comes into the world (Ps. 139:13-16). But he does so *providentially,* using the means of a father and mother and gestation in the womb.[2] By contrast, his original creation of Adam and Eve was unique. He did not merely bring into existence one man and one woman but also the human *race.* He laid once and for all a foundation for the subsequent developments in the human race. On the fourth day he created the sun and the moon, and now they are permanently there and do not need to be re-created. He created different kinds of animals. Now the different kinds are already here, and he does not continue to create new kinds every other day or so.[3]

Hence, the "rest" of Genesis 2:2 means "rest from acts of creation." The creation is "finished" (2:1), so God does not need to recommence with more acts of creation. We have reached a permanent endpoint. Consequently, the rest goes on forever. Then how do we understand passages that indicate that God is still "working"? Jesus, justifying his work of healing on the Sabbath day, says, "My Father is working until now, and I am working" (John 5:17). His statement does not conflict with Genesis 2:1-3. He is speaking primarily of acts of *redemption,* not acts of creation, and he may perhaps include acts of providence as well, but these also clearly do not belong on the same level as acts of the original creation.

Theologically speaking, God's plan includes not only redemption and providence but the coming of a "new heaven and a new earth" (Rev. 21:1; see Isa. 65:17). Redemption in Christ includes "new creation" (2 Cor. 5:17; Gal. 6:15; see Rom. 8:19-23). But these later reflections in the Bible do not deny the finishing of the *first* creation in Genesis 1. It is a mistake to import them directly

---

[2] The conception and birth of Christ involve another exception; but even here we see the involvement of Mary as a human mother.

[3] We must temporarily lay aside the disputes about microevolution and macroevolution, and look at the main point that Genesis 1 is making.

into Genesis 2:1-3, because they are talking on a plane different from the first creation. "The heavens and the earth were finished," according to Genesis 2:1, and in this context the "rest" in verses 2 and 3 is the rest from then onward.[4]

How long is the seventh day? For some years I thought that the seventh day might be only 24 hours long. God's rest goes on, while the seventh day is only the first day in which God begins to rest.[5] But now I believe that this approach does not work well theologically. The day is not just there with a very loose attachment to God's rest. The day has a special blessing and holiness, "because on it God rested from all his work . . ." (2:3). God's rest is the pattern for man's rest (Ex. 20:8-11). To conceive of God resting over many "days," of which only the first day is the Sabbath, breaks down the key analogy that Exodus 20:8-11 needs, not only to validate the single day of man's rest but to validate the holiness of the day. The holiness is first of all the holiness belonging to God's rest, not the holiness of the day. The holiness extends to the day precisely because it is *the* day of God's rest. The day must link closely to the rest, and on this one day man rests because on this one day God rested. I conclude, then, that since God's rest goes on forever, God's *day* of rest also goes on forever.[6] The seventh day, in order to deserve the consecration and holiness that it receives, must link itself closely to God's rest.

---

[4] Some people argue that God had to recommence work to respond to man's fall, which (perhaps) took place on the first day of the week. But (1) we do not know on what day of the week the fall occurred. (2) After the fall, God commences works of *redemption,* which is not the same as recommencing creation. (3) The full description in Genesis 2:1-3 presents the 6-and-1 pattern as derived from creation, and therefore as not depending essentially on the later fall into sin. Accordingly, the fall should not be imported into our definition of the seventh day.

[5] This position is represented in "Report of the Committee to Study the Views of Creation," *Minutes of the Seventy-First General Assembly . . . of the Orthodox Presbyterian Church* (Willow Grove, Pa.: Orthodox Presbyterian Church, 2004), 218-219.

[6] Note Augustine's affirmation of an everlasting seventh day: "But the seventh day has no evening and sinks toward no sunset, for you sanctified it that it might abide for ever. After completing your exceedingly good works you rested on the seventh day, though you achieved them in repose; and you willed your book to tell us this as a promise that when our works are finished (works exceedingly good inasmuch as they are your gift to us) we too may rest in you, in the Sabbath of eternal life" (Augustine, *Confessions* 13.36.51). John Murray comments: "There is the strongest presumption in favour of the interpretation that this seventh day is not one that terminated at a certain point in history, but that the whole period of time subsequent to the end of the sixth day is the Sabbath of rest alluded to in Genesis 2:2" (Murray, *Principles of Conduct: Aspects of Biblical Ethics* [Grand Rapids, Mich.: Eerdmans, 1957], 30). See also Henri Blocher, *In the Beginning: The Opening Chapters of Genesis* (Downers Grove, Ill.: InterVarsity Press, 1984), 44, 56-57; Franz Delitzsch, *A New Commentary on Genesis* (Edinburgh: T. & T. Clark, 1888), 110; and Johannes Oecolampadius: "if now you attend to the divine nature [i.e., God's rest rather than human rest], the seventh day will continue forever" (Johannes Oecolampadius, *D. Io. Oecolampadii in Genesim Enarratio.* [Basil, 1536], 27b, commenting on Genesis 2:2). The Latin of Oecolampadius runs as follows:

Nam operatur, & dum operatur quiescit, quandoquidem sola sua voluntate & verbo rem omnem perficit. *Si ipsam divinam naturam attenderis, dies ille septimus nunc semper durabit.* Nos juxta nostrum modum intelligendi septem dies facimus, apud ipsum tamen uno momento quodammodo comprehenduntur. Non possumus divina illa nostris corporeis comparare. Apud Ioannem habemus dictum: Pater meus usque operatur, & ego operor. Hic: Quievit. Illa facile possunt conciliari. Quievit deus ne nova opera conderet. Operatur, quia dedit illam virtutem rebus parturiendi fructus suos, ut initio decrevit, quae omnia suo verbo contingunt. Ita in ipso sumus & movemur.

Let me explain it in another way. Suppose that Genesis had explicitly said that God worked six 24-hour days, then rested from creating during one 24-hour day, and then recommenced with further acts of creation. It would certainly make sense to consecrate the one special day, and for man to imitate God by resting for one day. But now suppose instead that Genesis said that God worked six 24-hour days, then rested from creating for two months, then recommenced with further acts of creation. Would it then make sense for God to consecrate only the first day of the total period on which he rested, and for man to celebrate one day out of seven? Why one day rather than one month or two months? And if not two months, why not two days or a week or three hours? The selection of one 24-hour day seems unmotivated.

We must acknowledge that God can do anything he wants, and that we ought to obey his commands even if we do not understand their rationale. But Genesis 2:1-3 and Exodus 20:8-11 are not merely giving a Sabbath command to rest; they are providing a rationale for that command. The Sabbath is full of meaning for Israelites not just because God tells them to rest, but because he shows that their rest imitates *his* rest. They are imitating him, which is part of being in his image (note also Ex. 31:17). Detaching the idea of "day" from the idea of rest breaks down this meaning, and makes the Israelite Sabbath look like something that has been artificially imposed. That goes against the grain of Genesis 2:1-3 and Exodus 20:8-11.

These unacceptable consequences follow only if we assume that there must be an exact match in measurable length between God's days of activity and ours. If, on the other hand, the two are only *analogous,* the problems disappear. Analogy provides a firm basis for the Israelite Sabbath, just as it also provides a basis for the Sabbath and jubilee *years* in Leviticus 25.[7]

God rests forever from his initial work of creation, because it is "finished" (2:1). Man rests only in a preliminary way on his seventh day, because his work is not yet absolutely finished. He will recommence work on the first day of the next week. But all his work heads toward the time of absolute and

---

[7] Some critics of the analogical day theory have worried about whether speaking of "analogy" dissolves the historical character of God's work. No, it does not. The pattern in Leviticus 25 of Sabbath and jubilee years illustrates the kind of analogy we have in view. Longer periods (periods of years and weeks of years) are analogous to shorter ones, periods of seven days. The time periods are real, and the activities of working, resting, and releasing that take place during these times are also real—even though the details about the *kind* of rest and work differ depending on whether we are looking at days or years or weeks of years. Likewise, Genesis 1 indicates that man is to imitate God in many respects, including not only in his exercise of dominion but in his pattern of work and rest. But in the details, man does not work in precisely the same way as God does, nor does he work at precisely the same tasks in the precisely the same order.

In the case of sabbatical years, the Bible specifies how long a time is involved when the period in question is measured by the movements of heavenly bodies. In the case of the days of creation, we do not have this specification. But our lack of detailed knowledge about time measurement does not destroy the genuineness of the analogy.

final rest, of which Hebrews speaks: "So then, there remains a Sabbath rest for the people of God, for whoever has entered God's rest has also rested from his works as God did from his. Let us therefore strive to enter that rest, . . ." (Heb. 4:9-11).

Hebrews is speaking of the final rest into which we will enter in the consummation, the new heavens and the new earth (Rev. 21:1–22:5). This final Sabbath rest goes on forever. And it is the big "day" toward which the little celebrations of human Sabbaths look forward. Our human rest on one day of 24 hours looks not only backward to God's rest from creating but also forward to our final "day" of rest. The forward-looking reference clearly contains an analogy rather than a pure identity. Our rest now is preliminary and partial (we still do works of necessity and mercy). And it comes to an end after 24 hours. The consummate Sabbath involves final and complete and continuing rest—not in the form of inactivity, but rest from the particular labors toward fruitfulness and dominion to which human beings devote themselves in this life. We might say that the 24-hour human Sabbath rest foreshadows the final rest of human beings, as well as imitating the final rest of God, into which he has already entered (Heb. 4:10). This foreshadowing involves analogy to the reality to which it points, rather than pure identity of length.

Hence, God's seventh day in Genesis 2:2-3 is unending. It is *not* 24 hours long. And if this is so, then it is analogous rather than identical to a human day of 24 hours. But now if the seventh day is analogical and not identical, the whole structure is undeniably analogical. The entire pattern of God working six days and resting on the seventh forms a pattern analogical to man's work and rest.

Evening and Morning

Even the detail about the evening and the morning of each day finds an attractive interpretation within the analogical day theory. C. John Collins points to Psalm 104:23, "man goes out to his work and to his labor until the evening."[8] It says, "until the evening." Israelites work during the daylight, but at evening changes take place. Nocturnal animals come out at night: "You make darkness, and it is night, when all the beasts of the forest creep about" (verse 20). Man no longer works, but does what? He comes back home, rests, and sleeps. In fact, rest takes place not only on the seventh day, but in smaller pieces, namely each night during the six days of work.

---

[8] See the fuller discussion of the analogical day theory in Collins, "Reading Genesis 1:1–2:3"; Collins, *Science and Faith*, 77-96.

Now it turns out that this entire pattern of work and rest among human beings reflects God's original pattern. God worked to create distinct things during each of six days. He rested on the seventh day. But the language of evening and morning also indicates a pause in between the work of each day. Genesis pictures God as working for a period during each day, but at the end of the period of work, "there was evening," marking the end of the work, "and there was morning," marking the end of the pause in work. Man's period of rest during the night reflects these pauses between the days' work in Genesis 1.

The King James Version (KJV) translates these expressions in a different way: "And the evening and the morning were the first day" (Gen. 1:5; similarly for the subsequent days). This wording makes it sound as if the evening and the morning together make up or define the first day (much as we might say that daytime and nighttime make up one day). On this interpretation, the KJV sentence at the end of verse 5 defines and summarizes the time period during which the events of the preceding verses took place. But the KJV has mistranslated the Hebrew, which literally runs, "And was evening and was morning, day one." The verse contains two occurrences, not one, of the verb *was* (Hebrew *hayah*). The second occurrence, separating "evening" from "morning," makes it impossible to take the two terms together and equate them with "the first day." The error in the KJV has been corrected by more recent translations. The verse should read, "and there was evening and there was morning, the first day"; or, as Derek Kidner says, ". . . translate it 'evening came and morning came.'"[9] Each of the six days begins with God's work, not with "evening." The "evening" then comes *after* the work. The Hebrew introducing the expression "and there was evening" normally indicates narrative succession, and so it is here.

Many people think that "evening" gets mentioned because customarily the Jews thought of the 24-hour-period day as beginning at evening and ending at the next evening—unlike a modern American, who would trace the day from midnight to the next midnight. But there are difficulties with this suggestion. In fact, the information regarding Jewish thinking is complex. Jews could think of either the morning or the evening as a beginning, depending on the situation.[10] Second, this interpretation seems to make the expression

---

[9] Derek Kidner, *Genesis: An Introduction and Commentary,* Tyndale Old Testament Commentary (Downers Grove, Ill.: InterVarsity Press, 1967), 47.
[10] Psalm 104:23 offers an instance where the morning begins the day of work, which is followed by evening. For a fuller discussion, see H. R. Stroes, "Does the Day Begin in the Evening or Morning," *Vetus Testamentum* 16 (1966): 460-475; cited by Kidner, *Genesis,* 47.

"there was evening, and there was morning" almost superfluous. The reader's response might be, "Of course there was evening, and there was morning, because that is what makes up a day. Why are you telling us the obvious?" On the other hand, this culminating expression makes an important addition to the description if indeed it signifies God's temporary rest in between the times of work. Such a picture of a pause gives meaning and validity to man's temporary rest in between his days of work.[11]

God's Garden

The analogy between God's work and man's work occurs at other points as well. Consider God's work in planting the garden of Eden:

> And the LORD God planted a garden in Eden, in the east, and there he put the man whom he had formed. And out of the ground the LORD God made to spring up every tree that is pleasant to the sight and good for food. . . . (Gen. 2:8-9).

God planted a garden and made the trees spring up. Afterward he put Adam in the garden of Eden "to work it and keep it" (Gen. 2:15), and to enjoy the fruits (2:16).

God commissions Adam to be a gardener. But God himself was the first gardener, in his planting and making things spring up. God's action in "gardening" offers the analogical basis for Adam to imitate. Adam, made in the image of God, "images" God actively by continuing God's gardening project. One may infer that Adam also was to keep a pattern of six days of work and one of rest, in imitation of God's pattern. In both cases we must have analogy rather than identity. Adam is not God, and is not semidivine. He cannot create new kinds of trees. But within the framework that God has given him, he can imitate God's gardening *at a subordinate level*.

In fact, the transcendence of God and his great power and majesty stand out in Genesis 1–2 just as strongly as the exalted position that man has as the image of God. Man is made in the image of God and is therefore to imitate God, but always at a subordinate level, as creature and not Creator. God's works of creation, in their majesty, belong to an entirely different order than man's works of imitation. One aspect of this divine transcendence is that God's works are analogical to man's; and that analogy extends to the character of the days.

---

[11] For further valuable discussion of the "days," see Collins, *Science and Faith*, 360-367.

Look again at God's gardening. For a human being to plant trees and have them grow up takes days, months, even years. How long does it take God? If the analogy with God's gardening is an identity, it takes God just as long. It takes him years, using the ordinary means of his providence. But God, as God, is not confined to the ordinary. Perhaps the garden springs into being instantaneously. No, the language in 2:9 that says God "made the trees to spring up" suggests the passage of time. But how much time? Years? Or only a few minutes? We cannot tell, because God's actions are analogous to rather than identical to those of the human gardener. God and man are not on the same level. But likewise the days of God's work week are analogous to the time that a human being needs. To say that they are identical imposes on Genesis a direction that it does not endorse, and brings one into actual conflict with the seventh day and with the analogy of gardening.

One may choose to press the language about the six days, and to insist that they must be 24-hour days. But one might also choose to press the language about the seventh day, and argue that all the days are indefinitely long. One might choose to press the language about God's gardening, and then conclude that the garden must have come into being over a period of many years. All three of these moves press one piece of language into providing us very specific information about the length of time. But this process of pressing results in different, contradictory answers, warning us that we are pressing the language beyond its original intention. All three pieces give us analogy, not identity.

FOCUS ON CLOCKS OR ON INTERACTIVE EXPERIENCE

We should also consider different cultural approaches to time. Cultures differ in striking ways in their attitudes toward time.[12] Among these differences are differences concerning punctuality and "keeping to the clock." First, people can focus on the "objective" passing of time as shown by a clock. We may call this *clock orientation*. Second, they can focus on the more subjective, interactive time that they experience in the rhythms of human events. Human beings interact with one another in social groups or interact with created things, such as when they celebrate a wedding or harvest a field. These interactions involve natural groupings into beginnings, middles, and endings for human experiences and projects. We may call this focus *interactive orienta-*

---

[12] Edward T. Hall, *The Silent Language* (Garden City, N.Y.: Doubleday, 1959), especially 23-41; Robert Levine, *A Geography of Time* (New York: HarperCollins, 1997); Robert Levine and Ellen Wolff, "Social Time: The Heartbeat of Culture," in E. Angeloni, ed., *Annual Editions in Anthropology 88/89* (Guilford, Conn.: Dushkin, 1988), 78-81.

tion.[13] All human beings are aware to some extent of both kinds of orientation. Many of us have interactive experiences where we "lose track of time" and then suddenly realize that it is later on in clock time than we thought.

Different cultures can give priority to either one or the other of these orientations. Or they may have some mixture of the two approaches. In preindustrial societies, priority belongs mostly to interactive orientation.[14] A meeting starts not when the clock strikes nine (there may be no clocks) but when everyone is there and has had time to chat. The meeting lasts, not for one hour, but until the participants are "finished," that is, when people are satisfied with their social experience in their time together.

Postindustrial societies, by contrast, tend to run more by the clock (though there are still significant variations in custom and point of view between different cultures). American culture has a strong clock orientation. Someone says, "Sorry, I have to leave to meet Jim at 11:10" ("and he expects me to be not more than five minutes late"). Social experiences may start abruptly and terminate just as abruptly, because the clock governs the endpoints. And clock time is more merciless than nature's obvious rhythms. In the ancient world before the arrival of mechanical clocks, you experienced the rhythm of the seasons and the rhythm of day and night, but not the mechanical rhythm of the ticking clock.

How does all this apply to Genesis 1? If one goes to Genesis 1 with a clock orientation, one focuses primarily on how long it took, as measured by a clock. But if one goes to Genesis 1 with an interactive orientation, one asks what important events took place, and what was their human social meaning. Human beings did not appear on the scene until the sixth day of the creation week. But during the preceding days, God was on the scene, working with a rhythm like that of human work. A human worker naturally identifies with this rhythm, especially if he knows that he is made in the image of God. He immediately knows how long it took. It took six days, that is, six human-like cycles of work and rest, followed by a seventh day of longer rest.

---

[13] Robert Levine observes:

> One of the most significant differences in the pace of life is whether people use the hour on the clock to schedule the beginning and ending of activities, or whether the activities are allowed to transpire according to their own spontaneous schedule. These two approaches are known, respectively, as living by clock time and living by event time (Levine, *Geography of Time,* 82).

Levine and Wolff speak of "clock time" and "social time" ("Social Time," 79). See also Robert Lauer, *Temporal Man: The Meaning and Uses of Social Time* (New York: Praeger, 1981). I have introduced my own terminology in speaking of *clock orientation* and *interactive orientation.* But the difference is acknowledged by a number of authors, using a variety of terminology.

[14] See, e.g., Levine, *Geography of Time,* 81-100: "life on clock time is clearly out of line with virtually all of recorded history" (81-82).

The pattern that strikes him is the rhythm of work, not the question of ticks of the clock. These days in Genesis 1 are *really* days, because they match the human rhythm. (We will comment further about the reality of the days in chapter 16.) How long they took by ticks of the clock is a secondary question. Americans, by contrast, tend to press the question of clock ticks, because that clock orientation is a big factor in American culture.

In fact, this clock orientation shows up quite prominently when some of the advocates of the 24-hour-day approach say that the days of Genesis 1 were "ordinary days." In what way were they "ordinary"? In terms of the events that took place during the days, they were among the most extraordinary days in all of history! A person with an interactive orientation would never call them "ordinary." The term can fittingly apply only if we have already committed ourselves quite thoroughly and one-sidedly to a clock orientation. The person using the key word "ordinary" is claiming that the days were ordinary *by clock time*.

TIME MEASUREMENT

But we must still deal with the question of how Genesis 1 communicates to people who live primarily in terms of interactive orientation. Would they still arrive at roughly the same conclusions? To answer this question, we need first to consider what one means by a 24-hour day, and how one proposes to measure a length of time. The difficulty that we confront is that questions about *measurement* push us back toward the idea of an objective standard of measurement, a standard independent of human bodily rhythms and social interaction. An interest in exact measurement according to a mechanical standard characterizes clock orientation, not interactive orientation.

So suppose that we continue to press for a measurement of time length, according to the pattern of clock orientation. Suppose we could travel back to ancient Israel but still retain our own "excessive" cultural interest in clock ticks. The Israelites did not have mechanical clocks, so measurement by a mechanical clock literally does not make sense.[15] But if we are still concerned about exact measurement, can we find possible alternative routes?

---

[15] We must not oversimplify our picture of ancient cultures. Some cultures, both ancient and contemporary, have provided for themselves no special devices for time measurement beyond the movement of the sun, moon, and stars. But even in these cultures, the movement of the sun and the oscillation of day and night provide a nonhuman, objective background, making people aware that time transcends their individual and social horizons.

In the ancient Near East a professional caste of priests and wise men developed more focused interest in measurement of time. As early as the Old Kingdom in Egypt (2600–2200 B.C.) the night was divided into 12 subdivisions based on the rising of certain stars, and the day likewise was subdivided into 12 portions, which could be roughly measured by a sundial or a water clock (*The Encyclopaedia Britannica*

On the fourth day of creation, God supplied a means for measuring. He created the sun, the moon, and the stars, ". . . to separate the day from the night. And let them be for signs and for seasons, and for days and years" (1:14). We also hear that the heavenly bodies "rule over the day and the night" (1:18). An Israelite reader of Genesis 1 could grasp easily that the sun controlled ("ruled") the oscillation of day and night, and made them "separate," in the sense that one followed the other rather than having the two mixed. The seasons and the days and years indicate when the Israelites celebrate their special festivals such as the Passover and the Feast of Booths. The sun marks out the pattern of days, and the position of stars relative to the sun marks out the years, while the moon marks out months, within which the festivals take place. Together, these heavenly bodies function as timekeepers, telling the Israelites where they are in the cycle of days, months, and years. Here are natural rhythms for the marking out of time.

Now suppose that we ask an Israelite reader to calculate the exact time that passed during the creation week as a whole. He might tell us, "Seven days. Genesis 1 counts the days, and these days match my work on six days, followed by one day of rest." But this reply should not satisfy us, because he may be talking to us from the standpoint of interactive orientation. The rhythms of work and rest are what matter to him. So we have to press him to measure the length by some "objective" means, a means disconnected from human interactive interests.

When exact measurement of time matters, the Israelite keeps track by using the "old-fashioned," universal method of the sun, moon, and stars. But God put them in place and caused them to function in the familiar way only beginning with the fourth day. It makes no sense to ask the question, "How long did the first three days take by an external, objective measurement," because there is no obvious way of measuring the time. Human beings did not

---

[Chicago: Encyclopaedia Britannica, 1963], 8:49-50). Water clocks in Egypt from about 1400 B.C. consisted of "bucket-shaped vessels" with a small hole in the bottom, and with markings on the inside for the 12 parts of the day (*Encyclopaedia Britannica* [1963], 5:903). There were different markings for each month, because the total time for daylight varied with the season of the year. Thus the interest at this point was not mainly in an absolute, exact measurement of time intervals, but a practical division of both day and night into convenient subunits. This approach of breaking the day and the night each into 12 subunits spread from Egypt to the Greek and Roman world, leading to the terminology for "hour" (Latin *hora;* Greek *hora*). The mechanical escapement clock arose later in medieval Europe. From about 1290 onward there is mention of public striking clocks, the oldest surviving one in England (from 1386) being in the Salisbury cathedral (*Encyclopaedia Britannica* [1963], 5:933).

In short, in the Middle East, and later in the Roman Empire and in medieval Europe, we see some professional acquaintance with a concept of objective measurement of time. And ordinary people might have some familiarity with the basic ideas (especially in late medieval Europe, if a cathedral clock sounded out the hours to a whole town!). But clock-measured time did not dominate or control cultural practices, which still for the most part ran at the more natural pace of human rhythms of work and rest.

exist, so that one could not even appeal to a more "psychological," intuitive human sense of the passage of time. The ancient heavenly timekeepers did not exist either. The only reasonable answer is that it took three days in terms of interactive orientation, that is, in terms of the rhythms of work. But that is no answer at all to the modern question. The Bible simply does not give an answer, because it is not addressing our modern, clock-oriented question.

We meet a barrier here because we are creatures, not the Creator. Our Creator, through his works during the six days of creation, not only created the human race but provided us with a stable environment in which we may live, work, eat, and rest. Within that environment we function with some skill—though things have been disrupted by the fall. But when we try to ask the question concerning the technical details of the length of the creation week, we find ourselves moving outside that safe, stable environment. We are acting as if we could jump outside our skins, almost, and, like a god, observe the works of creation without the aid of any human environment. Most significantly, we want to observe and measure and time the length, without using the timing devices that God provides us only *within* a stable created environment. Can one do that? Can one even attempt it without ignoring the limitations that we have as creatures?

These reflections bring us back to the old point: God is Creator and we are *not*. That poses an ultimate barrier to the possibility of thinking of ourselves as if we were watching the work of creation *from outside*. We know what God has done in creation, because he has spoken to us and explained it to us in Scripture. But we always know what we know *as creatures*, as human beings made in the image of God but not ourselves divine.

We know by analogy. God is the supreme Father, and we have human fathers by imitation and analogy. God is the King, and we have human kings by analogy. And so on. The analogy in every case is real and valid and true. But we cannot get beyond analogy as if we could become divine ourselves and know God directly on his own level. The same, I would suggest, holds for our attempt to understand the days of creation. We understand, but we understand as creatures. And that means that there remains mystery. In particular the mystery of the seventh day shows that God's days do not necessarily have measured lengths identical to our ordinary clock-time human days. God does not provide us precise, specific information about the clock-time length of any of the six days of his work.[16] The six days *may* all be of 24-hour-day length, when

---

[16] People holding to the 24-hour-day viewpoint might reply that, of course, we cannot jump out of our skins and know *directly* how long the days are. We know because God has told us that they are "days." God, who is not subject to our creaturely limitations, knows; and if he knows, he can tell us.

With most of this reply I agree; but it misses two crucial points. First, we cannot stand outside of our creaturely status in order to get a godlike view of analogical language, and to pin down precisely all the points

measured by the speed of light or some other modern "objective" standard; but they also may not be. The passage in Genesis does not say.

Thus, when some advocates of the 24-hour-day view claim to have specific information about the length of the days, they fall short in hearing what Genesis does and does not say. They sincerely desire to honor God's word, and to follow God wherever he leads, but they have not done full justice to the passage. In harmony with the analogical day view, the passage simply teaches that God made the world in six days but does not provide details about how to measure the exact length of the days by some objective, nonhuman standard.

THE FRAMEWORK VIEW

The analogical day theory can be considered as one variant of the framework view. In agreement with the analogical day theory, the framework view maintains that the six days in Genesis 1 are God's work days, and as such are analogous to rather than identical to ordinary human days. But, in contrast to the approach of analogical days, advocates[17] of the framework view speak of the

---

of analogy. That is, we cannot specify *exactly* how the days of God's work of creation are like our human days of work, any more than we can specify *exactly* how God's Fatherhood is like human fatherhood. In each case we can make a beginning, and specify *some* points of analogy. But we never avoid mystery.

Second, we have unsolvable difficulties in trying to specify to ourselves what we mean by "length of time" for days 1-3 when we try to calculate it precisely by some objective standard of measurement. We are building out from Genesis 1 by several steps when we try to achieve precision. And we cannot achieve precision unless we have a clear public standard of measurement to apply—whether movements of heavenly bodies, or wind-up clocks, or the human psychological sense of passage of time, or cesium clocks, or the speed of light, or other means. This is part of our creaturely condition. If we grant that the universe operated according to present-day scientific laws during the six days of creation, then we have grounds for extrapolating backward and obtaining time estimates. But this assumption of constancy of laws during the six days is something that the young-earth creationist typically denies.

We can put it another way. What is a "day" without the sun? When we take away the sun, are we not left with work activity followed by rest? Then this pattern of work followed by rest is the built-in analogy for understanding "day."

Third, as we already observed, modern people tend to bring to Genesis 1 a strong bias toward clock orientation, rather than interactive orientation, and therefore miss completely the fact that Genesis appears to speak to Israelites using interactive orientation, and to focus on the human-like rhythm of work and rest. These seven days *really* are seven days, with evenings and mornings after each of the first six days. There is no illusion here. But a person dominated by clock orientation feels threatened unless he can know how many clock ticks we are talking about.

Of course, even people whose culture encourages primarily an interactive orientation toward time are aware of the background pattern of day and night governed by the sun. For them, a term like "day" has associations *both* with the rhythm of human work and rest *and* with the rhythm of the movement of the sun. But the Genesis 1 narrative speaks of a situation where the "greater light" did not exist until the fourth day. Only an interactive meaning remains with which to understand the pattern in the first three days. The presence of this interactive meaning in the first three days also invites us to extend its meaning as the dominant meaning in the remaining days. Hence, instinctively, ancient readers do not focus on the question of time length *as measured by* clock orientation.

[17] See especially Nicolaas H. Ridderbos, *Is There a Conflict Between Genesis 1 and Natural Science?* (Grand Rapids, Mich.: Eerdmans, 1957); Meredith G. Kline, "Because It Had Not Rained," *Westminster Theological Journal* 20 (1958): 146-157; Meredith G. Kline, "Space and Time in the Genesis Cosmogony," *Perspectives on Science and Christian Faith* 48/1 (1996): 2-15; note the answer to Kline's "Because It Had Not Rained" in Derek Kidner, "Genesis 2:5, 6: Wet or Dry?" *Tyndale Bulletin* 17 (1966): 109-114. See also the further discussion of the framework view in appendix 1.

pattern of the six days as "a literary framework" organizing the acts of creation. The principal architects of the framework view want to say that this framework is full of meaning.[18] But their intended message may not always come across. To some people the label "literary framework" suggests something completely artificial and extraneous to the content, the actual acts of creation. But if the framework is artificial, it drains force from the significance of the Sabbath pattern for man. Man, in observing the Sabbath pattern, seems to be imitating an illusion, a literary artifice. Moreover, since its original development, some Christians—not the original architects of the view[19]—have attempted to redefine or stretch the framework view into a large umbrella that includes views that do not really give much weight to Genesis 1. They treat Genesis 1 as if it were no more than a very vague and general affirmation that God created everything.

The framework view argues that the succession of days represents logical and topical and structural grouping, rather than chronological succession. (But it does acknowledge some degree of chronology: man is created last, and the seventh day follows the other six.[20]) This view is theoretically possible. But topical grouping does not exclude the possibility of chronological succession. We may have both, rather than choosing between them. Kidner thoughtfully observes,

> Yet to the present writer the march of the days is too majestic a progress to carry no implication of ordered sequence; it also seems over-subtle to adopt a view of the passage which discounts one of the primary impressions it makes on the ordinary reader. It is a story, not only a statement.[21]

But Kidner also reminds us that we should see how Genesis 1 is selective:

> As with all narrating, it demanded a choice of standpoint, of material to include, and of method in the telling. In each of these, simplicity has been a dominant concern. The language is that of every day, describing things by their appearance; the outlines of the story are bold, free of distracting exceptions and qualifications, free also to group together matters that

---

[18] See, in particular, Lee Irons with Meredith G. Kline, "The Framework View," in David G. Hagopian, ed., *The Genesis Debate: Three Views on the Days of Creation* (Mission Viejo, Calif.: Crux, 2001), 217-256, especially 236-247, which makes the pattern of days an analogical representation of the "upper register" of God's dwelling in the invisible heaven of the angels. This elaboration was not present in the initial development of the framework view by Arie Noordtzij and N. H. Ridderbos.

[19] Ibid., 220.

[20] Ibid., 221.

[21] Kidner, *Genesis*, 54-55.

belong together (so that trees, for example, anticipate their chronological place in order to be classified with vegetation), to achieve a grand design in which the demands now of time-sequence, now of subject-matter, control the presentation, and the whole reveals the Creator and His preparing a place for us.[22]

The intuitive impression of chronological progression in Genesis 1 arises partly from details that imply a logical progression. The dry land has to appear on day 3 before the land plants on day 3. The "expanse" ("firmament") created on day 2 must be there in order for the lights to be put in the expanse on day 4, and in order for the birds to "fly above the earth across *the expanse of the heavens*" on day 5. The sea and land, from day 3, furnish the habitat for the sea creatures and the land creatures on days 5 and 6. The plants from day 3 provide something for the animals to eat on day 6 (Gen. 1:30). The narrative as a whole gives the impression of a well-planned project. Nowhere, of course, does Genesis say explicitly that A must be prior to B. But the accumulation of instances of natural progression leaves a firm sense of an overall chronological movement.

I prefer the analogical day theory to the framework view because it retains a sense of chronological progression and affirms the reality of the structure of seven days as a pattern for man to imitate. (Further discussion of the framework view can be found in appendix 1.) If we grant that the grouping into days may ignore exceptions and may partly group together matters that belong together, we find that in fact its order corresponds roughly to the order of events in mainstream scientific accounts. Edwyn Bevan, without holding to a classical view of inspiration, observes that ". . . in principle they [the stages in Genesis 1] seem to anticipate the modern scientific account by a remarkable flash of imagination."[23]

---

[22] Ibid., 55.

[23] Edwyn Bevan, "The Religious Value of Myths in the Old Testament," in Samuel H. Hooke, *In the Beginning* (Oxford: Oxford University Press, 1947), 161; quoted in Kidner, *Genesis,* 55.

Many people worry about the fact that the sun, moon, and stars were made on the fourth day, because it seems out of place according to a mainstream scientific account. Some interpreters say that the heavenly bodies were actually created much earlier, but God "caused them to function" as they now do by removing a thick layer of obscuring mist and clouds that had previously hid them from the earth. But in a context like Genesis 1, the key verb *made* (Hebrew *'asah*) does not merely mean "cause to function." It surely includes or implies an idea of actual creation or "making." In Genesis 1:26, where God proposes to "make" man, we find the Hebrew word *'asah,* "make." Then in Genesis 1:27, where God "created man," we find the special verb for "create" (Hebrew *bara'*). In Genesis 1:21 "God created [Hebrew *bara'*] the great sea creatures." In verse 25, "God made [Hebrew *'asah*] the beasts of the earth." In the context of Genesis 1, there is not too much difference in the implications of the two Hebrew verbs.

I suggest that the difference in the point of view of ancient and modern readers helps our understanding. What is the sun? To a modern reader informed by planetary science, it is a huge ball of hydrogen plasma in whose hot core thermonuclear energy is generated. According to mainstream science, the

LOOKING BACK OVER THE DIFFERENT APPROACHES

Though I have expressed a preference for the analogical day theory, I should also stress that more than one of the theories offer us approaches with some strengths. The 24-hour-day view, mature creation, the day-age theory, the analogical day theory, and the framework view all affirm the main theological truths of Genesis 1–2. And they all attempt to exegete the details of Genesis 1–2 responsibly, though some are not as successful as others. In particular, the day-age theory has a weakness when it claims that the word *day* actually *means* an indefinitely long period, in the same way as it does in expressions like "the day of the LORD." If the word *day* is being used analogically in Genesis 1, the analogy belongs to the *whole chapter*, not merely to the word *day* in isolation. When the day-age theory admits this, it essentially turns itself into the analogical day theory.

In a similar manner, when the 24-hour-day view addresses at length concerns about modern science, it tends to turn itself into the mature creation view. The framework view turns itself into the analogical day theory if it admits that Genesis 1 retains a chronological progression. The shifts from one viewpoint to another leave us with two attractive theories, mature creation and the analogical day theory. I regard the analogical day theory as the stronger of the two, mostly because mature creation assumes too quickly that the days are 24 hours long, when measured by some technical instrument. It has not realized how strong is the exegetical evidence in Genesis 1–2 for an analogical rather than identical relation between God's days and man's.

The mature creation view remains a theoretically possible position. But it derives almost all its attractiveness from the prior conviction that the days are 24 hours in length. If indeed the Bible clearly teaches 24-hour days, God is directly telling us that we ought not to be deceived by apparent age in the

---

sun in this sense existed before even the most primitive plant life arose on earth. But what does "the greater light" (Gen. 1:16) mean to an ancient reader? Like the rest of Genesis 1, it is phenomenal language. "The greater light" is the bright disk of light that human beings can see in the sky. This visual phenomenon simply did not exist on earth until the atmosphere cleared. God made this phenomenon on the fourth day.

Modern readers have difficulty here mainly because a worldview associated with modern science (and to some extent philosophical thinking inherited from Aristotle) has given us distorted conceptions about what is real. According to a typical modern point of view, the ball of hydrogen plasma 93 million miles from earth is real; the visible disk in the sky is mere appearance. I disagree. See my discussion of what is real in chapter 16.

In fact, by choosing to focus on the sun as a visible phenomenon, namely a bright disk, God can address people in every culture of the world. All cultures can observe the sun as a disk. By contrast, if the Bible had chosen to speak of the sun as a ball of hydrogen plasma 93 million miles away, it would have been obscure except for those with the special information deriving from modern science. In this respect, the Bible remains culturally universal, while a modern scientific viewpoint (though true enough within its own sphere) is not culturally universal. Though the Bible may look foolish to those who pride themselves on their modern special knowledge, it is incredibly wise once we understand God's purposes (1 Cor. 1:18-31).

universe any more than we should be deceived by apparent age in Adam and Eve when they were first created. But in fact, careful attention to Genesis 1–2 shows that God does not indicate the length of the days by some instrumental standard; instead, some features of Genesis 1–2, like the unending seventh day of God's rest, actually caution us not to make quick inferences. Thus, God nowhere tells us that, if we look backward in time, we are looking at an "ideal time" or unreal past projection. Without this premise, the mature creation view ceases to be attractive. On the basis of the general faithfulness of God, and on the basis of his invitation to explore the world he has created, we have good reason to believe that the apparent ages found in astronomy are also real ages. That is, they are real from the point of view of the technical, calculational concerns of astronomy and modern science. But reality includes many dimensions, not least of which is the point of view of human interactive orientation. We shall take up this point in chapter 16.

11

THE ROLE OF MANKIND
IN SCIENCE

Now what about the role of human beings in science?

Because human beings have fallen and continue in rebellion against God, the products of human activity suffer corruption. The corruption may be subtle and still be serious, as in the corruption that takes place when scientists practice idolatry by substituting an impersonal idea of autonomous, self-sufficient law for the God of the Bible, whose word is law.

Thus we must exercise care in our reflection about the very nature of science. What people assume to be "obviously" right about science may not be so right. The obvious intellectual and technical triumphs of science tend to mesmerize us into uncritical acceptance of whatever cloaks itself in the name of science—as in the case of the philosophy of evolutionary naturalism (chapter 5). Science does indeed offer us impressive triumphs. But under the impressiveness may still lurk hairline cracks that represent serious flaws in thinking in the long run. And some of the impressiveness may have developed in spite of, rather than because of, the ways in which we think about science. As we saw in chapter 1, scientists in practice believe in God in spite of protestations to the contrary. They achieve success on the basis of this belief.

THE ROLE OF MAN IN GENESIS 1–2

In Genesis 1:26-30 God creates man in his image and gives him dominion over the plants and animals. In Genesis 2:15 God puts man in the garden of Eden "to work it and keep it." Together these passages give man significant responsibilities and privileges in relation to God and the created order. First, man is made in the image of God. He is a creature, not the Creator, and thus is subordinate to God. At the same time, being made in the image of God, he is like God in a variety of ways. Genesis 1:26-27 invites us to reflect on ways in which man is like God. He is a person, able to think, to speak, and to listen, and to respond to God in worship. The list could be extended. In addition, God makes man a subordinate ruler under God's rule. Though dominion does not define the totality of being in the image of God, it is obviously one of the ways in which man is like God and imitates God.

God clearly indicates man's superiority to the animals and plants. At the same time, man does not have a boundless, arbitrary freedom to exploit the things placed under him. He is ultimately a steward who must answer to God for how he uses the gifts and privileges that God gives him. The restriction placed on the tree of the knowledge of good and evil produces a concrete reminder of man's more general responsibility to be answerable to God (Gen. 2:16-17). Moreover, man's privilege of imitating God implies also imitating the bounty and goodness of God. As God has abundantly blessed man with a pleasant environment, man himself in his dominion is to be a kind master who values the creatures under his care.

We could, if we wish, draw some quick implications for modern discussions of ecology and conservation. Genesis 1–2 repudiates both modern extremes. On the one hand, it does not simply immerse man in nature so that he is just one more species, with no special privileges. Man is special. And his specialness does not consist first of all in his superior intelligence but in his status as a creature made in the image of God. Hence, we do not worship nature or place animals on the same level as man. Unlike some people who want to leave nature completely untouched, we can confidently domesticate animals or plant a garden that alters the untouched wilderness.

On the other hand, Genesis repudiates the view that man has carte blanche to do whatever suits him and to satisfy his own lusts at any price. God cares for his creation; he does not exploit it. Man must imitate God. Certainly man may use the fruit of the trees for his nourishment (Gen. 2:16), but his overall goal is to serve and glorify God, not merely serve his own desires. And the goal certainly ought not to be serving desires that become perverted after the fall! The "dominion" of Genesis 1:28 is thus to be understood as a thoughtful, caring dominion, a dominion expressing God's goodness and care, and not a heartless, brutal, crushing dominion. Genesis 1–2 repudiates the sinful perversion of dominion into destructive exploitation.

We can also see that Genesis 1–2 encourages human devotion to multiple goals rather than simply to material abundance. God shows his majesty in the world that he created (Ps. 19:1-6). Man in honoring God aims at magnifying God's glory. Man serves not himself, but God. So he beautifies the world, to display the beauty of God. He makes plants fruitful, to display the fruitfulness and bounty of God. He practices righteousness with fellow human beings, to display the righteousness of God. He makes machines that display the power of God. These represent not separate, competitive goals, but different aspects of the same overall goal. So the machines ought to enhance human living, but not at the expense of beauty.

But let us not move too quickly into contemporary discussion of science. We need to consider carefully the entire biblical picture about the role of human beings. Genesis 1–2 gives us a foundation, a beginning, for understanding human tasks. But it is only a beginning. It contained God's first words of instruction to man, but other words would come. God intended that man should live in fellowship with him, and this fellowship would include ongoing two-way conversation. Even after the fall had erected a barrier, God continued to speak. In the end, we should not try to derive all of our understanding of man's tasks merely from Genesis 1–2, because Genesis 1–2 was never intended to stand alone as a total explanation.

SUBSEQUENT DEVELOPMENT IN HISTORY

But the fall intervened, so that we never see how the history of mankind *should* have developed. We know that human beings would have multiplied, and we infer that their dominion would have grown in extent and in thoroughness. But what we actually see in the subsequent history is always corrupted by sin. As we illustrated in our consideration of idolatry in science, rebellion and sin infect in subtle ways even the best and most admirable of human works, and sin infects human works in ways that sometimes turn them into ugly horrors, as we see in instances of human cruelty.

Bearing in mind the effects of sin, we can still draw some reasonable conclusions about goals. The entrance of sin does not totally destroy mankind, nor does it totally destroy his task of dominion and care for the creation. God shows his grace even in Genesis 3 by giving a promise of redemption, as well as by refraining from totally destroying Adam and Eve on the spot. After the flood, God promises to continue a regular, providential pattern in the world:

> While the earth remains, seedtime and harvest, cold and heat, summer and winter, day and night, shall not cease (Gen. 8:22).

He also renews man's dominion as well as the creational command to be fruitful and multiply:

And God blessed Noah and his sons and said to them, "Be fruitful and multiply and fill the earth. The fear of you and the dread of you shall be upon
every beast of the earth and upon every bird of the heavens, upon everything that creeps on the ground and all the fish of the sea. Into your hand
they are delivered. Every moving thing that lives shall be food for you. And
as I gave you the green plants [referring to Gen. 1:29], I give you everything" (Gen. 9:1-3).

Genesis 4–11 gives at least some hints as to how man's dominion develops. Genesis 4–5 distinguishes the godly line of Abel and Seth from the
ungodly line of Cain. Abel was "a keeper of sheep," thereby exercising
dominion over some of the animal world. Cain was "a worker of the
ground," thereby exercising dominion over some of the plant world, as well
as over the ground itself. Interestingly, Cain's line shows further progress in
dominion. Cain built a city, which he named after his son Enoch (4:17). He
expressed dominion in architecture. Jabal his descendant "was the father of
those who dwell in tents and have livestock" (4:20), which suggests an expansion of animal husbandry on a much larger scale than Abel's. Jubal "was the
father of all those who play the lyre and pipe" (4:21), which implies not only
development of music but development of musical instruments, which take
some technical skill. Dominion is leading to skills in manufacture. Tubal-cain
"was the forger of all instruments of bronze and iron" (4:22), indicating a
growth in metallurgy. Genesis 2:12 mentions gold and bdellium and onyx
stone in Havilah, near Eden, which already shows God's provision for man
and hints at a possible later development in which man will use these provisions. Under Tubal-cain such development begins to take place.

The prominence of dominion work among the descendants of Cain
might make readers wonder whether Genesis intends to condemn such
dominion. After all, the line of Cain is leading up to the corruption in the days
of Noah (Gen. 6:1-8). But the original dominion command in Genesis 1:28,
as well as the participation of righteous Abel in keeping sheep, indicates that
the impulse to dominion represents a continuation of the original good creation. The corruption through sin does not utterly displace the creation, but
twists it in ugly directions.

Technical work reaches a climax of sorts with the tower of Babel (Gen.
11:1-9). "Let us build ourselves a city and a tower with its top in the heavens" (11:4). One sees here a vivid illustration not only of the development of
powerful human abilities but also of sinful twisting of these good abilities.
The ability to build a city or a tower is a good gift of God from creation. The

people twist this gift by using it in a prideful manner ("and let us make a name for ourselves"), by desiring to seize the divine ("its top in the heavens"), and by turning aside from the dispersal that would be a natural consequence of obeying the command to fill the earth (1:28). God frustrates their design and they leave off building (11:8). The failure illustrates what may happen also to later human projects that arise out of the impulse for dominion.

These projects involve developing human skill. We see here the skills of artisans, not the elaborate technical knowledge of modern science. Yet there are affinities between the two.

Artisans remain practical, focused on the particular materials with which they work. They typically do not mount large-scale projects of purely intellectual reflection. But they find new and better ways to use their materials, as in the production of bronze and iron. They find ways to improve the tone and ease of fingering in a lyre or a pipe. The farmer finds ways of plowing, sowing, weeding, and plant breeding that produce better crops. The animal husbandman finds ways of effectively tending and feeding his animals and then breeding them to produce a more robust herd in the next generation. In good times, some of this skill may accumulate over generations, as masters instruct apprentices. From time to time, challenges to do better lead to experimentation with the materials. What if we try a new material in the musical instrument? What if, in forging metals, we try a different mix of starting materials or a different technique in heating and shaping the metal?

The development in artisanship does not yet produce science in its modern form. But its experimental aspect brings it closer to science than the practice of theoretical reflection in isolation from experiment. The world derives from God's plan, not directly from man's mind. So we must go out and look at the world God made, not just deduce mentally what God "must" have done.

UNDERSTANDING GOD'S WORLD

Genesis 1–2 includes within its framework attention to the role of man's mental and verbal skills. Farming proceeds under a guarantee from God that seeds reproduce "each according to its kind" (1:11, 12). A farmer needs to understand this principle. If you plant an apple seed, you will get an apple tree, not an orange tree. If you plant oats, you will get oats. Farmers constantly rely on the creative word of God that established this regularity, and they rely on the faithfulness of God to his own word as he maintains the regularity year by year. Over time, they discover that one can improve crops by selecting the best seed for the next planting. The principle in Genesis 1, "according to its kind," turns out to apply to some extent even within a single species, when one is trying to produce the next generation of good crops. Similarly, animal husbandmen rely on the fact that sheep give birth to lambs who grow into sheep. Directly or indirectly, workers rely on the word of God that governs the plant world or the animal world or the mineral world.

This reliance encourages human reflection on God's word of command. Man is to "think God's thoughts after him."[1] He needs to do this thinking in order to grow in mastery and skill in managing plants and animals and the environment. And because God made man in his own image, man has a fundamental ability to do this thinking. His mind and his language automatically come with the capability of some understanding of God, of "being on the same wavelength," as it were, because his mind is "like" God's. At the same time, man is a creature, not the Creator, and all his thinking is dependent on God.

We see man exercising his privileges in thinking and speaking in Genesis 2:19-20, when he names the animals. In doing so, he imitates God, who also gave names: God called the light Day and the darkness Night (Gen. 1:5). Naming is an exercise of authority and sovereignty.

It is possible that Adam merely assigned sounds randomly in order to create names. But in Hebraic culture naming typically indicates something about the thing named. Adam's name for Eve had meaning ("The man called his wife's name Eve, because she was the mother of all living," Gen. 3:20). God's names of Day and Night certainly have meaning. God renames Abram "Abraham," that is, "father of a multitude," to seal his promise of many descendants to Abraham (Gen. 17:6). He renames Sarai "Sarah," meaning "princess," in the same context (verse 15). The name Jesus, meaning "the Lord saves," is given because "he will save his people from their sins" (Matt. 1:21).

Thus, when Adam gives names in Genesis 2:19-20, we should think of descriptive names, not merely arbitrary sounds. If Adam is to do this, he must give attention to the animals that he names. He must see what kind of ani-

---

[1] Cornelius Van Til especially uses the expression "thinking God's thoughts after him" to stress both the presence of God and man's dependence on God:

Over against this [modern autonomous thinking about science] Christianity holds that God is the creator of every fact. There are therefore no brute facts. Thus God's thought is placed back of every fact. Thereby man's thought is made subject to God's thought in the interpretation of every fact. There is not a single fact that man can interpret rightly without reference to God as the creator of that fact. Man cannot truly apply the category of causality to facts without the presupposition of God. It is God who has caused all facts to stand in a certain relation to one another. Man must seek to discover that relation (Van Til, *Christian-Theistic Evidences* [Philadelphia: Westminster Theological Seminary syllabus, 1961], 86).

See also Cornelius Van Til, *The Defense of the Faith,* 2nd ed. (Philadelphia: Presbyterian & Reformed, 1963), 31-50.

mal each is, and in particular must see that no animal is really a fit companion for him (2:20). It takes discernment, perhaps study. But we are still at the beginning, comparatively. Adam as a creature does not know everything, and must grow in knowledge. The names would perhaps pick out some obvious features that distinguish one animal from another, but they would not be full descriptions. They make a beginning at attention to detail, description, and classification. All of these functions continue in the early years of the development of biology into its full-blown modern scientific form. Adam is the first "scientist," if you will, though his science at that point would be elementary.

Above we discussed artisanship. But Adam's work of naming is reflective and verbal, not manipulative. In fact, these two aspects are complementary. God made man to function as prophet, king, and priest.[2] The terms and the specific offices of prophet, king, and priest appear in fully differentiated form only later. But the broad functions are already there at the beginning. God speaks truth, exercising a prophetic function. He rules, exercising a kingly function. And he blesses what he has made, exercising a priestly function. Adam as an image-bearer imitates God on the level of the creature. He speaks and thinks, functioning as a prophet. He rules over the animals and keeps the garden, functioning as king. He offers his service to God and through his work blesses his fellow human beings who will come after him, thereby functioning as priest. These functions overlap. Just as God rules the world by speaking, Adam can exercise authority over the animals (a kingly function) by naming them (a prophetic function).

Artisanship represents primarily a kingly activity. Man reshapes the structure and organization of things. Naming, on the other hand, involves speech, thought, and understanding, which falls more in line with the prophetic function. Both exist in harmony. To this day we see a division of labor between experimental science, which involves kingly interaction with experimental apparatus, and theoretical science, which involves prophetic interaction, in which people think about the rationality of the word of God governing the experiments. The two sides need plenty of interaction. Otherwise, experimental science loses the valuable input of brilliant new ideas that synthesize and organize the experimental observations, as well as suggesting new directions for experiments. Conversely, theoretical science, detached from experiment, runs into unfruitful speculation where no one knows what theory is right, because the theories have never been checked!

Technology as an application of science continues the kingly work of the

[2] Van Til, *Christian-Theistic Evidences,* 117.

artisan. And if it is done right, it aims to praise God and to bless the recipients and users of technology, continuing the priestly function.

Adam made a good beginning in science. He and his descendants could have made a good continuation, going from strength to strength in their understanding of God's world. But the fall intervened. Rather than humbly investigating God's ways, Adam and Eve decided they wanted to be "like God" (3:5). They decided not to submit themselves to God's instruction, but rather autonomously to make up their own minds about the tree. The attitude of autonomy and independence from God already corrupts science in an essential manner. One is no longer in love with God and therefore no longer desirous of really understanding his ways. One cuts oneself off from the original Source of instruction. One casts off the attitudes of humility and patience that are important to science.

And there are secondary effects as well. People like Abel die without passing on the knowledge that they gain. Wars and destruction and death and famine give people little leisure for any kind of patient, extended reflection on scientific questions. Great libraries perish in fire or in ruin. In order to gain power, people conceal knowledge rather than share it.

And finally, idolatry corrupts the prophetic and kingly impulse to understand and explore. The polytheist avoids science, because polytheism makes him despair of finding a rational order. He thinks that this world derives partly from the irrational interaction of petty gods. The animist avoids science for fear of offending the spirits. The Buddhist avoids science because meditation that empties the mind is the way to Nirvana.

SOLOMON AS SCIENTIST

Out of all the nations of the world, God chose Abraham and promised to be God to him and his offspring (Gen. 17:7). The ancient Near East of Abraham's time was filled with polytheism, which undermined one of the foundations for science, namely human confidence in a unified world order. God revealed himself to Abraham and his offspring as the one true God, the Creator of heaven and earth, thereby providing a platform that opened a possibility for the growth of science. Did it happen? Abraham's offspring flirted again and again with the polytheism of their surroundings. That did not help. And when they were few in number, or in distress in Egypt, they did not enjoy a situation favorable to science. After the conquest under Joshua, the period of Judges was chaotic. David finally established a secure kingdom through a series of wars.

Solomon's time enjoyed the resulting peace and security. The reign of Solomon provided a unique opportunity. Solomon knew the true God, and had peace. More significantly still, the Lord gave him great wisdom (1 Kings 3:12). The wisdom answered Solomon's request to know how to govern the people, which is a practical concern for practical skill. The focus is not purely theoretical or intellectual. We see the fruit not only in the story of Solomon's decision about the prostitute's son (1 Kings 3:16-28), but in the book of Proverbs. Proverbs gives wisdom about human nature and human conduct. It is more practical, more down-to-earth, more "proverbial" than modern social scientific work. It is not occupied with statistics, with methodology for research, with technical qualifications for exceptions. It is a beginning. And in its beginning it already exceeds modern social science in one respect, namely that it has the center right: "The fear of the LORD is the beginning of knowledge" (Prov. 1:7).

Solomon's achievements show the fruit of God's gift of wisdom:

> And God gave Solomon wisdom and understanding beyond measure, and breadth of mind like the sand on the seashore, so that Solomon's wisdom surpassed the wisdom of all the people of the east and all the wisdom of Egypt. For he was wiser than all other men, wiser than Ethan the Ezrahite, and Heman, Calcol, and Darda, the sons of Mahol, and his fame was in all the surrounding nations. He also spoke 3,000 proverbs, and his songs were 1,005. He spoke of trees, from the cedar that is in Lebanon to the hyssop that grows out of the wall. He spoke also of beasts, and of birds, and of reptiles, and of fish. And people of all nations came to hear the wisdom of Solomon, and from all the kings of the earth, who had heard of his wisdom (1 Kings 4:29-34).

It says that he spoke of trees, of beasts, of birds, of reptiles, and of fish. It sounds like the beginnings of descriptive science. Perhaps Solomon's speech merely used the animals as illustrations for human behavior, in the way that Proverbs 6:6 urges the sluggard to "go to the ant." Even this illustrative use requires some observation of the animal or plant world. But the language of 1 Kings 4:29-34 seems to describe a much more concerted focus on the plants and animals, and not *just* for the sake of illustrating human life. Solomon's discussion of plants and animals appears to be *in addition to* the 3,000 proverbs, proverbs that make observations about human life. Wisdom, in the ancient Near East, included wisdom not only concerning human life but also concerning the natural world. God challenged Job as to whether he was wise by asking him whether he knew secrets of nature (Job 38:4–41:34).

As far as we know, Solomon did not have a lot of technical experimental apparatus. But science does not start with its present fund of apparatus. It builds gradually. The beginnings of modern biology included much work in detailed observation and classification of animals and plants (especially Linnaeus, whose system of classification continues in use today, with appropriate modifications and enhancements). Solomon's utterances may well have begun explorations in this direction.

But, like the Proverbs, Solomon's utterances may have also included choice, amusing observations about striking features in animal behavior. The ants are so industrious (Prov. 6:6). And the humble lizards get into king's palaces (Prov. 30:28).

God created the animals not only so that we might classify them, but so that we might enjoy them, and perhaps be amused. Modern science in its single-minded focus on the classification, the causation, and the mechanical structures, has achieved much; but we can *also* appreciate the illustrations and the metaphors provided in the animal world. They too are something that God has provided. In fact, the fascination about animals that helps draw us into detailed investigation of their ways comes partly from their amusing and striking, curiosity-awakening features. The good teacher includes this side, and does not simply drone on about generalities. Moreover, he honors God in so doing, because God reveals himself in the particularities and the amusing and beautiful details as well as in the generalities.

So Solomon was a "scientist," after a fashion. He did not have the immense accumulations of knowledge in mature modern sciences, but he made a beginning. It was a good beginning, as we can see from the admiration that it evoked in its own time (1 Kings 4:34). Unfortunately, it was also the end! Solomon's work did not pass on to his successors. In his later years, Solomon slid back and strayed from his earlier devotion to the Lord. As a result, the Lord pronounced judgment and tore the kingdom in two after Solomon's death (1 Kings 11:9-12). Israel did not again see either the peace or the wisdom that they had seen in Solomon.

Solomon's time nevertheless leaves behind an important record. It gives us a picture of what could be, even if it is a miniature, a small picture of beginnings. Solomon shows that science is possible, that it is legitimate—more than this, that it is a blessing to be pursued. Like Solomon, we should pursue the wisdom that only God can give. And wisdom includes wisdom in understanding God's world. We rightly admire science, and desire the wisdom that science includes. The Christian view of the world affirms the legitimacy and value of science in an emphatic way, and shows that, far from being inimical to science, the Bible encourages the godly person through love of God to come to love God's wisdom and to love to reflect about the wonders of God's world. Doing so may honor God, and if done well may even attract the attention and admiration and wonder of others who do not know the true God who revealed himself uniquely to Israel.

PERSONAL EXPERIENCE

May I speak personally? I have found that science offers a wonderful window onto God's wisdom. It provides extraordinarily beautiful and wise and profound exhibitions of God's glory. I loved learning science and mathematics in high school, college, and graduate school. Not everyone does, I know, but I think almost anyone would if he could get over the academic difficulties and see the world with Christian eyes.

I now teach New Testament. But I have continued to love science and to read about science. Properly understood, it is a way of growing in love for God. Unfortunately, it does not seem so to many, and that is one reason why I am writing this book! Listen to the psalmist exult as he reflects on what he sees:

> O LORD, how manifold are your works!
>   In wisdom have you made them all;
>   the earth is full of your creatures.
> Here is the sea, great and wide,
>   which teems with creatures innumerable,
>   living things both small and great.
> There go the ships,
>   and Leviathan, which you formed to play in it.
> These all look to you,
>   to give them their food in due season. . . .
>
> May the glory of the LORD endure forever;
>   may the LORD rejoice in his works,
> who looks on the earth and it trembles,
>   who touches the mountains and they smoke!
> I will sing to the LORD as long as I live;
>   I will sing praise to my God while I have being (Ps. 104:24-27, 31-33).

As usual, the psalmist describes the level of ordinary appearances, so that others may easily share in his joy and admiration. But science, rightly understood, increases the joy and admiration. Science is all about discovering the mind of God.

HUMAN LIMITATIONS

Spectacular as modern science may be, it is still subject to limitations because human beings do the work. We are finite and fallible, and after the fall we are sinful. The Christian view of the world provides clear space for science, but also indicates some limits. Because we are not God, we never know in the way that he knows. We do not know everything, and what we do know remains in most cases tentative. Science, as we observed, does not directly hear the word of God, but reflects on the effects of the word of God. Scientists' constructions of scientific laws are not the *real* laws, but an approximation or the best guess about the laws.

The Bible also gives borders in time and space for human reflection. In some respects Genesis 8:22 provides a basis for science, because it guarantees a stable order of events: ". . . seedtime and harvest, cold and heat, summer and winter, day and night, shall not cease." But it also gives a qualification: "While the earth remains, . . ." And the promise clearly begins from the time when God gives it to Noah. The immediately preceding flood disrupted many of the ordinary regularities, which makes the promise all the more precious.

The promise also focuses on the level of ordinary events and addresses ordinary people, as we have seen to be true of Genesis 1–3 and Genesis 6–8. It does not directly focus on the concerns of scientists for technical details. Nevertheless, it is suggestive. It suggests that God will continue to govern the entire world in a consistent way from the time of Noah until the end of this present world. Hence, it invites scientists to proceed with confidence in investigating how God regularly governs the world during this period.

But we must also affirm clearly that God may work miraculously whenever he chooses, at any time during this period. The flood of Noah sits right before the promise of 8:22, as a gigantic reminder not only of God's power but of his right to do as he pleases. The promise of regularity in 8:22 does not involve an enslavement of God to man, so that God must never do anything out of the ordinary. God remains a personal God. His governance of the world is personal, not a mechanism. It is not a question of God "breaking in" from outside, to alter a mechanism that is running self-sufficiently; there is no such mechanism. *God* rules the world, including its more "mechanical-looking" features: "You cause the grass to grow for the livestock" (Ps. 104:14). His purposes are rational, but they are also personal. His rationality transcends our rationality. He has a good, rational purpose for raising Christ from the dead, even though (we might say precisely because!) resurrection is out of the normal course of things.

Let us think again about Genesis 8:22. God promises the regularities of the seasons. That gives us confidence that science can uncover regularities that apply during the whole period from Noah's flood until the second coming. But what about the period before Noah's flood? May we extend scientific investigation back to that time as well? By itself, the promise in Genesis 8:22 makes no guarantee. But as we look at Genesis 4:1–5:32, it sounds like a world in many respects like the world after the flood. So we may tentatively guess that the flood constituted a judgment in which God used ordinary means, at least for the most part. The flood marked a destruction and re-creation from a thematic, theological point of view, but it may or may not have involved a radical disruption of scientific laws such as modern science uncovers. The description in Genesis 7–8 does not indicate just what regularities God disrupted during the flood. To find out more, we can go and look at old rocks. This looking leads us into the discussions of flood geology, mainstream geology, and mature creation geology, which we already covered (chapter 9). Even mature creation geology, which thinks that geologists study "ideal time" or "apparent age," grants that they may fruitfully engage in this study using ordinary scientific assumptions. The other two approaches, flood geology and mainstream geology, think that, in the area of physical laws, God has governed the world in basically the same way from creation on through the time of the flood.

This conclusion also makes some sense theologically. Despite the fact that the flood in some respects functions like a "re-creation," it is not a creation from nothing (*ex nihilo*). God preserves Noah and his family. He preserves animals in the ark. So we might rather say that the flood is a small-scale picture or model of re-creation, but that it is not literally full-scale re-creation. And how could it be, since the sun, the moon, and the stars are not affected? The flood then takes place *within* the larger created order that God established in Genesis 1. This created order retains its regularity all the way from Genesis to Revelation, "while the earth remains."

But it is still not clear whether God acted in the same way during the six days of creation as we see him acting afterward, at the end of the six days. The mature creation view answers that he did not, while many mainstream scientists who are Christians think that he did. We cannot know for certain. That is part of our creaturely limitations. We were not there when God created the world (Job 38:4). We live firmly and completely within an environment that God has already finished establishing. We cannot dictate to God how he must have done the establishing. Mature creation may be right. Or the mainstream may be right. And what difference does it make? It makes no difference in practice, because the mature creation theory says that the scientist studies apparent age. For practical scientific purposes, this apparent age functions just like real age.

Knowing all about *how* God created matters only if we think we have to have absolute knowledge. We say to ourselves, "We must *know,* and not be cooped up under the onerous limitations that our environment may have temporarily forced upon us." But underneath, that is rebellious talk. We want godlike knowledge, and we make ourselves discontent with the situation in which God in his wisdom has placed us. I would say in reply, "Get a grip on your ambition, humble yourself, relax, and accept that you are a creature. It is okay not to know, if God does not give us the means of knowing. It is enough that he knows, and he will take care of the rest."

We may also have limitations in space. Genesis focuses very much on the "world" of the ancient Near East. And Genesis 1, though giving man dominion over plants and animals, does not give him dominion over the sun and the moon and the stars. Is outer space beyond the reach of science? We might think so. The ancients often supposed that the regions above followed different laws from the regions below. God could have done it that way. But once again we have to look and find out. We cannot dictate to God either that outer space will be the same or that it will be different. Detailed data about the motions of the planets and data about the motions of earthly bodies enabled Newton to make the daring guess that the two followed the same laws at a fundamental level of analysis. Modern astronomy has further developed Newton's views. But we must see this development as an extra gift from God. God need not have given us common physical laws for the two realms, but he did. All the more we should honor his glory, displayed in the magnificent beauty and consistency of these laws.

Finally, we have limitations when we move forward in time. Genesis 8:22 includes the limitation, "While the earth remains." We know from later Scripture that the earth will not *always* remain. God promises "a new heaven and a new earth" (Rev. 21:1). Its description so transcends our present experience that we suspect it may involve new physical laws, or transformations of the present laws, in ways that no human being can anticipate.

Modern scientists who look at the cosmos have gone their own way. They speak confidently of billions, even trillions of years in the future. They say that the sun will eventually burn out and become a nova. Long after this event, all useful energy will be dissipated into heat; it will be so spread out that it cannot do any useful work. They predict the "heat death" of the universe, which will also involve the extinction of all living things as we know them.

How do they know what will happen? They have extrapolated into the far future on the basis of fundamental laws of physics. But what are these laws of physics? They are the scientists' human descriptions of the way in which God governs the world now within the physical sphere. The postulation of the laws assumes the presence of God (chapter 1). And yet they want to say that God cannot do otherwise in the distant future.

But in fact, the expression "while the earth remains" presents an impenetrable barrier, beyond which these scientists cannot see or extrapolate. The extrapolation into the future passes into "ideal time," an unreality. We ask ourselves what *would* happen if the same physical processes continued to work indefinitely. But we know from a Christian point of view that this extrapolation is simply a "what if" question, because its assumption of continuity is invalid.

CHRISTIAN AND NON-CHRISTIAN THINKING

The extrapolation into the far future gives us a good example of the difference between Christian and non-Christian thinking.[3] Both Christians and non-Christians in practice are inconsistent. And there are many forms of religious and irreligious worldviews and commitments. There are forms of theism outside of Christianity (Islam, for example), and there are forms of pantheism, panentheism, polytheism, and spiritism, as well as various atheistic commitments. For the sake of simplicity and contrast, let us consider two positions in a "pure" or idealized form, namely consistent Christianity and consistent atheism.

A Christian looks forward to the second coming of Christ. An atheist looks forward to an endless continuation of the universe as it now is. According to his view, there can be no second coming. Here is a decisive difference. But to understand how the difference arises and how it operates, we must go more slowly.

A Christian has learned from the Bible about the true nature of God, and about the fact that God governs the world according to his word. God's immanence (presence) in the world, including God's creation of man in the

---

[3] For detailed reflection on the differences, see Cornelius Van Til's writings, and John M. Frame, *The Doctrine of the Knowledge of God* (Phillipsburg, N.J.: Presbyterian & Reformed, 1987).

image of God and his gracious redemptive revelation of himself to us in Christ, gives us confidence that we can know God and can conceivably come to understand his ways in governing the world. So a Christian does approach modern science with confidence that science is observing how God governs. A Christian can extrapolate into the future based on the constancy of God and the faithfulness of God to his own word.

But a Christian also knows that he is not God and cannot dictate to God how he must act. God is *transcendent* as well as immanent. The Christian knows from Genesis 8:22 and other passages that the present world will not last forever into the future. The time of Christ's second coming will bring radical transformation and disruption of the present order. Hence, all extrapolation beyond that time becomes extrapolation into "ideal time," a discussion of how things *would have* looked if God had delayed the second coming until a later time.

The atheist also uses assumptions about God's laws for the world, but they differ from Christian assumptions. Typically, the atheist says that the laws are *impersonal.* What effect does this have on his thinking about the future of the universe? It typically means that an atheist thinks of the present system as going on indefinitely, without interruption.

But if the laws actually were impersonal, they would not be laws at all. They might be anything. Irrationality lies at the bottom of this assumption. If "laws" come out of the void, why should we have any hope that they will in any respect match what the human mind can think or imagine? It is as if a plant on earth tried to grasp the thinking of a human being, or worse, the thinking of a martian. Why should we expect that the sun will rise tomorrow, just because we have seen it rise before? Maybe the laws governing human memory are changing on us, and our memory of the past is completely off base. Or, if our memory is okay, maybe the laws will change tomorrow. Maybe light will never return, or the face of a jack-o'-lantern will replace the sun! Once we abandon the idea of a personal, trustworthy God, little prevents our wildest nightmares from taking his place.

The atheist must ignore this difficulty, and believe in spite of himself that he can grasp the laws. Moreover, the atheist must know that there are no *other* laws pertinent to the extrapolation on which he works.

Let me illustrate. In thermodynamics, *entropy* is a technical concept used to measure the amount of disorder in a system. The Second Law of Thermodynamics says that in a closed physical system, the entropy never decreases, and a system with initially low entropy tends to evolve into a system of high entropy.

If we then take the visible universe as a whole and treat it as a closed system, we predict that it will increase in entropy until it reaches a final state of very high entropy, which takes the form of "heat death," in which energy is uniformly distributed and not available for useful work. Long before this final endpoint, human beings would not have enough available energy to sustain life. It is a gloomy picture.

But what assumptions have gone into this conclusion? For one thing, we have assumed that the visible universe as a whole is a closed system. Is this true? The universe is not "closed" to God's action. The atheist has nevertheless protected himself with the expression "closed *physical* system," which focuses on physical causality operating within the created world. But even on a strictly physical level, one cannot say what is happening at the far edges of the visible universe, because one can see out to that distance only dimly. And one cannot guarantee that one's "sight" is capable of detecting all possible kinds of physical input. Neither can one guarantee that there are no small and diffuse physical inputs nearby, provided that they are so small that they escape measurement. Some decades ago, some scientists actually advocated a "steady state" universe in which hydrogen atoms or elementary particles might be created out of nothing at a very slow rate throughout the visible cosmos.

Second, suppose that another law affects the Second Law of Thermodynamics. Suppose, for example, that another law says that entropy tends to increase during the opening stages of expansion of the visible universe, but that slowly this tendency to increase slows down and even reverses. The slowing down might be so gradual that it has not yet been detected, and would not be detected until far in the future.

Third, suppose that another "law" says that the universe is controlled by a personal God. This God normally validates the Second Law of Thermodynamics, but, whenever it suits his personal, rational purposes, he makes the behavior of the universe deviate from the Second Law.

Most atheist scientists would react quite differently to this third suggestion. The first two suggestions can still be made to fit within the overall atheistic assumption of impersonal laws, while the third does not fit. But the strong reaction shows that the atheist is making assumptions about the nature of law. How does he *know* that these assumptions are right? Has he seen "behind the veil," and checked out that there is no personal God, and that the laws are impersonal? He must claim to know what in fact he cannot know.

Moreover, how can an atheist judge what is probable among different possible laws? One can judge probabilities within a situation like dice-throwing, because we already think it is partially governed by specific laws. But how do we judge how likely it is that the universe is a closed physical system, or that the Second Law of Thermodynamics will one day go into reverse? If we know God, and know that we are made in his image, we have some hope that we can in many cases guess what is more likely. But without having God behind all the possibilities for specific laws that we could imagine, how do we know? An atheist might be disposed to admit that he cannot know, absolutely, whether he has missed some key factor in his extrapolation. In theory, he admits his limitations. But without God he seems to have no way of assessing the extent of the limitations, and whether he has the least chance at all of being right.

The Second Law of Thermodynamics is now known to be more complicated than my summary above. We should not literally say that entropy *never* decreases, but that statistically it almost never does, and that any small, fleeting decreases are soon overwhelmed and reversed. But how do we know whether still other laws lie behind the statistics? Is some unknown law influencing the statistics, so that, over time, the descriptive phrase "almost never" proves less and less accurate? Or can we envision that God may bring about a statistical exception in a particular situation for his own, personal purposes?

Christian and atheist alike agree that the Second Law of Thermodynamics holds—more or less. But this apparent "agreement" papers over differences that appear because of differing conceptions of the whole idea of law. A larger idea of law always lies there in the framework of assumptions that guides the way in which we view a particular law, and how we judge its applicability, particularly applicability beyond the bounds of what is most ordinary and familiar.

We may summarize some of the differences by saying that a Christian and an atheist have different views of law both in its transcendence and in its immanence. For a Christian, the transcendence and immanence of law express the transcendence and immanence of the one personal God. God who is personal is knowable to us who are persons made in his image. Hence we can have genuine knowledge of law. From our confidence in God's faithfulness and our knowledge of his larger purposes, we can make good estimates as to how his laws might apply even in cases where we extrapolate. But we always have the qualification that God is God, and we are not. He transcends our knowledge. He can surprise us.

For an atheist, on the other hand, transcendence leads to blank irrationality. Why should there be laws at all, and why should they be accessible to man at all? Why should his human mind be in harmony with impersonal laws out there? Actually God both creates the human mind and ordains the laws, but the atheist does not want to admit it. The atheist imagines the laws just to be out there, against a background inexplicability as to why. There is an ultimate irrationality at bottom, that transcends the laws themselves.

At the same time, an atheist must somehow come to know the physical laws, which means that the laws must be accessible to his mind. They must have some kind of immanence. Having come to know the laws, the atheist must know them perfectly, exhaustively, in order to extrapolate into an infinite future. The atheist knows at some level that all science is tentative, but he grasps what he knows as if it were ultimately and completely known. If the law is impersonal, then maybe it is subpersonal, and thus within the reach of human dominion. (Note that the atheist still relies covertly on the God-given confidence and impulse toward dominion.) The atheist then can pretend to himself that he has achieved total, godlike dominion. He has grasped all that there is to be grasped, or at least all that needs to be grasped, with virtually infinite precision. The infinite precision is needed because even small errors at the beginning result in huge differences when one extrapolates out to trillions of years in the future. The impersonality of the law enables the atheist to feel that he can "get on top" of it, subdue it, and claim infinite precision.

One can see tensions here. The claim that law is impersonal results in a false transcendence for the law that then makes the law inaccessible. The claim to know the law with perfection involves false immanence, because science is tentative. Neither the atheist's version of transcendence nor his version of immanence really works.[4] But they are close enough to working to create an illusion, because these conceptions distort in an idolatrous direction the actual truth about the transcendence and immanence of God, which are reflected in the transcendence and immanence of God's law.

The precise form of idolatrous distortion influences one's conception of the laws. The animist, as we have seen, does not undertake scientific investigation, because he fears offending the spirits. The spirits create a situation where laws probably do not exist but if they do exist they are inaccessible. On the other hand, modern scientific thinking typically distorts the law into *subpersonal* law. Because the law is still subpersonal, it cannot give him back-talk or cease to cooperate. It does what he wants, namely control the universe over which the atheist now sits in mastery.

---

[4] For extended discussion of Christian and non-Christian views of transcendence and immanence, see Frame, *Doctrine of the Knowledge of God.*

Atheistic thinking has two subtle effects. First, it makes the atheist an idolater, who is responsible for his rebelling against God in spite of knowing better. We might think that this personal, human side is the only effect, but idolatrous ways of thinking also have effects on other areas of knowledge. The atheist persuades himself that the world really will go on indefinitely into the future through the operation of the same physical laws. His *scientific* summary of the very meaning of the laws differs from the summary that a Christian would offer, because the impersonality of the law distorts his judgment.

12

THE ROLE OF CHRIST AS REDEEMER IN SCIENCE

Sin has infected human beings. It infects every human being born into the world, and it infects deeply. It infects the mind. It infects the products of the mind, including science. How do we find a remedy?

CHRIST'S FULFILLMENT OF DOMINION

We need redemption in science because science, as a human endeavor, shows the effects of sin. Sin in the form of idolatry, as well as the petty forms of sin among professional scientists, such as jealousy, rivalry, and occasional falsification of evidence, affect the character of scientific work. In fact, because one's conception of scientific law forms the guiding framework for the day-to-day work of science, idolatrous corruption of scientific law infects scientific work *pervasively.* The effects are all the more devastating when they are subtle. Non-Christians do not think with utter perversion, but think with a distorted concept of law that *is still close to the truth,* and borrows from the truth.

The Bible indicates that God did not stand aloof from our misery, but sent redemption through Christ. "For if while we were enemies we were reconciled to God by the death of his Son, much more, now that we are reconciled, shall we be saved by his life" (Rom. 5:10).

God did not send a recipe book or a philosophy, but his Son. And his Son did not hold aloof from those in need. He became man. He ate with tax collectors and sinners.

Redemption in its total compass provides responses to all the damages of the fall, including the damage to human dominion. Man after the fall continues to have impulses toward dominion, but these impulses get twisted into megalomania and oppression of fellow human beings. True dominion needs restoration.

The New Testament indicates that Christ came as the last Adam, one like Adam. He did what Adam failed to do, and became the head of the new humanity (Rom. 5:12-21; 1 Cor. 15:12-28, 42-49). Several passages echo the language of Adamic dominion from Psalm 8 and apply it to Christ: God put "everything in subjection under his feet" (Heb. 2:7-8; Ps. 8:6; 1 Cor. 15:24-28; Eph. 1:22).[1] Jesus Christ is the second person of the Trinity, who is God from all eternity. But the passages in question say something about his *humanity*. As man, he was raised from the dead. As man, he ascended to the Father. As man, he received dominion from the Father as the reward for his work. In Ephesians 1:22 the language about dominion echoes Psalm 8's language about Adamic dominion, and follows right after the mention of the resurrection of Christ and his sitting at the Father's right hand:

> . . . he worked in Christ when he raised him from the dead and seated him at his right hand in the heavenly places, far above all rule and authority and power and dominion, and above every name that is named, not only in this age but also in the one to come. And *he put all things under his feet* and gave him as head over all things to the church, . . . (Eph. 1:20-22).

In the next verse Paul indicates that Christ "fills all in all" (1:23). The language of filling echoes the command in Genesis 1:28 to "fill the earth." Christ through his ascension and reign has thus fulfilled both aspects of the creation mandate in Genesis 1:28—the one aspect involving filling the earth, the other involving exercising dominion ("subdue it and have dominion . . ."").

Christ also indicates this triumph in the well-known words of the Great Commission: "All authority in heaven and on earth has been given to me. Go therefore and make disciples of all nations . . ." (Matt. 28:18-19). "All authority" indicates comprehensive dominion. And this dominion serves as a foundation for a universal spread of the gospel and of discipleship, discipleship that involves submission and obedience to this one who has authority. In other words, discipleship *fills the earth* with human beings in God's image.

We might wonder whether the language of authority pertains to Christ's divine nature or his human nature. With respect to his divine nature, Christ is God and rules over the whole universe from all eternity (Heb. 1:3a). His

---

[1] Dan McCartney, "Ecce Homo: The Coming of the Kingdom as the Restoration of Human Vicegerency," *Westminster Theological Journal* 56/1 (1994): 1-21.

authority is complete and universal. The Great Commission presupposes the reality of his divinity. But its focus does not seem to be there, but more on his human nature. The wording says that "all authority *has been given* to me." This giving of authority from the Father belongs naturally with the events of resurrection, ascension, and being seated in his human nature at the right hand of the Father. Acts 2:33, for example, speaks of Jesus as "having received from the Father the promise of the Holy Spirit" in connection with the ascension. Gifts from the Father come as a consequence and reward for the accomplishments in the flesh, particularly the crucifixion and resurrection. In Matthew 28:18-19, the giving of authority is also the basis for mission: "Go *therefore* . . ." The word "therefore" also suggests that the "giving" of authority takes place at the time of ascension. Christ's triumph *in the flesh,* in his human nature, leads to his reward and the consequent mission on earth. (Note that Christ's present reign at the right hand of God is both the reign of the Son, the second person of the Trinity, and a reign that fulfills the promise concerning a *human* son of David who will reign [Isa. 9:6-7; Acts 13:33-34]. Jesus retains his human nature in his exalted state.)

The Great Commission also includes an aspect of "filling the earth." In the concluding statement Christ says, "Behold, I am with you always, to the end of the age." The expression "with you" indicates his presence, and indirectly suggests that in person he "fills" the world. But we also see a progressive "filling." Through the progress of the Great Commission, Christ will "fill" the world with his disciples, with whom he is especially present. He will therefore fill the world with them as his representatives and ambassadors.

To be sure, the fulfillment of the creation (or cultural) mandate has arrived in a surprising form, namely through the achievement of a single man. But this single man is representative for the new humanity, and through union with him others also exercise universal dominion: "and [God] raised us up with him [Christ] and seated *us* with him in the heavenly places in Christ Jesus" (Eph. 2:6). The language of being "seated" at God's right hand implies authority and rule. The heavenly position of the seat implies that the rule is universal. Likewise in Revelation Christ promises a position of rule, but this time it is in the future: "The one who conquers, I will grant him to *sit* with me on my *throne,* as I also conquered and sat down with my Father on his throne" (Rev. 3:21).

Taken together with Ephesians 2:6, the language of ruling in Revelation 3:21 shows the well-known already/yet-to-come pattern of New Testament eschatology. Because Christ has triumphed, his people share in the triumph *already.* But the implications of the triumph are still working out, so that we have hopes still to be realized in the future, hopes of what is *yet to come.* This characteristic two-pole fulfillment applies to the so-called cultural mandate in Genesis 1:28, the mandate to fill the earth and subdue it. The task has already come to completion in principle in Christ as representative head of the new humanity. But it has yet to come completely to realization in the individual members of the new humanity.

The issue of the cultural mandate is important for our purposes because it includes the call to exercise dominion. And this dominion, as we have seen, includes scientific investigation.

But now, since Christ has fulfilled the cultural mandate, scientific investigation needs to be rethought. If the mandate had already been fulfilled in every respect, we would have to say that science is at an end already. Its task has finished. But the twofold idea of "already" and "yet-to-come" means that something may yet remain. What remains nevertheless flows out of what has *already* been accomplished. That is, the cultural mandate, and with it the task of scientific investigation, still applies to human beings, but it addresses them in a new way, since Christ has completed the mandate in his representative triumph.

Christ's completion of the cultural mandate expresses itself not only in the kingly sphere of ruling but in the prophetic sphere of wisdom and understanding. According to Ephesians 1:21-22 Christ rules over all, as the last Adam ("under his feet" echoing Ps. 8:6). That is the kingly aspect. But he also has all wisdom: ". . . God's mystery, which is Christ, in whom are hidden all the treasures of wisdom and knowledge" (Col. 2:2-3). That is the prophetic aspect. Christ compares himself to Solomon, in a way that indicates his superiority even to the great wisdom of Solomon:

> The queen of the South [i.e. the queen of Sheba mentioned in 1 Kings 10:1-13] will rise up at the judgment with this generation and condemn it, for she came from the ends of the earth to hear the wisdom of Solomon, and behold, something *greater than Solomon* is here (Matt. 12:42; Luke 11:31).

Christ is the final Solomon. Solomon gave us only a picture, only a preliminary taste of what might be. And in the end he was flawed. He failed through his sin. He was a "type" or prefigure of what would come through Christ, his greatest descendant.

CHRIST THE FINAL SCIENTIST

Wisdom belongs to Christ innately with respect to his divine nature. As God, he knows everything from the beginning. But the comparison with Solomon shows that he is also consummately wise with respect to his human nature. So once again we should relate his wisdom to the cultural mandate and the task of science. The scientist pursues both wisdom and dominion in relation to the natural world. Christ, through his position of rule and wisdom, has achieved both fully. To say it boldly, Christ is the final and archetypal scientist!

But my claim about Christ ought not to transform our understanding of Christ; rather, it ought to transform our understanding of science. The corruption and idolatry in science manifests itself especially in this, that scientists seldom see their need for Christ *in the sphere of science*. Science needs redemption because of the turning of scientific law into an idol (chapter 1). And only Christ can provide that redemption:

"And there is salvation in no one else, for there is no other name under heaven given among men by which we must be saved" (Acts 4:12).

Jesus said to him, "I am the way, and the truth, and the life. No one comes to the Father except through me" (John 14:6).

". . . apart from me you can do nothing" (John 15:5).

Redemption of science, it turns out, does not take place merely through a faraway, arbitrary "magic" that waves a wand and fixes what is wrong. It takes place through Christ becoming our wisdom and ruler, and achieving what we fail to achieve because of sin. From now on, then, our achievements follow in his steps. As in issues of personal sanctification, so also in respect to science, we become imitators in fellowship with him. Science on earth becomes a process of coming to know Christ (Phil. 2:8-10) and participating more deeply in his wisdom.

Or that is what it *should* be. And maybe it has *actually* been that way in some cases, with scientists who are devout Christians (though even they will fall short of the ideal). But today it does not seem to be so with most practicing scientists. Then how can they ever succeed? How can science advance? As we already saw in chapter 1, scientists succeed largely in spite of themselves! They succeed by continuing to believe in God in their assumptions about scientific law, at the same time that they deny and disbelieve. Now we must extend this observation to include not only God the Father, but God the Son, God Incarnate as Redeemer.

Christ's accomplishment of redemption has borne fruit. He gives blessings even to those who are still in rebellion against him. Because of our rebellion, we do not deserve to retain functioning minds. (The mentally retarded and those who have suffered strokes remind us of this.) We do not deserve to have the ability and skill inherited from past generations who have been blessed. We do not deserve the leisure and prosperity necessary to build sophisticated measuring apparatus, nor the leisure and teachers helping us to study our way through layers of progressively more sophisticated scientific theories. If we nevertheless get benefits when we deserve the opposite, we are receiving a redemptive blessing. It does not mean that we ourselves as individuals have received personal salvation from Christ through faith. But if we are non-Christians, we have a kind of shadow of this faith in the confidence that we can receive and use what we do not deserve—although our confidence is distorted by ingratitude and pride.

WISDOM

Most of all, as part of God's blessing on the undeserving, scientists receive wisdom. Not all have the saving wisdom to know Christ personally and submit to him. But what they have, they have from God. "He who teaches man knowledge—the LORD—knows the thoughts of man, that they are but a breath" (Ps. 94:10-11). The context of the statement in Psalm 94:11 seems to be general. Not only does the Lord teach some people saving knowledge, but whatever knowledge people have, they have from the Lord. Knowledge comes through the teaching of the Holy Spirit: "But it is the spirit in man, the breath of the Almighty, that makes him understand" (Job 32:8). The expression "the spirit in man," with lowercase "s," indicates the human spirit. But the original Hebrew had no capitalization. Moreover, the parallel line, "the breath of the Almighty," indicates that man's understanding relies on a divine origin and gift. Whether or not the first line designates the human spirit, the second line hints that the divine Spirit, the Holy Spirit, lies behind the gift of knowledge to the human spirit.

Does God really give us all the knowledge we have? Some people might be disposed to divide knowledge into two parts, one supernatural in its source and the other natural. When God speaks from the top of Mount Sinai, that is a supernatural source of knowledge. When the scientist works through an experiment, or reasons through the implications of an equation in physics, or derives the implications of a theory in chemistry, he receives knowledge from nature. Are there then two distinct sources here? Yes, we can receive instruction in more than one way, and a supernatural source like Mount Sinai stands out as both spectacular and inexplicable.

But less spectacular and more explicable sources also derive from God. He is God who rules over the ordinary as well as the extraordinary. He sustains the experimental apparatus in its place, with its properties. He is also the Lord of logic, of the very reasoning processes that human beings use. The origin of logic lies in the self-consistency of God and his loyalty to himself. Logic spills over into the world through God's Son, who is the Word of God. As the Word, he is the divine reason behind the world and the original that all human reason reflects. He is the wisdom of God, according to Colossians 2:3.

In fact, the prologue of the Gospel of John, when it calls Christ the Word (Greek *logos*), may be alluding not only to the words that God spoke in creating the world but also to Greek thinking about a rational order governing the world. The Greek word *logos,* translated "word" in John 1:1-14, can designate not only verbal utterance but also a rule or reason. The Stoics speculated about reason as a principle not only in the human mind but also supplying the law of nature.[2]

Not only what seems to be accidental but also what seems to be necessary derives from the plan of God. What seems accidental derives from the freedom of God's choice, as he creates and rules the world. What seems necessary is necessary because it reflects the self-consistency in God's character. So necessity itself, including the necessities of logic, displays the character of God.[3]

Scientists, whether Christian or atheist, rely on the Father, the Son, and the Holy Spirit. They rely on the Father as the source of stable law. They rely on the Son, who is the Word of the Father and the true Law of the universe, the true source of rationality and logic. They rely on him also for providing, through his sacrifice, benefits and blessings that they do not deserve. They rely on the Holy Spirit to teach them. But the atheists do not see that they have this reliance.

Thus we are confirming the truth that the apostle Paul expressed in one of his sermons to pagans:

---

[2] See, e.g., T. Rees, "Stoics," in James Orr et al., eds., *The International Standard Bible Encyclopedia,* 5 vols. (Chicago: Howard-Severance, 1930), 5:2855.

[3] See the discussion in Vern S. Poythress, "Reforming Ontology and Logic in the Light of the Trinity: An Application of Van Til's Idea of Analogy," *Westminster Theological Journal* 57 (1995): 187-219.

> In past generations he [God] allowed all the nations to walk in their own ways. Yet he did not leave himself without witness, for he did good by giving you rains from heaven and fruitful seasons, satisfying your hearts with food and gladness (Acts 14:16-17).

God has supplied rain, food, and various comforts and pleasures even to the people who did not acknowledge him but rebelled against him. He has been "kind to the ungrateful and the evil" (Luke 6:35). "For he [God] makes his sun rise on the evil and on the good, and sends rain on the just and on the unjust" (Matt. 5:45). We may now extend this principle into the area of science. God provides scientific insights and scientific and technological success even to those who rebel against him. We get what we do not deserve.

13

The Word of God

in Science

What role does the word of God play in science? In fact, it plays a central role. In chapter 1 we saw that science studies the word of God governing the world. "Scientific law" really means the word of God, or else a human scientist's formulation of his approximation to that original, divine word.

Knowing God

The better one knows a human person, the better one may predict what he will do, or the kind of thing that he might do. Similarly, the better one knows God, the better one may predict how he governs the world. And so the better one predicts or discovers scientific laws.

If so, will not Christians be in a better position to predict or discover scientific laws? How can non-Christians do it? Non-Christians continue knowing God and relying on God, even when they verbally deny him. Thus they are able to have some sense of what he might do. They can guess beforehand the probable form that a scientific law might take.

We may put it another way. Since man is made in the image of God, by his very nature man thinks "like God." His thoughts in some ways will imitate God even when he is not conscious of the imitation. So non-Christians make progress in science precisely because they live in God's world, in which the law conforms to the rationality of God, and because their minds conform to the rationality of God.

Yet distorted conceptions of God, or an idolatrous substitute for God in the form of *impersonal* scientific law, can have subtle deleterious effects, as in the case of long-range predictions about the future of the universe. Moreover, if practitioners of science were to stray too far away from belief in the rationality of law, science could suffer more serious damage, as we can see from considering the difficulties that scientific study poses for an animist or an adherent to Shankara's Vedantic Hinduism.

GOD'S TRANSCENDENCE AND SURPRISE

We know that even human persons are never perfectly predictable. Neither is God. And the transcendence of God proclaims that, "My thoughts are not your thoughts, neither are your ways my ways, declares the LORD. For as the heavens are higher than the earth, so are my ways higher than your ways and my thoughts than your thoughts" (Isa. 55:8-9). God's superiority means that science takes work, and genius, and gifts from God, not just mundane knowing.

Christians who study the Bible come to know God better. They may have some advantage in their guesses about his ways in governing the world. But the Bible, as John Calvin reminds us, addresses itself to the ordinary person, not to the questions of the scientific specialist. The Bible focuses on telling us how God has acted in bringing about salvation. All that the Bible says is true. But it may not tell us so much about the details of how he governs the world in providence.

The Bible even gives some indication of the challenge of understanding God's works in providence. In Job 38–41 God challenges Job's wisdom and ability to judge what God should do in his life by asking whether Job understands God's creation and providence: the measurement of the earth (38:5), the stable separation between sea and dry land (38:8-11), the coming of snow and hail (38:22), and so on. Indirectly, he hints that understanding these things may be challenging and complex.

The Bible also indicates the special role that the second person of the Trinity has in creation and providence by calling him the Word (John 1:1-3). Against the background of the narrative in Genesis 1, the title "Word" indicates that the second person of the Trinity stands behind the particular words of command that God spoke in Genesis 1. God governs the world by wisdom (Prov. 8:22-31). The New Testament then reveals that the Son is the embodiment of wisdom (1 Cor. 1:30; Col. 2:3).

Can we attain this wisdom, and understand to the bottom God's governance of the world? We attain it partially. But the word of God in governance can be comprehended only as an expression of the One who is supremely the Word, who is God and who is with God (John 1:1). The word of God's governance is simultaneously a word commanded by God the Father and a word in union with God the Son. And "no one knows the Son except the Father, and no one knows the Father except the Son and anyone to whom the Son chooses to reveal him" (Matt. 11:27). In the end, the relation between the Father and the Son is "revealed" in part, but remains an incomprehensible mystery. We know and we understand, but we know in part; we do not "comprehend" in the sense of mastering what we know. If such is the case with the relation of the Son to the Father, it is derivatively the case with respect to God's word governing the world, which issues from the Father in union with the Son. Hence, God's word is incomprehensible. To comprehend the world would be to comprehend this wisdom of the word of God, which exceeds comprehension.

MIRACLE

What are we to think about the occurrence of miracle? We already addressed this issue briefly in chapter 1. Some miracles, like the resurrection of Christ, are totally inexplicable using modern scientific laws. Others, like the dividing of the waters of the Red Sea, used the means of "a strong east wind all night" (Ex. 14:21), but still seem virtually impossible by ordinary means. Still others, like the arrow that wounded Ahab (1 Kings 22:34), seem not to demand any exception to known scientific laws but are divinely controlled "coincidences."

The Bible shows us these miracles for theological reasons. They show God at work in startling, extraordinary ways to bring salvation or judgment, to show his power and faithfulness, and to arouse awe and wonder in human onlookers. It does not matter very much exactly *how* God did what he did; what matters is that he did it. And so, although Exodus 14:21 mentions at one point that God used a strong east wind, other descriptions of the exodus do not mention this detail but simply assert that God did it: "He rebuked the Red Sea, and it became dry" (Ps. 106:9).

God is free to work through ordinary means, or to work in extraordinary ways. Theologians have used the terminology of "primary cause" and "secondary cause." God as the *primary cause* is active in bringing about all the events in the world, both ordinary events and extraordinary ones. But in the case of ordinary events he works in conjunction with *secondary causes.* As Psalm 104:14 says, "You make the grass to grow for the livestock." In the growth of grass God is the primary cause. But scientists can investigate many secondary causes. They study the way in which water and nutrients travel from the soil through the roots into the grass, and how photosynthesis takes place to convert the energy of light into chemical energy for sustaining life. In other cases, God may work apart from any secondary cause, as he did in the initial creation of the world (Gen. 1:1).[1]

Many modern people suppose that "science has disproved the miraculous." But much depends on one's conception of science. If, as modern materialists believe, the world is nothing but atoms in motion, nothing but a machine, and if there is no God, then miracles in a biblical sense are impossible. If something weird happens, it may remain inexplicable, but it is just weird, not an act of God. On the other hand, within a Christian view of the world, scientific law is man's current best description approximating the word of God that governs the world. The word of God governs the regularities of the seasons, and of night and day. But it *also* governs the exceptional cases, where God may deviate from a hitherto observed regularity. Special acts of salvation or judgment provide special reason for God to deviate from the ordinary. The deviation is just as rational as the rationality of his continuing to govern the world in a regular way most of the time.[2]

All the works of God harmonize rationally into a unified plan for the entire world, and for the entirety of history. His goal, "a plan for the fullness of time," is "to unite all things in him [in Christ], things in heaven and things on earth" (Eph. 1:10). *How* his entire plan harmonizes is up to him. In many cases it may mean that the same general regularities that the scientist observes apply to unusual events as well. The arrow that struck Ahab may have flawlessly obeyed the usual laws of mechanics and aerodynamics. The flood of Noah may have taken place according to all the usual laws of mechanics and hydrodynamics and meteorology. Some of the events even during the six days of creation may have involved the use of present-day laws as means to God's end.

But we must always maintain the qualification, that it is up to God. This qualification does not destroy science, but it increases its tentativeness. We know enough to serve God in this world. However, we have no guarantee from God that through scientific progress we can know everything there is to know about origins.

---

[1] See further discussion in chapter 14.

[2] From Herman Bavinck: "For that reason a miracle is not a violation of natural law and no intervention in the natural order. From God's side it is an act that does not more immediately and directly have God as its cause than any ordinary event, and in the counsel of God and the plan of the world it occupies as much an equally well-ordered and harmonious place as any natural phenomenon" (Bavinck, *In the Beginning: Foundations of Creation Theology* [Grand Rapids, Mich.: Baker, 1999], 250).

COMPREHENSIVE RULE BY GOD

Readers may already see that I think that God rules the world by his word in a comprehensive way. He rules the big picture, and he rules the details. Nothing escapes his control. The word of God includes within its scope not only the general regularities and the overall patterns, such as the succession of day and night; it also controls the details like the arrow that struck Ahab through a crack between the pieces of his armor. Two different verses directly assert the comprehensiveness of God's rule:

> In him [Christ] we have obtained an inheritance, having been predestined according to the purpose of him who works *all things* according to the counsel of his will . . . (Eph. 1:11).

> Who has spoken and it came to pass,
>   unless the Lord has commanded it?
> Is it not from the mouth of the Most High
>   that good and bad come? (Lam. 3:37-38).

These verses are confirmed by a host of others that show God's control over many specific events: events in general (Neh. 9:6; Ps. 103:19; Dan. 4:34-35; Acts 17:28; Rom. 11:36; Eph. 4:6; Col. 1:17; Heb. 1:3); the physical world (Gen. 41:32; Ex. 9:26; Ps. 104; Isa. 40:12; Amos 4:7; Nah. 1:3; Matt. 5:45; Acts 14:17); animals (Ps. 104:21; 136:25; Dan. 6:22; Matt. 6:26; 10:29); nations (Josh. 21:44; Judg. 6:1; 1 Chron. 16:31; Ps. 33:10; 47:7; 75:6-7; Isa. 10:5; 40:15; Dan. 2:21; 4:17; Amos 3:6; Hab. 1:6); individual human beings (Ezra 8:31; Job 14:9; Ps. 34:7; 37:23; 118:6; 139:16; Prov. 16:9; 20:24; 21:1; 29:13; Isa. 64:8; Jer. 10:23; Dan. 3:17; John 9:3; Acts 18:9; James 4:15); free acts of humans (Ex. 12:36; Ezra 6:22; 7:6; Jer. 7:27; Ezek. 11:19-20; 36:27; Phil. 2:13); sinful acts of humans (Gen. 45:5; 50:20; Ex. 21:13; 1 Sam. 2:24-25; 2 Sam. 12:11-12; 16:21-22; 1 Kings 12:15; John 19:11; Acts 2:23; 3:18; 4:27-28; Rev. 17:17); "chance" events (Job 36:32; Prov. 16:33; Jonah 1:7; Acts 1:24-26); the devil and his angels (1 Sam. 16:14; 1 Kings 22:20-23; Job 1:6-7; 2 Thess. 2:9-11); and disasters (Isa. 45:7; Lam. 3:38; Amos 3:6; Rom. 8:28).

The most difficult issue concerns the sinful actions of evil people. How can these be under the control of God without impugning his goodness?[3] The crucifixion of Christ offers the answer. Herod and Pontius Pilate did as their

---

[3] For a larger discussion of the problem of evil, see, for example, C. John Collins, *The God of Miracles* (Wheaton, Ill.: Crossway, 2000), 156-162.

hearts inclined them to do, and they were responsible and guilty for condemning an innocent man. But it is also true that they did "whatever your hand and your plan had predestined to take place" (Acts 4:28). Reformed theologians offer more extensive discussion of these matters, in maintaining that we confront here one of the many mysteries that God's incomprehensible greatness presents to the human mind.[4] We should accept the biblical teaching without trying to "bring God down to our level" by mastering the idea of God's rule and trying to force reality into the confines of our human minds. I shall say a little more about genuine human responsibility in the next chapter. But an extended discussion could fill a whole volume.

CONTINGENCY

The rule of God over generalities implies that scientific laws come from him. The regularities that we see come from God's word, which specifies the regularities. But we need also to consider the particularities. Does God simply wave his hand at the universe in general, with no involvement with the particularities? The instance with the arrow that wounded Ahab shows otherwise. In fact, the verses listed above, together with many others, indicate that God controls *details* as well as generalities or regularities. He created Adam and Eve, not just "humanity." He formed David in his mother's womb and determined the number of his days (Ps. 139:13-16). God's rule over the particularities is important, both as an expression of the magnitude of his sovereignty and as an expression of his care for individuals, not merely for a broad course of historical development of a whole civilization. "Are not two sparrows sold for a penny? And not one of them will fall to the ground apart from your Father. But even the hairs of your head are all numbered" (Matt. 10:29-30).

The particularities affect science. In the nineteenth century, people impressed with the regularities veered in the direction of complete mechanical determinism. Some (LaPlace being the most famous) claimed that the behavior of the entire universe could be exactly calculated if only one had enough information about the positions and velocities of all the individual particles.

But in the twentieth century quantum mechanics appears to many interpreters to have put a permanent barrier in the way of physical determinism. Exact calculation is permanently impossible, not merely because of limita-

---

[4] For an extended, up-to-date discussion, see the excellent volume by John M. Frame, *The Doctrine of God* (Phillipsburg, N.J.: Presbyterian & Reformed, 2002). The doctrine of God impinges on theology of science in many ways, not just at the point of God's sovereignty, so the whole volume offers a useful background for us.

tions in measurement, but because quantum mechanics seems to say that contingent events at the quantum level are intrinsically contingent, intrinsically probabilistic. There is no way even in principle to predict a single contingent event, but only the statistical averages of many events. These single events occur at a microscopic level. But small initial differences magnify in time, so that a butterfly flapping its wings in South America can make the difference between stormy weather and mild weather a month later in the Northern Hemisphere.[5]

The control of God over particularities, including contingencies, guarantees that these contingencies themselves still belong to his plan. And that guarantees that contingent events in our lives and in the course of civilizations do not take him by surprise or frustrate him. What if the contingencies had turned out differently, and my mother's parents had never met? What if a stray bullet or an infection had struck down George Washington in the early stages of the American War of Independence, and the war had consequently been lost?[6] Possibilities like these abound, and God controls them all. There is no straying piece of dust or independent molecule in the universe.

God's control also guarantees for the scientist that he can study the rationality of patterns even within areas of the physical world where contingency appears to be ultimate. The contingency, we might say, is not contingent for God, inasmuch as he planned it. And granted that a particular fission of a particular radioactive atom was planned, it is certain that it would take place when it did. But this certainty belongs to God alone, not to us as finite creatures. Quantum mechanics shows that human beings will never be able to have complete physical knowledge or complete predictability. Quantum mechanics then serves as a testimony to the distinction between Creator and creature, and the limitations of creatures.

REGULARITIES AND EXCEPTIONS AND THE ISSUE OF REPEATABLE EVENTS

The comprehensiveness of God's rule gives us a firm basis for science, in that it implies that the world down to its smallest details conforms perfectly to God's word of governance. No detail is just "there," outside of God's purpose or control. On the other hand, the incomprehensibility of God implies

---

[5] This problem even has a name, "the butterfly effect"!
[6] Stephen Jay Gould envisions another such imaginary case where the North lost the Battle of Gettysburg (Gould, *The Structure of Evolutionary Theory* [Cambridge, Mass.: Harvard University Press, 2002], 1338, 1341-1342).

that science must retain its tentativeness. We can know truth. But we should acknowledge that in every truth about God's word we also have mystery.

Moreover, if we conceive of science as concerned primarily with the regularities, the generalities, its focus is narrower than God's word. It does not undertake to study God's word comprehensively, but only those aspects of God's word that address the regularities. The particularities of particular events, like the crucifixion and resurrection of Christ, remain beyond its scope, even though they too are comprehensively controlled by God's word.

In fact, though some people have tried to define "science" in a more rigorous way as *exclusively* the study of regularities, human curiosity does not stop with generalities. For example, we do have an interest in the past, even though the past is made up of many events that are never repeated in exactly the same way. Physical science does not focus on human history, but it does have subdivisions that focus on the past of physical processes. So we have historical geology, which tries to reconstruct the past history of the rocks. We have historical biology, which tries to reconstruct the past of animals and plants. We have historical cosmology (though it is seldom so designated), which tries to reconstruct the large-scale past of the universe and its galaxies.

In the case of astronomy and cosmology, though many questions remain about the time immediately after the Big Bang, many less challenging subareas have good, reasonably coherent explanations. These explanations harmonize either with the mature creation view or the analogical day theory or other theories that propose that God's original acts of creation may have taken more than six 24-hour days.

In the case of historical biology, however, we run into a difficulty. Mainstream non-Christian scientists think it likely that life originated only once. We have here a unique event, and one that cannot be easily reproduced in a modern laboratory. Here the influence of one's worldview and one's conception of law impinges more directly. If one is a materialist, if one's worldview says that matter in motion is all there is, then one "knows" that the first replicating "proto-cell" came into being *somehow*. One hopes, partly for the sake of defending one's materialist assumptions, that this "somehow" involved a series of steps, each of which had a probability that was not too low. But even if the overall probability was very low, it happened. Strange things happen. One interprets the event from the standpoint of materialism. Impersonal laws must somehow account for it, because there is no other way of accounting for it within a materialist worldview.

Conversely, suppose that one believes that the origin of the first proto-cell, along with the events in the whole universe, proceeded exactly in accord with the word of God. This word of God specified both the regularities and any exceptions. One sees the regularities when one examines large numbers of events. But this was a unique event, and there is no telling for sure how God did it. Maybe he used the regularities; maybe he did something exceptional and unaccountable.

If God did something exceptional the first time that life was created, maybe he did something exceptional in making other kinds of life. The origin of each new major kind of plant or animal might have represented a kind of decisive turning point, which was never repeated. Here again, one comes up against a unique event, rather than a general pattern replicable in the laboratory. Did God create different kinds of life by multiple distinct acts of creation, each of which used only nonliving materials in the construction? Or did God modify already existing life that he had created earlier?

We can see that the introduction of the possibility of exceptions alters the nature of judgments about the past, especially in cases where we confront one-time events. The past of astronomy contains many events with respect to the origin of individual stars or galaxies that never repeat for the same star, but they do repeat in similar form for other stars. So we still find a regularity. We may hope that, by applying present physical laws and mathematical models, we can show approximately what went on.

The first appearance of new kinds of living things confronts us with a more difficult challenge, because we cannot say beforehand just how similar are the distinct events involving these new appearances. On the basis of early-twenty-first-century understanding of the role of information contained in DNA and RNA, we may suspect that each introduction of a major new kind involved an introduction of information. But it was not the same information in each case. Might each case involve an exception to normal regularities in God's governance? If we have a Christian worldview, we cannot exclude this possibility a priori. Or maybe, if we knew enough, we could see regular patterns in examining the origin of many different new kinds. Then we could think in terms of a law-like regularity governing the many instances of the origins of new kinds. The study of the origin of new kinds is *not* quite like looking at modern science conducted in a modern laboratory with respect to repeatable events.

We shall return to consider the origin of living things in greater detail in chapter 19.

14

TRUTH IN SCIENCE AND
IN LIFE

We may now expand our vision beyond the idea of regularities and scientific law, by considering particular unrepeatable events.

As we saw in the previous chapter, God rules comprehensively. He determines the regularities. And he determines the particulars. The regularities lead us into the discussion of scientific law. But what about the particularities? What are they? No general law suffices to explain this particular apple in my refrigerator, or to explain Napoleon. General laws are pertinent to understanding apples, and they explain some aspects of the particulars. But they never explain absolutely everything. Every time we explain historically how the apple got to be in my refrigerator, we just expand our task, because then we would have to explain the antecedent events to our history: how the apple grew just as it did on one tree, and how the apple picker got it down, and so on. The general laws never suffice just by themselves.

The word of God unifies the two aspects, the general and the particular. God's word specifies both. He speaks to specify generalities, as when he promises that seedtime and harvest shall not cease (Gen. 8:22); and he speaks to specify particulars, as when he predicts the death of Ahab in battle (1 Kings 22:20) or the scattering of the disciples at the time of Jesus' crucifixion (Matt. 26:31, quoted from Zech. 13:7). The generalizing aspect of God's word leads to scientific study of scientific laws. The particularizing aspect leads to what? Apparently, it leads to ordinary truths about ordinary events and states of affairs. Ahab fell in the battle of Ramoth-Gilead; the disciples scattered when Jesus was arrested.

The word of God specifies these events and states of affairs; that is, it specifies the truth about the world. Since God's rule is comprehensive, the specification is comprehensive, and the truth is comprehensive. All truth is what God has specified through his word.

DIVINE ATTRIBUTES OF TRUTH

In chapter 1 we found that the law of God has divine attributes, because it is God speaking. Similarly, truth has divine attributes, because it is God speaking. In fact, we are simply expanding beyond the area of law to include God's speaking about the particularities. From a Christian worldview, truth does not receive its origin first from human beings who observe the world. Truth exists in the mind of God and in the plan of God, even before the foundation of the world. Truth, one may say, is what God knows. It includes what he knows about himself, which surely is divine, and what he knows about the world, which is included in his plan. His plan is comprehensive, so all truth is in the plan or in his self-knowledge. All truth is divine. We might have suspected as much when Jesus said, "I am the way, and the truth, and the life" (John 14:6). And elsewhere, "Your [God's] word is truth" (John 17:17). These verses in John focus on redemptive truth. But it should not be surprising that the principle applies more broadly, to any truth whatsoever.

We hasten to add that human *knowledge* of the truth is not divine, but limited. This human viewpoint does not define what the truth *is*, because God, not man, is the standard of truth and the origin of truth.

We may travel through the divine attributes one by one, to check whether they extend to include not only law, but truth.

Omnipresent and Eternal

First, consider omnipresence. Laws are the same in all places, by the very nature of the law. The same is not so obvious for particular, as opposed to general, truth. Each distinct situation has its own factuality and its own truths that pertain to it. At the moment it is true that I am seated in a chair in my office; my wife, by contrast, may be standing up at home. But if it is true that I am seated in a chair, it is true also for my wife who is at home that I am seated. The truth describes a situation at a particular location in time and space. But the truth so stated is true in whatever location from which we choose to state it.

We do have to pay attention to time and place in determining what someone means. "I am seated" depends on who "I" refers to and what time is in view. But if we find out the time and the circumstances, we can say that the statement is indeed true. And then the statement, so understood as referring to a particular time and place, is true wherever we ourselves may choose to go. The truth follows us everywhere; it is present everywhere.

And the truth is present in all times in the future. The past might seem to be more questionable, if this world allows genuine contingency. A human being situated in the past cannot predict beforehand whether I am seated just now or not. But if tomorrow at 4:00 P.M. I will be seated, it is true today that tomorrow at 4:00 P.M. I will be seated. We do not seem to be able to escape the impression that if something is true, it is true! And, at least to an ordinary way of thinking, this sameness does not make impossible the existence of contingent human decisions.

The truth, then, is everlasting. Do we need to distinguish between an everlastingness that means enduring within time, and eternity, which means being somehow "above" time? As in the discussion of law, the difference between the two is difficult, in fact impossible, to comprehend fully. But we may suspect that the truth is eternal. It is not subject to change. It is *immutable*.

Immaterial and Invisible

Next, truth is immaterial and invisible. We see that the apple is red. We do not with our physical eyes see the truth that the apple is red. We know it. This conclusion is also apparent from the fact that I know the truth that the apple is red even when I cease looking at the apple. Truth is ideational in character, not physical.

Omnipotent

Next, consider the attribute of power. Does the truth have power over the world? I observe a red apple, and I say, "That's a ripe, red apple." If what I say is really true, it matches the state of affairs in the world. In fact, it matches perfectly, not in the sense that it says everything in exhaustive detail, but in the sense that it is not deficient or incorrect in what it does say. The match between truth and the world is perfect, suggesting that one determines the other perfectly. Perfect determination means perfect control, perfect power. But which determines the other? Does truth determine the world, or does the world determine the truth?

At first glance, many people might think that the world determines the truth. In human experience, we observe the world and from observation find out what is true about the world. The order in our experience moves from the world to truth. But someone else might have observed the apple before I did. And still a third person might have predicted the ripening of the apple from still earlier observations, which precede the appearance of redness.

Human prediction, of course, is fallible. But it relies on regularities in the world. We thus come back to the issue of regularities, or general truths, and these seem to precede any particular case that conforms to the regularity. The regularity governs the particular instance, rather than vice versa.

Moreover, we always know truths in a context of other truths, which give meaning to any particular truth. We know what "red" is partly from earlier experiences of red, and we know what an "apple" is from earlier experiences with apples. The truth that "this apple is red" has meaning not in isolation but in relation to the familiarity of apples and of red colors. This familiarity itself presupposes regularities of very basic kinds, regularities that mean that there are apples and that certain familiar characteristics allow us (perhaps with occasional mistakes) to recognize an apple when we see one, and to group it together with other instances of the same kind. The relation between a universal ("apple") and a particular case ("this apple") presupposes both general regularities and particulars that manifest those regularities.[1] Thus the particular truth "this apple is red" can be grasped only as it coheres with other truths, about other apples and other instances of red color. This truth enjoys harmony with other truths.

The harmony is prior to any particular instance within the harmony, inasmuch as the instances cannot of themselves create harmony. And this implies that, at least at some level, truth is prior to the particular case. The particular case conforms to truth, rather than vice versa. So the truth has power over the world. And the power is perfect, that is to say, omnipotent. Because God is truth, all that he creates conforms to truth.

Our hesitancy about the omnipotence of truth arises because our human *formulation* of the truth is indeed secondary. But the truth exists before we *formulate* it. The origin of truth is in the mind of God. That truth, the truth that belongs to God, has power over the world.

Transcendent and Immanent

The truth is both *transcendent* and *immanent*. Particularly when we think of the harmony of many truths, the harmony transcends any one situation. At the same time, it applies to the situation, so that it is immanent in its application.

---

[1] This illustrates the famous issue of universals and particulars, or the one (the universal) and the many (the particulars), to which Cornelius Van Til devotes so much attention. See Cornelius Van Til, *The Defense of the Faith*, 2nd ed. (Philadelphia: Presbyterian & Reformed, 1963); Van Til, *A Survey of Christian Epistemology* (n.l.: den Dulk Christian Foundation, 1969).

Personal

Truth has many of the classical attributes of God. This conclusion should not be surprising, if we realize that truth is an expression of the word of God. The word of God controls not only the generalities, as we saw in the case of scientific law, but the particularities, that is, the cases of particular truth about particular situations.

As in the earlier discussion of scientific law in chapter 1, many try to escape acknowledging God by denying his personal character. In the case of truth, they may say that the truth is impersonal rather than personal. It is just "there" somehow.

As with law, so here, we may observe in reply that the truth is rational. We demonstrate that it is rational when we grasp truth with our minds; and we presuppose that it is rational when we search for truth and expect beforehand that it will fit our minds. Truth is also language-like, in that it can be expressed in human languages. These two characteristics, rationality and expression in language, belong to human beings as *persons*. Even though some may deny it in theory, our practical treatment of truth as rational and as linguistically graspable affirms its personal character.

Truth and the World

The same concern arises here as with scientific law, namely whether we are "deifying" an aspect of this world. God created the world, and each thing created is finite and limited. But the *truth* about this created thing is not limited in the same way. The truth remains forever, whereas the created animal perishes after a time. Truth transcends the world, as is particularly evident when we focus on the unity expressed in the harmony among many particular truths.[2] That unity cannot be explained as the product of any one fact in the world.

Righteous, Good, Pure, Loving, and Kind

We may now consider *moral* attributes of God, such as righteousness and goodness, as attributes of truth. Our earlier consideration on scientific law

---

[2] The thought of Gregory of Nyssa is similar: "For since God hath made all things in wisdom, and to His wisdom there is no limit (for "His understanding," saith the Scripture, "is infinite" [Ps. 147:5]), the world, that is bounded by limits of its own, cannot contain within itself the account of infinite wisdom" (Gregory of Nyssa, *Answer to Eunomius' Second Book,* in Philip Schaff and Henry Wace, eds., *A Select Library of Nicene and Post-Nicene Fathers of the Christian Church,* 2nd series, 14 vols. [reprint; Grand Rapids, Mich.: Eerdmans, 1979], 5:262. Similarly, William Young affirms the divine attributes of truth, basing his view on Augustine [Young, *Foundations of Theory* (Nutley, N.J.: Presbyterian & Reformed, 1967), 105-106; Augustine, *Soliloquia* 2.2; *De Libero Arbitrio,* 2.12-15; Anselm, *De Veritate* 1, 9.]).

(chapter 1) left morality to one side. Scientific law concerns regularities in the material world, not regularities in the moral world. But truth belongs to both worlds. For example, the commandment "You shall not steal" expresses a moral truth, namely the truth that human beings ought not to steal. Every moral principle or commandment is also a truth about moral standards. The truth is righteous, good, pure, loving, and kind, because it expresses the righteousness, goodness, purity, love, and kindness that moral principles enjoin.[3]

Of course one can evade this conclusion by denying that any kind of absolute moral standard exists. And some postmodern circles commonly make this denial. But it is inconsistent. Just as the scientist must believe in God in the actual practice of science, so the average human being must believe in morality when he reacts with moral indignation. The person who has just been robbed or slandered reacts with instinctive moral condemnation—even when his theoretical moral relativism tells him that there is no substance to his reaction. Moreover, the reaction presupposes absolute moral standards, not relative ones, since the condemnation of the thief and the slanderer does not wait to ask whether the other person has a different culture or environment, in the context of which he is perfectly justified in what he has done. Moral condemnation can of course sometimes make misjudgments, because of the fallibility of human beings. But mistaken or not, it presupposes that standards apply to the other person, not just to oneself.

We see here the inescapable effects of continued human knowledge of right and wrong. Even in the midst of rebellion against God, people continue to know God and his moral standards:

> Though they know God's decree that those who practice such things deserve to die, they not only do them but give approval to those who practice them (Rom. 1:32).

> For when Gentiles, who do not have the law, by nature do what the law requires, they are a law to themselves, even though they do not have the law. They show that the work of the law is written on their hearts, while their conscience also bears witness, and their conflicting thoughts accuse or even excuse them . . . (Rom. 2:14-15)

---

[3] Of course, human beings may verbally wound others through untimely and mean-spirited use of the truth. In such cases, the moral fault belongs to the human speaker, not to the truth itself. We must "speak the truth in love" (Eph. 4:15) if we are to conform to the moral truths about speaking.

TRUTH AS DIVINE WITNESS

In sum, human beings confront God, with his divine attributes, whenever they confront truth, because truth is what God thinks and what he specifies by his word. Truth is an inescapable aspect of thought and speech, and so God is inescapable. Our conception of truth presupposes God, and the affirmation of any particular truth presupposes God. How do unbelievers escape? They believe in a God of truth, and simultaneously they suppress the truth in unrighteousness (Rom. 1:18). "Although they knew God, they did not honor him as God or give thanks to him, but they became futile in their thinking, and their foolish hearts were darkened" (Rom. 1:21).

One may now understand better the situation of relativists who deny that there is truth, or other relativists who deny that the truth is accessible. The modern secular atmosphere has already taught people to be suspicious of transcendence. When they observe moral blind spots and ignorance in various human societies, they may conclude that there is no route to transcendence. They deny transcendence and then deny the truth. Denying God and denying truth go together.[4]

HUMAN RESPONSIBILITY

God's control over truth might seem to some people to hem in human freedom unbearably. If all truth belongs to God, what room is left for any kind of human independence? "In him [God] we live and move and have our being" (Acts 17:28).

We have already considered in chapter 13 some of the biblical evidence for God's comprehensive sovereignty. I believe that this sovereignty is real, and that human responsibility also is real. The relation between the two involves mystery, because of the limitations of our finite minds. I must leave to others a fuller discussion, because these matters could fill whole volumes.[5] Let the following remarks suffice for our own context.

First, when we affirm that truth has divine attributes, and therefore belongs to the sphere of the divine, we strongly affirm the incomprehensibil-

---

[4] Stephen Prickett seems to have arrived at similar conclusions by looking at meaning:

> If, so the argument seems to run, we push meaning back far enough, even beyond the practical everyday dictates of reason, science or law, we encounter only Humean scepticism or metaphysics—in other words, God. If, as both Stein and Hart seem to concur, meaning is ultimately guaranteed by God, we do not need that theologians' holy grail, a 'proof' of God. The concept of 'proof' itself is meaningless without God (Stephen Prickett, *Narrative, Religion, and Science: Fundamentalism Versus Irony, 1700–1999* [Cambridge: Cambridge University Press, 2002], 220).

[5] See, for example, John M. Frame, *The Doctrine of God* (Phillipsburg, N.J.: Presbyterian & Reformed, 2002), 119-159.

ity of truth as an aspect of the incomprehensibility of God. Human responsibility, as one issue within the truth, is also incomprehensible.

Second, it is literally meaningless to try to think of truth or meaning outside the plan of God, the wisdom of God, and the word of God. Human
responsibility has meaning by reference to God's wisdom. Removing human
responsibility from God's control removes it from meaning. The result would
then be the evaporation of both a meaningful idea of humanity and meaningful responsibility.

Third, the fullness of truth includes many sides. Consider the case where
I choose one morning to put on a striped blue tie rather than a checked blue
tie. God affirms, as part of his truth, that I put on the striped blue tie. He also
affirms that I *choose* to put on the tie. My choice is just as real as the wearing of the tie. God affirms a state of affairs (I am wearing the tie). He also
affirms causal connections between states of affairs. I am wearing the tie now
because I earlier put it on; and I earlier put it on because I chose to do so.

Consider a more crucial example. In God's mercy he ordains that I
should be saved; he also ordains the means through which I am to be saved.
". . . whoever believes in him should not perish but have eternal life" (John
3:16). John 3:16 is God's truth, affirming an unbreakable connection
between means and ends, between human choice ("whoever believes") and
salvation ("have eternal life"). All these statements are true, and they are true
because God affirms them, as part of his plan. God's affirmation and God's
truth, rightly understood, do not undermine human responsibility but support it. We get into trouble only if we try to reduce the meaning of the world
to one aspect. If we reduce it to God-appointed destinies, we will arrive at
fatalism. If we reduce it to human-appointed decisions, we will arrive at
human pride over having had enough sense to save ourselves.[6]

Fourth, as we earlier observed (chapter 13), God as primary cause does
not compete with secondary causes within the world. When God uses "a
strong east wind" (Ex. 14:21) to dry up the sea, God does it and the east wind
does it, but on different levels. God's control of human affairs affirms the reality of secondary causes from human beings and from the environment.

Fifth, I suspect that some people are disturbed by the prospect of God's
control for the wrong reason. They picture human freedom as freedom in

---

[6] See the discussion of reductionism in the next chapter. John Jefferson Davis (*The Frontiers of Science and Faith: Examining Questions from the Big Bang to the End of the Universe* [Downers Grove, Ill.: InterVarsity Press, 2002]) expresses dissatisfaction with the "problems" involved in traditional Calvinistic understandings of predestination (59). His instincts in rejecting reductionistic solutions elsewhere in his book could have served him well here, in that he could have observed that alleged problems with assur-ance and the offer of the gospel arise from reductionistic approaches to the meaning of divine truth.

independence from God. But such "independence" can be dangerously close to the desire of Adam and Eve to become independent by eating the forbidden fruit: Satan promises, "You will be like God, knowing good and evil" (Gen. 3:5).

If we think about it, even the persons of the Trinity do not act "in independence" of one another. With respect to his incarnate ministry, Jesus says, "The Son can do nothing of his own accord, but only what he sees the Father doing" (John 5:19). "The words that I say to you I do not speak on my own authority, but the Father who dwells in me does his works" (John 14:10). The Son cares nothing for "independence." Each person of the Trinity acts only in harmony with the other persons.

Now, what about human beings? Do they act in independence of God? Do they have greater "freedom" than the Son? It would be blasphemous to think so. Freedom as independence is simply the wrong way of thinking. It is not to be found in the Bible, and the character of the freedom in the Trinity suggests that in fact the idea of independence comes from a more nefarious source!

15

DEBATES ABOUT WHAT IS REAL: THE CHARACTER OF SCIENTIFIC KNOWLEDGE

Modern philosophy of science has extensively discussed the character of scientific knowledge. We cannot enter into all the details of the debates, but we may explore briefly how a Christian worldview addresses the discussion. For this purpose, we must simplify; we group together the major approaches under five main headings: realism, idealism, empiricism (including operationalism), pragmatism, and postmodern relativism.[1]

MAJOR APPROACHES OR SCHOOLS

The *realist* says that science describes real properties of the world "out there." Scientific knowledge objectively matches realities in the character of an objective world. The "critical" realist, in distinction from the naive realist, acknowledges that appearances can be deceptive, and that in practice science is always tentative and subject to revision. But science aims at true description and explanation. Though we cannot have perfect certainty about its descriptions in any particular case, we are traveling toward truth, and some of the descriptions are true to facts out there. For example, we describe bulk matter as being made up of atoms held together by chemical bonds, because there *are* atoms, and they *are* held together by chemical bonds.

By contrast, the *idealist* says that science describes the appearance of

---

[1] See the further discussion in J. P. Moreland, *Christianity and the Nature of Science: A Philosophical Investigation* (Grand Rapids, Mich.: Baker, 1989), 139-212. What I call "empiricism" Moreland subdivides into "phenomenalism" (A. J. Ayer and logical positivism) and "constructive empiricism" (Bas C. van Fraassen).

things according to the way in which the human mind naturally organizes them. We never grasp "the thing in itself," what is out there, but only the thing as already organized by our perception and our ways of thinking. So what happens in science? A description in science may be true as a description of this already-organized perception. We describe bulk matter as being made up of atoms because that is the reasonable way to think in organizing the phenomena; but atoms cannot actually be said to exist out there, because we can never get to them, but only to their effects at a phenomenal level.

The *empiricist* says that science studies the events and phenomena of immediate perception, and that the theoretical constructions of science do not directly describe real entities but are a convenient way of summarizing the patterns in empirical data.

According to strict empiricism, atoms are a convenient fiction for organizing our thinking about phenomena in chemical reactions. Scientific statements, when properly analyzed, are actually claims about the regularity in the phenomena, not claims about the existence of metaphysical entities such as atoms.

This view had greater plausibility before we had instruments by which we could project visually an image of a single atom. In the nineteenth century, no one could "see" atoms, and much was being deduced from the constant proportionalities seen in bulk chemical reactions, or in bulk behavior of gases. Atoms were postulated, but could not be seen. Empiricists rightly pointed out that the postulate was just that—a postulate. It could not be rigorously proved. Hence, one could plausibly claim that atoms might be a convenient fiction for explaining the proportionalities. Now, with atomic-force microscopes, we can construct an image of a single atom or a small number of atoms. Strict empiricist claims about the fictionality of atoms have lost plausibility.

The *pragmatist* says that science does not offer direct knowledge of the world as it is, but only a practical tool or means for achieving technical mastery of the world. The value of science lies wholly in its practical success.

The postmodern *relativist* says that science is a social product of groups with a certain social unity of purpose and knowledge-base. "Knowledge" is relative to one's group, and groups based on different kinds of assumptions would come up with different "knowledge." There is no way to adjudicate between incommeasurable groups.

THE PLAUSIBILITY OF CRITICAL REALISM

At first glance, critical realism might seem to offer the most compatibility with a Christian worldview. We believe that God created a world, not just human beings. The world is real. And God has so constructed us that we can know him and know about his world (creation in the image of God). This reality of the world and of God excludes the other positions. In particular, relativism could possibly be attractive only if there were no God who is the ultimate standard and can adjudicate between human groups with competing views. Idealism and empiricism and pragmatism would seem to be unduly restrictive in not allowing us to say that we know the real world out there. They confine science to the humanly organized phenomena or to empirical data and their regularities.

Moreover, in practice most scientists tend to be realists. Idealism, empiricism, pragmatism, and postmodern relativism have the air of being philosophical reflections that stand back at a distance from science and pronounce on the basis of philosophical insight what it all must mean. But the average scientist takes a more commonsense approach and just believes that he is studying the world out there.

In addition, the three nonrealist approaches have serious practical difficulties at points. Postmodern relativism has little way to account for the stupendous success of science, particularly in its technological applications. If truth is all relative to one's human group, why should one's transistor radio work in all human cultures? And how can the statement about the relativity of truth be universally true?

Empiricism and pragmatism suffered a setback when the early twentieth century probed into the inner structure of the atom and found increasing evidence from many diverse directions that confirmed that atoms were distinct entities, not merely convenient fiction. In the nineteenth century, while the data about atoms remained on the frontiers of science, it could be interpreted in empiricist ways. One could claim that the idea of atoms was merely a convenient fiction, because there were few ways of testing the idea in a more direct way. But in the twenty-first century, within fully consolidated science, the data are consistently interpreted in realist ways. This process suggests that empiricism is plausible in a particular area of science only until science makes enough progress to have many-directional confirmations.

Idealism seems difficult to maintain because of the ways in which the world "talks back" to us. We cannot just impose theories on the world, or guess right away what the phenomenal world must be, on the basis of what the organization of our psyche tells us. Rather, we go out and through experiment find out the way the world actually is. Moreover, idealism, which got some support from Immanuel Kant's philosophy, suffered a serious setback from the general theory of relativity. Kant assumed that spatial geometry was imposed on the world by the mind of man. Geometry was what it was because human intuition dictated it. But the theory of general relativity found that the actual world exhibited non-Euclidean geometry (nonstandard geometry, from the point of view of the Kantian tradition), which confounded human intuition.

So does critical realism clearly win? It appears to win when we look only at the deficiencies of competing positions. But let us not move too fast. The scientific study of perception clearly shows ways in which human perception *does* mold what it sees. A host of optical illusions show that our retina and our brains process the incoming patterns a good deal before they reach consciousness.

We may take as an illustration the experience of watching a film. We experience continuous motion on the screen, when in fact a careful analysis of the mechanism of a movie projector shows that the screen displays a series of discrete, distinct pictures so rapidly that we are not conscious of the discreteness. From such a phenomenon, does idealism gain new life for its contention that we see only our perceptions that have already been conformed to the human recipient?

Or consider the experience of watching a show on television. When we stand back at a normal distance from the television screen with good reception, we seem to see a continuous picture. But inspection of the screen with a magnifying glass shows that it is made up of discrete colored dots. So is the sense of continuity an illusion imposed by perceptual processing?

Consider a third example. Apart from blind or color-blind people, human beings see the world in color. But this color is what it is because of the organization of our retina (in particular, the cone cells, or color receptors) and of our brains. Bats "see" at night using sonar, not by utilizing visible light. What if we "saw" like bats, or "saw" using infrared light? The world would "look" very different. So what is "real"? Is it the world of color that we see in daylight, or the black-and-white world that we see in twilight, or the world that a bat "sees" in a pitch-black night?

A critical realist can reply in two ways. He might say that all these levels are "real," and that reality is "stratified," with complex connections between the levels.[2] This approach harmonizes with a Christian worldview. But, as a second alternative, the critical realist might reply that the complexities with

---

[2] If I understand him right, this is the position of Roy Bhaskar, *Scientific Realism and Human Emancipation* (London: Verso, 1986), 92: ". . . explanation and redescription of deeper strata of reality. In the ongoing process of science, as deeper and wider shores of reality come to be known . . ." Likewise Alister McGrath affirms a stratified reality (McGrath, *A Scientific Theology,* 3 vols. [Grand Rapids, Mich.: Eerdmans, 2001–2003], 3:82-84). For "dialectical critical realism," see Alan G. Padgett, *Science and the Study of God: A Mutuality Model for Theology and Science* (Grand Rapids, Mich.: Eerdmans, 2003), especially chapter 2.

perception support the "critical" aspect of critical realism. By critical reflection we pass beyond our initial impressions. The "real" is the world as science describes it.

If the critical realist takes this second route, one may then ask, "Which science, and at what historical stage?" The redness of the apple, which we thought was real, turns out upon further investigation to be a phenomenal effect within the eye and the brain. The scientist tells us that these phenomena are caused by what is real, namely the light waves with wavelength in the red part of the spectrum. But science continues to advance. With the coming of the special theory of relativity, the waves turn out not to be waves in a stable medium (called "ether") but waves with a complicated mathematical description. The description undergoes transformations in changing between different "inertial systems" (that is, different states of motion for the observer of the light). The waves which formerly seemed to be "real" become "phenomena" that a particular observer can measure, and which change when we choose another observer moving at a different speed.[3] In accordance with the Doppler effect, even the color of the light may change depending on the speed of the observer!

With the advent of quantum mechanics,[4] the equations of light that seemed to be "real" got displaced with a theory of photons, or corpuscles[5] of light, which are "real" behind the "phenomena." In addition, atoms, which are "real" from the standpoint of an ordinary chemical engineer, turn out to be "phenomena" underneath which is the reality of quantum mechanical description of electrons spread out around a nucleus.

How do we know when we have reached an "ultimate" level of descrip-

---

[3] One may read about this change in any of the popular expositions of relativity. See, for example, Barry Parker, *Einstein's Brainchild: Relativity Made Relatively Easy!* (Amherst, N.Y.: Prometheus, 2000). For a fuller, historical discussion, see A. d'Abro, *The Evolution of Scientific Thought from Newton to Einstein,* 2nd ed. (New York: Dover, 1950).

[4] Albert Einstein proposed the special theory of relativity in 1905. The first contribution toward quantum mechanics appeared a few years earlier, in Max Planck's 1901 paper on radiation. So in mentioning relativity first, do we have our dates backward? I am looking at how scientists would describe the red apple using coherent, well-built theories. Special relativity came into being in one swoop in 1905 as a full theory. By contrast, quantum theory grew up painfully through the addition of miscellaneous bits, until it arrived at a more satisfactory synthesis in 1925–1926 (Schrödinger, Heisenberg, and Dirac). And even this synthesis needed further development in quantum electrodynamics in order to explain more fully the character of light. See A. d'Abro, *The Rise of the New Physics: Its Mathematical and Physical Theories* (New York: Dover, 1951). For a nontechnical introduction to basic ideas of quantum mechanics, see J. C. Polkinghorne, *The Quantum World* (London: Longman, 1984); Nancy R. Pearcey and Charles B. Thaxton, *The Soul of Science: Christian Faith and Natural Philosophy* (Wheaton, Ill.: Crossway, 1994), chapter 9.

[5] My account still simplifies. These "corpuscles" of light are not fully corpuscular in a way that would match ordinary intuitions about golf balls and marbles. They display a complex interplay of wave-like and particle-like properties, which do not integrate into an intuitive picture based on either marbles or water waves.

tion? How do we know whether quantum mechanics will in turn be succeeded by something that gives a deeper account of the phenomena?

Quantum mechanics is particularly troubling, because Erwin Schrödinger and Werner Heisenberg developed two different versions, side by side. The two approaches later turned out to be mathematically equivalent, but they used two sharply differing pictorial starting points, which suggested two different philosophical interpretations. Schrödinger's approach suggested a more realist interpretation, because he represented an electron as a wave spread out around an atomic nucleus (but the wave in question involved complex numbers rather than real numbers, which would still be disconcerting to a conventional realist!). Moreover, in developing his equation he used intuitive guidance from a realist picture, earlier developed by de Broglie, of wave motion around the central nucleus of an atom. By contrast, Heisenberg represented an electron by infinite matrices that represented experimentally observable quantities. Heisenberg's model was more akin to empiricism. In fact, Max Born and Heisenberg self-consciously used an empiricist point of view in their search for the correct formulation, because they realized that an electron did not behave like a "real" macroscopic particle with fixed position and momentum.

In short, one mathematical representation (Schrödinger's) seems to support a realist interpretation, while the other (Heisenberg's) supports an empiricist interpretation. This situation should disturb both realists and empiricists, because the mathematical equivalence of the two approaches suggests that it makes no difference, or at least that we cannot tell which directly represents "reality." Maybe we are asking the wrong question. Or perhaps the equations of quantum mechanics are the "reality," and what we call an electron is nothing more than a convenient label for the unity that we conceptualize in the equations (a more idealist point of view).

COHERENT REALITY FROM A CHRISTIAN WORLDVIEW

When we believe that the word of God governs the world comprehensively, we have a standpoint from which we can begin to address these dilemmas. The word of God governs the phenomena (empiricist focus) and our ideas about the phenomena (idealist focus). He governs the regularities of the phenomena (focus on law) and whatever "realities" may still be hidden from us (realist focus). God governs the practical use of the phenomena (pragmatist focus), and the variations in perception that may occur among different groups of people (postmodernist relativist focus). He governs the differences in perception between color-seeing and color-blind people, and between human beings and bats. Because God is wise and his word embodies his wisdom, all these things are meaningful, and all are "real" in some sense. Then why should we fight about these issues?

THE REAL

God's word governs

{
red apple

human neuronal basis in cones and brain

vision by the color-blind

bats' sonar vision

light as electromagnetic waves

light as quantum corpuscles

mathematical description in quantum mechanics

"more ultimate" future theory
}

Herman Dooyeweerd, in his reflections about reductionism, provides a useful suggestion.[6] If people do not acknowledge God as the origin of all, they must still strive to explain the coherence of the world that God made. So they substitute an idol for God. And, in modern thought the idol is frequently an intellectual idol, namely some principle that a person holds to be the deepest thing about the world, and in terms of which the rest of the world is to be explained. The world is to be *reduced* to the one principle, or a number of closely related principles within a single area of life.[7]

So we find attempts to reduce everything to the material-physical aspect, or to the biological, or to the psychological, or to the social. Postmodern relativism looks like reduction to the social aspect. (Or in some forms it involves reduction to the linguistic aspect, because language is used as the tool by which we see the relativity of all human points of view.) Empiricism looks like a reduction to sense experience. Pragmatism looks like reduction to the tech-

---

[6] Herman Dooyeweerd, *In the Twilight of Western Thought* (Philadelphia: Presbyterian & Reformed, 1960).
[7] On the tendency of scientists to reduce societies to individuals and individuals to genes, see also Richard C. Lewontin, *Biology as Ideology: The Doctrine of DNA* (New York: HarperCollins, 1993).

nical or pragmatic aspect. Idealism looks like reduction to the mental or psychological or perceptual aspect.

And is critical realism reductionist? It depends on what one means by it. If one just means that there is a world out there about which one may know something, then many worldviews may affirm as much without really settling important questions. If it means that one must pass beyond the redness of the apple in order to get to the "real," it is reducing the world to whatever current science, or a supposed ultimate science, would say is at the bottom.[8]

A Christian worldview maintains that in a sense the world has no "bottom."[9] The doctrine of creation out of nothing (*ex nihilo*) denies the eternal existence of any "prime matter." There is no matter that is just "there," before God starts to work. Rather, God creates *everything,* not just structure on top of previously existing prime matter. And God creates everything by his *word.* The word introduces the structure and the meaning. The law of God is the continued structure for the world. The world has no ultimate independence from this word or law of God, but is *utterly* dependent. Understanding the world does not mean understanding the prime matter, because there is no such thing. It means understanding the world as governed by the word of God. And that can only mean understanding the word of God, for that word simply is the wisdom that gives rationality to everything that we see.

In particular, in seeing the redness of an apple, we see exactly what God's word specifies that we should see. We see a phenomenon specified by the word of God. And when you think about it, that is all we ever see. In doing so, we see "reality," that is, something that God has ordained for his purposes. The scientist reflecting about light waves and atoms also deals with reality. All the levels are "reality," because all are governed by the coherent, wise word of God.[10]

---

[8] Roy Bhaskar's critical realism talks about "stratified reality" to acknowledge the various levels of analysis at which science works. In principle, everyday human experience could be one of these levels. But the prestige of science tempts us to degrade everyday experience as a mere accident deriving from the arrangement of the human nervous system. The "real" is what science finds in its deepest theoretical constructions—and everything else gets reduced to that one level. "In modern culture science is accorded intellectual authority to define the way the world really is" (Nancy Pearcey, "You Guys Lost," in William A. Dembski, ed., *Mere Creation: Science, Faith and Intelligent Design* [Downers Grove, Ill.: InterVarsity Press, 1998], 74).

[9] Milbank reflects, "There is nothing, for Basil 'behind' the appearances, 'a base for the base', and nature is finally incomprehensible because 'all is sustained by the creator's power'" (John Milbank, *The Word Made Strange: Theology, Language, Culture* [Oxford: Blackwell, 1997], 98, and the surrounding discussion in chapter 4).

[10] Discussions of realism and antirealism often focus mainly on the status of theoretical entities, things such as atoms and electrons and magnetic fields. Because I take seriously the denial of "prime matter," I shift the focus from "entities" to the word of God: the word of God specifies structure and meaning. Atoms and electrons and magnetic fields are meaningful within a network of meaning at certain stratified levels of scientific explanation. All these meanings within human scientific work approximately reflect aspects of the word of God comprehensively governing the world. The meanings are in that sense "real." Likewise apples and dogs are meaningful within a network of meanings from ordinary life. All created reality is constituted by meaning networks specified by the creational word of God.

But then how is it possible to be mistaken in our analysis of the world? We move among these levels of reality with confidence, because God governs them all coherently, but sometimes the coherence takes forms that surprise us, as in the case of optical illusion. We *do* see continuous motion when we watch a film, and that continuous motion is real as ordained by God. But we then find a surprise in looking at the technical details of the operations of a movie projector. Its operation also is *real*. What one experiences in watching the film corresponds in a highly complex way to the discrete pictures on the celluloid. A person makes a mistake if he imagines that the correspondence must be simple and direct, and that since one level has continuous-looking motion, the other must as well.

The forms and levels of reality hold together by the coherence of the word of God, not by the artificiality of trying to reduce one reality to another. "And he [the Son] is before all things, and in him all things hold together" (Col. 1:17).

OVERTURNING EARLIER THEORIES

The appreciation of multidimensional reality can also account for cases where later science has overturned earlier scientific theories. Copernicus's sun-centered solar system displaced Ptolemy's earth-centered system. But both systems recognized a general pattern of cyclical motion in the planets. Even after it was displaced, Ptolemy's system of epicycles continued to show reasonable correlation between mathematical calculations on the one hand and physical locations in the sky on the other hand. The system was not wrong to notice the correlations; but it was oversimple, and to that extent wrong, in postulating a direct correlation between mathematics of epicycles and position in *three* dimensions.

Consider another example. At an early point, chemists thought that in combustion a substance called "phlogiston" escaped from the combustible substance into the air. Only after a considerable struggle did they come to abandon this theory for one in which oxygen from the air combined with the combustible substance. They were right to see commonalities in various types of combustion. And they were right to think in terms of a special element ("phlogiston"), whose behavior would be analogous to other chemical elements. But they had guessed exactly the reverse of the truth in postulating that combustion involved the loss of an element into the air. They saw a correlation, but reversed a crucial piece in trying to explain the details. Even the early theory already had a significant degree of contact with what was real.[11] But the understanding needed refinement in order to grasp more fully the details of the various correlations—between chemical elements, between various forms of combustion, between the behavior of gaseous components in the process, and between the quantities of elements involved in various reactions.

AFFIRMING THE ORDINARY

It is important to affirm the reality of our ordinary experience of apples. Otherwise, we depreciate subtly—or not so subtly—our ordinary level of living. On this level we struggle and fight out much of the human drama, of love and hate, riches and poverty, loyalty and betrayal, worship and apostasy. Is our human drama an illusion or a vapor, a merely accidental bubble of foam cast up from the real ocean of scientifically described reality underneath? Did God give us the beauty of the sunset, or is it just an accidental confluence of effects on the brain due to physical causes that alone are real? Is beauty real, or is it a cheat that shows us only "epiphenomena," a surface whose real meaning lies buried beneath in a scientific analysis of light as electromagnetic radiation, and of rods and cones in the retina, and neural processing in the visual cortex?

Beauty is real; it is a manifestation of the beauty of God who made the world to reflect his beauty. From time to time people recognize real beauty in ordinary experience. One of my friends, when younger, found himself one day overwhelmed by the beauty of a field, so overwhelmed that he felt that he should worship. But he did not yet know that there was anyone to worship!

Beauty also appears in the technical explorations in science. From an early age I was attracted by the beauty of mathematics, and then of physics and other sciences, and that beauty lured me into study. Stephen Jay Gould, wrapping up his last book on evolutionary theory with more personal remarks, eloquently expresses his fascination with the living world and its history, showing his delight in a way that also indicates the beauty that he perceives:

> . . . hardly a natural historian, dead or alive, has ever failed to locate his chief delight in the lovely puzzles, the enchanting beauty, and the excruciating complexity and intractability of actual organisms in real places. We become natural historians because we loved those dinosaurs in museums, scrambled after those beetles in our backyard, or smelled the flowers of a hundred particular delights. Thus, we yearn to know, and cannot be satis-

---

[11] On knowledge as contact with reality, rather than perfectly precise correspondence, see Esther Meek, *Longing to Know* (Grand Rapids, Mich.: Baker, 2003).

fied until we do, both the general principles of how mass extinction helps to craft the patterns of life's history, and the particular reason why Pete the *Protoceratops* perished that day in the sands of the Gobi.

... We care [about Charles Darwin's life] for the same reason that we love okapis, delight in the fossil evidence of trilobites, and mourn the passage of the dodo. We care because the broad events that had to happen, happened to happen *in a certain particular way*. And something unspeakably holy—I don't know how else to say this—underlies our discovery and confirmation of the actual details that made our world and also, in realms of contingency, assured the minutiae of its construction in the manner we know, and not in any one of a trillion other ways, ... [12]

A Christian worldview, by discerning the foundational role of the governing word of God, enables us confidently to affirm not only the reality of beauty in science but the reality of ordinary human experience *in all its textures*. The beauty of a sunset is real, and not a mere "accidental" consequence of the properties of light and atmosphere and our visual system. In fact, this "ordinary" level enjoys a centrality in the entire purpose of God. On this level, and not primarily elsewhere, we see and hear and understand the great turning points in God's plan, namely creation, fall, redemption, and consummation. Man does enjoy a kind of centrality, whatever may be his physical size in comparison to the size of a galactic supercluster, or whatever may be his location on the third planet of an ordinary sun somewhere in a spiral arm of a typical spiral galaxy.

God dignifies man by making him in the image of God, and gives him the dominion of a subordinate ruler. Through the incarnation of Christ and his acts of redemption, God makes the one man, Jesus Christ, the center point through which the whole universe is governed and will reach its goal (Eph. 1:10). A human point of view is special, not merely because, from a practical standpoint, we must concern ourselves with how to take the next step in human action, but because God himself gives us significance.

STRENGTHS AND WEAKNESSES IN THE FIVE SCHOOLS

In contrast to this nonreductive approach, many a person thinking about the progress of science hopes to find an ultimate bottom to the world. He hopes

---

[12] Stephen Jay Gould, *The Structure of Evolutionary Theory* (Cambridge, Mass.: Harvard University Press, 2002), 1338, 1342. We will look at macroevolutionary theory in chapters 18 and 19; my point here is not to discuss the theory, but the theorist, who knows that there is beauty.

to achieve some godlike vision that leaves behind as less than "real" the red-ness of the apple and the colors of a sunset. He wants a final analysis that exposes the skeleton, the world framework, on which everything else is built up. This search hopes to reduce the phenomena on all levels to the skeleton, and that is already an idolatrous move. But this move also misconstrues the whole character of the world, because the word of God is the framework of the world. Or, to put it in another way, the comprehensive plan of God for the world and all its details provides the ultimate rationality in terms of which we understand anything at all. That "framework" specifies that all the levels are real. But each is real in connection with its coherence within the whole, a coherence sustained by God.

Our problem is spiritual. As sinners (and I include myself), we do not want such a world, because God confronts us too overwhelmingly. So we dis-tract ourselves with our idols.

From a standpoint of a nonreductive affirmation of comprehensive coherence, one can see both strengths and weaknesses in each of the five schools delineated above. For this purpose, we must again simplify the schools.

First, realism postulates the metaphysical priority of the external world to the world of thought. As good experimentalists, we must go out and find what the world is like. Idealism, by contrast, postulates a certain metaphys-ical priority of thought over against the external world. The categories of thought are already there, and we experience the world only within an already existing framework.

So which is really prior, the external world (as realism believes) or the world of thought (as idealism believes)? To answer rightly, we must first dis-tinguish the Creator from the creature. Metaphysically, the world is prior to *human* thought, since God created the world and then created man to have a place in it. On the other hand, God's thought is metaphysically prior to the world, since he had a plan (his thoughts) even before he created the world. And man created in the image of God can in some ways access God's thoughts. So he experiences indirectly something of the priority of thought to event. Both realism and idealism turn out to be both right and wrong, because they fail to reckon with the distinct position of the Creator.

Empiricism gives epistemic priority (priority in knowledge) to human sense experience. Pragmatism gives epistemic priority to the practical process of prediction and manipulation of the environment. These priorities make some sense for human beings, because in our finiteness we cannot say dog-matically what lies "at the bottom," beyond appearances and practice. On the other hand, practical purposes and comprehensive knowledge go together in God, with no "priority."

Postmodernism gives epistemic priority to the *distinctiveness* of different individuals and groups. "Truth" is only truth for a particular individual or a particular group, and may differ when we go over to another group. In contrast, idealism gives priority to the *commonality* of rationality in all human beings. But God created human beings both as individuals and as members of humanity; we need not prioritize either what is common or what is distinctive.

God's word
governs
{
distinctive individuals
    (postmodern individualism)

distinctive groups
    (postmodern collectivism)

common rationality
    (idealist viewpoint)

The comprehensive coherence entailed by the unity of the plan of God also involves coherence among different points of view or different emphases that people may use in understanding God's world. I have discussed this principle of coherence among viewpoints at some length in *Symphonic Theology,* and John Frame's works exhibit extensive instances.[13] For example, the four Gospels each present the person and work of Christ with different emphases. But, rightly understood, they harmonize. Christ is both the great king in the line of David (Matthew) and the revealer of the Father (John).

Consider another example of harmony. With a Christian worldview, we find harmony between different aspects of ethics. A *normative* perspective focuses on the norms or laws or standards for right and wrong. A *personal* perspective focuses on the attitudes and motives that drive behavior. A *situational* perspective focuses on what helps in practice in a situation, in promoting the glory of God.[14] Because God issues the norms, governs the people, and

---

[13] Vern S. Poythress, *Symphonic Theology: The Validity of Multiple Perspectives in Theology* (reprint; Phillipsburg, N.J.: Presbyterian & Reformed, 2001); John M. Frame, *Perspectives on the Word of God: An Introduction to Christian Ethics* (Phillipsburg, N.J.: Presbyterian & Reformed, 1990); Frame, *The Doctrine of God* (Phillipsburg, N.J.: Presbyterian & Reformed, 2002); Frame, *The Doctrine of the Knowledge of God* (Phillipsburg, N.J.: Presbyterian & Reformed, 1987); see also Vern S. Poythress, *God-Centered Biblical Interpretation* (Phillipsburg, N.J.: Presbyterian & Reformed, 1999).

[14] See Frame, *Perspectives on the Word of God.*

governs the situation, all three in principle exist in harmony. But non-Christian thought, not having God as an ultimate source for all, tends to polarize and treat one pole or another as ultimate. Deontological ethics starts with norms, existential ethics with persons, and utilitarian ethics with situations.

The three perspectives on ethics show kinship with the five schools and their views of science. Realism, in its concern for real laws out there, focuses on norms (the laws) and on the situation to which the norms apply. Idealism focuses on thoughts, which connect it to the personal perspective. Empiricism focuses on sense experience, which connects it to the personal perspective. Pragmatism focuses on practice in the world, which connects it to the situational perspective. It pulls man back down to earth by observing that God created man to fill the earth and subdue it, both practical tasks; and neither task guarantees that man will ever penetrate to some ultimate ontological skeleton, if it even exists. Finally, postmodern relativism may be seen as a form of idealism that champions the diversity rather than the unity among human persons.

Within a Christian worldview, all five of these "isms" belong together as perspectives on the one plan of God. No one of them makes sense without the others. Human beings need to be there to do science, and to think the thoughts about scientific theory. Science without persons is a mere vapor. And human beings exist in their diversity as well as unity, as postmodernism would like to remind us. In addition science requires something that the persons will investigate: an external world both with lawful regularity (realism) and with particular data that we may organize for practical purposes (empiricism and pragmatism). One does not choose between these perspectives, but chooses all of them at once as fruitful options. At the same time, one chooses none of them in their non-Christian forms, in which they are set against one another, or in which they remain unclear as to whether man is to proceed as if he had an autonomous mind or as a creature in submission to God.

CRITICAL REALISM OFFERING UNITY

Since critical realism appears to be growing in popularity, I may say a word more about it. As we already observed, much depends on what one means by the term. Does "critical realism" simply mean that the external world exists and that we can know truths about it (the "realism" part)? Does the "critical" part mean merely that we are finite and sometimes turn out to be mistaken?

Critical realism may attract people precisely because it seems to offer some kind of common ground. But commonness is achieved by vagueness. A vague definition sweeps aside crucial questions as to what sort of "critical" stance we take and what sort of "realism" we hold. Does realism live within a world that God made? Or is God irrelevant or nonexistent? What sort of God or substitute for God do we believe in, when we come to consider scientific law?

And what about the "critical" aspect? Does criticism presuppose that man's mind is normal, or that it is fallen?

The attractiveness of common ground grows when we hope that we can achieve peaceful cooperation by means of it. So can there be peace? Achieving peace is one aspect of achieving "salvation," the fulfillment of the deepest human hopes. Questions about true and false ways of salvation lurk in the background whenever we seek so exalted a goal as peace, even if we conceive of this peace as partial and provisional. Peace in the fullest sense has been given by Christ, and by no one else: "I have said these things to you, that in me you may have peace. In the world you will have tribulation. But take heart; I have overcome the world" (John 16:33). And perfect peace comes with his coming, and in no other way.

At the same time, Christ brings division between those who follow him and those who do not:

> Do not think that I have come to bring peace to the earth. I have not come to bring peace, but a sword. For I have come to set a man against his father, and a daughter against her mother, and a daughter-in-law against her mother-in-law. And a person's enemies will be those of his own household. Whoever loves father or mother more than me is not worthy of me, and whoever loves son or daughter more than me is not worthy of me. And whoever does not take his cross and follow me is not worthy of me (Matt. 10:34-38).

Christ demands absolute allegiance, and that is a bitter pill for sinful people to swallow. The New Testament is therefore realistic about the offensive aspects of its message. We cannot avoid the offense of the cross (1 Cor. 1:18-30) or the offense involved in submission to Christ's lordship. The exclusivity of biblical claims also causes offense. If we appear to have unity short of unity in Christ, we have not yet exposed the deeper issues.

"Yet," the questioner replies, "unity already exists in science. Christian and non-Christian work side by side, each making a contribution." Yes, unity exists after a fashion because all scientists must believe in God (chapter 1).

But they do so in spite of themselves. This unity does not really need critical realism, because people with very bizarre beliefs, including idealism, empiricism, pragmatism, and relativism, as well as simple materialism, may already cooperate, provided they are happily inconsistent with their beliefs. Nevertheless, in subtle ways the inconsistency of believing and not believing affects the course of science. Critical realism as usually defined does not help the inconsistency in a fundamental way, because the solution requires Christ's redemption.

Consider finally the atmosphere that realism may produce. Some realist writing can emanate an atmosphere of normalcy and sanity. If so, it is both a strength and a weakness. Most people, most of the time, intend to operate in the sphere of what is normal and sane. We know that an external world exists and that we have knowledge of it. Realist discussion can reassure us by showing up the fallacies and deficiencies of alternative, "strange" approaches.

Yes, other approaches have their failings. But I wonder whether some realists, before turning their backs on the failings, have sufficiently appreciated why others might adopt such strange, deficient approaches. I sympathize deeply with those others, because I suspect that underneath they are discontent with the "normal." Something is radically wrong, and they feel desperation. One follows normalcy if normalcy holds promise of giving what one wants. But if the world is desperately sick, and if normalcy appears to be unaware of it—if perchance normalcy itself displays symptoms of the sickness—one casts about for alternatives. One becomes radicalized. And the more desperately sick the world is, the more desperate the alternatives. The realists are like contented bourgeois managers of factories, while the radicals are like the visionaries who plot for a bloody communist revolution. I sympathize, because I think the radicals are right to be desperate (chapter 3); but I regret that the desperation may break out in ways that make the sickness worse (the bloodshed in revolution). That is the nature of sin. Christ came to bring the true remedy for sin, through his death and resurrection.

MULTIPLE PERSPECTIVES

So we have ended up affirming all five of the different schools, provided that one does not take them up unchanged but treats them as perspectives on science, or even perspectives on all of life. For example, one redefines and reshapes postmodern relativism by dropping the relativism that despairs of finding truth but continuing to affirm a God-ordained diversity in ways of expounding truth, whether that diversity is seen in the four Gospels, or in

Schrödinger's and Heisenberg's two approaches to quantum mechanics, or in the contrast between starting with human capabilities (idealism) and starting with pointer readings on instruments (a form of empiricism).

In fact, the diversity in human thinking does not represent merely some frustrating quirk but at its best reflects that original diversity in the persons of the Trinity. One God knows the whole truth, guaranteeing the unity and stability of truth. At the same time, the Father knows all things in knowing the Son; and the Son knows all things in knowing the Father. Thus we can see diversity in the persons of the Trinity.[15]

The acknowledgment of multiple perspectives enables us to make some sense of the diversity of "levels" with which we may analyze the perception of a red apple. We may affirm the value both of ordinary human experience and of special modes of analysis that science introduces. We affirm our ordinary visual experience, and we also study scientifically the cellular and neurological processes involved in human vision. We study the physics of light, or we look at light from the standpoint of special relativity, or quantum theory, or perhaps even further theories still to be developed. These viewpoints are like different perspectives on the world. But they are not isolated from one another. Through our ordinary world we learn of science, and we expand that ordinary world as we develop a capacity to occupy more of the specialized standpoints that science offers. And those specialized standpoints, rightly understood, also lead to affirming the reality of what we experience in the ordinary world.

---

[15] Poythress, *Symphonic Theology*, 47-51; Poythress, *God-Centered Biblical Interpretation*, 36-47.

16

ORDINARY EXPERIENCE OF THE WORLD IN RELATION TO SCIENTIFIC THEORY

We may now reflect on the relation of ordinary human experience to scientific theorizing.

THE COPERNICAN REVOLUTION

Consider the struggle that people experienced in adjusting to modern astronomy. What happened when Copernicus said that the sun was at the center of the solar system?[1] Earlier, the Greek astronomer Ptolemy (second century A.D.) had maintained that the sun, moon, stars, and planets all traveled in orbits around a stationary earth. Then Nicolaus Copernicus (1473–1543) postulated that the earth rotated on its axis, and that both the earth and planets traveled around the sun as center. The stars could be considered as fixed relative to the sun. Tycho Brahe (1546–1601) offered a compromise view in which the sun traveled around the fixed earth, and all the planets around the sun.

In the time of Copernicus, telescopes had not yet been invented. So astronomical observations at the time did not have the accuracy they have today, and it was not so easy from a scientific point of view to say which theory had the most promise. Copernicus's approach resulted in a simplification, but that, rather than any clearly superior accuracy, was the main argument in its favor.[2]

---

[1] I simplify, because Copernicus initially offered his approach as merely a hypothesis and a way of simplifying the mathematical model of the planets. He was careful not to say that the sun was literally the center.
[2] In fact, Tycho Brahe's failure to observe any parallax (slight variation) in the position of the stars at different times of year seemed to disconfirm the Copernican theory. No one at the time dreamed that the stars were trillions of miles distant (*The Encyclopaedia Britannica* [Chicago: Encyclopaedia Britannica, 1963], 2:645).

The matter might have remained a technical dispute among astronomers had it not seemed to threaten the thinking of a larger world. Socially and culturally, some were concerned that it might invite people to question tradition, thereby threatening the status quo.[3] Philosophically, some people saw it as threatening the central role of man in the cosmos, by displacing the earth from the center. Religiously, some people saw it as threatening the authority of the Bible, because they thought that the Bible declared that the sun moved ("The sun rises, and the sun goes down, and hastens to the place where it rises," Eccles. 1:5), and the earth was immobile ("the world is established; it shall never be moved," Ps. 93:1).

DIFFERENCES IN PERSPECTIVE

Copernicus's theory did threaten the status quo, no doubt. As for the other issues, in hindsight it is much easier to see that the dispute neglected to consider differences in perspective, that is, differences in the framework within which the questions arose. The Bible addresses the ordinary person, and adopts the ordinary language of how things appear. The sun does rise, and the ground does remain stable underfoot (Eccles. 1:5; Ps. 93:1).[4] By contrast, the astronomer asks recondite questions about the motions of heavenly bodies relative to one another. He takes the perspective of the specialist and the one who inquires into quantitative details about positions. The philosopher asks whether man enjoys a central role in the cosmos, and that question differs from whether man enjoys a central position from the standpoint of astronomical space. Such a distinction, however, could easily escape people who were expecting a simple match-up between spatial location and importance.

WHAT IS REAL?

Seeing the differences in perspective therefore provides us with a partial solution. But lurking in the background is the question of what is real. Copernican astronomy seemed to undermine people's naive sense of what is real. It threat-

---

[3] Alister McGrath points out the relation between the rejection of Galileo and religious polemics: "[the controversy over Galileo] is to be set against the long-standing and bitter debate . . . between Protestantism and Roman Catholicism over whether the former was an innovation or a recovery of authentic Christianity. The idea of the unchangeability of the catholic tradition became an integral element of Roman Catholic polemic against Protestantism. . . . The interpretation which he [Galileo] offered had never been offered before—and it was, for that reason alone, wrong" (McGrath, *Science and Religion: An Introduction* [Oxford: Blackwell, 1999], 14). See also Richard J. Blackwell, *Galileo, Bellarmine, and the Bible* (Notre Dame, Ind.: University of Notre Dame Press, 1991).

[4] Also, it is possible that Psalm 93 intends to speak metaphorically about the "world" of human activity, using pictures of physical activity (or stability). In any case, it is a misunderstanding to read it as if it asserted a particular scientific theory about the physical position of the earth.

ened Bible readers and the philosophical vision of mankind because people were trying to find from one source alone all the answers about the "bottom" of the world. They were tempted to see Copernican astronomy as a claim to give us a more ultimate analysis, a rock-bottom analysis, of the "real" nature of things, as opposed to the way in which they appear. That kind of search for ontological ultimates goes astray because it does not really find rest in the ontological ultimacy of God and his word. God simultaneously makes real all the perspectives. In the long run, the search for ultimacy forces us into a choice between perspectives; then one perspective is ultimate and gives us our ontology, while the others are merely derivative, and maybe even illusory.

In Copernicus's time, if people insisted on finding an ultimate ontology, they produced warfare between philosophy, science, and the Bible. Once a war started, each position might proclaim that it offered the ultimate ontology. Philosophy, after proclaiming the centrality of man, wants to debunk astronomy by claiming that it is a mere illusory play with numbers, a fruitless speculation for the sake of mathematical simplicity. Or astronomy, proclaiming the ultimacy of scientific insight, debunks philosophy as a spatially parochial vision, and debunks the Bible as outdated or only addressed to narrowly "spiritual" concerns. Or the defenders of the Bible understand the Bible reductionistically. They then proclaim the exclusivity of ordinary perception, and condemn the ungodliness of astronomers who will not simply submit to it and do their research in conformity with the Bible's "clear teaching."

Today we are no longer conducting much debate about the position of the sun. But temptations of a similar kind remain in play. Bible defenders can become too certain too quickly that they know what the Bible means. And they may not attend to the differences in perspective between the Bible's ordinary view and a scientist's technical view. Conversely, lovers of science can convert science into a materialist worldview that gives them, as they suppose, the final ontological answers. Then they debunk the Bible and philosophy.

Is a scientific analysis in terms of light waves more *ultimate* than a human being's perception of a red apple? One should first ask, "More ultimate for what purposes, and in what context?" And then one may answer to the general question of ultimacy, "No, neither one is more ultimate." Reality has many levels, and human beings have many legitimate perspectives.

Amusingly, even the story about Copernicus and the position of the sun has not yet come to a full end. Yes, Copernicus's view has taken over, first among scientists, then more broadly. Because of the impressive triumphs of science over decades and centuries, and its continued influence on general culture, nearly every educated person in the civilized world accepts that the earth rotates and orbits around the sun.

TWENTIETH-CENTURY DEVELOPMENTS

But that is not the end of the story. Twentieth-century astronomy found that the sun is not motionless, but travels in a very large orbit around the center of the Milky Way galaxy. The Milky Way galaxy in turn sits in no particularly central location, but simply in one location among many local and distant galaxies. It is in motion with respect to the local cluster of galaxies. The sun is not motionless and is not the center; there is no center.

The Copernican view, and later the Newtonian view, had assumed that, underneath the phenomena, there was an absolute fixed space and fixed time in terms of which planetary motion took place. This assumption was convenient, but flawed. Albert Einstein in his general theory of relativity (1916) showed that, mathematically, the equations of motion were transformable from one state of motion to another, in such a way that no one state was intrinsically more fixed than another.[5] No absolute space or absolute time existed, but only an intertwining of space and time in a way that depended on the state of motion and of acceleration of the observer. Hence, the standpoint of an observer standing on the surface of the earth was *just as ultimate,* mathematically, as the standpoint where the sun was fixed, or where the center of the Milky Way galaxy was fixed. The common person, who accepts the sun as the stationary center of the solar system, has not caught up with a phase of science that overturns the very idea of fixing one thing as stationary. A person who thinks that the Bible is scientifically outmoded, because it treats the ground as fixed, turns out himself to be scientifically outmoded![6]

But we should not try to vindicate the Bible in this way with the latest scientific theory. The latest theory may itself eventually become outmoded. Rather, we need to recognize that the Bible is giving a description from the perspective of ordinary language and ordinary human observation. And, I

---

[5] The special theory of relativity (1905) constructed the appropriate mathematical equivalence between different states of motion without acceleration. The general theory extended the principle to include accelerated states and states within gravitational fields.

[6] Even this is not the end of the discussion, because the general theory of relativity can be interpreted in more than one way. Alvin Plantinga observes:

> One can also interpret relativity theory as nothing more than a recipe for translation from one frame of reference to another; so taken it makes no pronouncements on the question whether there is a frame at absolute rest. So taken, the claim that there is such a frame is quite consistent with it; perhaps the frame at absolute rest is given by the way God sees things. (And hence it could be, so far as knock-down drag-out demonstration goes, that the earth is the center of the universe after all!) (Plantinga, "Evolution, Neutrality, and Antecedent Probability: A Reply to McMullin and Van Till," *Christian Scholars Review* 21 [1991/1992]: 92n8.)

suggest, we need to recognize the perspectival character of *any* technical scientific theory, as showing us a wondrous reality in God's wisdom but not a reality that replaces ordinary reality or is ontologically more ultimate.[7]

THE INDISPENSABILITY OF THE ORDINARY

The reality of the ordinary is worth underlining. Every adult with reasonable mental functions and with a normally functioning body knows intuitively through his body that he is at the center of the spatial, auditory, and tactile world that he perceives. He sees a world *from the perspective* of his body. He knows this unavoidably. He knows it indispensably. To cease to know it would put him in jeopardy of life and limb. Without understanding his own spatial location he would not be able to judge the danger of putting his body in front of a speeding car or walking off the edge of a high building.

This world of one's personal bodily perception is joined in human understanding to the worlds of other human beings with whom we are in communion. Through imagination, through human communication, and through the experience of occupying multiple spatial positions at different times, we understand that we inhabit a common world that we share with others in time and in space. But that commonality cannot erase or displace the individuality of our bodily position. The two complement one another. To understand the common world of humanity, we build on the individual world of perception. These experiences all occur under the providential control of God. God's word specifies and guarantees that we will have experiences of these kinds. Such experiences are real in that they are the purposeful, meaningful effect of the word of God.

In science we come to understand new perspectives about the very small, about the very large, about very different spatial locations, about very different forms of life, about correlations between mathematics and the physical world. These new perspectives *necessarily* rely on ordinary perception as a starting point. Rightly understood, they grow out of the ordinary rather than displacing or undermining the reality of the ordinary. It takes a powerful ideology to maintain, contrary to our deepest intuitions, that the "real" is only what science uncovers. And yet the ideology is so strong in our time that it often conceals from us the obvious, namely the reality of human bodily existence. In an extreme case of denial, we can even analyze ourselves into

---

[7] For more on perspectives, see Vern S. Poythress, *Symphonic Theology: The Validity of Multiple Perspectives in Theology* (Grand Rapids, Mich.: Zondervan, 1987).

virtual nonexistence, claiming materialistically that our conscious experience is little better than an illusion cast up by electrical signals in the brain.

ULTIMACY IN PERSPECTIVES ON TIME

Similar observations hold for two different perspectives on time. On the one hand, science proclaims that the universe is 14 billion years old. On the other hand, the Bible, according to one interpretation, says that the universe is only thousands of years old. But we have seen (chapter 10) that the differences are due partly to cultural differences between clock orientation and interactive orientation. Clock orientation means mechanical orientation toward the measurement of time with objective numbers. Combined with scientific extrapolation of clock time into the past, it gives the figure of 14 billion years. But interactive orientation sees that creation took place in six days of human-like rhythm of work and rest.

Modern people assume that science gives us *the reality*. What science gives is indeed real; but it is one aspect of reality, one perspective, at which we naturally arrive when, with extreme consistency and zeal, we pursue the clock orientation and its quantitative measurements.

The ordinary, interactive human way of looking at temporal rhythms, the way familiar to all prescientific cultures, is still valid in God's eyes, and we ought therefore to open our eyes to its grasp of *reality*. Reality does not reduce itself to scientific focus, but is richly controlled by the wisdom of God in his word. Human rhythms still offer a valid way of looking at the history of creation! And in a sense, because they are human, because the human rhythms belong to the natural rhythms of our bodies, they remain more central to ordinary human meanings than the technical reflections of science, beautiful though these may be in their own sphere.

God really did create the world in six days. That is to say, when we speak in everyday human terms, and think in terms of the human rhythms of work and rest, we are right to say that God created the world in six days, because we are thinking of days within an interactive orientation. Only within the technical sphere of consistent clock orientation and calculation do we develop another, complementary perspective on time. Within that sphere, where we define "time" in an unusual, precise way that separates it from human rhythms, we obtain a figure of 14 billion years.

Copernicus and Einstein provided beautiful technical perspectives for the needs of scientific reflections on space. Modern scientific calculations of time likewise provide beautiful technical perspectives for the needs of scientific reflections on time. In neither case should we reductionistically think that these technical perspectives overthrow ordinary human perception, or the experience of time as a human rhythm of work and rest.[8]

AVOIDING THE IDEOLOGY OF REDUCING MEANING

In the case of both space and time, philosophical reductionism—an ideology—promotes the illusion that science displaces and negates ordinary human experience. *Ideology* tells us that human perceptions about the fixity of the earth and the temporal rhythms of Genesis 1 are "unreal." But that ideology is wrong.

God is rich in wisdom and gives bountifully to human beings, blessing them with both the richness of ordinary human experience and the richness of the technical perspectives of science (Acts 14:17; James 1:17). This richness invites us to give thanks.

But we are ungrateful rebels. We displace the richness of God with a counterfeit substitute, in the form of an abstract impersonal something, a principle of scientific law, or a principle of matter, from which everything else must flow impersonally. So we then have the need for postulating that some "reality" within the world must offer the final explanation for human experience, and must reduce that human experience down to something "deeper" behind it, thereby making it ultimately unreal. The ideology of philosophical reductionism springs from a corrupt root, human idol-making.

We have nearly come full circle. God created the world in six days. That does not contradict technical science, because we say it from the standpoint of interactive orientation. Interactive orientation, rooted in the depths of human bodily experience, instinctively focuses on the event content of the days. Days are days because of their event content. People in various preindustrial cultures, through the centuries, have read Genesis 1 and understood it in this way, because they too naturally used an interactive orientation. They

---

[8] For some modern people, a figure of 14 billion years might also seem to be a matter of ordinary human perception. But actually our understanding of long periods of time is a product of complex education in a modern society.

The bodily rhythm of work and rest is common to human beings everywhere, because the need for sleep and rest is built into the human body. By contrast, the idea of a year is more complex, being related in most premodern societies to the succession of seasons. And the idea of a billion is not immediately graspable. We need first the concept of 10, and then the concept of multiplication, and then the concept of multiple acts of multiplication. And then a billion (in the American system) can be defined as ten times ten times ten . . . for a total of eight multiplications. This kind of thing has to be learned by a complex process. But in a modern society, after it is learned, it becomes through repetition something "ordinary," something common. All this goes to show how far technical scientific and mathematical concepts—like the concept of a billion—have penetrated modern minds. It takes an effort to realize that such concepts are neither ordinary nor common to human nature as such. And God in his wisdom designed the Bible to address human beings everywhere, not just those who inhabit modern societies.

were right in their understanding. And this understanding harmonizes naturally with modern science once we understand the difference between the perspectives, the clock orientation in science and the interactive orientation in ordinary human experience in preindustrial cultures.

We are nearly, but not quite, saying the same thing as the modern 24-hour-day viewpoint. The 24-hour-day viewpoint differs from an older, prescientific viewpoint in a subtle but profound way. In its usual form, it adopts a clock orientation, and it concerns itself with applying a quantitative clock measurement to the days.[9] One may wonder whether this approach has unconsciously given in to the *philosophical* primacy of a modern scientific orientation toward precise, quantitative measurement of time. In other words, it may have swallowed an ideological, philosophical assumption that it fervently wants to avoid!

HUMILITY

In all this perhaps there is another lesson about the nature of the Bible. By using the phenomenal language, interactive orientation, and a focus on the world as it appears to normal human perception, God has made Genesis 1 *accessible*. Not only ancient Israelites but people in many different cultures can understand Genesis. They do not first need to become "modern" or "scientific." Moreover, all the various cultures of the world *need* to understand Genesis, as a means for escaping the idolatries and false religions that offer

---

[9] Both St. Basil and St. Ambrose speak of "24 hours" in the context of homilies on the days of creation (J. Ligon Duncan and David W. Hall, "The 24-Hour View," in David G. Hagopian, ed., *The Genesis Debate: Three Views on the Days of Creation* [Mission Viejo, Calif.: Crux, 2001], 47; from Basil, *Hexaemeron* 2.8, in J. P. Migne et al., ed., *Patrologia Graecae* [Paris, 1857–1866] 29:50-52; English translation in Philip Schaff and Henry Wace, eds., *A Select Library of Nicene and Post-Nicene Fathers of the Christian Church*, 2nd series, 14 vols. [Grand Rapids, Mich.: Eerdmans, 1978], 8:64-65; Ambrose, *Hexaemeron* 1.10.37, in J. P. Migne et al., ed., *Patrologia Latina* [Paris 1878–1890], 14:155; English translation in Hermigild Dressler et al., eds., *The Fathers of the Church* [New York: Catholic University of America Press, 1961], 42:42).

But in understanding statements from outside modern culture, one must be aware of the difference between clock orientation and interactive orientation. What are the meaning associations of a word like "hours"? Does the meaning belong to a modern context? Then the dominance of science and the dominance of clock orientation in cultural practice define "hour" by ultimate reference to a scientifically precise, calculable, objective, nonhuman standard of measurement.

Or does the meaning belong to an ancient context? In the Roman Empire, to be sure, there was some capability for measurement with water clocks, and a custom of dividing the daytime into 12 parts. But where the predominant rhythms are interactive, and time in both its minor and major divisions has close ties with human activity, "hour" as well as "day" still has associations with humanly familiar rhythms. The Egyptians and the Romans divided the daytime into twelve "hours," but a daytime "hour" for a Roman meant one-twelfth of the time of daylight, whether the total time of daylight was long or short when measured by some mechanical clock. When viewed from our modern clock orientation, these daytime "hours" were actually longer in summer than in winter, because the daytime was longer in summer. And in summer the daytime "hours" would be longer than the nighttime "hours." When measured by clock orientation, an "hour" in the daytime in the summer in Rome would be longer than an "hour" in the daytime in Egypt, because the daytime lasts longer in Rome's more northerly location. Clearly the whole ancient system is still closely related to ordinary human rhythms, not based on recondite, scientific, objective, precise, quantitative time-measuring apparatus.

other accounts of gods and the world. So God shows great wisdom in the way that he wrote Genesis.

In fact, on the average, people from prescientific cultures probably understand Genesis 1 a good deal *better* than people under the heavy influence of modernity. The modern person brings to Genesis a loaded framework. He expects Genesis to "measure up" to the prestige of modern science by imitating it and offering the same kind of quantitative, precise, mechanical account. If it fails to do that, he regards it as primitive, antiquated, and inferior. Into his blood has seeped the pride of the modern world in the superiority of its technological and epistemological achievements, the pride in the superiority of modernity to its predecessors. The modern person finds it difficult to humble himself to accept that the ordinariness of human perception and the ordinariness of human experience in the body might still be a deep *reality*. God's decision to address the ordinary, to address people in the bodily frailty of their immediately "lived" world, might represent wisdom, not naivete. But can the modern person see it?

Pride interferes with understanding. The modern person does not really understand Genesis. Not because it is intrinsically inaccessible but precisely because it is too accessible! It is humiliatingly accessible. But for this very reason it becomes opaque to the person who holds fast to his pride.

Modern people, as we have observed (chapter 1), can become captive to various idols within their mental furniture. And in this case the idol in question is modernity itself, reinforced by a worldview that assumes that modern scientific accounts have made obsolete ordinary perception, rather than adding extra dimensions beyond the ordinary.

The modern person who prides himself on his superior wisdom gets trapped by the Bible's simplicities. The saying in Scripture proves true, "He [God] catches the wise in their craftiness" (1 Cor. 3:19). If you insist on being wise in your own eyes (Prov. 3:7), you may attain a position in which you have the delicious satisfaction of knowing with assurance that your own modern reading of Scripture, anchored in the triumphs of a modern worldview, is superior to the benighted darkness of all previous generations. But in this very triumph you will have proved yourself a fool, a dupe to modern ideology, and—more devastatingly—a dupe to your own pride.

To put it another way, the Bible is full of traps that God has set for the proud.

17

THE RELATION OF CREATION
TO RE-CREATION

What resources does the Bible provide for thinking about science? We have already seen some of them. The biblical doctrine of the sovereignty of God and the word of God provides a framework for science (chapters 1 and 13). Biblical teaching about man and his tasks provides important points for reflection (chapter 11). Teaching about Christ has implications for the redemption of science (chapter 12). The biblical teaching about sin and its effects on human endeavor has implications for the question of the noetic effects of sin on the intellectual work of science. Should we look in still other directions? Biblical teaching about wisdom is significant; but for our purposes we have taken it together with the doctrine of the word of God and the doctrine of truth (chapter 14).

CREATION AND REDEMPTIVE RE-CREATION

The Bible focuses on addressing ordinary people, and on instructing us about the remedy for sin. So we should beware of forcing it to address directly the questions of modern science. Yet, I suggest, the Bible has at least one more way of providing insights into the framework for doing science, namely through the link between creation and redemption. Creation took place through the work of the Trinitarian God. The Son of God, who is the image of God, had a role as the mediator of all the work of creation:

> He [the Son] is the image of the invisible God, the firstborn of all creation. For by him all things were created, in heaven and on earth, visible and invisible, whether thrones or dominions or rulers or authorities—all things were created through him and for him. And he is before all things, and in him all things hold together (Col. 1:15-17).

Right after this wonderful passage, the apostle Paul describes Christ's work as mediator of redemption:

> And he is the head of the body, the church. He is the beginning, the first-born from the dead, that in everything he might be preeminent. For in him all the fullness of God was pleased to dwell, and through him to reconcile to himself all things, whether on earth or in heaven, making peace by the blood of his cross (Col. 1:18-20).

Some tantalizing parallels invite us to compare the two kinds of mediation. The terms "through him," "firstborn," "all things," and "heaven/earth" link the two, as well as subtler relations between the holding together of creation and the redemptive reconciling of alienated creation. Mediation in creation forms one of the backgrounds and guarantees for effective mediation in re-creation. Similar connections between creation and redemption can be found in John 1, Revelation 21, and Hebrews 1:1-3.

Certainly, then, what we learn of Christ in redemption remains pertinent when we reflect on creation. But how is it pertinent? It is not easy to say, since the incomprehensibility of God, and the incomprehensibility of Trinitarian relations, prevent us from simply deducing what God planned to do in creation.

The correlation between creation and redemptive re-creation does not spring into being in the New Testament without antecedents in the Old Testament. We saw how Psalm 19 contains parts reflecting on general revelation (based on creation) and special revelation (pertaining to redemption). Psalm 148 calls for praise on the basis of God's creational and redemptive goodness. Isaiah looks forward to a renewal of the created order as an aspect of the fruit of redemption (Isa. 65:17-25). Proverbs 8 draws a connection between the wisdom by which God created the world and the wisdom needed to conduct human life.

The tabernacle of Moses also includes creational and redemptive motifs in a striking unity (Exodus 25–40). I have commented on the tabernacle at some length in *The Shadow of Christ in the Law of Moses,*[1] and I would refer readers to this earlier work for more extended discussion of what we will here sketch.[2]

When God gives plans to Moses for the tabernacle, he describes it as "a

---

[1] Vern S. Poythress, *The Shadow of Christ in the Law of Moses* (reprint; Phillipsburg, N.J.: Presbyterian & Reformed, 1995), 3-117, especially 9-40.

[2] Meredith G. Kline, *Images of the Spirit* (Grand Rapids, Mich.: Baker, 1980), has also provided useful input.

sanctuary, that I may dwell in their midst" (Ex. 25:8). It is a place where God draws near to Israel, and Israel to God. But it makes these provisions in a situation where sin still bars the way to God's holiness. Redemptive concerns obviously dominate the description. At the same time, the instruction says, "See that you make them [pieces of the tabernacle] after the pattern for them, which is being shown you on the mountain" (Ex. 25:40). The tabernacle replicates a pattern. And it turns out that the pattern is not merely arbitrary but is the pattern of God's dwelling in heaven (and on the mountain, when God comes down to meet Moses on the mountain).

Later in history God commissions Solomon to build a temple, which replicates many of the features of the Mosaic tabernacle on a larger scale. Solomon shows an understanding of this correspondence between God's dwelling in heaven and the dwelling on earth when, at the dedication of the temple, he mentions "heaven your dwelling place" (1 Kings 8:30, 39, 49), and at the same time affirms that God's name (representing his presence) will be in the earthly temple (1 Kings 8:29). Hebrews comments explicitly on the relation between the tabernacle "copy" and the heavenly original (Heb. 9:11, 23-28).

One can then see specific features in the tabernacle that suggest reminiscences of heaven. The cherubim on the lid of the ark are copies or images of the angelic living creatures that serve God in heaven (Ex. 25:18, 22). More cherubim woven into the curtain guard the way into the presence of God in the inner room (Ex. 26:31). The table with bread on it reminds Israel of God's provision of manna, which came "from heaven" (Ex. 16:4). The lampstand, with its lights, reminds one of the lights of heaven. The sun, moon, and five visible planets may even correspond to the sevenness of the seven lamps!

The tabernacle thus offers a kind of small-scale model of the macrocosmic dwelling of God in heaven. And although God is described as dwelling preeminently in heaven, heaven does not confine him: "Behold, heaven and the highest heaven cannot contain you; how much less this house that I have built!" (1 Kings 8:27). In a larger sense, the whole universe is God's dwelling. "Do I not fill heaven and earth? declares the LORD" (Jer. 23:24). Other Scriptures picture God's creation of heaven and earth as house-building: "who builds his upper chambers in the heavens and founds his vault upon the earth" (Amos 9:6); "Where were you when I laid the foundation of the earth?" (Job 38:4); "On what were its [earth's] bases sunk, or who laid its cornerstone, . . . ?" (Job 38:6). Not only heaven but the universe as a whole corresponds to the model house of the tabernacle.

The New Testament shows how these strands of thinking come together in Christ. When John says, "In the beginning was the Word, . . ." it evokes

the background of Genesis 1, with its expression, "In the beginning . . ."
Creation takes place through the Word, according to John 1:3: "All things
were made through him." This assertion about creation forms the background for the redemptive work of Christ, on which the rest of John focuses.
John 1:4 speaks of the Word as light in a redemptive sense, against the background of the creational light in Genesis 1:3. Later in John 1, Jesus Christ's
coming in the flesh is compared to the Old Testament tabernacle: "And the
Word became flesh and *dwelt* among us, and we have seen his glory" (John
1:14). The word for "dwelt" (Greek *eskenosen*) evokes thoughts of the tent
in the wilderness, and the mention of glory alludes to the fact that God's glory
appeared to Israel in connection with the tabernacle. Jesus' body is also compared to the temple (John 2:19-22). The tabernacle, like the creation itself,
was constructed according to the word of God. Behind the particular words
of instruction is the eternal Word that John 1:1-18 contemplates. The Word
who is God (John 1:1) is the source for creation, for re-creation, for tabernacle, and for all instances of God's dwelling with man.

IMAGING

The idea of copying or imaging features prominently in the tabernacle. The
tabernacle as a whole is a copy or image of the macrocosmic dwelling of God
in the world. More particularly, it is an image of heaven. The inner room, the
Most Holy Place, offers something closer to a picture of the immediate
dwelling of God in the presence of heavenly beings, the cherubim. The curtain separating the Most Holy Place from the Holy Place corresponds in a natural way to the blue sky, which conceals the invisible presence of God in the
heavenly places. The Holy Place "images" the Most Holy Place at a lower
level of holiness, and the courtyard beyond "images" the holiness of the two
rooms at a still lower level of holiness.

The idea of imaging does not disappear in John 1, but rather gets under-
lined in subtle ways by the affirmation that the Word is the source of all the
images. "In him was life, and the life was the light of men" (John 1:4). One
must allow this verse in John to resonate with the rest of John, where "life"
and "light" are important themes. Jesus later proclaims that he is the life
(John 14:6) as well as the light of the world (John 8:12; 9:5). He is such in a
redemptive sense; that is, he gives life to those who are spiritually dead, and
light to those who are spiritually in the darkness (John 5:24; 8:12; 9:39). But
the immediately preceding context in John 1:3 speaks of creation. Thus we
think of the creation of light on the first day, and the creation of life on the

third, fifth, and sixth days. John then invites us to see that the source of light and life in both senses lies in the Word, who *is* light and life. He is not just a bringer of light and life, as if these things were quite alien to him. Rather, he *is* light and life. The light and life within the created order reflect his original light and life.

This pattern, then, constitutes a form of imaging. The Word is light and life, in himself. He also gives an image of his light and life in creating light and life in this world. And he gives an image of his light and life to those who follow him redemptively.

The language about the "word" shows an analogous pattern. The second person of the Trinity is the original Word. The words of creation, "Let there be light," are images of this Word. The words of redemption given in Jesus' earthly instruction are equally images.

IMAGING IN THEOPHANIES

The coming of Christ to earth was anticipated in the Old Testament not only through the symbol of the tabernacle but also through biblical descriptions of *theophanies,* that is, appearances of God.[3] At special times God has appeared to human beings using spectacular visual displays. He appeared to Abraham in human form (Gen. 18:1ff.), to Moses in the burning bush (Ex. 3:1-6), to the Israelites in cloud and thunder at Mount Sinai (Ex. 19:16-25), and to Ezekiel in an elaborate vision (Ezekiel 1).

Ezekiel 1 shows ways in which a loose kind of imaging can operate. Roughly speaking, the theophany in Ezekiel 1 has three layers. The outer layer is a storm cloud (1:4). Then there are four living creatures and the associated wheels (1:5-25). Finally, in the center is a throne with a human figure on it (1:26-28). Several features reoccur in each layer: fire (1:4, 13, 27), gleaming metal (1:4, 7, 27), a voice or sound (1:24, 25; 1:28; 9:3-4). These features each suggest something relating to the character of God. The fire suggests the fire of God's consuming judgment (see Heb. 12:29). The gleaming metal suggests both the brightness of God's holiness and the firmness of his judgment. The voice suggests his ability to speak and pronounce judgment (see Rev. 1:15). These features fit the overall mood of judgment that appears in the first part of Ezekiel.

Theophanies thus reveal something about God at the same time that they also remain mysterious and make us aware of God's transcendence. The rev-

---

[3] The connection between theophany and imaging was earlier explored in Kline, *Images of the Spirit.*

elation of God takes place partly through physical displays: fire, cloud, light, motion, and sound. The physical display itself reflects some of the attributes of God, and in this respect we might say that it images God. Like some of the other instances of imaging, these images are partial. Ultimately the theophanies in the Old Testament point forward to the great and *permanent* theophany, the appearance of God in the person of Christ:

> And the Word became flesh and dwelt among us, and we have seen his glory, glory as of the only Son from the Father, full of grace and truth (John 1:14).

> Whoever has seen me has seen the Father. How can you say, "Show us the Father"? (John 14:9).

The small images are images of the Son, who is the perfect and full image (Col. 1:15).

These small images in the Old Testament are quite spectacular and extraordinary in their own way. But they also point to the ordinary. The thunderstorm-like phenomena at Mount Sinai were never to be repeated. Yet they also remind us of ordinary thunderstorms. The fire and lightning and thunder at Mount Sinai revealed the power and majesty and holiness of God in a unique way. But can we also affirm that an *ordinary* thunderstorm reveals the power and majesty and holiness of God? Surely it does, particularly after we have been taught about God through Mount Sinai. The Mount Sinai events, precisely because they revealed God intensively, can awaken us to what happens at a less intensive level in an ordinary thunderstorm.

Consider another example, that of fire. The fire at Mount Sinai revealed God's holiness and reminded Israel of his ability to consume unholiness. Does *ordinary* fire dimly reflect the same truth? Or consider light. The Bible says that "God is light, and in him is no darkness at all" (1 John 1:5). In the context, it focuses primarily on God's ethical purity. But it also hints at his ability to search out what is hidden and to expose it:

> And this is the judgment: the light has come into the world, and people loved the darkness rather than the light because their works were evil. For everyone who does wicked things hates the light and does not come to the light, lest his works should be exposed. But whoever does what is true comes to the light, so that it may be clearly seen that his works have been carried out in God (John 3:19-21; see also Eph. 5:8-14).

The bright light in theophanies obviously represents this characteristic of God. But so, at a lesser level, does ordinary light, because ordinary light is itself a reflection and reminder of the light that occurred in the extraordinary context of theophany. Thus, when in Genesis 1:3 God created light, he created something that reflects or images himself.

According to Romans 1, created things reveal the character of God:

> For his invisible attributes, namely, his eternal power and divine nature, have been clearly perceived, ever since the creation of the world, in the things that have been made (Rom. 1:20).

Everything that God made shows the power of God who made it. But from looking at theophanies, we can say more. Some specific things that God made, like light and thunderstorms and fire, not only reflect the general truth that God is their Creator but illustrate or reflect specific aspects of God's character. Of course, we also affirm that they are created reflections. Rightly understood, they do not lead to worshiping the creature but to worshiping God who made them.

DIVINE REALITY AND HUMAN KNOWLEDGE OF GOD

We may reflect for a moment on the relation of divine reality to human knowledge. Biblical teaching regarding God's transcendence and immanence implies both that we can have true knowledge of God (immanence) and that our knowledge is partial, limited, and derivative, whereas God's knowledge is complete, unlimited, and original (transcendence).[4] We must take care to guard both the genuineness of our knowledge of God and our subordination as creatures to God the Creator. These principles apply whenever we describe God, or when we describe the relations among persons of the Trinity, or when we describe God's actions in this world.

We may illustrate with the assertion that God is king of the universe. In making that assertion, we use an analogy between God and human kings. God is both like and unlike human kings. If we say that God is a king exactly like a human king, we reduce him to the level of the creature, and we deny his transcendence. On the other hand, suppose that we say that he is completely unlike a human king, and that the word *king* when used of God has a sense completely unrelated to human kings. Then the word *king* is no bet-

---

[4] For an extended discussion of knowledge of God in relation to transcendence and immanence, see John M. Frame, *The Doctrine of the Knowledge of God* (Phillipsburg, N.J.: Presbyterian & Reformed, 1987), 11-40.

ter than a nonsense word like *glak*. It means nothing, and we are not really saying anything definite about God. He remains unknown, and we are then denying his immanence.

When the Bible describes God as a king, it is following neither of these unacceptable extremes. The context in the Bible makes us understand that God is the Creator, immeasurably greater than a human king; he is not on the same level. But the Bible means something when it says that God is a king. It clearly intends to communicate that God is like a human king, and that we can learn about God from the comparison. The word *king* does not function *univocally*, to say exactly the same thing with respect to both God and man (making God a creature). Nor does it function *equivocally*, to say two different, unrelated things (making the word *king* useless and unknowable). Rather, it functions *analogically*, relying on the analogy that God himself has established as meaningful.

In fact, in various places the Bible gives us further indications about the nature of the analogy. God created man in his image, and gave him dominion, according to Genesis 1. The capacity for human dominion derives from God's dominion, and his decision to give to man this capacity. Moreover, God in his providence appoints specific human beings to positions of governmental authority (Ps. 75:7; Dan. 2:21; Rom. 13:1). God out of his authority appoints human authorities. Thus the use of the word *king* for both God and humans does not amount merely to an accident of language. It rests on a genuine analogy between God and man. We have first the general analogy arising from God's creating man in his image. And then we have the specific analogy between God's authority and the authority of a human being whom he appoints. If we start, as many people do, from the earthly level, we might claim that human kings are literally kings, whereas God is a king only in an extended, metaphorical sense. But when we remember that the use of the word *king* relies on an already existing analogy, we might well reverse the order of thinking. God is the original king, of which a human king is only a shadow, a copy, or an image.

Similarly, God is the original Father, who is Father to the Son. Human fathers are copies, images of the divine Fatherhood. God is not "father" at the same level as a human father; but he *is* a father, in fact the supreme Father, and our language remains meaningful when we call him Father. (It is once again analogical language.) The Son is also the Word, according to John 1:1. This "Word" is not on the same level with merely human words. But it is still meaningful to say that he is the Word. In fact, ontologically he is the original Word, of which human words and discourse are images.

Christ is the image of the invisible God (Col. 1:15). As in the other cases, the word *image* functions analogically. It is analogous to an imaging relation within creation, such as the relation between God and a man made in his image, or between Adam and Seth, who was fathered in the image of Adam. And then an inanimate body like a stone or a rubber ball can "image" the positions, motions, and forces of a human being. Thus we can have confidence that we are seeing a genuine analogy here. A skeptic might deny that there is an analogy. But then he would be saying that the word *image* when used for a physical body has nothing to do with the word *image* for the creation of man. We must reply that since we understand God through analogical relations, *image* applied to God is indeed related to the analogical relations that we see *within* creation. We must always affirm the distinction between Creator and creature (transcendence); but equally, we must affirm the accessibility of God to man the creature (immanence)—an accessibility that depends on God having established real and manifold analogies within creation that testify to his character and bear his imprint.

Man made in the image of God is of course by far the most noteworthy example of a testimony within creation to God who made him. But why should not this testimony extend at a derivative and attenuated level to other creatures? Plants and animals "image" the life of God by producing offspring in their image. Why should not we expect that even the inanimate things image something about the character of God? And they do, as we see from the illustrations with thunder, light, and clouds.

REALITY

Now, which is the "real" light, or the "real" life or word? The word "real" should throw up a red flag. As we saw in chapter 15, within a world whose ontology is exhaustively defined by the divine word, all things conforming to that word are "real." "Reality" turns out to be rich, wonderful, and multidimensional. Physical light is real; redemptive "light" of revelation is real, and the source of light in the Second Person is real. A modern atmosphere may tempt us to describe one or more of these levels as "merely" metaphorical, in a depreciatory sense. But we need a theology of language and a theology of metaphor that eliminates the depreciatory element.[5] Human language is an image of the Word, and as such it points to depths. A metaphor given by God is not "mere" metaphor, but an unveiling of these depths.

---

[5] For a beginning in addressing language and metaphor, see Vern S. Poythress, *God-Centered Biblical Interpretation* (Phillipsburg, N.J.: Presbyterian & Reformed, 1999).

To put it another way, from an ontological point of view, the original light and life and word is the eternal Word, the Son of the Father. Earthly manifestations are "metaphorical" reflections designed by God, but designed so that they actually show us the real. They reveal the Son who is their source, just as a window reveals the landscape beyond. One can look at the glass in the window, or one can look through the window, as one chooses. But the analogy is imperfect, because the window is a created thing distinct from the created landscape, whereas the light and life and word in this world exist only as sustained by the One original Light and Life and Word who give them.

The light in this world has no "substance" independent of the original Light, but is wholly dependent. Is it then so transparent to the uncreated Light that we cannot distinguish the two? Yes, we can distinguish. The light in this world has physical, mathematical, and aesthetic relations that we can describe in some detail and subject to analysis. The uncreated Light is light indeed, not subject to being "decomposed" into analytical relations. But then he is also Life and Word and Truth and Wisdom and Bread and Vine, so that we have to think of relations with other meanings after all. All meaning resides within the governance of the true Wisdom of God.

What God created is real and is distinct from God. But it is not independent of God. God governs the world he has made, and also displays within the world many reflections of his character.

18

THE MYSTERY OF

LIFE

Now let us consider a particular area of scientific research, biology. The Bible as usual does not directly provide technical information for the researcher. But it is trustworthy and true in what it says, and provides a framework within which research may proceed.

KINDS OF PLANTS AND ANIMALS

God specifically indicates in Genesis 1 that he created plants on the third day, birds and fish on the fifth day, and land animals on the sixth day. God gives to man dominion over plants and animals (1:28-29), and explicitly distinguishes the two by indicating that animals have been given plants for food.

Genesis also indicates that these living things appear "according to their kinds." The repetition of that phrase confirms what Israelites could see around them, that plants and animals belong to distinct classes. We find sheep, goats, and camels, but no intermediate animals that are half goat and half camel. The word of God gives order and division within the world. The order among animals forms one part of the total organization of the world.[1] Moreover, reproduction takes place along the lines that God's word establishes. "The earth brought forth vegetation, plants yielding seed according to their own kinds, and trees bearing fruit in which is their seed, each according to its kind" (Gen. 1:12). Each plant yields a particular kind of seed, "seed according to their own kinds," or a particular fruit. Israelites know that this seed gives rise to the new plants and trees, in accordance with the particular

[1] On the theme of order, see Henri Blocher, *In the Beginning: The Opening Chapters of Genesis* (Downers Grove, Ill.: InterVarsity Press, 1984), 70-74.

kind. Oat seeds lead to a crop of growing oat plants. The pattern carries over to the animal world as well. Sheep give birth to sheep. The command to "Be fruitful and multiply" directed to the water creatures assumes that the multiplication takes place according to the kinds that the word of God specifies. Hence, the word of God specifies and controls not only an original act of creation but also the continued pattern of growth and reproduction according to kinds. Israel needs to recognize that every day, as farmers and husbandmen tend crops and livestock, they are depending on God's faithfulness to his word.

God's instruction in Genesis 1 thus has practical functions. But as human beings grow in knowledge and continue to reflect on animals and plants, Genesis also provides hints for the beginnings of taxonomic classification of animals and plants. The word "kinds" cannot be equated with species or genus or family or any other of the later terms used in *technical* taxonomic classification. It is a more ordinary, general term to denote what ordinary Israelites could observe, namely that one goat is in most respects more like other goats than like dogs or rats, and that goats give birth to more goats like themselves.

In fact, observant Israelites would find that the principle of reproduction according to kinds applies in an altered sense even *within* a single species. If one picks the best seed or the best goats to reproduce in the next generation, one is more likely to get good results. By selective breeding over a number of generations, one can produce a distinct *variety* or subline within a species.

But right away a complaint arises: The account in Genesis 1 seems to get the classification "wrong" by grouping all the water creatures together, rather than classifying whales and dolphins separately with mammals. The scientist classifies whales and dolphins with mammals, while classifying bony fish separately and crustaceans and shellfish and sponges into still other groups. The scientist might also complain that bats should be classified with mammals, rather than with birds. Genesis, however, groups all the flying creatures together. But actually there is nothing wrong with the classification in Genesis. Once more it helps to distinguish the ordinary language of observation from the technical language and technical concerns of science. The Bible does not here interrupt its grand narrative to deal with every possible exception. And at an ordinary level whales and dolphins and bats are not "exceptions," since whales and dolphins live in the sea and bats fly in the air. The animals are being grouped together not in terms of technical morphological or genetic similarities but in terms of the obvious similarity of habitat. An early Israelite might easily assume that similarity of habitat dictates similarity at every other level. But God is full of surprises, and eventually the detailed investigator finds out that whales and dolphins are among the surprises. Technical study adds an additional layer of richness onto our understanding of the word of God governing kinds. But it does not undermine the obvious differences in habitat or other characteristics.

IMAGING IN LIFE

When animals reproduce "according to their kinds," they produce other animals who look and behave like the parent and grandparent animals. They produce copies or likenesses of themselves. This whole pattern reminds one of the imaging that we saw in the tabernacle. So what, if anything, does it have to do with imaging?

In Genesis 1 God "created man in his own image, in the image of God he created him" (Gen. 1:27). At a minimum, that means that man is made like God. And we do see ways in which man is like God. Man is like God in the dominion that God gives to man, in man's ability to use language, and in his ability to name animals.

Genesis 5:1-3 picks up the language from Genesis 1, as it looks at Adam's posterity:

> When God created man, he made him in the likeness of God. Male and female he created them, and he blessed them and named them Man when they were created. When Adam had lived 130 years, he fathered a son in his own likeness, after his image, and named him Seth.

Seth was born "in his own likeness, after his image," a description that clearly echoes the creation of man in the image of God, after his likeness. Adam, of course, is not God. But he imitates God on a creaturely level by producing "in his own likeness." In context, it means in the likeness of Adam, not in the likeness of God. But since Genesis 5:1 just affirmed that God made Adam in the likeness of God, Seth is clearly in the likeness of God as well. In fact, we easily infer that all the descendants will display the same pattern, as is confirmed by Genesis 9:6, 1 Corinthians 11:7, and other passages.[2]

Man is distinct from all the animals in being made in the image of God.

---

[2] Some people argue that man lost the image of God in the fall; but it is difficult to evade the implication of Genesis 5:1-3, not to mention 1 Corinthians 11:7; man remains in God's image in some sense. In the Bible we do not yet meet the expression "image of God" as a fully technical theological term, but rather as part of broader assertions about the character of man, who still imitates God in some respects, even in the midst of sin. On technical terms, see Vern S. Poythress, *Symphonic Theology: The Validity of Multiple Perspectives in Theology* (Grand Rapids, Mich.: Zondervan, 1987), 55-82.

But in this very distinctness one also ironically perceives a likeness, because animals reproduce "after their kinds." The text never says in so many words that man reproduces after his kind. But reproduction "after his image" is quite similar. Mankind is not just one more kind of animal, on the level of other animals, so the avoidance of "after his kind" is warranted. But the idea is similar—similar enough to suggest that, though animals are not on the level of mankind, they mirror mankind on their own lower level. May we say that animal reproduction images human reproduction? Genesis 1 does not spell out the relationship between man and animal with perfect explicitness. But it hints at it, and the more people begin to look at the biological aspects of reproduction among animals, the more they will see striking analogies between man and animals.

So if animal reproduction images human reproduction, does imaging occur in any other way? Does animal behavior image human behavior? One has only to watch monkeys to be amused by the similarities. Does animal physiology image human physiology? Explorations of the organs and bodily organization show many analogies between humans and primates, and more broadly between humans and mammals. We should be most grateful for these analogies when it comes to the treatment of human disease. Many hypotheses and treatments for human disease can be tested on animals first, precisely because of the analogies between animals and humans.

So imaging among animals is analogous to imaging among human beings. Does this imply that animals are *merely* an image of man, who is the *real* image? No. Animals have their own existence and integrity. They are, after all, a creation of God and not of man. God reflects his own uncreated life in the things that he has made. One of the ways in which he shows his glory is through the mystery of created life on earth, both animal and plant life.

How are we supposed to think about God's reflections of himself in the created world? God is distinct from his creation. We are not to mix together or confuse the Creator with his creatures. God's uncreated life is distinct from the created life of creatures. But God does show something about himself in creation, and creates reflections of his character and his activity, not only in man who is the crown of creation, but in the other creatures as well. That is why there are analogies between the life and reproduction of animals and the life and reproduction among human beings. Both animal and man reflect, each in its own way, the character and life of God.

Imaging, or more broadly analogical relationships, extends through many aspects of the biological world. Even at the molecular level, DNA and proteins show striking analogies. We can compare the DNA and proteins contained in the cells of different kinds of animals and plants, and they show notable similarities. For example, cytochrome c, a protein involved in cell metabolism, occurs in cells throughout almost the entire kingdom of plants and animals, including bacteria. But the exact sequence of amino acids making up the protein differs as we move from one taxonomic group to another.

The replication of DNA during cell division is a kind of reproduction of an original. The copy is an "image" of the original DNA. This replication of DNA at the molecular level is analogous to the replication of a cell by cellular division. And cellular division is analogous to the replication of an animal through reproduction, either sexual or asexual. All these cases of replication are forms of imaging.

From where does the imaging come? We are not asking about material causes, but about a pattern that expresses an idea. Human reproduction images the creation of man in the image of God. The origin is in God, and of course in his word that controls the expression of the idea among humans and animals and plants. But imaging is not just an idea in the mind of God. It expresses an ultimate reality of the divine being, inasmuch as the Son is the original image of the Father (Col. 1:15; Heb. 1:3). This disclosure about the Son comes later in time than the Old Testament material about creation. But the reality it discloses precedes and founds creation. God made man in his image, because, even prior to the creation of man, the Father loved the Son, who was his image. God's making of man mirrored or imaged the Son, who is the original image.

But dissimilarity also confronts us. The Son was "begotten, not made," as the Nicene Creed reminds us. Man was *made,* made as a creature. In contrast, the Son is eternal. Then why do we say that he was "begotten"? "Begotten" in ordinary usage describes the relation between a father and a son among human beings. Adam begat Seth. In more modern English, we say that he fathered him (Gen. 5:3). When we use the term "father" or "beget" with respect to God, we obviously use it analogically. But we have a clear basis for the analogy in the fact that Adam fathered Seth "in his own likeness," clearly imitating God, who fathered Adam "in his own image," which imitates the Son being in the image of the Father. The origin of these imitations lies in the Father, who is Father to the Son, and whose Trinitarian life is the Original for these derivations.

The Bible indicates that the Father sent the Son into the world, to be born of the virgin Mary (Gal. 4:4; cf. Matt. 1:18, 23). The language about "sending" the Son implies that the Son was the Son in relation to the Father even before he came into the world in the incarnation. When he became man and was born of the virgin Mary, his special birth displayed and confirmed that he was the eternal Son. What happened in time and space in the incarnation gave us a window into understanding who the Son always was, namely the Son of the Father. The incarnation without a human father was a reflection of God the Father's eternal relation to the Son. We underline the character of this reflection of eternal relationships when we say that the Father eternally *begets* the Son. The Nicene Creed speaks of Christ as "the only-*begotten* Son of God, *begotten* of the Father before all worlds, God of God, Light of Light, very God of very God, *begotten,* not made, being of one substance with the Father." The word *begotten* indicates that the Father *begets* or *fathers* the Son eternally. We confess this not because we understand it but because we thereby indicate that the incarnation shows us who God is, and always was, namely Father relating as Father to the Son through the power of the Holy Spirit (Matt. 1:18; Luke 1:35). God exhibits the true character of Trinitarian relations through the once-for-all event of the incarnation.

Thus with reverence and mystery we may say that God is not eternally idle or immobile, but eternally active. The Father loves the Son and the Son loves the Father (John 3:35; 14:31). The Father fathers the Son and the Son renders his Son's service to the Father. The Father images himself in the Son and the Son images the Father, as is beautifully expressed in a redemptive context: "Truly, truly, I say to you, the Son can do nothing of his own accord, but only what he sees the Father doing. For whatever the Father does, that the Son does likewise" (John 5:19). The eternal activity of the Father with the Son through the Spirit produced an imaging in time when God created man in his image. Man as created son must imitate the Son who is the original image; and man must imitate the Father who made him an image. And he imitates the imaging climactically by also engaging in imaging—Adam fathered a son. For what more exalted achievement could a man have than to have produced a new creature who is himself in the image of God!

"As the Father has life in himself, so he has granted the Son also to have life in himself" (John 5:26). The context of this statement in John is redemptive. But, as usual, we may infer that the principle extends to creation. From all eternity the Father has life in himself; he fathers the Son as his image and therefore the Son also has life in himself. Now Adam is given life, but as a creature he does not have life merely "in himself"; he is able to propagate life to Seth, but only because he lives and moves and has his being in God (Acts 17:28). Life and propagation of life thus find their root in God. Not only does God control and ordain life; he controls it and ordains it in imitation of himself. God is the *living* God (Matt. 16:16; etc.). He has divine life. He then images his own life in the life of the world. He loves the Son, and out of love produces images of love all through the world. He loves the Son, and the drive of this active love gives to creatures, as an image of itself, the creaturely power to love, to act, to father.

Imaging and copying display themselves particularly in the biological world, the world of life. In fact, biology today has some special terms for such patterns. *Analogy* means "correspondence in function between anatomical parts of different structure and origin," while *homology* means "likeness in structure between parts of different organisms due to evolutionary differentiation from the same or a corresponding part of a remote ancestor."[3] The second definition, at least as commonly understood, presumes the evolutionary principle of descent from a common ancestor, but that is not our point of focus at the moment. God through his word designed analogies between different kinds of organisms, as well as the principle of reproduction according to kind within any single kind of organism. Moreover, analogies show themselves at different levels. Organisms reproduce, or produce images of themselves. Cells within a multicellular organism divide and produce images. DNA replicates and produces images. These replicative processes are similar to one another across many different kinds of organisms, and thus they mirror one another. Many other processes in organic life besides directly reproductive processes mirror one another among different kinds as well as within one kind.

In addition, the discovery of DNA and RNA confronts us with biological *information*. Information encoded in the particular sequence of nucleotides in a particular molecule of DNA or RNA contains the recipe for building a protein with an exactly specified sequence of amino acids. Any living cell, like a factory, manufactures proteins using the "blueprint" information in the cell's DNA. This information seems analogous to the original "information" in God's word. The processing of that information in a cell seems analogous to the means that God used in creation to work out a product that conforms to his word. The word of God specifies the "manufacturing" of a created thing. The cell contains in its molecular information a kind of created analogue or image of the uncreated Word.

If we wish, we may trace out little images of the eternal Word within this world. We start with the second person of the Trinity who "was with God and was God" even "in the beginning" (John 1:1). The specific words

---

[3] *Webster's Ninth New Collegiate Dictionary* (Springfield, Mass.: Merriam-Webster, 1987).

that God speaks to create light and to create animals and plants are like images of the Original Word. God also speaks words to human beings. And human beings speak words to one another, all in imitation of God's original speaking.

What about animals? Animals do not speak in language. They have animal cries and calls, but these represent only a rudimentary communication in comparison to human language. And yet even here, can we say that these calls are distantly analogous to human language? Both animal calls and human language reflect, each at its own level, divine language. We have found that some animals communicate not with audible sounds but with other means: bees communicate using a special dance, while ants communicate with chemical signals. And these represent dim images of the word of God.

Individual cells communicate chemically in a large variety of ways, which we are still in the process of discovering. The most notable cellular communication in higher animals comes through the nervous system, which also proves to play a central role in human action and reaction. Within a single cell, various communication systems carry information in and out from the cell membrane, back and forth from the nucleus, and specialized subsystems may control the cell's shape, its process of division, and its chemical manufacturing subsystems. DNA and RNA, as well noted, communicate their information content.

All these patterns are tiny images of the Word of God. They display the wisdom of the Father, a wisdom bound up with the Son who *is* Wisdom. We can admire and praise God for the mysterious activity and fecundity of life as it displays itself at the level of ordinary living, and as it comes into living rooms in fascinating TV programs about nature. We can admire and praise him all the more when with microscopic care we examine details and see intricate imitations of the life of God traced even in these details. The biological world gives us an invitation to worship God—the Father, the Son, and the Spirit.

THE SPIRIT GIVING LIFE

What role does the Holy Spirit play? We remember that the Holy Spirit was hovering over the waters in preparation for the works of creation (Gen. 1:2). In the New Testament the Holy Spirit has a distinct role in giving new life, redemptive life:

> But if Christ is in you, although the body is dead because of sin, *the Spirit is life* because of righteousness. If the Spirit of him who raised

Jesus from the dead dwells in you, he who raised Christ Jesus from the dead will also give *life* to your mortal bodies *through his Spirit* who dwells in you (Rom. 8:10-11).

It is the *Spirit who gives life;* the flesh is of no avail (John 6:63).

Ezekiel 37 prophesies about the giving of life by describing a vision of a valley of dry bones. The dry bones receive life as Ezekiel prophesies to them, and breath comes into them, signifying the giving of the Spirit: "And I will put my Spirit within you, and you shall live, . . ." (Ezek. 37:14). In fact, Ezekiel 37 plays on three meanings of the Hebrew word *ruach,* which can mean "breath," "wind," or "Spirit" (or "spirit," the human spirit). The Spirit is depicted as being like the breath of God, which comes and breathes life into the dead bodies. The picture is reminiscent of Genesis 2:7, where "the LORD God formed the man of dust from the ground and *breathed* into his nostrils *the breath of life,* and the man became a living creature."

The energy of the Holy Spirit in redemptive life, in new creation, mirrors the energy that God used in bringing creational life to man. We may infer that creational life comes *through the Spirit.* Job 32:8 provides a confirmation: "But it is the *spirit* in man, the breath of the Almighty, that makes him understand." In Hebrew "spirit" is the same word (*ruach*) normally used for the Holy Spirit. The English translation (ESV) is right not to capitalize "spirit." This verse speaks of the spirit "in man," pointing to the human spirit. But the next line puts the human spirit into connection with "the breath of the Almighty," indicating that God himself energizes human understanding. He does so through his "breath," hinting at the presence and activity of the Holy Spirit.

The Bible consistently distinguishes between God the Creator and his creatures. God is God, and the Holy Spirit is God. Man's human spirit is not God. And yet God is also present in his creation, and his presence and power touch the inmost life of man, including his spirit. Without the Holy Spirit sustaining us, we would immediately die. "If he [God] should set his heart to it and gather to himself his *spirit* and his *breath,* all flesh would perish together, and man would return to dust" (Job 34:14-15). Psalm 104:30 extends this principle beyond human beings and applies it to animals: "When you send forth your *Spirit,* they [animals] are created, and you renew the face of the ground." "Renew the face of the ground" refers to production of vegetation. So both new animal life and new plant life arise from God sending forth his Spirit and bringing them to life.

For man, life is associated with breath. God gave the initial "breath of life" to Adam in Genesis 2:7. The psalmist observes about man that, "When his breath departs, he returns to the earth; on that very day his plans perish" (Ps. 146:4). "The Spirit of God has made me, and the breath of the Almighty gives me life" (Job 33:4). The breath comes from God, especially from the Spirit of God. Thus we seem to have within creation a series of "images" or reflections of the life in God.

First, God has life in himself. In particular, he shows himself as the source of life through his Spirit, who is life (Rom. 8:10). Second, the life of the Spirit comes to human beings, so that they breathe. Their breath reflects the breath of the Spirit. Third, animals, as reflectors of God's life and as analogues to human life, are breathing creatures. When the animals died in Noah's flood, "Everything on the dry land in whose nostrils was the *breath of life* died" (Gen. 7:22). Fourth, even plants derive their life from the Spirit. After the first half of Psalm 104:30 mentions God sending his Spirit, the second half says, "and you renew the face of the ground," which is describing the renewal of plant life. Scientists have now found that higher plants have a system of "respiration." Though respiration does not take place through active muscular movement, air channels ("stomata") in leaves let in air, and a chemical exchange of oxygen and carbon dioxide takes place analogous to that in animals. Individual cells have to engage in a similar process of respiration, or more generally metabolic consumption of energy, in order to maintain life. Evidence for God's care and the presence of his life-giving Spirit is all around us, including these little images of "breath."

PURPOSEFULNESS IN LIFE

We have seen, then, how reproduction, storage and communication of information, and breathing (more generally metabolism) offer analogical images of the original uncreated life of God. Other processes in living things also offer analogues. Consider the whole area of purposes and goals. God acts with purpose, to achieve goals. The supreme goal of the Father is to glorify the Son, and the supreme goal of the Son is to glorify the Father (John 13:31-32; 17:4-5). These supreme goals are worked out in God's subordinate goals in his works of creation and providence. The dynamicity of divine life expresses itself in goal-directed action within creation.

Human beings, in imitation of God, also formulate goals and set out to achieve them. Only through attention to the goals involved do we really understand how other human beings build houses, write books, and tend crops.

Animals and plants, though they do not appear to have *conscious* long-term plans, also act in a goal-directed manner, to preserve their life and to grow and reproduce. It is not popular in modern biology officially to acknowledge goals, but both scientists and popularizers of science inevitably end up using explanations involving goals, because they are so obviously part of the pattern of life and so much a key to understanding life at an ordinary level.

As usual, a Christian worldview rejects the idea that this apparent goal-seeking is merely illusory. As Michael Polanyi demonstrated years ago, even the analysis of man-made machines requires reference to purpose.[4] Only through knowing what a machine is *for* (its purpose) can we say whether it is intact or broken, working or idle, effective or ineffective, efficient or inefficient. Similar principles hold when we look at living organisms, a single living cell, or even the molecular machines inside a cell.

When we speak in such ways, we are not trying to revive a philosophy of vitalism that says that a spooky life-force appears in living things in addition to ordinary chemical and physical forces. The chemical and physical analyses are valid and discover real truths through their analyses. But God's word has many dimensions, controlling not only physical and chemical actions but the distinctive activities of living things, which have purposes *according to his plan,* purposes that man can in part discern because he is made in the image of God.

Descriptions of purpose complement descriptions of physical energy, rather than postulating another *type* of energy on the same level. Suppose that Sally gets into her car to go to work. We might choose to focus on the physical, chemical, and mechanical activities involved in Sally's muscle contractions and bodily movement. Or we can focus on Sally's purpose, namely to go to work. These two ways of looking at Sally are complementary. Sally's purpose is not an extra form of *physical* energy or *physical* movement. It stands alongside the physical aspect as an explanation at another level. Similarly, at a cellular level we can observe the chromosomes of a cell duplicating and lining up on a central axis in preparation for cell division. We can focus on the physical forces and the chemical processes involved in duplicating the chromosomes and lining them up. Or we can focus on the purpose, and say that the cell is preparing to divide. Both are true analyses, but on different levels. We resist reduction of the physical to purpose, or purpose to the

---

[4] On the irreducibility of purpose to mere physics, see Michael Polanyi, *Personal Knowledge: Towards a Post-Critical Philosophy* (Chicago: University of Chicago Press, 1958), 327-380.

physical, because God's word is rich enough to impart a distinct meaning and structure to both.

POWER AND CONTROL IN LIVING THINGS

The concept of purpose has links to patterns of *control* in living things. To achieve the purpose for which a living thing is designed, it typically must control subordinate processes, both within itself and in the environment. The control executes a purpose. We can therefore trace analogies between different levels of control.

First, God controls all events according to his plan. ". . . according to the purpose of him who works all things according to the counsel of his will" (Eph. 1:11). "Who has spoken and it came to pass, unless the Lord has commanded it? Is it not from the mouth of the Most High that good and bad come?" (Lam. 3:37-38). The Son of God exerts control to execute the plan of the Father. "My food is to do the will of him who sent me and to accomplish his work" (John 4:34). Human beings, having been given dominion by God, control creatures under them. Animals control not only their own bodies but their food, and interact in complex ways to exercise some control of their environment: making nests and dens, hunting prey, digging up seeds, and so on. Plants control their growth in an orderly way, and control the processes of their reproduction. Even individual cells control their shape and the chemical composition of their protoplasm.

EVALUATING EVOLUTION

When one takes seriously the display of the glory of the Father and the Son and the Spirit in life, it raises questions about modern evolutionary theory. We earlier distinguished three meanings of evolution (chapter 5). *Microevolution* describes small variations that can be observed to occur from generation to generation, through the operation of mutation, natural selection,[5] and human-controlled selection in breeding. *Macroevolution* describes the hypothesis that the operation of microevolution over a large number of generations produced from a small beginning—probably a single first protocell—the entire panoply of life that we observe today. *Evolutionary naturalism* describes the materialist worldview that appeals to macroevolution for

---

[5] "Natural selection" describes the process in which some, but not all, of the offspring of one generation survive to reproduce offspring in the next generation. Those who survive and reproduce are more likely to be those better adapted to the current environment.

support. We have already rejected evolutionary naturalism. We will now focus on macroevolutionary theory.

The theory musters evidence in its favor in the form of analogies and homologies. In embryology, in fossils, in genetics, in morphology, and in molecular analysis, we find analogies between organisms. The analogies are so pervasive and so impressive that they point to common ancestry from a single origin in the remote past. Or do they? By following a trail of reasoning set in motion by the Bible, we have arrived at an alternative account, namely that the analogies derive from a common pattern in God himself. This pattern is mirrored and imaged and replicated countlessly by reflecting the one eternal Word in the words of God with respect to the living world. The analogies show common design by a common designer.

But what of the fossil record? The proponents of macroevolution argue that the fossils show the pattern of an evolutionary tree (though there remain serious gaps between major branches). From where did this tree pattern come, if not from common ancestry? More than one possible answer can be offered. In contrast to the conventional macroevolutionary answer, one may simply observe that God designed the pattern; it is not an illusion. A single living tree has twigs and smaller branches and larger branches and trunk, which in many respects image one another. The growth of a tree shows the pattern of offshoots that replicate the growth of an original single stem. What if the pattern of life through geologic ages mirrors life on a small scale, the life of a tree? It then becomes another instance of imaging.[6]

The motif of imaging shows that we can organize the entire evidence cited in favor of evolutionary theory within a framework of design. God designed all of life, from its microscopic minutiae to its grandest sweeps. And he used as a pattern for the design—himself. The Father fathers the Son as his image. In harmony with this, Stephen Jay Gould says that "something almost unspeakably holy . . . underlies our discovery and confirmation of the actual details that made our world."[7]

---

[6] Uncannily, Stephen Jay Gould concludes his monumental book on evolutionary theory by alluding in the final two sentences to wisdom and the tree of life: Darwin, he says, was

clothing the structure of his thought in that apotheosis of human achievement—wisdom, which the *Book of Proverbs*, citing the same icon that Darwin would borrow more than two millennia later, called Etz Chayim, the tree of life. "Length of days is in her right hand," for "she is a tree of life to them that lay hold upon her; and happy is every one that retaineth her" (Gould, *The Structure of Evolutionary Theory* [Cambridge, Mass.: Harvard University Press, 2002], 1343; see Prov. 3:18).

[7] Ibid., 1342.

SECONDARY CAUSES

But now we need to return to the observation that God as primary cause governs secondary causes, and that secondary causes do not compete with the primary cause as though they were on the same level (chapter 13). We affirm that God designs all of life, down to its smallest particulars: this particular beetle, not merely the larger species of which this beetle is a representative. The Bible says as much when it says that God rules over the death and life of individual animals:

> When you hide your face, they [animals] are dismayed;
>   when you take away their breath, they die
>   and return to their dust.
> When you send forth your Spirit, they are created,
>   and you renew the face of the ground (Ps. 104:29-30).

The psalm at this point describes God's providential sustenance of animals. So the "creation" of which it speaks is not the original creation in Genesis 1, but the creation of a new generation of individual animals, after an older generation has largely died out. Similarly the psalmist describes the care of God in creating him as an individual:

> For you formed my inward parts;
>   you knitted me together in my mother's womb.
> I praise you, for I am fearfully and wonderfully made (Ps. 139:13-14).

In theological terms, we say that God acts as primary cause for the creation of new animals or a new individual human being, but he brings about the result through secondary causes, that is, the normal processes of conception, gestation, and birth.

EXCEPTIONS IN THE MEANS FOR PRODUCING NEW INDIVIDUALS

Do secondary causes always operate in the same way in making new individuals? They did not in the case of the birth of Christ, because he was born from a virgin (Matt. 1:18-25). They did not in the case of Eve, because she was made from Adam's rib (Gen. 2:21-23).

We can find people who dispute both of these exceptions; that is, they deny the virgin birth of Christ or the special creation of Eve. We should expect this reaction in an age that is dominated by science, because contemporary culture tends to interpret "science" as implying impersonal laws that allow no exceptions. By contrast, when the laws are generalities about the rule of a personal God, the framework for science shifts in a radical way, and the answers come out different.

An exception is appropriate in the case of Christ, because he is the only Son of God. And, like Adam, he is the beginning of a new race, the renewed humanity of the "new creation" (2 Cor. 5:17). An exception does not result in absurdity, but rationally coheres with the plan of our personal God. An exception is also appropriate in the case of Eve, because she is the very first woman. If Adam had been left alone, new human beings could not yet come forth using the normal course of secondary causes. Finally, an exception is appropriate in the case of Adam, because he is the first man.

CREATION OF EVE FROM ADAM'S RIB

Did Eve really come from a rib of Adam? Some interpreters prefer a figurative interpretation of the rib. So we need to look more carefully at the meaning of Genesis 2:21-22. We will consider Henri Blocher as a representative of a figurative interpretation (though he refuses to be dogmatic).[8]

First, Blocher claims that Paul's statement in 1 Corinthians 11:8, "woman was made from (*ek*) man" does not require a literal interpretation. He explains,

> There are different kinds of causality, and that which the apostle has in mind may be exemplary or final. It could perfectly well be said that the woman is 'from' (*ek*) the man if he played the part of a prototype and if God created the woman because of the need the man had of her. Such a conclusion emerges by itself from Genesis 2, even if the text does not reveal the detailed method of the divine procedure.[9]

But Blocher is not expressing himself convincingly here. In 1 Corinthians 11:8 Paul expected his readers to see his allusion to Genesis 2. Given that allusion, and given the fact that Genesis 2:21-22 pictures Eve as physically deriving from Adam, the readers are bound to think in terms of that concrete picture, not just in terms of a vague idea of a prototype or of human need.

---

[8] Blocher, *In the Beginning*, 100: "Since other scriptural references do not settle the issue, however, we refuse to be dogmatic about it; if someone insists on the literal meaning, we have no objection, but let him make sure he also sees the symbolic richness of the account!" Others besides Blocher hold a similar view; I focus on him because he offers more explicit reasons.

[9] Ibid., 99.

The question remains whether the concrete picture in Genesis 2:21-22 functions literally or figuratively. Even if it functions wholly figuratively to express only woman's close relation to man and the purpose of God in meeting man's need, it serves Paul's theological point in 1 Corinthians 11:8. Paul need not be making an assertion about either its literal or its figurative character, but may simply be referring to the picture in Genesis 2:21-22 as it stands, in order to draw his own legitimate theological inferences. Hence, I do not think that 1 Corinthians 11:8 by itself is decisive, but not for the reasons that Blocher gives.

Blocher next says that

> The author [of Genesis 2] plays on the double meaning for rib, which also means 'side' and therefore 'alter ego'. The Arabs apparently use the expression, 'He is my rib' to mean 'He is my close friend'. We use a similar turn of phrase when referring to one's 'better half'.[10]

Blocher makes several misjudgments in these sentences. To begin with, the part from "alter ego" onward should simply be cut out, because it has no sound foundation. "Side" does not mean or imply "alter ego," even in English. And Hebrew does not necessarily match either Arabic or English. The data from biblical Hebrew provide no firm basis for such loose associations.

The Hebrew word in question, *tsela'*, does possess the two meanings, "rib" and "side." The meaning "rib" occurs in the Old Testament only in Genesis 2:21-22, while elsewhere we find the "side" of the ark (Ex. 25:12), the side of the tabernacle (Ex. 26:20), and the sides of the altar (Ex. 27:7). We also find the word used to refer to side chambers or some other adjoining part of the temple (1 Kings 6:5, 6; Ezek. 41:5), to refer to boards (rib-like supports?) of the temple wall (1 Kings 6:15, 16), and to refer to the side (or ridge?) of a hill (2 Sam. 16:13).[11]

Victor Hamilton's commentary expresses doubts as to whether the meaning "rib" is appropriate in Genesis 2:21-22, since the meaning "rib" does not occur anywhere else in the Old Testament.[12] Such a meaning does, however, occur in later rabbinic Hebrew when referring to animals' ribs.[13] Moreover,

---

[10] Ibid. In the original French, Blocher has "moitié" but also provides the English expression "better half."
[11] Francis Brown, S. R. Driver, and C. A. Briggs, eds., *A Hebrew and English Lexicon of the Old Testament* (Oxford: Oxford University, 1953), 854; Ludwig Koehler and Walter Baumgartner, *The Hebrew and Aramaic Lexicon of the Old Testament*, 5 vols. (Leiden/New York/Köln: Brill, 1996), 3:1030.
[12] Victor P. Hamilton, *The Book of Genesis: Chapters 1–17,* New International Commentary on the Old Testament (Grand Rapids, Mich.: Eerdmans, 1990), 178.
[13] Marcus Jastrow, *A Dictionary of the Targumim, the Talmud Babli and Yerushalmi, and the Midrashic Literature* (New York: Pardes, 1950).

the other possible meaning, the meaning "side," does not fit Genesis 2:21-22, where God "took one of his ribs/sides and closed up its place with flesh." This description requires something smaller than a whole side. Hence, the word means "rib" here, just as it does in later Hebrew. In fact, it is not at all certain that the Hebrew word ever has the meaning "side" *in the narrow context where it designates a bodily part.* All the extant cases occurring in this context have the meaning "rib." The word has the meaning "side" when it applies to a building or to a piece of furniture.

We should note also that none of the biblical passages in question contains any hint of an established metaphorical or figurative usage—nothing like Blocher's "better half." Theoretically, a figurative meaning is possible; but there is no hard linguistic evidence for it, and if the meaning of the passage is figurative, the figure almost certainly belongs to the passage as a whole, not to the term "rib" in isolation.

The attractiveness of a figurative interpretation really arises from theological considerations. Blocher quotes Matthew Henry:

> God did not make the woman 'out of his head to rule over him, nor out of his feet to be trampled upon by him, but out of his side to be equal with him, under his arm to be protected, and near his heart to be beloved'.[14]

Theologically, Henry describes woman's role acceptably and colorfully, and Genesis 2 may indeed suggest such things. But the theological conclusions do not undermine the physicality of the original picture. Just as human sexual intercourse signifies full personal communion, not merely physical union, so God's mode of creation contains significations about the nature of the woman so created, but neither observation undercuts the reality of the physical aspect. In fact, one might even wonder whether some people take flight from the physical into a wholly figurative interpretation due to Platonic embarrassment with the physical, as if it were something unworthy of God's direct involvement, or something irrelevant to understanding the real core of human personality.

I conclude, then, that Genesis 2:21-22, though it ends in mystery, does indicate something about the means through which God made Eve. He did use natural means, namely the deep sleep and the rib. They were not the normal means that we see operative in reproduction today.

---

[14] Blocher, *In the Beginning,* 99-100, quoting from Matthew Henry, *Commentary on Holy Scripture* (1708–1710).

INITIAL CREATION OF KINDS

Eve, the first woman, is like no other woman, and certainly not like an animal. Her creation is unique. But we have already seen analogical parallels between human beings and animals and plants. So we need to raise the question whether the creation of the first goat and the first donkey was unique in an analogous way. Did God operate without ordinary means, or did he use ordinary means but in an unusual way that we cannot anticipate and may not fathom? We do not know. Certainly nothing in Genesis precludes unusual means.

But then mainstream evolutionists cannot rightly say beforehand that the processes involved in the creation of plants and animals are "natural" in the sense of being fully intelligible in the light of the ordinary processes of reproduction. When evolutionists bar exceptions *beforehand,* they act with dogmatism for which they can give no rational ground. They have only a belief in materialism, or a belief that other possibilities are impossible, or a lack of awareness of prior assumptions in the scientific tradition in which they float along.

The Bible opens the possibility that other cases may, like Eve's, involve unusual processes. But can we say more? Does the Bible give us positive information about how God created various kinds of plants and animals?

ALTERNATIVE VIEWS ABOUT THE ORIGIN OF DIFFERENT KINDS

Christians looking at Genesis 1 have developed three different views of the origin of plants and animals. *Fiat creationism* says that God created each distinct kind in a moment, and that the entire process of creation of kinds took place over a comparatively short period (typically, six 24-hour days). *Progressive creationism* allows that the acts of creation may be spread over a period of millions of years, but the distinct kinds still came into being through distinct special acts of creation. A third view maintains that God used the normal means of reproduction over millions of years to bring out gradual changes that led to the existing species. This final view is usually called *theistic evolution.*[15] Theistic evolution would agree almost completely with the overall factual history of life that mainstream evolutionists postulate. Theistic evolutionists might say that mainstream evolutionists have their facts

---

[15] For a discussion of these views, see Bernard Ramm, *The Christian View of Science and Scripture* (Grand Rapids, Mich.: Eerdmans, 1954), 253-293.

right, but that the hand of God supervised the entire process of gradual change in forms of life over the millennia.

In the minds of many, the word "evolution" has now become closely associated with the anti-theistic worldview of evolutionary naturalism. "Theistic evolution" therefore seems to be a contradiction in terms. We need a better label, perhaps "divinely controlled gradual production of kinds of life." However, "theistic evolution" is the traditional label, so I will continue to use it, with the understanding that one should not import secularism into the label just because of the word "evolution." "Theistic evolution" is simply a convenient label for the position that thinks that God consistently used ordinary means during the past. Some theistic evolutionists would allow that God's creation of Adam and Eve may have been exceptional. This allowance for exceptions seems to me wise, not only because of the particularities that the Bible gives in describing the creation of Eve, but also because the transcendence of God implies that he has power to act exceptionally, and we as creatures do not know beforehand exactly when he may do so.

The interesting debate, then, concerns not the mere abstract possibility of what God might do, but what he is likely to have done in most cases, given the testimony of Scripture and evidence that scientists can explore.

If creation took place during six 24-hour days, or during any reasonably short period, there was not enough time to bring about the different kinds of life by normal reproductive variation. Conceivably, God could have greatly speeded up the process that theistic evolutionists depict. But it seems unlikely. Therefore, the 24-hour-day view leads most people quickly to adopt fiat creation of life. We then still have to deal with fossil evidence, and that leads us back into the discussion of flood geology and mature creation. The mature creation view can say that the fossils belong to "ideal time," but the question still confronts the scientist as to how best to picture the development within ideal time, which shows processes analogous to those within real time. So, even in a situation with ideal time, we are left with a debate between progressive creation and theistic evolution.

One argument against theistic evolution observes that Genesis 1 pictures creation in a startlingly simple way. God spoke, and it happened. The origin of plants, the origin of animals, and the origin of everything else came about by the mere utterance of God's word. For example, Genesis 1 mentions no means through which God brought into existence the sun, the moon, or the stars. So we must conclude that there *were* no means.

But such reasoning is fallacious. Absence of *mention* does not imply absence of *existence*. For example, Exodus 15 and Psalm 106:9, in describing the exodus from Egypt, mention no created means used in dividing the waters. "He rebuked the Red Sea, and it became dry" (Ps. 106:9); "At the blast of your nostrils the waters piled up" (Ex. 15:8). But Exodus 14:21 mentions "a strong east wind." The mere silence about the wind in one passage does not eliminate the possibility that another passage may mention the wind. The silence about means allows us more effectively to concentrate on the main point: that God did it. Whether he used one particular means, or another, or no means at all, is completely secondary. So it is with Genesis 1. Genesis 1 gives us the main point, that God did it. It does not tell us how. Genesis 1:26-28 also tells us that God created man but does not add the detail given in Genesis 2:7, that he used an ordinary means, namely dust, in doing so.[16]

---

[16] In favor of fiat creation, J. Ligon Duncan and David W. Hall approvingly cite Herman Witsius:

> . . . for since they [the prophets and God Himself] expressly declare, that God stretcheth forth the heavens ALONE, they exclude every other cause of every sort; and since it added that God spreadeth abroad the earth BY HIMSELF, we are taught that this is an *immediate* act, in which no cause, not even one that is instrumental, and that operates by power derived from another, has any place (Herman Witsius, *Sacred Dissertations on What Is Commonly Called the Apostles' Creed* [reprint; Escondido, Calif.: den Dulk Christian Foundation, 1993], 198; cited with some variations by J. Ligon Duncan III and David W. Hall, "The 24-Hour View," in David G. Hagopian, ed., *The Genesis Debate: Three Views on the Days of Creation* [Mission Viejo, Calif.: Crux, 2001], 59-60).

The Scripture in question comes from Isaiah 44:24. Witsius maintains that the addition of the words "alone" and "by Himself" ("by myself" in KJV) exclude all secondary causes. Witsius does not intend to exclude the use of previously available materials that God himself has made (196; see Gen. 1:6-10).

But there is an alternative explanation for Isaiah 44:24 (and its companion, Job 9:8). A similar Hebrew expression for "alone" (Hebrew *lbad* with pronominal suffix) is used elsewhere in describing God's wonders. Psalm 136:4 says, "to him who *alone* does great wonders, . . ." The first "wonder" the psalm then describes is the making of the heavens (verse 5), and then the spreading of the earth (verse 6). It also includes the dividing of the waters of the Red Sea (verse 13), where we have already seen that God used "a strong east wind" as a secondary cause (Ex. 14:21). In context, "alone" does not in fact exclude all secondary causation but affirms that God alone is God, and that he alone has power to do these wonders, in contrast to idols and in contrast to the puny abilities of human beings.

Psalm 72:18 speaks in a similar way: "Blessed be the LORD, the God of Israel, who *alone* does wondrous things." The immediate context in the psalm does not obviously specify any particular "wondrous things." It invites us to think broadly of all the wondrous things that God does—in creation, in miracles, and in providential care—in a manner like the wide enumeration in Psalm 136. Earlier on, Psalm 72 mentions particular mercies toward the needy and the poor (verses 12-14). Should these be included among the "wonders"?

Moreover, the concern to recognize and serve the Lord *alone* occurs in a number of places: "For you are great and do wondrous things; you *alone* are God" (Ps. 86:10; see also Deut. 4:35; 1 Sam. 7:3, 4; Neh. 9:6; Ps. 83:18; Isa. 2:11, 17; 37:16, 20). These verses confirm that, in the culture of the Israelites, the real danger was not a temptation to be fascinated by secondary causes, but to cease to trust God and to put one's trust in false gods or in human ability, whether one's own or someone else's (Ps. 146:3-5). Thus, Isaiah 44:24 proclaims God's unique power but does not speak one way or the other about whether God used any secondary causes.

Herman Bavinck confirms the propriety of this kind of language by using "by himself" in describing *providence:*

> Just as he created the world by himself, so he also preserves and governs it by himself. Although God works through secondary causes, this is not to be interpreted, in the manner of Deism, to mean that they come in between God and the effects with their consequences and separate these from him. "God's immediate provision over everything extends to the exemplar of the order" (Bavinck, *In the Beginning: Foundations of Creation Theology* [Grand Rapids, Mich.: Baker, 1999], 250; Bavinck cites Thomas Aquinas, *Summa theologicae* 1 Q 22, Art. 3; Q 103, Art. 6; Q 103, Art. 2; and *Summa Contra Gentiles*, 3:76ff.).

I conclude, then, that Genesis 1 harmonizes with fiat creation. Yes, God could have created each kind of animal instantly, by his word. But it also harmonizes with theistic evolution, because it does not teach that God used no means. Rather, it is silent about means in order to concentrate on the main point.

Other people have rejected theistic evolution on the basis of the language in Genesis 1 about kinds. Each kind of plant or animal reproduces according to its kind. That pronouncement suggests to them that each kind is permanently fixed by the word of God, and could never gradually evolve into another kind. But here again we must be cautious about how we read Genesis 1. As modern people, interested in science, we come to Genesis 1 with scientific questions about evolution already in mind. But Genesis 1 originally addressed Israelite readers, who had no such questions. They knew that oat seeds lead to oat plants, olive seeds lead to olive trees, and goats give birth to goats. Genesis 1 showed them that God had established this order, and that they could depend on it. As usual, Genesis 1 is addressing the "unlearned" (both premodern and modern man), and speaks to ordinary experience rather than to the technicalities that arise in advanced science. It says, in effect, that you can count on the fixity of kinds when you are dealing with the next generation, and the generation after that. It does not tell us what may or may not happen over millions of years of generations. Maybe there might be a gradual drift, or a splitting apart of one species into two with somewhat different characteristics and habitats. Or maybe not. Maybe things are very fixed, no matter how many generations one travels into the future. The Bible really does not say one way or the other.

As in many other areas, the Bible does not directly answer every technical question that we may have. It gives us the big picture, telling us about God and man and sin. And it invites mankind, as part of the exercise of dominion and the exploration of God's wisdom, to go out and look. Find out how God governs the world in detail. "It is the glory of God to conceal things, but the glory of kings is to search things out" (Prov. 25:2).

For instance, find out what the limits of breeding are. Dog breeding leads to nothing but dogs; and if we inbreed too much, the progeny may be less healthy, more delicate, and may show more unwanted side-effects. We know this because we have done it. We might have guessed beforehand, but a guess is not as good as a concrete result, partly because God is transcendent and our guesses do not always correspond to his word.

Or go and look at fossils. Centuries before, when fossils came to human attention, people were not sure what they were looking at. Was this a remnant from a long-dead animal, or was it simply a strange pattern in a rock? Could we have guessed beforehand that God created other kinds of plants and animals, that are now extinct?[17] And what kinds of patterns do we find in these extinct animals, that show similarities and differences with the kinds alive today? And how long ago did they live? And—the current controversial question—how did God bring into existence the whole kind? By what means, or by no means at all? Does the fossil record suggest that one sort of answer is more probable than another?

PROCEEDING WITH IMPERFECT KNOWLEDGE

Christians occupy a variety of positions in their reading of Genesis 1–2 and the conclusions they may draw from it with respect to science and evolution. We must live with the fact that any of our interpretations are fallible in principle. But we are also bound to act on the basis of what we believe Genesis 1–2 teaches. I have indicated how I understand Genesis 1–2, in expressing my preference for an analogical day approach. Given that approach, Genesis 1–2 does not specify a particular clock-time length for the totality of the acts of creation. And, as I have argued above, neither does it give us much detail about means that God may or may not have used in creating the plants and animals. That leaves open *any* of the three main options: fiat creationism, progressive creationism, and theistic evolution (provided that we allow for exceptions). We may tentatively decide for one of these views only by examining evidence outside Scripture, that is, evidence deriving from general revelation and the world that God rules.

Nowadays, the evidence in the areas of biology and historical geology is massive. Whole books are devoted to it, arguing in favor of one of the three views, or in favor of an evolutionary view without the benefit of specifically *theistic* evolution.[18] Because of the massiveness of the evidence, I cannot get into all the details here. But we may set the tone for wise evaluation. In evaluating the evidence, a Christian worldview should have its guiding role. We know that worldviews have an influence on the character of science, partly through influencing one's conception of scientific law. So one must sift

---

[17] In a mature creation approach, the fossils may bring us into ideal time, but the same questions remain when we try to understand the patterns of evidence in ideal time.

[18] As an introduction, see Michael Denton, *Evolution: A Theory in Crisis* (Bethesda, Md.: Adler & Adler, 1985); Philip E. Johnson, *Darwin on Trial* (Downers Grove, Ill.: InterVarsity Press, 1991); and for specialized focus on intelligent design and irreducible complexity, Michael Behe, *Darwin's Black Box: The Biochemical Challenge to Evolution* (New York: Free Press, 1996); William A. Dembski, *No Free Lunch: Why Specified Complexity Cannot Be Purchased Without Intelligence* (Lanham/Boulder/New York/Oxford: Rowman & Littlefield, 2002). For defense of gapless macroevolution, see, for example, Gould, *Structure of Evolutionary Theory*.

through evidence critically. One must realize that evolutionary naturalism confuses the picture, by prejudicing those who are ideologically committed to it. And, among the opponents of naturalism, it can result in a kind of reverse prejudice against anything to do with evolution—including theistic evolution.

EVALUATING MACROEVOLUTION

In detail, the dispute focuses mostly on *macroevolution,* that is, the hypothesis that major differences between kinds of plants and animals were bridged in the past through normal, gradual processes of reproduction and selection through many generations. Microevolution (small variations within a species) is not in dispute. And evolutionary naturalism ought not to be merely disputed but vigorously rejected.

So what about macroevolution? The fossil record is piecemeal, with gaps between major kinds. People already committed to macroevolution, either on philosophical grounds or because it has been accepted by the mainstream of scientists, fill in the gaps by postulating that there were intermediate forms, or some gradualist explanation. We should be suspicious, because the current atmosphere, in the general culture and within the subculture of scientists, includes the assumption either that there are absolutely no exceptions (closed regularity) or that no exceptions ought to be allowed as a matter of "scientific principle" (see the discussion of methodological naturalism in the following chapter). The assumptions predetermine the answer.

On the other hand, let us not be too quick to embrace the alternative (some kind of progressive creationism) without looking to see whether it has weaknesses of its own. Sometimes people operate here with an improper dualism between primary and secondary causes, so that one excludes the other. So ordinary reproduction (with secondary causes) does not involve God, and only an extraordinary act of creation (with no secondary causes) shows his existence, care, and involvement. This view has allowed unbiblical assumptions about secondary causation. And these assumptions put pressure on people not to look for secondary causes at all. So the accusation comes from the defenders of evolution that we have given up too early on looking for an explanation. To say God did it and stop there does not give us a scientific explanation but instead brings an end to science. There is a grain of truth here. But it is only a half-truth, because we need not *stop* with saying that God did it. Maybe there are ordinary secondary causes through which he did it. And even if there are not, God has reasons for what he does, and we may be able to discern a pattern that gives us some understanding of his reasons.

From a Christian worldview, we should affirm that, in principle, God could create animals either instantaneously or gradually, as he chooses. He could use a preexisting life-form as his starting point, just as he used Adam's rib to create Eve. Whether he used extraordinary or ordinary means remains a secondary issue. We should avoid putting pressure on science artificially to prefer the extraordinary. But we should also avoid locking in the assumption that we must *exclude* the extraordinary. In fact, given the current atmosphere in science that wants absolutely to forbid the extraordinary, some pressure in the other direction is appropriate!

19

ORIGIN OF NEW KINDS OF LIFE:

INTELLIGENT DESIGN

How did new kinds of living things originate? Did they come into being by gradual evolution or by a sudden act of direct creation by God? In considering these questions, we need to assess the movement called *intelligent design*,[1] which uses the idea of *irreducible complexity*.

IRREDUCIBLE COMPLEXITY

Briefly, irreducible complexity describes a system with many coordinated parts, all of which are necessary for the function of the system as a whole.[2] Michael Behe offers as an illustration the ordinary spring mouse trap. The mouse trap needs all five parts, in a coordinated arrangement, or it will catch no mice (it has no effective function). He then offers examples of cellular

[1] The movement of intelligent design has now produced quite a few books. One of the early, groundbreaking books was Phillip E. Johnson, *Darwin on Trial* (Downers Grove, Ill.: InterVarsity Press, 1991). See also Johnson, *Evolution as Dogma: The Establishment of Naturalism* (Dallas: Haughton, 1990); Michael Behe, *Darwin's Black Box: The Biochemical Challenge to Evolution* (New York: Free Press, 1996); and William A. Dembski, *No Free Lunch: Why Specified Complexity Cannot Be Purchased Without Intelligence* (Lanham/Boulder/New York/Oxford: Rowman & Littlefield, 2002); William A. Dembski, ed., *Mere Creation: Science, Faith and Intelligent Design* (Downers Grove, Ill.: InterVarsity Press, 1998); William A. Dembski, *The Design Revolution: Answering the Toughest Questions About Intelligent Design* (Downers Grove, Ill.: InterVarsity Press, 2004). For a historical account, see Thomas Woodward, *Doubts About Darwin: A History of Intelligent Design* (Grand Rapids, Mich.: Baker, 2003).

[2] See Behe, *Darwin's Black Box*. Dembski (*No Free Lunch*) introduces the more general idea of "complex specified information" or "specified complexity." Behe's concept of irreducible complexity deals specifically with biological machines. Dembski's concept is intended to include biological machines but also explores the issue of design much more broadly, including the detection of intelligent design in texts, archaeological artifacts, criminological investigations, and possible signals from extraterrestrial civilizations.

The two conceptions, Behe's and Dembski's, should not be confused. It seems to me that Dembski's concept of complex specified information is too broad for my purpose, inasmuch as complex specified information would potentially include not only Behe's irreducibly complex biological machines but also *reducibly* complex biological systems that at least conceivably could have been put together "gradualistically," through a series of steps each of which would yield increasing functionality (see, e.g., Dembski's own remarks to this effect in *No Free Lunch,* 212, 343ff.). Hence, Dembski's concept does not frame the question in a way that focuses on the tenability of Darwinian gradualism.

machinery, such as the bacterial flagellum, with similar coordination of parts. These systems are *complex,* in that they involve a number of coordinated parts. And they are *irreducible,* in the sense that they cannot be reduced to a simpler system, by eliminating one or more of the parts, and still perform their intended function *at all.*

Instances of irreducible complexity produce a problem for Darwinian gradualism. Darwinian gradualism postulates that the present order of living things originated over millions of years from a single original proto-cell (common descent). In addition, it postulates that the changes from one generation to another were gradual,[3] and that the existing differentiations came about through selective death of all but the "fittest" in any one generation.

Darwinian gradualism might conceivably produce a complex machine gradually, if one part produces some benefit, and adding a second part produces a greater benefit, and so on. Over a period of time, selecting "the fittest" gradually weeds out everything but a system with all its parts in place. But a system with *irreducible* complexity does not allow a gradual build-up, because the system does not function at all until all the parts are both present and in place, ready to perform cooperatively.

An intelligent designer, by contrast, can construct an irreducibly complex system, because he can assemble the parts one by one by intelligent selection, knowing the end-product to which he is heading.

So how did the first bacterial flagellum come to be? We know that God brought it about, but how? We do not know. We may not ever know, because the events took place so long ago, and because fossils do not leave behind detailed molecular evidence. Everyone, then, has no more than a guess.

But this example nevertheless remains valuable, because it brings out the influence of ideology on science. *Naturalistic* ideology wants to exclude from the beginning the possibility that the flagellum was put together by intelligent design. The label usually given is *methodological naturalism,* which we need to discuss.

---

[3] George Gaylord Simpson, "Uniformitarianism: An Inquiry into Principle, Theory, and Method in Geohistory and Biohistory," in M. K. Kecht and W. C. Steere, eds., *Essays in Evolution and Genetics in Honor of Theodosius Dobzhansky* (New York: Appleton-Century-Crofts, 1970), 72-81. Simpson notes that a small mutation may on occasion result in large somatic effects; but most of these are lethal (80). Gradualism allows for such large-scale effects but still postulates that they arise from small differences in initial conditions at an earlier time (say, when a single mutation occurred).

THE ATMOSPHERE OF SCIENCE

First we need to consider more broadly the atmosphere of assumptions that weave their way into science.

Science pursues truth about the physical world, and explores its lawful regularities. But science also involves the participation of human beings, as individuals and as groups, who hand on an atmosphere and an attitude toward the business of science. The conception of science is not fixed once-for-all by its task, but may change according to the dominant worldview within which scientists work.[4] And change has come over the centuries from Copernicus to now.

Many of the early scientists were Christian believers, and those whose personal religious views deviated from orthodox Christianity still lived within an atmosphere where it was natural to think of scientific laws as the product of a wise, rational Creator. They sometimes talked about God even within their scientific discussions.

We now see a situation where scientists who are Christians, Jews, agnostics, or atheists work together within many specialties, but where they have mostly stopped bringing God into the discussion. And this cessation of open discussion can also affect the way in which one tries to help science forward. One ceases not only to talk about God, but even to think about God as the origin of laws. One thinks of the laws as impersonal.

METHODOLOGICAL NATURALISM AS A GUIDE FOR SCIENCE

People have a term for this situation, namely *methodological naturalism.* Methodological naturalism says roughly that modern science does conduct itself and should continue to conduct itself with the assumption that in the areas that it investigates, all the particular events and all the general patterns take place according to general laws that for practical purposes can be regarded as impersonal; and even if there are some exceptions, these are best ignored for the sake of getting on with the task of science.

Methodological naturalism can be converted in some people's minds into *ontological* or *metaphysical naturalism,* the view that there is no personal God and that the physical domain is all that there is. For philosophical and religious reasons, some people use methodological naturalism as a stepping-

---

[4] Thomas S. Kuhn, *The Structure of Scientific Revolutions,* 2nd ed. (Chicago: University of Chicago Press, 1970), offers a pertinent exploration of the social atmosphere in which science carries on. See also Richard C. Lewontin, *Biology as Ideology: The Doctrine of DNA* (New York: HarperCollins, 1993).

stone toward ontological naturalism. But logically the two are distinct. Methodological naturalism more modestly proposes a practical restriction on the kind of hypotheses that scientists may consider, based partly on the pragmatic argument that the restriction will help science make progress rather than getting caught in fruitless byways. A number of people maintain that science *by definition* has a firm commitment to excluding the supernatural.[5]

What shall we say about methodological naturalism? We first need to acknowledge that various conceptions of methodological naturalism may exist, and that some people might not agree with my definition above. It is not easy to pin down what people mean by the term. To illustrate the difficulty, let us consider Robert T. Pennock's discussion.[6] Pennock introduces methodological naturalism first by observing that it should be distinguished from ontological naturalism. He then continues:

> The methodological naturalist does not make a commitment directly to a picture of what exists in the world [in contrast to the ontological naturalist, who does do this], but rather to a set of methods as a reliable way to find out about the world—typically the methods of the natural sciences, and perhaps extensions that are continuous with them—and indirectly to what those methods discover. An important feature of science is that its conclusions are defeasible on the basis of new evidence, so whatever tentative substantive claims the methodological naturalist makes are always open to revision or abandonment on the basis of new, countervailing evidence. Because the base commitment of a methodological naturalist is to a mode of investigation that is good for finding out about the empirical world, even the specific methods themselves are open to change and improvement; science might adopt promising new methods and refine existing ones if doing so would provide better evidential warrant.[7]

One can find in this description a good deal that fits well into a Christian worldview, provided one is allowed to interpret it in one's own way. As a whole the description sets a pragmatic, practical tone. Whatever works, one

---

[5] "[A]ny reliance on a supernatural force, a Creator intervening in a natural world by supernatural processes, is necessarily not science" (Michael Ruse, "Witness Testimony Sheet, McLean v. Arkansas" in *But Is It Science?* [Buffalo, N.Y.: Prometheus, 1998], 300-301). "By definition, science cannot consider supernatural explanations. . . . So by definition, if an individual is attempting to explain some aspect of the natural world using science he or she must act as if there were no supernatural forces operating on it" (Eugenie Scott, "Creationism, Ideology, and Science," *Annals of the NY Academy of Science* 775 [June 24, 1996]). I was alerted to these quotes by Del Ratzsch.

[6] Robert T. Pennock, *Tower of Babel: The Evidence Against the New Creationism* (Cambridge, Mass./London: MIT Press, 1999), 189-196.

[7] Ibid., 191.

adopts. It vigorously affirms the tentativeness of science and its ability to adjust to new evidence, both of which harmonize with a Christian worldview. But it is in danger of being so loose a definition that it excludes very little.

In the book from which this passage comes, Pennock is criticizing the proponents of intelligent design. But the passage in question might easily allow research based on intelligent design. Intelligent design as a new addition has only to show that it introduces "extensions that are continuous with" current methods of science. But what counts as "continuous"? Science might adopt "promising new methods," according to Pennock, but what counts as "promising"? Biases in favor of an impersonal conception of law can easily enter under the apparently innocent umbrella of current scientific practice, to which one then adds the condition that the new must be continuous with this kind of science, and must be promising.

Pennock argues later on that intelligent design can never become fruitful, because it merely stops all attempts at naturalistic explanation.[8] That is, if one says that God created the flagellum through a special supernatural act, it brings an end to scientific exploration. The origin of the flagellum remains forever beyond the bounds of science. But this is not necessarily how proponents of intelligent design understand their proposals; Dembski proposes ways in which design might undergird a positive research program.[9] Has Pennock simply failed to imagine how a positive development of intelligent design might be scientifically fruitful?

A little later in his discussion Pennock becomes more specific in his questioning: "Does science put forward the methodological principle not to appeal to supernatural powers or divine agency simply on authority?"[10] The issue is whether one appeals to supernatural or divine agency. Pennock believes that in science one should not resort to such an appeal. At this point Pennock is influenced by earlier parts of his book, where he tends to lump together all forms of "creationism" and to see intelligent design as a new but minor variation on an old theme. But "intelligent design" in fact does not mean "designed by God." It means designed by an intelligence, whether the intelligence is human or extraterrestrial or angelic or divine. Francis Crick, one of the discoverers of

---

[8] Ibid., 194-197.

[9] See Dembski, No Free Lunch, 311-379. In fairness to Pennock, one should note that Dembski's 2002 book was not available when Pennock wrote. The intelligent design movement is still developing, and Pennock could not easily anticipate the positive directions that it might suggest for research. Nevertheless, even in 1996 Michael Behe quite distinctly addressed Pennock's concern by distinguishing between the investigation of repeated events, where one might safely assume regularity, and once-for-all events, like the origin of the first cell, that might involve exceptions to familiar regularities (Behe, Darwin's Black Box, 241-243; see Woodward, Doubts About Darwin, 166-170).

[10] Pennock, Tower of Babel, 194.

the structure of DNA, actually proposed that life was initially implanted on the earth by aliens, precisely because he could not see how it could have come about without intelligent intervention.[11] Such a view involved intelligent design but is nevertheless completely consistent with ontological naturalism. To be sure, the present-day advocates of intelligent design believe that God was the designer in question. But their proposal does not require such a specific belief. It poses the question more broadly, in terms of "intelligence." Hence, Pennock cannot avoid the question of whether life on earth is the product of intelligent design merely by excluding the supernatural.

EXCLUDE THE SUPERNATURAL?

But let us consider the issue of the supernatural. Pennock argues that science must exclude the supernatural and the divine, because its observations depend on "lawful regularity":

> Lawful regularity is at the very heart of the naturalistic worldview and to say that some power is supernatural is, by definition, to say that it can violate natural laws. So, when Johnson [Phillip E. Johnson, a proponent of intelligent design] argues that science should allow in supernatural powers and intelligences he is in effect saying that it should allow beings that are above the law (a rather strange position for a lawyer to take). But without the constraint of lawful regularity, inductive evidential inference cannot get off the ground. Controlled, repeatable experimentation, for example, . . . would not be possible without the methodological assumption that supernatural entities do not intervene to negate lawful natural regularities.[12]

Curiously, Pennock uses the expression "the naturalistic worldview," not "naturalistic methodology." The expression "naturalistic worldview" sounds as if it entails ontological naturalism. In that case, Pennock tacitly admits that one must have ontological naturalism to support methodological naturalism in science. If it is not a pure ontological naturalism that emphatically denies the existence of the supernatural, one must at least have a practical naturalism that emphatically denies the active influence of the supernatural. But let us suppose that this is just a slip of the pen.

The crucial points come later in the quotation. In this argument Pennock brings in questionable assumptions about the supernatural and the natural

---

[11] Francis Crick and Leslie E. Orgel, "Directed Panspermia," *Icarus* 19 (1973): 341-346.
[12] Pennock, *Tower of Babel*, 195.

that guarantee his conclusions. He says that "by definition" the supernatural "can violate natural laws." In so doing he does not reckon with a genuinely Christian worldview. In a Christian worldview, as we have seen, "natural laws" are shorthand for God's word, which is never violated. Exceptions to regularities that human beings observe all have a rational purpose within the plan of God, and all conform to his word.

Pennock also supposes that if we allow exceptions, "inductive evidential inference cannot get off the ground." On the contrary, inductive evidential inference is based on the faithfulness of God as manifested in his word (remember Gen. 8:22). Pennock may be thinking that if we allow exceptions, they must be purely irrational exceptions, and that the whole of the supernatural must be purely irrational, so that it would destroy inference. If so, he is not taking into account the rationality of God that is constantly involved in his actions.

One must not be too hard on Pennock. It may be that he is partly responding to theists who have wrongly assumed a dichotomy between God's action and physical causation.[13] He is also partly right, namely, that one must give careful thought to the role of the supernatural. Depending on how the supernatural is understood, it may or may not bring a premature end to the attempt to understand the way in which a past event came about through immanent physical causes.[14]

Moreover, Pennock is representative of others who have struggled with some of the same issues. In an article that Pennock cites on "uniformitarianism," Stephen Jay Gould reasons similarly. Divine intervention would mean "the suspension of natural laws"; and inductive inference needs to exclude exceptions.[15]

---

[13] In the immediate context of his book, Pennock is responding most explicitly to Johnson, *Evolution as Dogma;* and Johnson, *Darwin on Trial.* But "creationism" as a broader movement lies in the background. Moreover, Johnson's books, because of their focus on the weaknesses of naturalism, have not said much about what an alternative positive theistic approach would look like.

[14] See also Behe, *Darwin's Black Box*, 241-243, who addresses this very issue.

[15] Stephen Jay Gould, "Is Uniformitarianism Necessary?" *American Journal of Science* 263 (March 1965): 223-228:

> He [Lyell, one of the early developers of geology] thus postulated another, very different, type of uniformity that asserted the invariability of natural laws in space and time as a necessary condition to his contention that reference need only be made to observable processes in explaining past changes. The main force of this proposition was to eliminate supernatural explanations of material phenomena; for this uniformity denies divine intervention (the suspension of natural laws) and affirms that elucidation of earth history belongs to the domain of science, not, as Buckland might have preferred, to quasi-theological inquiry suited more for proving God's grace than understanding natural processes . . . (224).
>
> However, the assumption of spatial and temporal invariance of natural laws is by no means unique to geology since it amounts to a warrant for inductive inference which, as Bacon showed nearly four hundred years ago, is the basic mode of reasoning in empirical science. Without assuming this spatial and temporal invariance, we have no basis for extrapolating from the known to the unknown and, therefore, no way of reaching general conclusions from a finite number of observations (226).

SECONDARY CAUSES, AND GOD AS PRIMARY CAUSE

One cannot ascertain all of Pennock's or Gould's assumptions. But for many people this type of reasoning gains its appeal from the assumption that there is only one mode of causality:[16] if an event comes about because of antecedent causes within the visible world, that excludes "the supernatural"; conversely, the supernatural excludes antecedent causes within the physical world. But the Bible contradicts this thinking at a most basic level. God is the Creator, and not merely another finite cause within the world. He is not one being alongside other beings on a common level. God "works *all things* according to the counsel of his will" (Eph. 1:11), not just those things that we currently deem miraculous or inexplicable. "You cause the grass to grow for the livestock" (Ps. 104:14).

The theologians have therefore for centuries distinguished *primary* and

---

One may note that the language about "spatial and temporal invariance" conceals an ambiguity. On one interpretation, it simply reiterates our point (chapter 1) that the law of God is omnipresent (spatially invariant) and eternal (temporally invariant). Gould rightly observes that invariance characterizes science as a whole, not just geology (227). So he appears to be speaking a virtual tautology. But, within a Christian worldview, this kind of invariance would be consistent with God's acting differently in special circumstances, just as a human being's consistent character might lead to exceptional actions in special circumstances. For that matter, a fox with previous experience of being pursued by hunting dogs might act exceptionally when he finds himself pursued once again, in order to try to throw the dogs off the scent. Everything depends on the kind of "invariance" one has in view. In practice, readers are going to take it to mean the kind of invariance that can be postulated using impersonal laws. The discussion thus conceals the difference in conceptuality between a Christian and an atheistic view of scientific law. Gould is right to be suspicious of past centuries, where the postulate of divinely governed catastrophism (first cause) often served as an alternative to explanation through secondary causes. But a triumph for one type of explanation in these cases does not logically lead to its universal triumph, unless one secretly introduces a conception of impersonal law.

George Gaylord Simpson, in a longer article, has space to devote to a more extended and nuanced discussion of uniformitarianism, and rightly zeroes in on the issue of the "preternatural":

Hutton's theory [of geological history] included catastrophic events, but he considered them to be naturalistic and actualistic, that is excluding the miraculous or preternatural and involving only second causes, defined as forces now extant in nature (Simpson, "Uniformitarianism," 48).

Simpson's discussion is quite precise in its expression, "involving only second causes." Hutton, a theist, favored second causes for heuristic reasons, because they promised to provide an explanation beyond the bare fact that God did it. Note the discussion of secondary cause below.

[16] And one may ask whether some people's thinking about intelligent design has in part fallen into the same trap. The *whole* world, not simply those pieces of cellular machinery that *look* designed, has been designed by God. Design does not belong to a piece only because we can find no way to explain it through appeal to current scientific laws. In fact, scientific laws are themselves a prime case of design. Design shows itself not only in a particular case like a bacterial flagellum but in a general law like the conservation of energy. Once we grasp deeply that God rules the entire world, we begin to see that everything testifies to him, and we see everywhere evidence of his design. Unbelief fails to see design, not because of lack of evidence but because unbelief suppresses the truth about God (Rom. 1:18-23), which is crucial in acknowledging the evidence. To be sure, those pieces that look designed and that cannot easily be explained on a naturalistic basis may prove to be particularly useful in apologetic discussion. But one should beware of giving the impression that unbelief is innocent until it confronts such special evidence, such as in the design of the bacterial flagellum.

William Dembski, for one, shows some care in his discussion. He distinguishes clearly between a product that is designed and a product from which we can detect clear *evidence* of design (Dembski, *No Free Lunch*, 23, 114). Dembski is, moreover, justified in exploring the ways in which God's activity of design may be like human activity in design, by virtue of creation in the image of God. But more could be said. A theologian could wish that the ontological distinction between Creator and creature as designers received pointed attention, and that Dembski had pointed out the comprehensive presence of God's design. But one must respect the limited purpose of Dembski's book.

secondary causes.[17] God is the primary cause of the grass growing. Secondary causes include the movements of water and minerals in the soil, the sunshine, and the multitude of chemical and biotic processes taking place within the grass. The two do not exclude one another. God acts and achieves his purposes by means of the secondary causes, which he ordains and controls. He controls the outcomes (specific events) and the means (secondary causes leading to the outcomes). Theologians call this concurrence (Latin, *concursus*), the joint operation of primary and secondary causes.[18]

Using Job 1–2, we may include the operation of angelic beings as well. Job's sons and daughters died because "a great wind came across the wilderness and struck the four corners of the house, and it fell upon the young people, and they are dead" (Job 1:19). The great wind acted as a secondary cause. Job ascribed to God the primary causation: "The LORD gave, and the LORD has taken away; blessed be the name of the LORD" (Job 1:21). The text affirms that Job was right in his words: "In all this Job did not sin or charge God with wrong" (1:22). The book of Job also reveals that Satan had a hand in it: "Behold, all that he [Job] has is in your [Satan's] hand" (1:12). Later, when the Lord gives permission with respect to Job's body, the text explicitly says that "Satan went out from the presence of the LORD and struck Job with loathsome sores . . ." (2:7). Satan, we may say, serves as a tertiary, supernatural cause for Job's sores, alongside God as primary cause and any secondary causes that a doctor might have seen for the sores. At times, then, as many as three different causes stand alongside one another, each on a different level, and none excluding the others.

Likewise we may look at Noah's flood. It clearly has God as its primary cause. God also uses secondary causes at some points, as when the water is used to drown people and animals outside the ark. Perhaps God's primary causation is concurrent at all points with secondary causation, in such a way that we might be able to understand the flood using current scientific laws. But also perhaps not. Perhaps God used unusual means, and acted in a manner at odds with the current regularities. Scientific investigation has reason to hope that it can understand. But it cannot demand that it can understand.

A Christian understanding of both the transcendence and the immanence of the rationality of God influences one's expectations here.[19] Because God's

---

[17] This terminology is useful. But it can be abused to suggest that, because we use a common word "cause," the two kinds of cause exist *on the same level,* which then undermines the whole point of the distinction.
[18] John M. Frame, *The Doctrine of God* (Phillipsburg, N.J.: Presbyterian & Reformed, 2002), 287-288; Herman Bavinck, *In the Beginning: Foundations of Creation Theology* (Grand Rapids, Mich.: Baker, 1999), 229-260, especially 248-256.
[19] On transcendence and immanence, see John M. Frame, *The Doctrine of the Knowledge of God* (Phillipsburg, N.J.: Presbyterian & Reformed, 1987), especially 13-18.

rationality is analogous to ours, we can hope to understand (an implication of God's immanence). On the other hand, because God is transcendent, his rationality transcends ours, and he may surprise us (as in the case of the resurrection of Christ). We should also be influenced by a sense of human finiteness and the need for humility. We cannot keep theology out of the discussion. And neither can Pennock or anyone else, because the transcendence and immanence of law form the very foundation on which the entire edifice of science is built. Pennock uses assumptions about God, law, and the supernatural that may seem to be harmless general assumptions for philosophical reasoning, but they beg the important theological questions about transcendence and immanence.

THEOLOGIES AND WORLDVIEWS

It only remains for us to ask, "Whose theology do we use to determine our concept of God and our concepts of transcendence and immanence?" It can be a theology based on biblical instruction, or it can be a substitute, a counterfeit theology based partly on a vague theism or on scraps borrowed from cultural remnants of Christian influence. Then this might be combined with a doctrine of impersonal law and the complete rationality of law in principle. But underneath the doctrine of impersonal law lies complete irrationality, because it has no way to account for the fact that there is law rather than complete chaos.[20]

We could simplify our task if we could confine ourselves to two simple options: either we allow repeated supernaturalist "interference" with regularities, or we forbid it. Unfortunately, things are not so simple. Science relies on a conception of scientific law and regularity. And there are as many such conceptions of law as there are variations in the conception of God or gods. We confront a multidimensional spectrum of options, including not only variations on classical deism and Spinozan pantheism,[21] but polytheisms, animisms, spiritisms, gnosticisms, and materialisms.

These systems differ in what they think exists; that is, they differ in "ontology." These differences inevitably have their effect on science, because ontology justifies methodology. Animism, for example, frustrates scientific method because the spirits can randomly interfere with experi-

---

[20] The point that God supplies the foundation for rationality is made repeatedly in Cornelius Van Til, *The Defense of the Faith*, 2nd ed. (Philadelphia: Presbyterian & Reformed, 1963); see also John M. Frame, *Apologetics to the Glory of God: An Introduction* (Phillipsburg, N.J.: Presbyterian & Reformed, 1994).

[21] Pennock (*Tower of Babel*, 190, 192) mentions deism and Spinoza but does not pursue the differences between different views.

ments. Science must therefore reject animism *as an ontological option,* not merely as a methodological proposal, in order to get started. Not only animism, but any kind of chaotic or semichaotic ontology, threatens to overwhelm order with chaos, and accordingly has already been rejected in practice by working scientists.[22]

So we may focus on orderly ontologies, that is, worldviews that believe in a regular order open to human rational investigation. This wide collection may roughly be subdivided into two subgroups, *closed regularity* and *open regularity.* Closed regularity allows no exceptions to the operation of general laws, impersonally conceived. Strict ontological materialism is an example of closed regularity. Open regularity allows exceptions, but restricts their occurrence somehow. (Without the restriction, we are back into chaotic or semichaotic ontologies.) Various kinds of theism, for example, might restrict the exceptions by saying that exceptions remain low in overall frequency, and that each exception has a good reason within the mind of the deity (he does not needlessly throw things into confusion every once in awhile just for the fun of it!). The promise of God in Genesis 8:22 gives Christians a basis for being confident about regularity.

Human beings can never know enough to be sure of closed regularity. How can you know that the laws have no exceptions, without exhaustive knowledge or divine revelation? And a system of closed regularity typically excludes the possibility of divine revelation as well. So Pennock must allow for the ontological possibility of open regularity. Methodological naturalism must allow for ontologies of both closed regularity and open regularity, and not prematurely terminate the discussion.

---

[22] Pennock pushes into the background the influence of ontological naturalism on the actual practice of science. He carefully distinguishes ontological naturalism from methodological naturalism in order to champion the latter. But one may doubt how well scientists separate the two in practice. A background of ontological commitments always influences one's judgment about what lines of research to pursue.

For example, if ghosts do not exist, it is fruitless to investigate them; one rather investigates the psychology of people who imagine that ghosts exist. Because Pennock holds firmly to an exclusively methodological principle, he allows that ghosts may exist:

> This is not to say, however, that things we now think of as supernatural necessarily are so. It could turn out, for example, that ghosts exist but that unlike our fictional view of them, they are subject to natural law. In such a case we would have learned something new about the natural world (which may require revising current theories), and would not have truly found anything supernatural (Pennock, *Tower of Babel,* 389n36).

Pennock conveniently assumes that "our fictional view of [ghosts]" includes immunity from natural law. But one may doubt whether this is accurate. Some people view ghosts as personalities, much like embodied human beings but having gossamer-like appearance and finite powers analogous to those of embodied human beings. They would presumably be subject to many laws (because they are not infinitely powerful), in a manner analogous to human beings. A typical contemporary scientist would oppose grant money for the investigation of ghosts, not because he believes that they are immune to natural law but because he believes they do not exist. Ontological rather than methodological factors dominate. In short, methodology never operates in a vacuum. It justifies itself against the background of ontological assumptions.

Now suppose the scientist confronts an anomaly.[23] Methodological naturalism must treat the anomaly *as if* it were not an exception but conformed to general laws.

Pennock reasons that this is the only sensible route to take, because otherwise one gives up too quickly the task of trying to understand rationally. One tries to bring the anomaly under the power of known laws or extensions of them or modifications of them. Yes, there is a good deal of sense here. But what if the anomalies accumulate?

Michael Behe accumulates examples of "irreducible complexity" in microbiology, examples that seem to be beyond the reach of Darwinian gradual selection process.[24] One then asks what science should do. Should it insist that the examples of complexity be explicated wholly from already known physical laws? Or should it allow an explanation in terms of design? And if we allow design, is it only design from extraterrestrials, or do we permit design by God or angels?

If we are scientists, dilemmas confront us. Suppose we give the first answer, namely, that explanation can take place only within the framework of known physical laws. Either the true explanation *must* be found in this way, or not. If we affirm the "must," we are tacitly affirming closed regularity. We think we already know that irreducible complexity is actually reducible. We think we know that there are no real exceptions to existing laws. We thus end with ontological naturalism. And we also exclude the possibility of extraterrestrial intelligences or other kinds of explanations. This end is not only dogmatic; it is also contrary to the tentativeness of science and its customary willingness to acknowledge its own limitations.

So perhaps the true explanation of irreducible complexity lies outside of what we can find with methodological naturalism. But just the same, we propose to pursue methodological naturalism, that is, an explanation in terms of secondary causes. If that proves to be a correct explanation, we have gained understanding. So far, so good. But what if we come up with no satisfying explanation? Do we automatically disallow the possibility that the true explanation lies elsewhere? Do we pursue methodological naturalism to the bitter end, even though it does not always lead to the true explanation? That answer is clearly unsatisfactory, because it threatens to convert science into an artificial game. We are "game-playing" at understanding the world.

---

[23] On the key roles of anomalies in normal science and scientific revolution, see Kuhn, *Structure of Scientific Revolutions*.

[24] Behe, *Darwin's Black Box*.

It is now only a game, because we know all along that the rules we have adopted may sometimes lead us only to incorrect explanations. Methodological naturalism of this sort devalues science.

So we are left with the second answer to the question above. We should allow an explanation in terms of design. Or perhaps we seek for still another kind of explanation, neither by design nor by Darwinian gradualism. Pennock understandably shrinks from design as an alternative, because he thinks that it spells an end to rational explanation or rational weighing of evidence. But his arguments have succeeded in rejecting only chaotic ontologies, not open regularity (and not extraterrestrials). Moreover, design has its own rationality. In the case of God's design, it may also include secondary causes in addition to the primary cause. So scientific investigation is not at an end.

Scientists deal with anomalies here and there throughout the practice of science. As a practical matter, they cannot take the time to pursue an explanation for every anomaly, or they would constantly find themselves deflected from one minor problem to another. They must temporarily "throw out" most of the anomalies to get on with their business—whether these anomalies represent "real" exceptions to law (open regularity) or not. But when one confronts a whole pattern of anomalies of similar kind, it may be worth looking into. And if those anomalies do not easily succumb to one's current framework, one looks further afield and becomes more venturesome in one's hypotheses. No one can say beforehand just when anomalies might offer a clue to deeper understanding. And no one can say beforehand exactly what *kind* of hypotheses may prove most fruitful.

In the end, an appeal to methodological naturalism will not magically dissolve the challenge of the intelligent design movement. We have already seen the alternatives. (1) Methodological naturalism really conceals an underlying ontological naturalism, which already thinks it knows what kind of world we live in (including the exclusion of extraterrestrials). Or (2) methodological naturalism becomes a rule for game-playing instead of pursuing the truth. Or (3) methodological naturalism falsely claims that it knows beforehand that thinking in terms of design can never lead to greater understanding. Or (4) methodological naturalism is only a rough recipe for what scientists do under ordinary conditions, until they come up against anomalies that fail to harmonize with current naturalistic explanations. But they are free to explore other kinds of hypotheses when dealing with anomalies. In this fourth case, naturalism dissolves itself by admitting that it does not dogmatically exclude explanations outside its current framework of comfort. Or (5) we explain everything by saying that God did it (which is true enough), but then never wondering about *how* he may have done it. This last position Pennock rightly rejects as inadequate for the task of science. But rejecting this position does not lead to rejecting intelligent design in its best form.

In sum, when confronting the challenge of the intelligent design movement, methodological naturalism decomposes into various alternatives, none of which offers a sound basis for excluding the hypothesis of design. As we have seen, scientists understandably show a preference for first considering various kinds of explanation that lie well within the framework of current modes of explanation and current understanding of scientific laws. Scientists want to conduct their current research programs in peace. But when anomalies accumulate, one cannot dogmatically exclude explanations that travel into unfamiliar territory, including the territory of intelligent design. In such a situation, a simple appeal to methodological naturalism does not help the debate. In its original formulation early on in Pennock's book,[25] methodological naturalism is too vague to offer much help; and if one tries to make it less vague, it entrains unfounded metaphysical assumptions that undermine its value.

Moreover, methodological naturalism has always been incoherent, because it has always secretly depended on God to dispel the threat of irrationality, and to govern the world in a way that guarantees the regularities that we observe in scientific law. And yet methodological naturalism is close to the truth, because God invites people made in his image to explore the regularities. God as primary cause does not evaporate the secondary causes. We cannot grant ourselves any divine certainty that God will not make exceptions to the normal course of things, but we do have grounds for exploring the normal course.

A CONTINUING FIGHT

Confronted with the challenge of intelligent design, scientists will fight over alternative hypotheses and explanatory frameworks, just as they have fought during some of the earlier scientific revolutions that Thomas Kuhn catalogues. Sometimes the fights will be vigorous. Such is the way science grows when deeply conflicting explanations compete. In many respects, the fight over intelligent design does not differ so much from earlier fights. But it produces greater tensions due to at least five factors:

(1) Materialist, quasi-materialist, and hedonist worldviews have grown

---

[25] Pennock, *Tower of Babel,* 191, quoted earlier.

in popularity partly on the back of Darwinian macroevolutionary theory, using as their starting point the worldview of evolutionary naturalism (chapter 5). The issues of worldview engage the larger public and engage people's religious commitments either to conventional religions or to modern ideological substitutes for religion. The engagement of the larger public means that, even more than usual, desires to retain or claim power heat up the debates. Money and research grants and livelihoods may be at stake.

(2) The differences in worldviews threaten to split the unity of science, if ontological naturalists within science (closed regularity) come to differ in approach from people who hold to some kind of open regularity.

(3) The differences in worldviews make their effects felt partly through the difference in conception of scientific law. Does human thinking approximate God's personal law? In that case, we must allow that we may find exceptions to our normal expectations. Or are the laws impersonal and absolutely immune to exception? Then the idea of impersonal law has become a God-substitute, a false god. A conflict in this area threatens people's commitment to their god.

(4) Mainstream scientists see the conflict as a recapitulation of earlier struggles between science and religion, in which they think that religion deforms, suppresses, and mutilates science on the basis of ignorant dogmatism. So this fight gets construed not as a fight with fellow scientists who are "well-meaning but misguided," but as a fight against "barbarism."

(5) Intelligent design questions the foundational assumptions of current mainstream science by asking whether the reductionistic program of interpreting biology in terms of chemistry and chemistry in terms of physics and physics in terms of mathematics is adequate to the nature of the world.

RETURNING TO THE FLAGELLUM

We can illustrate the tensions by returning to the design of the flagellum. If one excludes extraterrestrials, the ontological naturalist *must* say that the flagellum came about by evolutionary gradualism, because that is the only thing that his worldview—his ontology—allows. "There must be some gradualist explanation," he says, "and we just have not found it yet." He must say it even though he has no positive evidence concerning this particular case; and he is staring at the negative evidence of irreducible complexity, which suggests that the machinery could not have come about gradually. He is acting on *faith* in his ontology.

The methodological naturalist typically ends up saying that within science we must not ask questions that invoke design. But the flagellum is begging for an explanation. So it becomes easier to see that a methodological naturalism that disallows any exceptions either conceals an underlying ontological naturalism, or is proposing to play a game that bans certain kinds of questions, rather than pursue the evidence wherever it leads.[26]

DESIGN AND CHANCE

So how might the flagellum have come about? A robust Christian theism means we confess that God did it. God created the various kinds of bacteria, and he created the flagella belonging to each kind. But how? The Bible encourages humility, in which we admit that we do not know.

But we can imagine. Let us imagine for a bit, in order to exhibit further the influences of ideology. We can imagine a purely instantaneous, fiat creation in which a whole bacterium came into being in a moment, all of its atoms being created from nothing.

Or did God appear in a theophany, like the pillar of cloud and fire in the wilderness of Sinai, and through the power of the whirling cloud assemble the atoms and molecules into a bacterium in a few seconds? Then, rather than creating extra atoms, did he assemble atoms already created at an earlier point? Here he is using a means, namely the previously created atom.

Or suppose there was no theophany. The onlooker would only see atoms coming together from hither and yon to assemble a complete bacterium within a few seconds. This option is an interesting one, because it could take place within the boundaries of known physical laws. The physical laws do not in themselves specify the prior locations of every atom. They only tell us how the atoms can be expected to behave. The atheistic observer might say

---

[26] Alan Padgett recommends an *interdisciplinary* study in such a case (Padgett, *Science and the Study of God: A Mutuality Model for Theology and Science* [Grand Rapids, Mich.: Eerdmans, 2003], 84). He likens it to a hypothetical case where astronomers discover signs of extraterrestrial intelligence and then call for the help of anthropologists and linguists in analyzing the signs. Likewise, cell researchers might call for interdisciplinary study of signs of intelligent design within a cell.

Yes, such a response sounds reasonable. In dealing with new challenges, the exact boundaries between disciplines matter little. In principle, either an expansion of the bounds of astronomy or biology or an interdisciplinary interaction might work; it depends largely on relative efficiencies. Eventually, there would probably arise a subdiscipline labeled "study of intelligence in solar system X" or "study of intelligent design within the cell" that would draw on a host of resources. But all these are secondary issues. The primary issue is whether we may reasonably expect to detect intelligence at all, and if so, how.

The advocates of intelligent design are saying that much evidence is already in hand, yet for ideological reasons people both within science and outside it are fighting hard *not* to face the evidence. The current reigning atmosphere wants to bury the primary issue, to disallow it with the mantra that it lies "outside science." At the same time, the same atmosphere wants to tell the social scientists and theologians and other interested parties that nothing pertinent to their fields has been discovered within the cell. The reaction is far different than it would be to, say, a discovery of an information-carrying signal from outer space. One therefore suspects that ideology is dominating the scene.

that "by chance" they just "happened" to come together in the right time and place. It is exceedingly unlikely, if one calculates probabilities. On the average it would not take place even once in a trillion universes, in their entire expanse, even if one gives each universe a lifetime of a trillion years. But it does not violate any physical law that the materialist knows.

But we need not take an example even this improbable. Suppose God has already created bacteria without a flagellum. He chooses one species of bacteria. Over centuries of time this species reproduces again and again. At one point, God sees to it that a section of DNA is "accidentally" duplicated, so that the offspring carry two copies of this section of DNA. The second copy, however, does not have a starting section, so that it produces no protein. The nonfunctioning DNA over the generations gradually mutates by "accidental" replacement of single bases. God sees to it that these mutations gradually lead to the full complement of genetic information that will be needed to produce a flagellum. This information includes not only the information for producing the proteins that make up a completed flagellum, but the equivalent of "assembly" instructions to make sure that the proteins come together in the right configuration, all in one place. When everything is ready, God, by a few more mutations, "turns on" the genetic information so that it is used to manufacture proteins and assemble them into the completed flagellum.

This process is thoroughly gradualistic. Any one step in the process does not have that low a probability. All the steps operate in accordance with well-known phenomena that take place in bacterial mutations. Would the typical advocate of macroevolution be satisfied? This process still challenges Darwinian thinking, because typically Darwinism does not allow "designed" or directed gradualism. It allows that bacteria that already have flagella can mindlessly evolve in the direction of better flagella, because the ones with better functioning flagella survive to the next generation. But here the flagellum does not exist until the last step. The individual steps could be viewed as mindless. But the accumulation of so many steps, *before* any advantage in fitness appears, stretches the credibility of a "naturalist" explanation. This kind of scenario effectively illustrates the point being made about irreducible complexity. If the flagellum is irreducibly complex, any scenario leading to its construction involves taking steps beforehand that already anticipate the endpoint.

Most evolutionists, I think, would answer that this kind of scenario should be eliminated from consideration, not because it is literally impossible, but because it is too improbable. If the laws were indeed impersonal, their elimination of the scenario would be reasonable.

To be more precise, we have to distinguish between deterministic and indeterministic laws. Deterministic laws allow virtually certain prediction of a result. "The sun will rise tomorrow."[27] "The trajectory of a marble shot into a vacuum will have parabolic shape, according to Newton's laws of motion."[28] Other laws govern chance events, any one of which remains unpredictable. "If you flip a coin 1,000 times, it will come up heads about half the time." In fact, God's control extends to both types of events, and both types of law.

In our imaginary scenario, the information for constructing a flagellum gradually builds up in total conformity to deterministic laws. Any one mutation conforms to indeterministic laws as well, since the laws cannot by definition predict a single event. But the totality of mutations seems not to conform, since the probability of having all of the events take place is much too low.[29]

REDUNDANCY IN BIOLOGICAL SYSTEMS

We are still welcome to explore possible gradualistic means that might avoid this low probability estimate. Niall Shanks tries this route by looking at redundancy in biological systems.[30] Some biological systems exhibit "redundant complexity." They could lose one part and still continue to function, because the function of that one part is duplicated by an alternate protein or an alternate chemical route. How is this pertinent?

Suppose for simplicity that the bacterial flagellum is composed of distinct parts A, C, E, H, I, M, and N (actually, many more parts than this are needed). When arranged in the proper configuration, they form a functional whole, which we can represent thus: MACHINE. If we remove any one letter from the word MACHINE, it is no longer a correctly spelled word. Likewise, if we remove any one part from the bacterial flagellum, it no longer functions to propel the bacterium. Even if we have every part but one,

---

[27] Though even this "law" has an exception: "unless Christ returns before tomorrow."

[28] We are here ignoring the fact that at a quantum level we may still face an irreducible indeterminacy, which could in theory affect macroscopic events.

[29] One can be more precise about the issue of low probability. Suppose one repeatedly shuffles a deck of 52 cards and then looks at the resulting exact order of cards in the whole deck. Any particular order for the cards has a very small probability, and yet *some* one order will actually occur. What makes the situation with the flagellum different is that the outcome has complex specified information, as discussed in Dembski, *No Free Lunch*. The outcome with specific genetic information for a flagellum is akin to shuffling the cards and finding that each of the four suits has been separated out, and that the cards within each suit are arranged exactly in ascending order. That result would be evidence for a trick shuffle or some other intervention by an intelligent designer of the outcome.

[30] Niall Shanks, *God, the Devil, and Darwinism: A Critique of Intelligent Design Theory* (Oxford: Oxford University Press, 2004), 180-190.

MACHIN, the result confers no advantage. It is therefore not feasible to explain how all the parts M, A, C, H, I, N, and E could be produced and assembled by an evolutionary process that gradually increases functionality and fitness.

But now suppose we postulate an earlier, "redundant" stage, with parts M, A, C, H, I, N, E, and e. The letter "e" represents a protein distinct from "E" but capable of fulfilling at least some of its role. Then the combination "MACHINE + e" would still be functional. If through a mutation the bacterium lost the ability to produce part E, it could still have a functioning machine in the form MACHINe. We can easily imagine a gradualistic transition from "MACHINE + e" either to MACHINe or to MACHINE. In fact, we can imagine that there might sometimes be multiple redundancies: "MACHINE + e + m" could lose some parts and become a still functional machine MACHINE or mACHINE or MACHINe or mACHINe.

This observation does show that an irreducibly complex machine with parts M, A, C, H, I, N, and E could have gradualistically evolved from a redundant machine with additional parts e or m or both. This step is in fact fairly easy, because the loss of redundancy means the loss of information. The difficult part is to get extra information.

Suppose that we postulate an earlier stage when the bacterium had the configuration MACHINE + e. The redundant machine MACHINE + e could in turn have evolved gradualistically from a machine with parts MACHINe, which is still a functioning machine. This step is quite a bit trickier, because it involves adding a new part E. If E represents a single protein, it already contains a massive amount of information. So one would have to explain how this protein could be obtained gradualistically. It could be done by the process of "exaption," which describes a hypothetical situation where a protein E with an existing function somewhere else in a cell or in an organism gets appropriated for a new job, namely to function as part of the flagellum MACHINE.

So now we have obtained a hypothetical picture in which MACHINe becomes MACHINE + e, which becomes MACHINE. But has this process helped? No, because the hypothetical starting point, MACHINe, is still irreducibly complex. The machine will not function without all the parts being already there. The barrier of irreducible complexity arises when we try to explain how there could have evolved complex machines that do not function until many individual parts are already in place. What the exact parts are—whether part E or a substitute part e—is not the main question.

Shanks, following Alexander G. Cairns-Smith, uses the analogy of a free-standing arch of stones.[31] The arch, which is seemingly impossible to construct gradualistically, can be constructed using scaffolding that one removes afterward. By analogy, a complex biological machine might be constructed by means of extra "scaffolding." The scaffolding would afterwards disappear, because once the construction was complete, the scaffolding would be redundant.

This illustration does show that the question of redundancy (the extra scaffolding) is important. But in the case of the arch, the scaffolding is put in place by an intelligent human designer who knows that he has as his goal the building of an arch. The analog in undesigned evolutionary gradualism would have to find a way by which, at every point in the addition of pieces of scaffolding and pieces of arch, the practical functionality of the whole is increased. That is the heart of the problem, because neither arches nor their scaffolding perform any useful architectural function until the whole is virtually complete. They require intelligent design. The same goes for irreducibly complex machines.

Shanks thinks he has solved the problem of irreducible complexity by introducing redundancy, but he has not. Neither the analogy with an arch nor the presence of redundant complexity solves the problems posed by complex machines that require many parts in order to perform any useful function. Darwinian gradualism needs to obtain a useful function at a very early stage, when one has only a very few parts. Otherwise, the few parts would be discarded.

One could therefore proceed to another stage of hypotheses. Suppose that MACHINE arose from an earlier redundant machine, namely MACHINE + e, which in turn came from MACHINEe. But now suppose that part e contains some capability of multifunctionality. It can, somewhat clumsily, take over part of the function of part N. Hence, MACHIe, without the N, can still exist as a clumsily functioning machine. By a similar process, we hypothesize that MACHIe can come from a redundant machine MACHIe + i, which comes from MACHie. Part i is also multifunctional, capable of taking over the function of H. And so we obtain a functioning machine in the form MACie. Now the gradualistic process has more hope, because there are fewer parts left.

Michael Behe already anticipates this kind of possibility in his initial book on irreducible complexity:

---

[31] Ibid., 184.

Even if a system is irreducibly complex (and thus cannot have been produced directly), however, one can not definitively rule out the possibility of an indirect, circuitous route. As the complexity of an interacting system increases, though, the likelihood of such an indirect route drops precipitously.[32]

In the end, there are still three problems with the above proposal using MACHINE. One is that, in general, it is harder to find multifunctional parts than single-function parts. Indeed, it may be impossible. Second, there may be a point at which no way can be found to produce any functional success with only a small number of parts. Third, it is all hypothetical. At this point in time, when we look at a flagellum, we do not know whether parts like "e" or "i" even could exist, much less that they did exist. Is such a series of unsupported guesses any better than the "guess" of intelligent design? What is more probable?

PROBABILITIES FOR THE FLAGELLUM AND FOR A COURT CASE

We operate with this sort of probabilistic situation in everyday life. The courtroom demands that guilt be established "beyond reasonable doubt." It does not say, "with perfect certainty." Many situations would still allow far-fetched explanations. The lawyer for the defense says, "My client didn't murder him. They had a heated argument, and he happened to have a gun in his hand. He pointed the gun to threaten the victim, and in the middle of the argument he intentionally pulled the trigger, but he didn't want to cause any harm." Will the jury believe it? It is possible, but it does not constitute a reasonable doubt.

So does a criterion of reasonable doubt apply to the flagellum? God rules the world with regularity. And the regularities do extend both to the courtroom and to the bacteria. That is, they do extend to situations involving probabilities. We are right not to be swept off our feet by the enticing rhetoric of a desperate defense lawyer. We can rely on God in matters of this kind as well as in matters of science. But God does not guarantee that a good, conscientious jury will make no mistakes. Divine justice is perfect, because God knows everything. Human justice will never be perfect. We convict a person when his guilt is "beyond reasonable doubt," not because we know that there are no exceptions, but because it is our duty to do the best we can. We compro-

---

[32] Behe, *Darwin's Black Box,* 40. I thank Del Ratzsch for drawing my attention to this quote.

mise between two extremes: one extreme convicts people in spite of serious doubts, and produces too many false convictions; the other extreme lets innumerable guilty people escape punishment because of outlandish doubts about very low probability alternatives.

Similarly, with a flagellum, we may make a mistake in judgment about how it came about. We may convict the innocent or free the guilty. But what if we use something like a criterion of "reasonable doubt"? At first glance it looks like the instantaneous assemblage of the total information for the complete flagellum, or the gradual buildup of information without any beneficial functionality for it, is a totally implausible explanation *from the standpoint of secondary causes*. Both of these options get put into the category of something that we know does not happen. Such reasoning would seem to favor an explanation more in line with theistic evolution. This view would say that somehow, in a way that we do not yet know, God added the flagellum through a gradual process that involved incremental benefits in fitness. Maybe there was a route through MACie to MACHIe to MACHINE.

But difficulties still confront theistic evolution. We have traveled beyond a first look at the flagellum. To use the courtroom analogy, we have looked carefully at the scene of the crime, and have already eliminated most explanations. We have no evidence that there exists functioning machines like MACie, nor do we even know what a part like "i" or "e" might be like. The postulated route through MACie to MACHIe to MACHINE is no more than a desperate guess, perhaps just as improbable as the hypothetical assemblage of information without functionality.

Go back to Darwin's time. It might be reasonable for a theist, looking at the evidence that Darwin observed, to make a daring extrapolation and to guess that God may have created all the species (with possible exceptions) through gradualist means. But it would still be a daring extrapolation needing to be checked out. The flagellum does not seem to check out well. When we try to envision a way by which God did it, and still stay within the bounds of theistic evolution, we end up with stories that sound curiously like the desperate defense lawyer. Why not instead try telling a story in which God, like an intelligent human designer, organizes the parts and puts them together?

But God is not quite like a human designer. He is first cause, not a secondary cause. Methodological naturalists might complain that when we invoke God, we mix causal levels, and so evade "scientific" explanation. But think again. The human designer, in gathering and organizing the parts of a machine, does not act contrary to deterministic physical laws. The molecules and the forces from his fingers, and contractions of his muscles, function in an ordinary way. Human intentionality is mysterious. It is not a "cause" on the same level as the physical causes immediately impinging on one machine part. The human being plans and looks ahead and plots the shape of the finished machine. Then he acts in an external world where he uses ordinary secondary causes. His planning and intentionality are like a primary cause in relation to these secondary causes, though of course he in turn also has God as *his* primary cause.

So the analogy with a human designer does help. We reject as outlandish a picture in which parts of a mouse trap or a complex machine randomly come together in a garbage dump to form the finished machine. We accept with equanimity the coming together of those same parts, under the control of the same general laws of physics, when human intention comes in. Human intention gives high probability to a result that otherwise has laughably low probability.

We can estimate probabilities only with some knowledge of the situation for which we are estimating. If a given complex machine requires 10 parts, and we are told that those 10 parts are dumped at random in a garbage dump with an area of 10,000 square meters, we may estimate a very low probability that we will find them one day later all linked together to form a machine. But if we are told that a human being intends to visit the dump during the night and put them together into a machine, our probability estimate has to be completely revised. Probabilities are tricky, because of the way in which they depend on prior knowledge. And strange things can happen, because our prior knowledge may lack some crucial piece of information. The man accused of murder, we find out, was acting out a scene for movie filming. The gun was supposed to have blanks. But unknown to him, a stagehand with a grudge for the victim put in real bullets. Suddenly, now that we have this extra piece of knowledge, the probability that the accused is guilty shifts radically.

Does analogous reasoning apply to the case where God is going to create a bacterial flagellum? Does it make a difference to the probabilities if we know beforehand what God's intentions are? Presumably it would. But in fact we know of God's intentions only after observing the result, the completed flagellum.

The analogy between God and a human designer still helps. When a human being constructs a motor, we can follow two levels of causes. We can focus on the secondary causes, involving physical motion and chemistry. By carefully analyzing a single metallic part, we might possibly deduce not only what factory manufactured it, but from what mineral deposit the iron ore came. But suppose that we tried to explain exclusively through secondary causes how the whole motor came together as a whole in one place. We could not do it. Physical causes exist all the way through, in the form of pressures from human fingers, or pressures from machines or robotic fingers set up by a human being. But this kind of causal chain is far too complex to follow, and looks very improbable unless we invoke a "primary" cause, namely the human designer or assembler.

Scientists feel little discomfort about abandoning an attempt at explaining a motor purely through secondary causes, that is, physical and chemical causes.[33] There is nothing unscientific about recognizing the limitations of chemical explanation, when confronted by human assembly of a motor. Might the same conclusion hold by analogy when we consider God's assembly of the first flagellum? Preference for one vision of "science" over another might incline us to prefer one type of explanation over another, or to want to disallow one option. But we cannot tell God beforehand how he had to do it.

REMAINING OPEN

I do not think that there is one obviously right answer to the flagellum. We need to recognize the difficulty. And we need to recognize that people's desires may run away with them, and lead them to choose one option when they should have a more open mind. On the one hand, scientists, both Christian and non-Christian, desire understanding. This desire inclines them to hope that the origin of the flagellum involved high probability transitions through "ordinary" mutations and increasing fitness. Then, with enough cumulative information, we might be able to trace in some detail how God brought about the first flagellum.

On the other hand, apologists and participants in the culture wars desire to have arguments that challenge the reigning ideology of materialism inside and outside the world of science. This desire inclines them to hope that God brought about the flagellum through a strange low-probability situation, which we will never be able to reconstruct.

Or maybe a third alternative can arise, still inconceivable in the present state of science, whereby we could see a pattern common to many cases of irreducible complexity, and the pattern might suggest something about the low-probability routes through which the complex configurations initially

---

[33] Simpson correctly observes that "Historical causation of the Empire State Building is by action of a species of animals [i.e. human beings]" (Simpson, "Uniformitarianism," 87). But, in practice, narrowly biological principles are here being supplemented by knowledge of human intentionality, which, as we noted, is not on the same level.

came about. By analogy with the human designer putting together a machine, we might learn enough about the designer to make a good guess as to how he did it. We may find that it involved means that do not amount to the unbelievable claim that 10 pieces of a machine came together overnight in the garbage heap with no intelligent guidance.

However things may turn out in the long run, in my opinion the predominant methodological naturalism in science needs to change, however painful that may be for those who currently hold cultural power. In particular, cultural space needs to be made for the hypothesis of intelligent design, as *one reasonable alternative to pursue,* rather than stigmatizing it as many cultural gatekeepers now do. The reigning methodological naturalism either conceals ontological naturalism, which is an ungrounded metaphysical and religious assumption, or it artificially excludes some answers by ruling them out of bounds from the beginning even though they may be right. Either alternative rests on unsound foundations. Now that both are being openly challenged by the intelligent design movement, only dishonesty or suppression of free exchange of opinion can permanently conceal the inadequacy of this ideological captivity within current scientific method.

20

GOD AND PHYSICAL
DISPLAYS

Now let us consider the implications of a Christian worldview for the study of the physical world, including nonliving things.

Does a pattern of imaging extend to nonliving things, as it does to living things? God made man in his own image, while plants and animals were made "according to their kinds" (Gen. 1:21, 26-27; 5:1). Man is unique among the creatures of the earth. Yet, as we saw in chapter 18, plants and animals, by reproducing according to their kinds, are analogous to Adam, who fathers a son in his image (5:3). Reproduction, a key process in living things, results in more living things "in the image of" the parents. While respecting the uniqueness of mankind, we might say that biological reproduction also offers us a process of imaging.

Reproduction in the usual sense does not extend to nonliving things. Yet nonliving things share some general physical properties with living things, namely the properties investigated by physics and chemistry. Does the idea of imaging reoccur in this area? Possibly it does, as a still more attenuated expression of the principle of imaging.

IMAGING IN NONLIVING THINGS IN THEOPHANY

In fact, we have already seen examples of imaging in nonliving things in connection with our earlier discussion of theophanies (chapter 17). Thunderstorms, fire, light, and clouds appear in connection with theophanies. They also appear in ordinary life, and even here they reflect some specific aspects of God's character. Likewise, the thrones of earthly kings reflect the original throne of God, symbolizing his power and authority. The jewels on earth reflect the jewel-like splendor in theophany (Rev. 4:3), and this splendor in turn reflects the beauty of God. Houses and temples on earth reflect the dwelling of God in heaven, and this in turn reflects the original dwelling of God in himself, expressed in the mutual indwelling of the persons of the Trinity (John 17:21). The life-giving character of God is reflected in the water of life in theophany in Revelation 22:1-2. In a subordinate way it is reflected in ordinary water on earth. The sun as a source of light reflects the original brightness of God (see Rev. 21:23). And so on. When our eyes are opened, we can see many reflections of the character of God. The Bible through its use of a variety of images suggests many such reflections.

PROPORTIONS

The tabernacle, as we saw in chapter 17, contains a number of imaging relations. We may consider one specific example of imagery within the tabernacle, namely the measurements. The tabernacle has many features that show simple proportions. The Holy Place is the same width as the Most Holy Place, but *twice* as long. The table with the bread of the Presence has dimensions of two cubits in length, one cubit in breadth, and a cubit and a half in height (Ex. 25:23). That is, the dimensions are 2 X 1 X 1½. Length and breadth are in the proportion of 2 to 1. Breadth and height are in the proportion of 1 to 1½, which is the same as a ratio of 2 to 3. Length and height are in the proportion of 2 to 1½, which is the same as 4 to 3. The court of the tabernacle has a length of 100 cubits and a breadth of 50, again with a ratio of 2 to 1. The court is 5 times the dimensions of the Holy Place, which has a length of 20 cubits and a breadth of 10 cubits.

What are we to make of this? There are perhaps some practical reasons for some of the dimensions. The dimensions had to be reasonable for human use. And the simple lengths in terms of cubits are easier to measure. But the symmetries also suggest beauty and harmony. Consider also that the outer of the two rooms, the Holy Place, possesses attenuated holiness in comparison with the Most Holy Place. The Most Holy Place is the image of the dwelling place of God. The Holy Place is then a kind of image of an image. And it is proportional to the inner room that it images. Proportionalities offer one expression of the principle of imaging.

So an Israelite could come to recognize that the principle of imaging is broader than its principal embodiment in human nature, man made in the image of God. Imaging in an attenuated way expresses itself in animals, plants, and now nonliving things, the spatial structure of the tabernacle.

Remember also that the symbolism in the tabernacle suggests a relation between several "dwellings" of God, among them a relation between the "macrocosmic house" of the universe and the "microcosmic house" of the tabernacle (see chapter 17).

And when the Israelite then contemplated the macrocosmic house, he might wonder whether it showed similar beauties and harmonies. Does the world at large, the macrocosm, show numerical symmetries or harmonies?

If we just look narrowly at the spatial character of the world, we are starting to explore geometry. When the Greeks like Pythagoras did so, they found profound relationships in proportions, which made some of them think that mathematical harmonies offered the key to the universe.

But for now we are focusing on the physical aspects of the world, not simply mathematics. One such area is music. The Greeks discovered simple proportionalities in the character of musical harmonies. Let us start with a string on a lyre. If we take a second string, half as long, and put it under the same tension as the first, it produces a note one octave higher. A simple proportionality in length, namely a length of 1 versus a length of 2, produces a simple harmony in musical notes.

In fact, we can say more. The note one octave higher has a fundamental frequency of vibration twice as high as the original note. The frequencies are related to one another in a ratio of 1 to 2, and this is the origin of the harmonious sound that we hear. Our ears and the mental processing of sound have a sense of proportionalities built into them. Using standard musical notation, we can depict the ratio by a simple illustration:

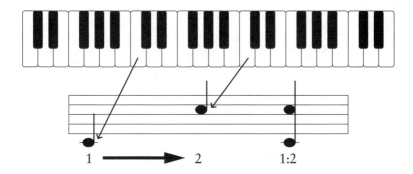

The first note is middle C, the second is a C one octave higher. The notes can also be played simultaneously, producing an octave chord.

Proportionalities occur more broadly. The other notes in scales and in melodies are also related by proportionalities. In fact, the chords that sound most harmonious to the ear are those that produce simple proportionalities in frequencies. The illustration below shows common chords and the related proportionalities:

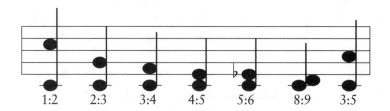

The first chord (on the left of the illustration) is an octave chord. As we have seen, the higher note has a frequency twice the frequency of the low note, resulting in a proportionality of 1 to 2 (1:2). The next chord is a major fifth, also an important harmony, with a ratio of frequencies of 2:3. The next, a major fourth, has a proportionality of 3:4. Then comes the major third, with a proportionality of 4:5. The minor third is 5:6. The major second has a proportionality of 8:9, which no longer sounds nearly as harmonious. Finally, the major sixth, the right-most chord, has a proportionality of 3:5.[1]

More complex chords show additional proportionalities. For example, the C major chord, consisting of C, E, and G in harmony, involves the ratios 4:5:6 among the three notes. If we take a G major chord, consisting of G, B, and D, it involves the same proportions: 4:5:6. The simplest chord progressions often move from C major to G major, or G major to C major, or some other sequence that involves a relation of a major fifth. The proportion between C and G is 2:3. Thus chord *progressions* utilize simple proportionalities:

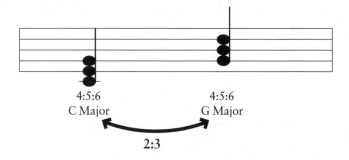

---

[1] Technically, the situation with chords is more complicated. On pianos and some other instruments, tuning typically aims to have equal "temperament," that is, an adjustment that enables the instrument to play in any key. The adjustment is a kind of compromise between keys that attempts to create exactly the same musical "distance" for each half step, namely a proportionality of $2^{1/12} = 1.059463...$. This is obviously not a simple proportionality, but the chords produced by such an instrument are still quite close to the simple ratios of ideal chords, and they are heard by the human ear as simple harmonious chords.

We hear natural harmonies when we hear these chords and progressions of chords. Dissonances can also be fit into the picture, because they are heard as disharmonies that we want to be dissolved into harmony. In all this, we are not consciously aware of the simple numerical proportionalities that underlie the chords. But the effects of the proportions are built into our brains in the way in which they detect proportions. We hear harmony and beauty—or sometimes dissonance that calls for resolution. In so doing, we are responding to the beauty and harmony of God. His harmony is reflected in the proportions of the tabernacle, and also, it turns out, in the proportions in music. In addition, the movement from dissonance to harmony appears to be analogous to the more general movement from chaos to order, a movement that we see taking place in God's creation of the world, and in God's re-creation responding to the chaos introduced by sin.

We could consider further echoes of proportionalities within music, but let us turn to consider other areas.

Proportions in Time and Space

Even before the Greeks discovered the proportionalities in music, astronomers began exploring proportionalities in the motion of heavenly bodies. God laid the foundation for this possibility when he created the heavenly bodies. In Genesis 1 God indicates that the heavenly lights function to mark off time: "And let them be for signs and for seasons, and for days and years" (Gen. 1:14). The first and most elementary level of theory—scarcely deserving the name of theory—simply observes the obvious regularities governed by the heavenly bodies. The sun brings daytime in a regular cycle. The moon marks out the division into months. And in a more complicated way, the position of the sun at its rising and setting, as well as the positions of the stars, mark out the cycle of the year.

Israelites had to know something about days, months, and years, because God commanded them to celebrate festivals at certain fixed times. For example, the morning sacrifice took place once a day (Num. 28:4), the Sabbath once every seven days (Lev. 23:3), the Passover once a year on the fourteenth day of the first month (Lev. 23:5), and at the beginning of each month there took place the blowing of trumpets and special offerings (Num. 10:10; 28:11). Any Israelite could observe that God had established for his benefit a regular correlation between the spatial positions of the heavenly bodies and the times when specific events took place.

Consider how things would look to an Israelite, when he examined the heavens and started thinking about the correlations between time and the positions of the heavenly bodies. The most obvious correlation of all connects the sun to the cycle of a day. One cycle of the sun makes one day. Seven cycles of the sun makes seven days. And within the daytime, the position of the sun in the sky shows the time of day—the basis for a sundial. These correlations establish a proportionality between the motion of the sun and the passage of time. One complete rotation of the sun makes one day; two rotations makes two days, and so on. There is a 1-to-1 correlation between rotations and days. And one can also see a correlation between positions of the sun in the sky and hours of the day.

Now remember that the tabernacle showed simple proportionalities in its physical dimensions. It also showed some instances of correlations between time and space. The cycle of seven days in the week corresponded to the spatial arrangement of seven lamps on the lampstand. The tabernacle as God's microcosmic model suggested that proportionalities might occur also in God's macrocosmic house, the universe. And the regularities in the motion of the sun confirmed this guess.

So now we have a proportionality between the sun's spatial position and the passing of time. That suggests that proportionalities may appear also with respect to other heavenly bodies. And they do. The moon varies in position and appearance in a way that regularly repeats itself in a cycle of about 29½ days. The position of the stars and the position of the sun at its rising and setting varies in a more complicated way that repeats itself every year, that is, every 365¼ days (approximately).

Observations of this kind open up a challenge to study the movements of heavenly bodies with greater and greater precision. Mathematics must develop in order effectively to manipulate fractional parts and large numbers. Geometry must develop means for representing and analyzing movement in three dimensions.

A first approximation says that the sun and the moon move in a circle. The sun has a cycle one day long, while the moon has a cycle relative to the sun's position of 29½ days. The intersection of the circle with the horizon, and the angle of inclination to the horizon, vary according to the time of year. Let us call this stage of development level 2 of theory.

But development of mathematics and of close observation shows some complexities, particularly with the movement of the planets. For the detail that the Babylonians and later the Greeks achieved, considerable mathematical calculation becomes necessary. In the third level of theory, made famous by Ptolemy, the movements of the heavenly bodies can be represented by circles to which are attached smaller circles or "epicycles." A large circle with its center at the earth rotates at a constant rate. To a fixed point on the circumference of this rotating circle we imagine that we attach the center of a smaller circle, which rotates at its own rate, which may differ from the main circle. If the approximation achieved by this representation proves not to be sufficiently good, we can attach still a third circle, producing an epicycle on the epicycle, and so on.

God has provided in the heavenly bodies a natural starting point for physics, especially the mechanics of motion. Ordinary motion on earth experiences the influence of friction, as well as the influence of wind and atmospheric pressure, all of which present obstacles to grasping the underlying simplicity that Galileo and Newton uncovered. The heavenly bodies, by contrast, move without the effects of friction or the atmosphere. They therefore show simplicity and regularity more directly at an immediately visible level.

People living in the modern world can observe still more proportionalities within the earthly sphere, provided that we overcome or ignore the effects of friction. Suppose we are traveling in a car to a distant place. In the first hour we travel 50 miles (about 80 kilometers). In the second hour we travel another 50 miles, for a total of 100 miles. By the end of the third hour we have traveled 150 miles. And so on. We draw up a table to summarize our trip:

TIME	1 hr.	2 hrs.	3 hrs.	4 hrs.	5 hrs.
DISTANCE	50 miles	100 miles	150 miles	200 miles	250 miles

The table expresses a proportionality connecting time and distance. Every hour corresponds to another 50 miles. We say that the car travels at 50 miles per hour over the entire distance. The constant proportionality between time and distance leads to a conception of speed, defined as the ratio between distance and time.

Now we can look at a similar situation in which the speed is varying. Imagine that we are in an airplane on the runway. The airplane engines come up to full power, and the pilot releases the brakes. The plane starts to travel along the runway, faster and faster. We can keep track of this travel in a second table:

TIME	0 sec.	1 sec.	2 sec.	3 sec.	4 sec.
SPEED	0 ft./sec.	2 ft./sec.	4 ft./sec.	6 ft./sec.	8 ft./sec.

The plane starts from rest, that is, traveling at 0 feet per second (ft/sec). After one second, it is traveling at 2 feet per second (about .6 meter per second). After 2 seconds, it travels at 4 feet per second. And so on. We find that there is a regular proportionality between time and speed. This proportionality leads to the idea of *acceleration.* Acceleration can be defined as the change in speed per unit of time. In the example with the plane, the plane is accelerating at a rate of 2 feet per second per second. The repetition of the phrase "per second" sounds odd at first, but it is accurate. Speed is measured in units like feet per second or meters per second. Acceleration deals with change in speed *per unit of time.* Every second, the speed becomes 2 feet per second more. The rate of change is therefore 2 feet per second, every second, or 2 feet per second, per second.

The world around us offers a host of examples of such proportionalities. The very concept of speed has built into it the idea of a proportionality between distance on the one hand and time on the other. Such a concept could originally be stimulated by observing the motion of the sun and the moon. But then it can be extended to analyzing the motion of a car or a plane. And then we come to the concept of acceleration, which applies an analogous analysis to situations in which the speed changes. The concepts of speed and acceleration lie near the foundations in the study of the whole area of physics. We now turn to consider physics as it has developed in its modern form.

21

A CHRISTIAN APPROACH TO
PHYSICS AND CHEMISTRY

What about the laws and theories explored in modern physics? When we explore the ins and outs of modern physics, we confront more abstract thinking and more complex mathematics than what we have previously discussed. Some readers may therefore find the details challenging. But everyone can appreciate to some extent the ways in which God has impressed signs of his wisdom and character onto the very laws of physics. I would therefore encourage even readers without backgrounds in science to look into these matters and consider them in order to gain a new way of looking at physics.

Let us first consider the unifying principles articulated by Sir Isaac Newton.

NEWTON'S THREE LAWS OF MOTION
Newton formulated three laws of motion.

> 1. Every body perseveres in its state of rest, or of uniform motion in a right line, unless it is compelled to change that state by forces impressed thereon.
>
> 2. The alteration of motion is ever proportional to the motive force impressed; and is made in the direction of the right line in which that force is impressed.
>
> 3. To every action there is always opposed an equal and opposite reaction: or the mutual actions of two bodies upon each other are always equal, and directed to contrary parts.[1]

---

[1] http://galileoandeinstein.physics.virginia.edu/lectures/newtongl.html, quoting from "an 1803 translation," presumably Isaac Newton, *The Mathematical Principles of Natural Philosophy* (London: H. D. Symonds, 1803). See my earlier discussion of Newton's laws in Vern S. Poythress, "Newton's Laws as Allegory," *Journal of the American Scientific Affiliation* 35/3 (1983): 156-161.

(The expression "right line" designates what we would now call a straight line.)

The First Law talks about a "body." The term "body" in ordinary usage often refers to the human body or to the bodies of animals. By contrast, Newton's laws involve a special, more technical use of that term, an extended use that would include not only human bodies but inanimate lumps. But in the background of this special usage there lingers the suggestion that there is an analogy between the human body and an inanimate body in motion. This analogy recalls our earlier exploration of imaging. It suggests that an inanimate "body" is analogous to the human body, and may show some form of imaging. In its own way it may then reflect something about the character of God. Is this so?

Newton's laws form part of an extended treatment of force and motion, which Newton developed in his whole work *The Mathematical Principles of Natural Philosophy.* This work in turn formed the basis for further development of impressive technical precision. As a result of this process, the concepts of a "body," "force," and "motion" all now have a technical or semitechnical meaning, as do the related concepts of "mass," "velocity," and "acceleration," which are necessary to interpret the meaning and application of Newton's laws.[2]

ANALOGY WITH HUMAN EXPERIENCE

But when Newton or later scientists introduce apprentices to science, they must start their explanation somewhere. They use language that starts with the ordinary and moves in the direction of a technical concept. Apprentices begin to understand by starting with ordinary experiences of bodies and motions, including their own bodies and motions.

Thus, we understand a "body" in Newtonian terms by first having experience of our own "body" in the ordinary sense, and experience of other "bodies." We draw an analogy between our body and the behavior of an inanimate ball or stone. For the purpose at hand, the ball or stone can be treated as a unity when we look at its behavior. This unity is analogous to the unity that a human being has when he moves from one location to another.

---

[2] Actually, the process of forming these technical terms started well before Newton. In the fourteenth century, Oresme "had a clear conception not only of acceleration in general but also of uniform acceleration in particular" (Carl B. Boyer, *The History of the Calculus and Its Conceptual Development (The Concepts of the Calculus)* [reprint; New York: Dover, 1959], 83). In Oresme, velocity is *velocitas* and acceleration is *velocitatio. Velocity* is the more precise term used by physicists to denote speed of motion in a particular direction.

The motion of the ball is like the motion that we experience when we move our bodies.

Even more striking is the concept of "motive force" (mentioned in Newton's Second Law). What is "force"? It is a fairly abstract and difficult concept, since we do not see "force" with the same obviousness that we see a ball or a human body. We kinesthetically feel the tension in our muscles and the pressure on our hand as we hold a stone in our hand. That direct personal experience of "force" in an intuitive sense gives the apprentice scientist a handle for conceiving of "force" in the abstract—that is, "force" as the physicist means it.

When we stretch a spring with our hand, we feel the tension in our muscles, and the resistance and tension increase as the amount of stretch increases. But now suppose that the spring is attached to a ball, instead of to our hand, and suppose that the spring is in a stretched shape. We postulate that the spring exerts "force" on the ball even though we cannot see anything noticeable taking place directly between the spring and the ball. Nor can we kinesthetically feel any tension in our muscles, and the spring does not have muscles of its own with which it could feel. We speak of tension in the spring, or force that the spring exerts, by analogy with the kinesthetic force of our muscles and our sense of pressure on the skin. "Force" in the spring is analogous to the force that we feel in our muscles.

Now consider the Third Law of Motion. It says, "To every action there is always opposed an equal and opposite reaction." For an apprentice physicist to understand this law, he must take successively two points of view. He first identifies with body A, and imagines himself exerting a force on body B. He then identifies with body B, and imagines himself exerting a force on body A. The Third Law says that the two forces are equal, but in opposite directions. The formulation of the Third Law, like the first two, depends on an analogy between human bodily experience of force ("force" in a more ordinary, intuitive sense) and force in inanimate bodies ("force" in the technical sense). It depends on the analogy between human bodies and inanimate "bodies"—a kind of imaging relation.

It also relies on the ability of human beings to adopt two or more different points of view, and to understand reciprocal interactions among two human beings. This capacity to relate to other human beings and their points of view mirrors the relation between the persons of the Trinity.[3] The Father,

---

[3] See Vern S. Poythress, *Symphonic Theology: The Validity of Multiple Perspectives in Theology* (Grand Rapids, Mich.: Zondervan, 1987), 50-54.

the Son, and the Holy Spirit each have full knowledge of one another and of the world. But their knowledge also involves the personal perspective of the person. The Son knows all things in knowing the Father; the Father knows all things in knowing the Son. Harmonious knowledge exists within the Trinity in three "perspectives." This unity in diversity reflects itself in human experience, in that we can take a diversity of perspectives and imagine what things look like from someone else's point of view. This capacity for perspectives gets used in the understanding of Newton's Third Law.

Man made in the image of God is of course by far the most noteworthy example of a testimony within creation to God who made him. But why should not this testimony extend at a derivative and attenuated level to other creatures? Plants and animals "image" the life of God by producing offspring in their image (chapter 18). Why should we not expect that even the inanimate things image some of the simpler capabilities of human beings? And they do; namely they show capacity to move, to rest, and to exert force on another body. Thus they too reflect the glory of God in their own way.

GROWING IN KNOWLEDGE

Let us think a bit about the history of astronomy and physics. The developments have extended over many centuries, with later scientists building on and revising the earlier results. Human beings typically do not come to know complex, rich truths by a single leap. We are finite and need to learn by simple steps.

God in his goodness has given us physical laws that enable us to proceed by relatively simple steps. Historically, man did not need to start with the extremely complex results in twentieth-century quantum field theory or general relativity. Physics has developed by steps, through observations of planetary motion, through Archimedes's experiments and reasoning, through Galileo's experiments with inclined planes, through Newton, through Einstein's special theory of relativity and general theory of relativity, and through quantum mechanics in its various phases of development.

We now know that Newton's laws are only approximate. Deviations appear when we are dealing with velocities approaching the speed of light, or strong gravitational fields, or very small objects where quantum effects become significant. But Newton's laws still find use outside of these extreme situations. God's laws are so ordained that there can be "levels" of theory. The deeper theories are more accurate, but also more complex. And we come to understand them using the stepping-stones provided by the shallower and simpler theories. Thus the simpler theories have not in every sense been super-seded. We have a different perspective on them in the light of later and more advanced knowledge, but they remain part of the intellectual "furniture" with which God has supplied the world. In agreement with our anti-reductionist reflections earlier, simpler theories like Newton's laws remain in place as part of the meaning of God's law. Even though they are approximate, they illus-trate God's goodness and wisdom. And they illustrate God's kindness in pro-viding "stepping-stones" toward more complex and richer theories.[4]

We have already considered more elementary levels of theory about astronomy. On the first level, the observer sees the obvious correlation, or proportionality, between the movement of the sun and the number of days. On a second level, he extends these observations to try to describe the motions of the moon and the planets. On a third level, we come to the com-plex theory of Ptolemy, involving a detailed model for describing the position of the planets. The planets moved in something like circular orbits. But each of these circles had "epicycles" attached to them in the form of smaller cir-cles with their own rate of rotation. That is as far as astronomy came in the ancient world.

It took several developments to bring a deeper understanding of motion within reach of human thought. First, continued observations of the heavenly bodies, over centuries, produced a growing body of data that required more complicated patterns of epicycles to describe. Second, Copernicus found that the number and complexity of epicycles could be considerably reduced if he postulated that the earth rotated, and that the planets moved around the sun rather than around the earth. Third, the shift to a sun-centered system enabled Kepler to study the regularities more carefully, and to dispense alto-gether with epicycles by replacing the many circles with a single ellipse for each planet. Fourth, Galileo's experiments with falling bodies and inclined planes uncovered regularities in the movements of earthly bodies. Isaac Newton was then able to describe the motion of both heavenly and earthly

---

[4] Paul Davies, in thinking about physical laws, remarks on the balance between depth and accessibility:
    What is remarkable is that human beings are actually able to carry out this code-breaking oper-ation, that the human mind has the necessary intellectual equipment for us to "unlock the secrets of nature" and make a passable attempt at completing nature's "cryptic crossword." It would be easy to imagine a world in which the regularities of nature were transparent and obvi-ous to all at a glance. We can also imagine another world in which either there were no regu-larities, or the regularities were so well hidden, so subtle, that the cosmic code would require vastly more brainpower than humans possess. But instead we find a situation in which the dif-ficulty of the cosmic code seems almost to be attuned to human capabilities. To be sure, we have a pretty tough struggle decoding nature, but so far we have had a good deal of success. The challenge is just hard enough to attract some of the best brains available, but not so hard as to defeat their combined efforts and deflect them onto easier tasks (Davies, *The Mind of God: The Scientific Basis for a Rational World* [New York: Simon & Schuster, 1992], 148-149).

bodies within a single coherent theory. Newton's theory we may call a fourth level of theory—or perhaps fifth or sixth or seventh, if we think of Copernicus or Kepler or Galileo as producing intermediate theories.

All these thinkers looked for correlations or analogies between arithmetical calculations, simple geometric figures, and physical positions and motions.[5] In doing so they agreed with the suggestion seen in the tabernacle model, the suggestion of simplicity, beauty, and proportionality. But it remained to find just what simplicities and proportionalities God was using and displaying in the macrocosm.

Copernicus preferred the sun-centered system partly for his own philosophical reasons, but partly because it simplified the system of epicycles. He was looking for simplicity. And he used the human ability to change one's point of view. He moved from the earth-centered viewpoint of Ptolemaic astronomy to a viewpoint with the sun as center. Remember that Newton's Third Law uses human ability to move from the point of view that identifies with body A to the point of view that identifies with body B. A Christian worldview finds the roots for this ability ultimately in the diversity of "viewpoints" of the three persons of the Trinity. The diversity-within-unity in the Trinity invites us to expect, as an imaging within the created world, instances of diversity-within-unity. We enjoy the unity of a single coherent world, a universe, and at the same time the ability to look at that world from any of a number of angles, *more than one* of which may prove to be illuminating.

Many intellectuals opposed Copernicus in favor of the status quo. One regrets that they did not have a better understanding of the Christian principle of different viewpoints, which would have encouraged greater openness. And one must point to the biblical principle that man must grow in understanding the world, rather than simply resting content with past authorities like Aristotle.

Kepler also struggled to find simplicity. Even with Copernicus's sun-centered system, some epicycles remained. This complexity was ugly and counterintuitive. Kepler found to his delight that it could be replaced with a single ellipse for each planet. The ellipse is a simple, elegant geometric figure, and thus reintroduces the beauty and simplicity that the themes of the tabernacle suggest.

Galileo looked for a simple mathematical description for bodies moving on earth. He could not totally eliminate friction, but when friction was min-

---

[5] Carl Boyer points out how medieval thinking offered a bridge toward modern physics partly through its attention to quantitative variation and motion (Boyer, *History of the Calculus*, 71). Greek thinking, by contrast, thought of both geometry and number "statically."

imal he found that horizontal motion was constant and vertical motion had constant acceleration. Both of these represent simple relations between motion at one time and motion at another time. There are proportionalities in motion within the earthly sphere as well as in the heavenly bodies.

BEAUTY AND PROPORTIONALITY IN NEWTON'S LAWS

Newton was able to put all these previous advances together into a single coherent picture, which also has its own elegance, beauty, and simplicity, including the use of proportionality. The Second Law of Motion says that the alteration of motion (we would say acceleration) is proportional to the force. The constant of proportionality is the "mass" of the object. In modern notation, Newton's Second Law can be written as

$$F = ma$$

where F is the force, m is the mass, and a is the acceleration. The apprentice physicist understands mass by starting with the ordinary experience of weight. Different objects held in the hand feel relatively light or heavy. Newton tacitly relies on human experience as a starting point for the abstract generalizations. And then he says $F = ma$, postulating a simple proportionality between force (F) and acceleration (a).

A relation of proportionality between alteration of motion and force is certainly among the simplest of possible relations that one might guess. God has been gracious in establishing a law that is simple enough to grasp, and beautiful in its simplicity. Moreover, proportionality is a simple form of analogy, and analogy in turn is closely related to the pattern of imaging. The acceleration a, we might say, is a kind of "image" of the force F.

In fact, another form of proportionality is concealed within Newton's law, in the term "a," standing for acceleration. In the Second Law Newton talks about "alteration of motion." In our later vocabulary, we would say, "alteration of velocity," or "change in velocity," or "acceleration." Velocity is the change in position per unit of time. It captures a proportionality between position and time, as we saw in the previous chapter. Acceleration, which means change in velocity per unit of time, involves a proportionality between velocity and time (again, recalling the preceding chapter). Thus, two distinct proportionalities are already built into the concept of acceleration, represented by the single symbol "a" in Newton's Second Law.

In fact, when we consider acceleration in more detail, things get more complicated. Consider again an airplane accelerating down a runway in order to take off. The plane is not going at a constant velocity. So we cannot measure the velocity simply by directly comparing distance and time. Suppose we measure the distance covered after one second. We find that the airplane has traveled 1 foot. After 2 seconds, it has traveled 4 feet. After 3 seconds, it has traveled 9 feet. We draw up a table:

TIME	1 sec.	2 sec.	3 sec.	4 sec.	5 sec.
DISTANCE	1 ft.	4 ft.	9 ft.	16 ft.	25 ft.

We can still see a correlation between time and distance. The distance in feet is the square of the time in seconds. After 4 seconds, the distance is 4 X 4 = 16 feet. This correlation is more complicated than the simple proportionalities that we saw earlier. There is no simple method of saying right away exactly how fast the plane is going after 3 seconds. If we look at the distance traveled in the preceding second (between second 2 and second 3), it is 9 - 4 = 5 feet. This leads to an estimate that the speed is about 5 feet per second. If we look at the distance traveled in the subsequent second (between second 3 and second 4), it is 16 - 9 = 7 feet, leading to an estimate of speed of 7 feet per second. But both are estimates. Because of the acceleration of the plane, the speed is in fact constantly changing. The estimate of 5 feet per second cannot be exactly right, because at the beginning of the interval the plane would have been traveling somewhat more slowly than 5 ft/sec, while by the end of the interval the plane would have been traveling somewhat faster than 5 ft/sec. The estimate of 5 ft/sec is only an average value for the period of time between second 2 and second 3.

To get around this problem, Newton invented calculus as a mathematical tool to calculate "instantaneous" velocities instead of average velocities.[6] Calculus starts with the more intuitive idea of an average velocity. It then shortens the period of time over which one makes the estimate. It then uses algebraic manipulation to calculate how the estimate changes as the time becomes indefinitely ("infinitesimally") short. Newton built not only on the work of Copernicus, Kepler, and Galileo, but on Descartes' and Fermat's invention of analytic geometry, which established a powerful correlation or analogy between geometry (analysis of space) and algebra (analysis of num-

---

[6] Leibniz coinvented calculus at about the same time as Newton; for predecessors, see Boyer, *History of the Calculus*.

ber). Newton used the resources of analytic geometry in the process of building numerical descriptions of physical phenomena in space.

GOD'S PROVISION OF STEPPING-STONES

Copernicus, Kepler, Galileo, and Descartes provided stepping-stones toward Newton's results. But in a sense the physical phenomena themselves provided propitious opportunities for these stepping-stones. Over a short period of time, any one of the heavenly bodies moved roughly in a straight line, with roughly constant speed. The constant speed invited human beings to notice the relation of proportionality between distance and time. But closer study then showed that the proportionalities were not always exact.

Some motions on earth also showed roughly constant speed: the speed of a runner or the speed of a rolling ball on a level surface. But in other situations the speed changed over time. So then it was natural to study the change of speed (the acceleration). Galileo found that the downwards acceleration of a falling object was roughly constant. But this result was again inexact, because of air resistance and because the gravitational force varies slowly with altitude. The approximation to a constant proportionality held out a promise of regularity. At the same time, deviations from constancy invited further study.

Moreover, changes in velocity over time implied that average velocity was only an approximation. This lack of accuracy invited Newton to invent some way of calculating instantaneous velocity, which led to the invention of calculus.

BEAUTY AND SIMPLICITY

Newton contributed two more important pieces to physical theory. First, he postulated a specific rule for gravitational force (Newton's Law of Gravitation). The gravitational force has to be known in order to explain in detail the actual motions of the heavenly bodies. Suppose that the earth has a mass M and the moon a mass m, and that the distance between them is r. Then Newton postulates that the gravitational force F is given by the equation

$$F = GMm/r^2$$

The force F is proportional to M, proportional to m, and inversely proportional to the square of the distance r. The constant of proportionality, G, called the "gravitational constant," is initially unknown, and must be determined by experimental measurement. The important thing is that it is the same for all gravitating objects. (In metric units, $G = 6.673 \times 10^{-11}$ m³/kg-sec².) Newton also specified that the force acted in the direction of the line connecting the two bodies (in this case, the line between the center of the earth and the center of the moon).

Again we see simple proportionalities in the equation. The force F is proportional to M, the mass of the earth; it is proportional to m, the mass of the moon; it is inversely proportional to the r times r, where r is the distance between the earth and the moon. The fact that the force F is proportional to the mass m is particularly significant, because it means that the resulting acceleration of a mass m due to gravitation is independent of its mass. Thus, a marble and a bowling ball released from the top of a tall building will hit the ground at about the same time. This is what Galileo had earlier found in experimenting with falling objects.

Some features of gravitation could not have been guessed apart from experimental evidence. Why is r in the denominator instead of the numerator? And why is it r² (r times r) instead of a simple r? Astronomers already knew that the planets further away from the sun took a much longer time to complete an orbit around the sun. For Newton this meant that the force dropped off with distance rather than being independent of distance or increasing with distance. Newton also knew Kepler's laws, that the planets moved in ellipses around the sun, with the sun at one focus of the ellipse; and that the line joining a planet to the sun swept through equal areas in equal times. These laws could be deduced from a force law with a factor of r², but not from any other.

Newton thus uncovered a simple, beautiful law based on the earlier simplicities and beauties of Kepler's laws. At the same time, he found that Kepler's laws were only an approximation. A single planet, all by itself, would travel in an ellipse around the sun.[7] But once other planets were present, those planets exerted their own gravitational force on the first planet. Then its course did not follow an ellipse, but an exceedingly complex pattern that did not correspond to any geometrically simple figure. Fortunately for Kepler, the sun's mass dominated all the other masses in the solar system, so that ignoring the influence of all the other planets still gave a reasonable approximation, and allowed Kepler to discern the simple pattern of the ellipse.

---

[7] Technically, both the sun and the planet would travel in ellipses around their common center of mass. The earlier stages of investigation could overlook this fine point, because the mass of the sun is so much greater than the masses of the planets. Here is another way in which God provided small stepping-stones toward the more complex final formulation.

A second insight is more implicit in Newton's formulations. Newton assumed that forces from different sources could be added together.[8] For example, the total force on the moon could be obtained by adding the force from the attraction of the earth, the force from the attraction of the sun, and then the small forces from other planets. That is similar to saying that those forces are independent of one another. The force from the earth on the moon causes a certain amount of acceleration, and the force from the sun on the moon causes its own additional acceleration, independent of the first acceleration. Galileo had earlier observed that motion of a body in a horizontal direction seemed to be relatively independent of its motion in a vertical direction. Newton generalized this principle, so that it applied to all bodies, both on earth and in heaven, in all three dimensions.

The apprentice scientist starts with a naive, intuitive understanding that rocks, balls, and human beings are created things with an integrity and "relative" independence in relation to other created things. By analogy, this feeling about independence gets extended into reasoning about physical forces. So it seems natural to postulate that forces from independent sources just get added to one another. Moreover, this process of addition corresponds to human experiences where one person is being pushed by two people together, in which case he experiences a stronger force in one direction; or where he is being pushed by two people in opposite directions, and experiences an effect similar to subtracting one force from the other.

In fact, Newton needed the principle of adding forces in order to work out even the simpler effects of gravitation. In principle, every particle anywhere on earth attracts every particle anywhere on the moon. The earth and the moon are not simple mathematical points, but large material objects. The distance r in the formula for gravity varies for every distinct particle on the earth or the moon. Fortunately, a spherically shaped mass of uniform density exerts exactly the same gravitational force as if all the mass were concentrated at its center. So for most purposes we can treat the planets as if they were points.[9] Here we see another happy simplification that God's rule over the world has provided for us.

Thus, Newton's systematization included several components. (1) Newton's three laws stated the general relations between force, mass, and acceleration. (2) Newton's Law of Gravitation specified the gravitational

[8] The principle of superposition of forces was already known before Newton.
[9] However, tidal effects on the earth, due to the gravitation of the moon and the sun, show a case where the greater attraction exerted on the nearer side of the earth must be taken into account.

force between two bodies. (3) Newton postulated that forces from different sources were additive, and that a force in a diagonal direction could be broken up into its components in two perpendicular directions. With these foundations, Newton had provided a system into which one could fit other kinds of forces, such as forces of pressure in a gas, forces of viscosity in a liquid, forces of strain in a solid, and electric and magnetic forces.

Newton's system also included ideas for how to translate between physical situations and mathematical representations. He used mathematical models that represented the forces and motions within the physical situations. Three principles for mathematical representation may be singled out.

First, through his invention of calculus, Newton provided a general tool for representing proportionalities between position and time, or between motion and time, or between other varying quantities. Calculus enabled one to calculate an *instantaneous* proportionality even when the proportionality changed with time. In modern calculus, the usual notation for the instantaneous rate of change of distance s with time t would be ds/dt (or $\partial s/\partial t$ if s depends on other quantities as well as time). To bring to the fore the idea of proportionality, I will temporarily represent this using a nonstandard notation, namely s:t. "s:t" is a shorthand notation for the normal notations used in calculus, ds/dt or $\partial s/\partial t$. s:t means that s (distance) *is proportional to* t (time). But in this context the notation represents an *instantaneous* proportionality. That is the way modern physics defines velocity: the velocity v is the instantaneous proportionality between distance s and time t, v = s:t. If the distance s changes in a complicated way, the velocity may itself gradually change, and then we may also consider the rate of change of v, which leads us to a *second* proportionality, v:t, the instantaneous change of velocity with respect to time. That is what we mean by acceleration. The acceleration can be represented compactly as s:t:t. This notation draws attention to each proportionality involved in the description. Each occurrence of the colon sign (":") represents a distinct proportionality. This notation then serves to remind us of the relation of calculus to the idea of proportionality. And this idea of proportionality, as we have seen, reflects the proportions in the tabernacle, and these reflect the imaging process that has its origin in God himself. God has left a witness to himself inside the mathematics that Newton used to describe force and motion!

Second, the principle of addition of forces leads to relatively simple mathematical equations that add together the contributions from various sources. This principle of addition goes back to the intuition that diverse creatures are relatively independent of one another. And behind this principle of diversity among creatures lies the archetype in God: God has both unity and diversity in himself. He is one God, in unity, and three persons, in diversity.

Third, one finds that, like gravitation, most other common forces involve simple proportionalities, which one expresses mathematically with multiplication. These simple proportionalities ultimately go back to the imaging relation within the Trinity. Imaging is the original of which proportionalities are copies.

Mathematical Models for Various Physical Systems

Together, the three principles offer a framework for producing mathematical tools or models for analyzing many common physical systems.

For example, consider a vibrating string. Suppose that the string is stretched out horizontally, and that we measure positions along the string by the number x. x is the distance from one end of the string to the point on the string that we are studying. Let h be the vertical position of the string at a point a distance x from the end. The vibration of the string over time obeys the equation

$$k\ h{:}x{:}x = m\ h{:}t{:}t \quad [10]$$

Here k is a constant measuring the tension in the string; h:x:x is the curvature of the string at point x.[11] m is the mass density per unit length of the string. h:t:t is the acceleration. The equation shows a simple relation of proportionality between the curvature h:x:x and the acceleration h:t:t. It is an application of Newton's Second Law, $F = ma$. The left-hand side, k h:x:x, represents the force (per unit length of string), and the right-hand side represents the mass times the acceleration.[12] In addition, each occurrence of a colon (":") represents a proportionality.

Instead of a string, we can consider water waves traveling in two dimensions. Suppose that we are studying water in a pool. Let x and y measure distances in two perpendicular directions along the surface of the water. Let h be the height of the water at any one point. The movement of waves obeys the equation

---

[10] The university sites on the Internet now provide excellent explanations of this and other equations in this chapter. Search for "equation for vibrating string" or "equation for waves."

[11] More precisely, h:x:x, or (h:x):x, is the second partial derivative of h with respect to x; in the usual notation, $\partial^2 h/\partial x^2$.

[12] More precisely, m is the mass per unit length, or mass density.

$$\text{h:x:x} + \text{h:y:y} = \text{k h:t:t}$$

k, the constant of proportionality, is $1/v^2$, where v is the wave velocity. Again we find that a simple, elegant equation using proportionalities describes the motion of the water.

For sound waves moving through the air in three dimensions, we have an analogous equation in three dimensions in space. These three dimensions can be represented by three measured distances, x, y, and z. x, let us say, measures straight ahead, y measures to one side, and z measures straight up. The resulting equation for sound waves is

$$\text{h:x:x} + \text{h:y:y} + \text{h:z:z} = \text{k h:t:t}$$

Here h represents the air pressure at any one point.

Or we may consider motions involving viscosity (like moving through molasses). Newton's law can still be applied to each small element of volume within a fluid, leading to the equation

$$\text{-p:x} + \text{k (u:x:x} + \text{u:y:y} + \text{u:z:z)} = \text{m (u:t} + \text{u u:x} + \text{v u:y} + \text{w u:z)} \text{ }^{13}$$

The left-hand side calculates the forces and the right side calculates mass times acceleration. Despite the appearance of complexity, this formula is really an instance of F = ma. -p:x is the force due to variations in pressure p. The expression with the factor of k, namely "k (u:x:x + u:y:y + u:z:z)," represents the force due to viscosity. k is a constant of proportionality whose value indicates the viscosity. Together these two forces represent the total force impinging on a small volume of fluid. On the right side of the equation, m represents the mass per unit of volume. u:t is the acceleration due to the change in velocity at any one fixed point. The other terms represent the acceleration due to the fact that the volume element in a flowing fluid is gradually moving to a new location, where the velocity is different from the original location.

One can see here the repeated use of addition of forces and simple proportionalities used in calculating the forces. Actually, the above equation calculates forces and accelerations only in the x-direction. There are two other equations, in the y-direction and z-direction. But the other two equations

---

[13] p is the pressure, k is the coefficient of viscosity, m is the mass density per unit volume, and u, v, and w are the components of velocity in the x, y, and z directions, respectively. This and the analogous equations in the y- and z-directions are known as the Navier-Stokes equations.

look essentially the same, since it does not matter how we choose the coordinate axes.

As physicists applied Newton's laws to many situations, it became more plain that fundamental physical laws could be expected to "look the same" in any direction. No direction was singled out for special treatment. This principle uses the idea of multiple perspectives. One perspective looks straight forward (the x-axis), while another looks to one side (the y-axis). A third looks straight up (the z-axis). The fundamental laws should look the same in any direction. One can generalize from these perspectives, to talk about any possible orientation for the three coordinate axes. Laws should look the same after an arbitrary rotation in space. Physicists would say that the laws are *invariant* under rotation.

We can tie this principle to biblical categories by saying that the truth, God's word, remains the truth as we change personal perspective. Physical laws thus reflect the character of God in a variety of ways. In the first place, the omnipresence and eternity of God are reflected in the law of God, in the fact that the law is invariant under changes in position and in time. But, in addition, the distinction of persons in the Trinity introduces the possibility of distinctions in personal perspective. These in turn have a reflection within the earthly sphere, in the form of distinct orientations in spatial direction. And the law is invariant under these changes in personal perspective.

From the standpoint of the ancient world, this result is surprising. Ancient Greek thinking about the physical world tended to regard the earth as a special location, and the downwards direction on earth as a special direction. The Bible itself could appear to endorse this intuition, since it describes events from the standpoint of an ordinary human observer on earth. To make the transition to Newton's science, or even that of Copernicus, one must grasp the possibility of multiple points of view, and distinguish between different possible choices of starting point for the measurements. One must also distinguish the overall attitude in ordinary human living from the attitude in scientific investigation.

To highlight the invariance of physical laws under rotational transformation, physics has made use of the mathematical device called "vector notation." Vector notation offers a way of describing physical or mathematical relationships in space without referring to any one particular coordinate system. Instead of writing three separate equations for motion in the x-direction, the y-direction, and the z-direction in space, one writes a single equation that represents all three directions, but does so independent of any specific choice of the direction of the three axes. The wave equation in three dimensions looks like this:

$$\nabla \bullet \nabla h = h{:}t{:}t$$

The "gradient" operator ∇, when applied to h, finds the direction in space in which h increases at a maximum rate, and its magnitude is the magnitude of that increase. (This procedure looks at a simple proportionality, namely the proportionality between change in h and change in spatial position.)[14] Thus the formula above is independent of any particular choice of axes x, y, and z as reference axes for our measurements.

The equations for fluid motion can similarly be rewritten:

$$-\nabla p + k \, [\nabla \bullet \nabla u] = m \, [u{:}t + (u \bullet \nabla)\, u] \ ^{15}$$

To people without a background in higher mathematics, this equation may look formidable, because of the symbol "∇." But in practice it amounts to a system of equations each of which involve (1) simple additions (going back to the idea of addition of force), (2) simple multiplications (going back to the idea of proportionality between force and other numerical quantities), and (3) calculating instantaneous proportionalities (going back to Newton's idea of how to capture a proportionality that is changing over time). Each of the proportionalities is analogous to the proportionalities in the tabernacle of Moses; and these in turn are analogous to the Son, who is the image of the Father. The laws of physics reflect the beauty and harmony in God.

The use of vector notation is only *one* way of highlighting invariant properties in physical laws. The century after Newton also saw the introduction of "generalized coordinates." As an example, consider a spinning ceiling fan. How do we describe the position of a chalk mark on one of the blades of the fan? Everything depends on the center of the fan, the axis on which it spins. In a case like this, instead of specifying a system by the location of particles in three dimensions, x, y, and z, one could specify the location with respect to its central axis. This kind of specification might lead to a simplification and to new physical insight for a body spinning around the axis. For this purpose

---

[14] The special dot sitting between the two gradient operators designates a vector "dot product," a special kind of generalized multiplication that applies to vectors. A vector is a mathematical object with both a magnitude (so many units long) and a direction in space (north, south, up or down, etc.). The generalized multiplication using a dot product can be defined as a series of simple multiplications and additions.

[15] In this equation, u is the vector representing the velocity of the fluid at any point in space. In the early equation, by contrast, u represented only the x-component of the velocity.

one uses three coordinates, r for the "radius," the distance away from the axis, θ (Greek theta) for the angle of rotation around the axis, and z for the distance parallel to the axis (the up-and-down direction for the ceiling fan). These are called "cylindrical coordinates." One can then rewrite Newton's law using this system of three coordinates, r, θ, and z, instead of x, y, and z. Or still other coordinate systems could be used.

Joseph-Louis Lagrange found a way of compactly describing Newton's laws of motion in many such systems. Suppose that instead of x, y, and z, we have coordinates q, r, and s. (These may have a simple or complicated relation to the original system in x, y, and z.) Suppose also that there may be more than one particle involved, so that we have in addition coordinates t, u, v for a second particle. For a total of 10 particles, we would have 30 coordinates. Lagrange considered very general systems with an arbitrarily large number of coordinates. For many systems, if L (the "Lagrangian") is the difference between the kinetic energy and the potential energy, Newton's equation F = ma is equivalent to

$$L{:}q = (L{:}(q{:}t)){:}t \ ^{16}$$

for each of the generalized coordinates q. This formulation shows an elegant simplicity, and in addition allows mathematical transformation of many physical problems into a form where they allow a much easier solution. As usual, each occurrence of the colon symbol (":") represents a distinct proportionality.

The idea of invariance under a change of perspective translates mathematically into equations that are invariant when we change the "perspective," that is, when we change the basic measurable quantities that we use in describing and analyzing the physical reality. Physical law exists, independent of our perspective. We can also say that physical laws show "symmetry." They have the same form after a mathematical transformation, just as a symmetrical column in a building has the same form after we rotate it. Symmetry is closely related to beauty. For example, we can see beauty in the tabernacle in the fact that the Most Holy Place has dimensions of 10 cubits *in all three directions*. It is 10 cubits long, 10 cubits wide, and 10 cubits high, so that any of the dimensions can be interchanged and leave the overall shape the same.

Symmetry and invariance have come to play a central role in twentieth-

---

[16] In standard calculus notation, Lagrange's equations are ∂L/∂q = (d/dt)[∂L/∂(dq/dt)], for each generalized coordinate q.

century physics. Physicists used symmetry assumptions again and again as they searched for deeper and more comprehensive laws. Because of its invariance under change of coordinates, Lagrange's formulation and a related one by William Hamilton served as clues in making the transition from classical physics to quantum mechanics. We cannot explore fully the role of symmetry and invariance without entering into much of the technical detail of powerful developments in the twentieth century. We will content ourselves with providing a kind of first taste, by considering Einstein's development of the theory of relativity.

EINSTEIN'S THEORY AS A STUDY IN SYMMETRY AND INVARIANCE

Conceptually, the theory of relativity started with reflections on symmetry and invariance. Earlier developments in physics had already made it clear that fundamental physical laws were invariant under rotation and under any choice of starting location (mathematicians would say invariance under translation). It looked like they were also invariant if you moved at a constant velocity. Suppose you wake up inside a train or an airplane. As long as you do not look out the window, and as long as there are no bumps or jerks in the ride, you cannot tell whether you are moving or how fast you are moving relative to the ground. The laws of physics are the same inside the airplane no matter how fast it is moving.

Newton's laws already have an invariant form in this respect. They depend on the acceleration, but *not* on the velocity. On the other hand, the laws for wave motion and fluid motion *do* depend on velocity, but that is only because everything takes place relative to the string or fluid through which a wave is propagating. If the entire string or fluid is itself moving along, that must be taken into account.

Einstein had the benefit of earlier developments. In particular, extended investigation of electricity and magnetism had eventually led to Maxwell's equations. These equations could be written in vector form, showing that they were invariant under rotation. But they were not invariant under changes in speed. The speed of light should change, depending on the velocity of the measuring system. But experimental tests seemed to show that the speed of light in a vacuum was always the same.

Einstein took the radical step of assuming that the speed of light was indeed always the same, but that underlying assumptions about the relation between measurement on a train and measurement on the ground needed reexamination. Einstein affirmed the invariance of fundamental physical laws, but showed that measurements of length and time differed subtly depending on one's perspective (one's "inertial system").

Suppose an observer on the train has a meter stick in his hand, and an observer on the stationary platform beside the train has a second meter stick. The observer on the platform would measure the train's meter stick as *less* than a meter long. A moving object appears to shrink.

This result seems at first glance highly paradoxical. But it is bound up with the fact that there is no uniform way of establishing that two different events at different locations are simultaneous. And the measurements of time in the two different systems also differ. The observer on the platform sees the clock on the train car as running slow. Nevertheless, if one sticks completely to descriptions from the standpoint of a single observer, the descriptions are completely coherent and in harmony with general physical laws.

The discrepancies between the two observers had never been noticed because at ordinary speeds the differences are tiny. If an airplane is going at 600 miles per hour or 1,000 kilometers per hour, the difference in length amounts to 1 part out of about 2 trillion (2×10^{12}). It is not measurable. The differences become significant only when speeds approach the speed of light, that is, 3×10^8 meters per second (three hundred million meters per second). (At this speed, one could go around the world 7 times in one second!)

So far, we have been looking at Einstein's special theory of relativity, which he published in 1905. In 1916 Einstein published the general theory of relativity, where he was able to take a further step. He used the mathematical technique of generalized coordinates, similar to Lagrange. And he followed the requirement that the fundamental law of gravitation should have invariant form even in accelerated systems, such as a falling elevator. He was motivated by observing that just as one cannot tell whether a train is moving without looking outside, one cannot tell whether one is being accelerated or being subjected to a gravitational field without looking outside. In short, he used the postulate of invariance between gravitation and acceleration to arrive at general equations that covered both. The equations of general relativity take considerable mathematical training to understand in detail. But they are built up from simple additions, multiplicative constants, and the proportionalities that Newton described with the invention of calculus.

The development of quantum mechanics in the twentieth century shows a similar reliance on principles of symmetry and on the search for elegant, beautiful mathematics that would express fundamental laws. We have here a rich stock of examples, but it can wait for another day.

Physicist Eugene Wigner, surveying the remarkable scientific triumphs in relativity theory and quantum theory, expresses astonishment at the harmony between beautiful mathematics and actual physical processes:

> The first point is that the enormous usefulness of mathematics in the natural sciences is something bordering on the mysterious and that there is no rational explanation of it. . . .
>
> It is not at all natural that "laws of nature" exist, much less that man is able to discover them.[17]

We too should express astonishment, but along with it, gratitude to God. Christians know who gave us the laws of nature. The Word, the second person of the Trinity, expresses himself in the words or laws concerning nature. They bear the imprint of his person, so they reveal awesome wisdom, power, and beauty. The simple proportionalities in physical laws are a form of "imaging," like the proportionalities in the tabernacle of Moses. God impressed these symmetries and proportionalities on the world as a reflection of himself and his own beauty and symmetry.

CHEMISTRY

Let us now turn for a moment to consider chemistry. What about patterns and laws in chemistry? Do they show symmetries and proportionalities? The periodic table of elements displays one of the more impressive patterns. Over a long period of time chemists gradually discovered that ordinary matter was composed of distinct chemical "elements" like hydrogen and oxygen that could not be further decomposed. Some elements showed pronounced similarities to one another in their chemical behavior, and that led gradually to the present-day arrangement of the periodic table. (See diagram.) The elements appear in horizontal rows in the order of their atomic numbers. (The atomic number is the number of protons in a single atom, and also the maximum electronic charge that the atom can have when ionized, that is, when electrons are stripped away.) Elements in any one column of the table show similar behavior. The elements in the rightmost column, the inert gases (helium, neon, argon, etc.), rarely combine to form complex molecules. Elements in the left-most column (column I A), the alkali metals (lithium,

---

[17] Eugene Wigner, "The Unreasonable Effectiveness of Mathematics in the Natural Sciences," *Communications on Pure and Applied Mathematics* 13 (1960): 2, 5.

sodium, potassium, etc.) easily give up one electron,[18] while elements in the column "VII A," the halogens (fluorine, chlorine, bromine, etc.), easily take up one extra electron. Together, these two columns (columns I A and VII A) combine to form salts. Thus table salt, sodium chloride, NaCl, is formed from an equal number of atoms of sodium (from column I A) and chlorine (from column VII A).

The similar properties in any one column of the periodic table mean that we could speak loosely of each element in a column as imaging the others in the same column. The behavior of one element is strikingly analogous to the behavior of any other element in the same column. The occurrence of imaging or analogy repeats what we have seen in many areas of biology and physics.

THE PERIODIC TABLE[19]

IA	II A	III B	IV B	V B	VI B	VIIB	VIII			I B	II B	III A	IVA	VA	VI A	VIIA	inert gases
H																	He
Li	Be											B	C	N	O	F	Ne
Na	Mg											Al	Si	P	S	Cl	A
K	Ca	Sc	Ti	V	Cr	Mn	Fe	Co	Ni	Cu	Zn	Ga	Ge	As	Se	Br	Kr
Rb	Sr	Y	Zr	Nb	Mo	Tc	Ru	Rh	Pd	Ag	Cd	In	Sn	Sb	Te	I	Xe
Cs	Ba	La	Hf	Ta	W	Re	Os	Ir	Pt	Au	Hg	Tl	Pb	Bi	Po	At	Rn
Fr	Ra	Ac															

In chemistry we also see extensive occurrences of proportionalities in many areas. The periodic table is closely related to one of the most important and pervasive systems of proportionalities, namely, the proportionalities in molecular combinations of elements. In the nineteenth century, chemical experiments gradually showed that many elements consistently combined in fixed proportions. Water, for example, is H_2O, meaning that it contains two atoms of hydrogen (H) for every atom of oxygen (O). Methane is CH_4, meaning that it contains four atoms of hydrogen for every atom of carbon (C). Carbon dioxide, CO_2, contains two atoms of oxygen (O) for every one of carbon (C).

Remarkably, chemists worked out all the relationships without ever seeing individual atoms. They had to reason from the constant proportions that

---

[18] In the light of twentieth-century knowledge of atomic structure, we now explain the properties of different elements in terms of electrons and electron "shells." The nineteenth century did not know about this subatomic structure but nevertheless succeeded in working out bonding relationships by experiment.

[19] For simplicity, the rare earth elements (Lanthanum series) and the Actinium series have been omitted.

they observed when combining macroscopic quantities of the different elements. The familiarity of our present-day thinking about atoms should not blind us to the sense of wonder. God has displayed before us a marvelous host of beautiful relationships in the phenomena of chemical bonding, and has made it simple enough so that, by patient work, chemists could discover elegant proportionalities even before we had a conception of atomic structure.

Numerical proportionalities also occur in many properties of materials. Consider, for example, the formula for pressure and volume in a perfect gas:

$$PV = nkT$$

where P is the pressure, V is the volume, T is the temperature (measured from absolute zero), n is the number of molecules, and k is Boltzmann's constant, which has to be measured empirically but is the same for any gas. When one thinks about it, this is a wonderful formula involving simple proportionalities. What right would we have to expect that God's world would display such consistency and so many instances of proportionality?

There is a further explanation for this formula. In 1738 Daniel Bernoulli hypothesized that the pressure of a gas was due to the motion of many individual molecules. This insight was further developed by a succession of scientists into the "kinetic theory of gases," which succeeded in deriving the perfect gas formula from first principles. The theory pictured gases as made up of a large number of individual molecules moving around at high speed, occasionally colliding with one another. These molecules would also sometimes collide with the surface of the container holding the gas, and bounce back. The effect of a large number of such collisions would be a steady pressure on the surface. The pressure P would obviously be proportional to the number of molecules (n), and inversely proportional to the volume (V), because molecules spread out over a larger volume would hit the sides less often.

This explanation of gases based on molecular motion might seem to take the fascination and beauty out of the formula. The formula and its proportionalities become "merely" a secondary effect of the underlying reality, which is individual molecules moving around. Yet our commitment to a Christian worldview, with its affirmation of multilevel reality, should encourage us to retain the sense of fascination and beauty. God wants us to enjoy the large-scale, tangible effects, with our observations of pressure and volume, as well as to enjoy probing underlying levels that provide a further explanation for the formula. God is author and artist for all the levels, not just the molecular one.

There is still more to this story. No actual gas is a "perfect" gas, but actual measurements conform closely to the formula when the pressure is not too high nor the temperature too low. Again, we can see the kindness of God in providing us with simplicity at first, simplicity that is easier to discover, and then leading us to discover that the simplicity does not cover the facts perfectly. There is more to be discovered. A more exact formula, taking into account the finite size of individual molecules and the slight attractive force between them, is Van der Waal's equation:

$$(P + an^2/V^2)(V - nb) = nkT$$

Here a and b are constants. a corresponds to a small force of attraction between molecules, while b corresponds to the finite size of individual molecules. If a and b are both zero, Van der Waal's equation simplifies and becomes $PV = nkT$, the formula for a perfect gas. Van der Waal's formula, though more complicated than the earlier one, still involves simple arithmetical processes of addition, subtraction, multiplication, and division.

Historically, many of the basic quantitative laws of chemistry were discovered in the nineteenth century, before the discovery of subatomic structure and before the discovery of quantum mechanics as an explanation of that structure. Quantum mechanics has now given us an extremely comprehensive and satisfying explanation for the periodic table, the properties of valence, and a wide range of chemical phenomena—all on the basis of a single fundamental equation of physics, Schrödinger's equation.[20] This deeper explanation again may tempt us into reductionism. We "reduce" chemistry to physics by saying that chemistry is "merely" an "accidental" effect of quantum mechanics. Once again we would wrongly be evaporating the mystery and beauty out of chemistry, which God has put there for us to appreciate and enjoy. As the Westminster Shorter Catechism reminds us, "Man's chief end is to glorify God, and to enjoy him forever" (Q. 1).

We can praise God both for the deep mysteries in physics and chemistry and for the consistency of God's rule in our ordinary affairs. Imagine a world

---

[20] But Schrödinger's equation, important as it is, does not stand by itself. One must mention Wolfgang Pauli's exclusion principle, which says that two electrons can never occupy the same quantum state. This principle is necessary to explain why electron shells fill up. One must know also that electrons have spin, and that atomic nuclei can have various compositions. The solution of one mystery still leaves others that are even more profound.

without the regularities that we take for granted: the rising of the sun, the supply of oxygen in the air, the consistent freezing and boiling properties of water,
the consistency of muscle behavior, the consistency of the transmission of
nerve impulses, the consistency of the chemical forces that underlie muscles
and nerves, and the consistency of our heartbeat. Our bodily existence
depends in countless ways on the consistency of God's rule over the physical
and chemical realms.

22

A CHRISTIAN APPROACH TO

MATHEMATICS

Like physics, mathematics fits well into the Christian worldview that we have developed. The word of God comprehensively controls the world that we observe. So the word of God includes a control of the mathematical aspects of the world. The coherence between mathematical expressions and physical laws that we saw in the previous chapter arises from the unity of the word of God. The word of God is a harmonious whole, and produces harmony between physics and mathematics. Indeed, it gives a foundation for the use of mathematics in all the sciences, and in other areas of life as well.

HINTS FOR MATHEMATICS IN BIBLICAL TEACHING

The biblical doctrine of God, plus the doctrine of creation, provide a sound basis for human beings to explore and appreciate the many-sided coherence in creation. "In him [Christ] all things hold together" (Col. 1:17). In addition, specific information from the Bible encourages the development of mathematics in connection with astronomy. We saw in chapter 20 that Genesis 1:14 points out the regularity of the movement of the heavenly bodies and invites human beings to use this regularity in keeping track of time. Keeping track in detail leads to the development of mathematical tools for calculations.

The tabernacle as a model of God's macrocosmic house also shows numerical and spatial beauty and harmony. In chapter 20 we observed the use of simple ratios in the dimensions of its construction. Since the tabernacle is a model of the macrocosm, that already suggests that the universe as macrocosm may show numerical and spatial regularities.

SYMMETRIES

The beauty of the tabernacle, which reflects the beauty of God, consists partly in simple symmetries. The shape of the tabernacle structure displays a north-south symmetry; it is the same on both sides of a central axis through the middle, as shown in the illustration below.

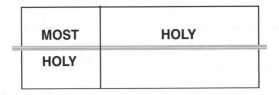

The Most Holy Place has the shape of a perfect cube, 10 cubits on a side and 10 cubits high. It thus has a further symmetry, as shown:

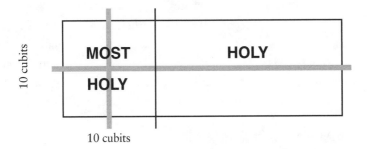

We instinctively see beauty in symmetries. And now the tabernacle beauty invites us to look for beauties and symmetries not only in the "microcosm," the tabernacle as a model, but in the "macrocosm," the universe as a whole. Yes, there are symmetries and beauties there. A butterfly, a honeycomb, a sea shell, a fern leaf—each touches us with its appearance. When our eyes are open in the wonder and fascination of the world, we ought to be drawn to worship God whose beauty is here reflected.

Symmetries crop up directly within mathematics as well, both in advanced mathematics and at a very elementary level. For example, there is a simple symmetry in the very fact that addition and multiplication have the same result regardless of the order of the numbers. $3 + 5 = 8$ and $5 + 3 = 8$. $3 \times 5 = 15$ and $5 \times 3 = 15$. We can write it in a way that shows the symmetry:

$3 + 5 = 8$

$5 + 3 = 8$

This property might seem to be utterly trivial. But it is not so trivial when we take a more complicated case. Consider the addition problem:

```
   549
    30
   156
   662
   987
   808
   235
+  421
_____
```

Does it matter whether we start from the top or from the bottom? That is, do we first have 549, then add 30 to it, then add 156 to the result, and so on? Or do we begin with 421 at the bottom, and add 235 to it, and so on? Will we come out with the same answer either way? What if we use the conventional shortcut in which we add all the units digits first, $9 + 0 + 6 + 2 \ldots$, and the add the 10s digits, and so on? Do we do this kind of addition starting at the bottom with the units digit 1 and then 5? How do we know that we will come out with the same answer?

People who regularly do addition problems by hand learn to check their work by doing the problem two different ways, perhaps from the top down and from the bottom up. Sometimes the results do not agree, but a closer look always turns up a mistake. When the mistakes are eliminated, the results always agree. The agreement shows a harmony and beauty derived from the word of God concerning numbers.

Return for a moment to the simple problem: does $3 + 5 = 5 + 3$? The agreement here seems utterly trivial, because we are so used to it. We learned it when we learned our addition table. We memorized the fact that $3 + 5 = 8$. We probably did not memorize the fact that $5 + 3 = 8$ separately. Rather, we eased the burden on our memory by learning the general rule that the result of addition is the same when you reverse the order.

How do we know that? We know because our teachers told us. But how did they know? Addition depends on the more basic idea of counting.

Suppose you have a collection of three dots: • • • You count the dots, "One, two, three." You also have a collection of five pluses: + + + + + You count the pluses, "One, two, three, four, five." Now you take the total collection:

• • • + + + + +

How will you count them? Will you count the dots first, or the pluses first? Counting the dots first is like adding 3 + 5. Counting the pluses first is like adding 5 + 3. Will the result be the same? How do you know?

One way of assuring yourself is by drawing a geometric picture. We picture the entire collection in space with the dots first:

• • • + + + + +

Then we picture it with the pluses first:

+ + + + + • • •

We can see that the two collections have the same number of pieces, because we can pair them off, one pair at a time. But this introduces still another idea. The idea of pairing off in order to check the relative size of two collections depends on human knowledge of the fact that, in any case whatsoever, pairing off will allow a reliable comparison of magnitude. We can also imagine that we physically move the dots in space. We pick them up and move them from the beginning of the row to the end of the row. We depend on the assumption that physical things have continuing existence, and that they do not randomly appear and disappear while we are doing the moving. The stability of physical objects, and the stability of the number of objects, depends on the stability of God's word governing the objects. We are depending on the faithfulness of God. God is so faithful in this area that we tend to take it for granted. We also tend to take for granted the harmony that God has established between numerical and spatial truths. When we see 3+5 represented in spatial terms by dots and plus signs, we know that it enjoys a harmonious relation to 3+5 represented in numerical terms, by counting.

Mathematicians have looked at other kinds of situations in which the results *do* depend on the order in which one does things. Consider a situation in which a cubical die is sitting on the table in front of you. The top of the die has one spot on it, while the face on its front has two spots on it (see the diagrams). Roll the die 90 degrees to the right. Now there is a four on top, while the face on its front is still the one with two spots on it. Now roll the die 90 degrees toward you. The four flips to the front, and now there is a five on top:

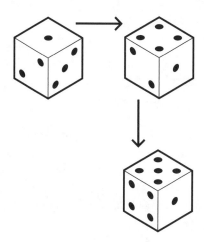

Now go back to the original position, with one spot on top of the die. This time, do the two rotations in the reverse order. First roll the die 90 degrees toward you. The five is now on top. Then roll 90 degrees to the right. There is now a four on top. The total result is different from the result when the roll to the right is followed by the roll forward. That is, the result of two rotations depends on the order:

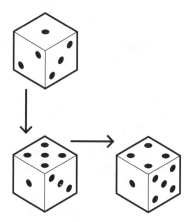

So why do two numbers always add up to the same result, *regardless* of order? It is a harmony ordained by God.

CORRELATING SPACE WITH NUMBERS

In the preceding discussion we have more than once employed a picture in space in order to reassure ourselves about the behavior of numbers. These pictures exploit an impressive correlation between numbers and space. The tabernacle suggests such a correlation. The spatial regions are marked out by measurements of length. The Holy Place has dimensions of 20 cubits by 10 cubits, which are numerical specifications. The Most Holy Place has dimensions of 10 cubits by 10 cubits, which invite a comparison between it and the Holy Place. Space is correlated with numbers. These simple relationships invite man to understand *spatial* regions in the macrocosm through *numerical* measurements and calculations of lengths. They invite us to explore in detail correlations between space and number. In other words, they invite the development of geometry, and they do so in a way that already relates geometry to arithmetic. Unfortunately, though the Greeks had an interest in spatial proportions, they did not sufficiently explore the relation of geometry to arithmetic. Only centuries later did Descartes invent analytic geometry, which provided a thoroughgoing and systematic way for drawing relations between number and space.

IMAGING IN THE TABERNACLE

The tabernacle model shows that mathematics in its roots originates from God. Both the spatial and numerical aspects of the tabernacle are an integral part of the structure of imaging or modeling. In particular, the Holy Place is an attenuated "image" of the Most Holy Place, which in turn is an "image" of the macrocosm and of God's dwelling in heaven.

Let us first consider the spatial structure. The spatial structure of the rooms is an image of God's dwelling in heaven. And, as we learn from the further revelation in the New Testament, God's dwelling in heaven has an analogue in God himself, namely in the indwelling of the persons of the Trinity (called coinherence or perichoresis). The Father is in the Son and the Son in the Father (John 17:21). The Holy Spirit is in fellowship with both the Father and the Son (John 3:34). This original uncreated indwelling is analogous to the dwelling of the Father, the Son, and the Spirit in human beings. And this indwelling in the created world is symbolically foreshadowed by the dwelling of God in the tabernacle and the temple. Hence, all the spatial rooms go back originally to an original pattern, an archetype, namely, the Trinitarian indwelling.

What about the numerical relations? The second room, the Holy Place, is twice as long as the first, the Most Holy Place. But it has the same width and the same height as the Most Holy Place. In two dimensions, the width and the height, the "image" matches the original in a one-to-one fashion. In the third dimension, the image is twice as large. Thus imaging is related to simple properties of addition and multiplication.

The root of imaging, as we saw in chapter 18, is the Son who is the original image of the Father. The Father is one, and begets a second in his image. Here, if you like, is the original one and the original two. Repeated imaging within the creation leads to a number sequence. So mankind, now thinking God's thoughts after him, can think not only one but two, and not only two but an indefinite number of additions to two. He then contemplates a series of numbers stretching out indefinitely: 1, 2, 3, 4, . . . But of course God is responsible not only for the utmost simplicities in number, the very conception of the number series, but for whatever complex and beautiful properties we find in this series.

CONCEPTIONS OF MATHEMATICS

We saw in chapter 1 that scientific laws have divine attributes. We are dealing with God's word, God's speech. The same can be said concerning mathematical truth. One can go through a process exactly parallel to chapter 1 and see divine attributes in mathematical truth, because mathematical truth is an expression of God's word.

Many people have thought that mathematics is quite distinct from the sciences, because it seems to be independent of the physical structure of the world. Physics, chemistry, biology, and other sciences have to go out and look at the world; they have to make sure that their descriptions match the behavior of the world, and from time to time scientists correct older theories on the basis of new evidence. By contrast, mathematics appears to involve only pure reasoning, and cannot be falsified by the world.

This picture of mathematics has some truth in it, particularly when applied to mathematics in more axiomatized form. (Axioms are starting assumptions from which many conclusions can be deduced.) But the origins of mathematics involved practical interaction with the world. The early developments in arithmetical calculation and in geometry involved practical projects of measurement, record keeping, and physical construction. Later geometry attained a "pure" axiomatic form under Euclid, who arranged the system of geometry in such a way that many theorems could be deduced from a few starting postulates. The deduction apparently took place without any necessity of testing conclusions in the physical world. But in the end the deductions could still be applied to the physical world. The results demonstrated an impressive harmony between mathematics, logic, and the physical world.

Even though mathematics shows logical structure, from the standpoint of the ordinary person axiomatized mathematics is only one subdivision of practical mathematics. And the practical use of mathematics does involve interaction with the world. Moreover, as in science, the development of technical concepts in mathematics starts with human intuitions about counting and space, which are rooted in experience.

In addition, people learning mathematics understand better if we keep illustrating the truths with examples in the world. We keep exploring the relations that various parts of mathematics enjoy with one another and with the physical world. Moreover, the history of mathematics shows how physical needs led to the development of mathematical tools. Newton developed calculus to deal with the description of physical motion. But the flow of knowledge sometimes went the other way: mathematical tools were sometimes already on hand for use in more thorough understanding of physical problems. For example, Einstein found the mathematics of curvature in manifolds (multidimensional mathematical spaces) already in place when he began to envision the theory of general relativity. Both directions of influence—from mathematics to the physical world, and from the physical world to mathematics—depend on harmony that God has established between space, number, and the physical world.

VIEWS ABOUT THE NATURE OF MATHEMATICS

Reflections about mathematics have given rise to three main approaches in describing its essence.[1] According to *intuitionism,* mathematics is ultimately about human intuitions concerning irreducibly basic concepts of number and space. The other two approaches take mathematics in its axiomatic form. *Logicism* says that mathematics is ultimately a branch of logic and is reducible to logic. *Formalism* says that mathematics is about the manipulation of formal language systems. Each such system has a fixed alphabet, fixed rules for writing formulas, axioms, and rules for deriving theorems.

All of these approaches have difficulties in explaining why and how mathematics can apply so effectively to the physical world. Intuitionism

---

[1] See Paul Benacerraf and Hilary Putnam, eds., *Philosophy of Mathematics: Selected Readings* (Englewood Cliffs, N.J.: Prentice-Hall, 1964).

seems to lock mathematics away within the human mind. Formalism makes it just a seemingly arbitrary game played with a language that obeys certain rules. But why these rules? Logicism has the best chance for explanation, since it claims that mathematical truths are truly universal. But it has not succeeded in reducing the ideas of number and space to pure logic. In human intuition, we do think about number and space in relation to our *experience* of a world that has numerical and spatial order.[2]

These approaches to explaining mathematics have the marks of reductionism, such as we discussed in chapter 15. God has ordained a coherence among a number of aspects of the world. First, the *human mind* has intuitions about numbers and space. Second, numerical and spatial order characterize the external *physical world*. Third, this order has an impressive *logical* organization, so that many consequences follow from a few starting assumptions. Fourth, the logical order can be organized rigorously into a representation in a formalized *language* system, with axioms and rules of derivation. The human mind, the physical world, logic, and language cohere. But if someone denies that God is the source of coherence, he is tempted to explain it by *reducing* the many aspects of the world to one aspect, which is then seen as the ultimate explanation.

UNITY AND DIVERSITY IN THE WORLD

Non-Christian approaches to mathematics have an even more basic problem. They cannot explain the interlocking and harmony between unity and diversity in the world. Unity and diversity in relation to one another are necessary for mathematics even to begin. Parmenides, the Greek philosopher, said that reality had unity but no diversity. All is one. Then counting is impossible, and spatial distinctions between one place and another are impossible. On the other hand, suppose, as atomistic and nominalistic philosophies tend to claim, that there is diversity and no unity. Then one could not confidently identify two instances of the same number, because being "the same" would have no meaning (sameness implies unity). One cannot get started without a coherent interlocking in which distinct, diverse things share unities.

Unity and diversity cohere in the world that God created because God is

---

[2] In addition, these philosophies have difficulty accounting for Gödel's proof, which shows the limitations of any formal system rich enough to include elementary number theory (thus questioning the formalist approach, and the logicist hope of reducing mathematics to axioms of logic). See the discussion in Vern S. Poythress, "A Biblical View of Mathematics," in Gary North, ed., *Foundations of Christian Scholarship: Essays in the Van Til Perspective* (Vallecito, Calif.: Ross, 1976), 171-172; James Nickel, *Mathematics: Is God Silent?* 2nd ed. (Vallecito, Calif.: Ross, 2001), 190-194; D. F. M. Strauss, "Is a Christian Mathematics Possible?" *Tydskrif vir Christelike Wetenskap* [*Journal for Christian Scholarship*] 39 (2003): 31-49.

One and is also Three. Both unity and diversity originate in the Trinity. Cornelius Van Til observes:

> ... if one begins with an ultimate plurality in the world, or we may say by regarding plurality as ultimate, there is no way of ever coming to an equally fundamental unity. On the other hand, if one should begin with the assumption of an ultimate abstract, impersonal unity, one cannot account for the fact of plurality. No system of thought can escape this dilemma. No system of thought has escaped this dilemma. ...
>
> What Augustine and all theistic thinkers after him have done is to say that in God, and more specifically in the triune God, lies the solution of this difficulty.[3]

SIMPLE BEAUTIES IN NUMBERS

Mathematicians see elegance and beauty in higher mathematics. But beauty also occurs in elementary mathematics, if we have eyes to see it. Reductionist philosophy of mathematics tends to drain the beauty away with the claim that all the surface manifestations of beauty are merely "accidental" by-products of more fundamental laws. In mathematics the opportunities for reduction are particularly strong, because one can deduce many mathematical properties from a few axioms. (For example, Euclid's book on geometry deduced many theorems from a few axioms of geometry.) But once we reject reductionism and see the entire field of mathematics as a display of God's wisdom and beauty, opportunities for admiration open up on every side. Not only the axioms but the deductions themselves show elegance. We affirm the reality of both "surface" manifestations and fundamental laws. Nothing is merely an accidental by-product.

Examples of Simple Beauties

We earlier considered the simple case of addition. $3 + 5 = 5 + 3$. Now consider the multiplication of two numbers. Is the result independent of order? Does $5 \times 3 = 3 \times 5$? Yes. Once again, the result may seem trivial, because that is how we learned our multiplication table. But the operations are different. 5×3 may be interpreted to mean the result of taking 3 five times, like this:

---

[3] Cornelius Van Til, *Survey of Christian Epistemology* (n.l.: den Dulk Christian Foundation, 1969), 47; see further discussion in James Nickel, *Mathematics: Is God Silent?* 231-232, 253-255; Poythress, "Biblical View of Mathematics," 168-173.

$$3 + 3 + 3 + 3 + 3$$

3 X 5 means taking 5 three times:

$$5 + 5 + 5$$

At first glance, it is not at all clear that these will come out the same. We can reassure ourselves using a geometric figure:

If we group together each column by itself, we get a collection of three dots in each column. Adding up the columns, we get $3 + 3 + 3 + 3 + 3 = 15$. On the other hand, if we first group each row by itself, we get a collection of five dots in each row. Adding up the rows, we get $5 + 5 + 5 = 15$. The number of dots is the same no matter how we choose to group them together. The analogy between geometry and arithmetic assures us that the geometric picture of the dots faithfully represents the arithmetic realities of addition and multiplication. We are depending on the coherent relation between space and number, established and maintained by God. And we are depending on the coherence of physical objects, that the dots stay there while we are counting. And we are depending on the coherence of the entire system of addition, in which, as we saw, the result of an addition is well-defined and independent of the order of the addition.

Let us consider a slightly more complicated case. 3 X 50 = 150. How do we know this result? When we learned our multiplication table, we learned it only up to 10 or maybe 12. We did not learn up to 50. But we later learned how to deal with large numbers using a recipe. To calculate 3 X 50, we first do 3 X 0 and obtain 0. Then we do 3 X 5 and obtain 15. And we know that we put the 15 to the left of the 0, obtaining 150. This system of multiplication depends on a coherent proportionality between multiplication of 3 X 5 on the one hand, and multiplication of 3 X 50 on the other. If you add a zero to one of the factors, you will get an extra 0 in the result. Everything else will remain the same. Here is a representation of some of the proportionality:

0 X 5 = 0	0 X 50 = 00
1 X 5 = 5	1 X 50 = 50

2 X 5 = 10   2 X 50 = 100
3 X 5 = 15   3 X 50 = 150
4 X 5 = 20   4 X 50 = 200
5 X 5 = 25   5 X 50 = 250
6 X 5 = 30   6 X 50 = 300
7 X 5 = 35   7 X 50 = 350
8 X 5 = 40   8 X 50 = 400
9 X 5 = 45   9 X 50 = 450

0 X 6 = 0   0 X 60 = 00
1 X 6 = 6   1 X 60 = 60
2 X 6 = 12   2 X 60 = 120
3 X 6 = 18   3 X 60 = 180
4 X 6 = 24   4 X 60 = 240
5 X 6 = 30   5 X 60 = 300
6 X 6 = 36   6 X 60 = 360
7 X 6 = 42   7 X 60 = 420
8 X 6 = 48   8 X 60 = 480
9 X 6 = 54   9 X 60 = 540

0 X 7 = 0   0 X 70 = 00
1 X 7 = 7   1 X 70 = 70
2 X 7 = 14   2 X 70 = 140
3 X 7 = 21   3 X 70 = 210

. . .

This is an impressive, extended proportionality. It says that the entire multi-plication table, as we originally learned it, replicates itself (images itself) when one of the factors is 10 times bigger. And it replicates itself again when a fac-tor is 100 times bigger, and then when it is 1,000 times bigger. We depend on this series of images whenever we use the normal routine for multiplying mul-tidigit numbers by hand.

We can also represent this process of imaging geometrically. Here is the diagram representing the multiplication of 3 X 5:

Now consider the following diagram:

```
• • • • •   • • • • •   • • • • •     • • • • •
• • • • •   • • • • •   • • • • •   • • • • •

• • • • •   • • • • •   • • • • •     • • • • •
• • • • •   • • • • •   • • • • •   • • • • •

• • • • •   • • • • •   • • • • •   • • • • •
• • • • •   • • • • •   • • • • •   • • • • •
```

We have 15 groups of 10 dots each. The first five groups of ten dots on the top comprise altogether 50 dots. Multiplying by three is equivalent to taking all 15 groups together, that is, 3 X 50 = 150. The diagram is analogous to the simpler diagram with 3 X 5 = 15 dots. But now each individual dot among the 15 has been replaced by a subcollection of 10 dots. Comparison between the two diagrams, with 15 dots and 150 dots respectively, shows that there is a geometric analogy between the two. The geometric analogy (or proportionality, as we have been calling it) assures us that we can calculate 3 X 50 (or 30 X 5) by first doing 3 X 5, and then adding the zero on. This proportionality between single dots and subcollections of 10 dots offers the basis for the entire process of multiplying multidigit numbers.

These are wonderful and beautiful harmonies established by God. And they were not so obvious to past generations. It took time for the decimal system to be invented, which allowed convenient representation of large numbers by using multiples of 10, 100, 1,000, and so on, and allowed an extremely efficient way of performing additions, subtractions, multiplications, and divisions on large numbers. The decimal system also allows greater facility in working with very small quantities, less than the size of ordinary units of measurement. That in turn opens the way to greater appreciation for the proportionalities that extend into the realm of the very small. Not only is 3 X 50 = 150; in addition, 3 X .000005 = .000015. Physically, three lengths of 5 microns (5×10^{-6} meter, smaller than the diameter of human hair) make a total of 15 microns.

Nowadays, most complex calculations are done on computers or hand-held calculators. These also depend on the same basic proportionalities, though internally they use the base 2 system (binary system) rather than the base 10 (decimal) system to perform calculations. Exploring how and why arithmetic operations can be represented using different arithmetical bases would lead us into still more mathematical beauties. When we use a calculator or balance a checkbook, we depend on the consistency and coherence of a huge number of proportionalities and stabilities in the number system. We depend on the faithfulness of God who establishes these consistencies.

Triangular Numbers

As another example, consider the "triangular numbers," which are simply numbers representing the number of dots in a triangular array. One can form triangular arrangements with rows of dots, as follows:

The first triangle has 1 dot. The second has 1 + 2 = 3 dots. The third has 1 + 2 + 3 = 6 dots. And so on. We observe that the number of dots in any one triangle is the sum of consecutive integers beginning with 1.

This observation already relies on the God-ordained coherence between the spatial arrangements of dots and the additive properties of numbers. It shows an analogy or "imaging" relation between space and number. As we have already said, "in him [Christ] all things hold together" (Col. 1:17). This "holding together" must include the holding together of spatial and numerical truths. So we are already depending on the Word, the second person of the Trinity, in our reasoning. And we are depending on the Father, the first person, who ordains all truth. We are depending on the Spirit, the third person, who teaches all truth (Ps. 94:10; Job 32:8). The imaging of space in number represents an attenuated reflection of the Son, who is the image of the Father. Our subsequent reflections on triangular numbers draw out further ways in which we can see harmony and coherence deriving from God.

How many dots are there altogether in the 1,000-th triangle in this series? In the triangle's first row we would find one dot. In the second row we would find two more dots, for a total of 1 + 2 dots. In the third row we would find three dots. Altogether we have 1 + 2 + 3 + 4 + . . . + 1,000 dots. Adding up all the numbers from 1 to 1,000 would be exceedingly time-consuming, and a mistake might easily creep in somewhere. The power of mathematics comes partly from seeing God-ordained patterns and finding ways to shorten our labor.

In the 1,000-th triangle there are (1,000 X 1,001)/2 (1,000 times 1,001 divided by 2) dots, that is, 500,500 dots. How do we know? There is a general principle or pattern. For any positive integer n, the n-th triangle, with n dots on its bottom row, has a total of n X (n+1)/2 dots. You can check it out with the first few cases. The first triangle has 1 X 2/2 = 1 dot. The second has 2 X 3/2 = 3 dots. The third has 3 X 4/2 = 6 dots. The fourth has 4 X 5/2 = 10 dots. And so on.

But how do we know that this formula always works? There are several ways of showing that it is true. First, let us use geometric reasoning. The number of dots is roughly analogous to the area of the triangle in which the dots reside. From somewhere in the past, you may remember that the area of any triangle is ½ times the base times the height. This formula is at least close to the formula n X (n+1)/2. Division by 2 corresponds to the factor of ½; n is the base, and n+1 is close to being the height, measured in rows of dots. But how can we go beyond these rough reasonings to something precise?

The formula for the area of a triangle is usually derived by placing two triangles of the same shape next to one another:

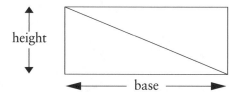

The area of the entire rectangle including the two triangles is height times base. Since this area is divided into two equal pieces, the area of one triangle is ½ of the height times the base.

If we see an analogy between this situation and our triangle of dots, we can use the analogy to construct an argument. Instead of one triangle of dots, let us produce two, with the second one upside down:

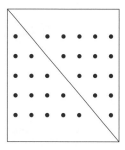

We then have two triangles, each with five dots on the longest row. There are five rows in all. But with the two triangles together, there are six dots in each row. The total number of dots is 5 X 6. The number of dots in one triangle must be half of this, or 5 X 6/2 = 15. This argument can clearly be generalized. The step of generalization involves seeing the God-ordained general pattern that occurs in triangles of any size. If we take two triangles with 1,000 dots on a side, there are 1,000 rows, and each row has 1,001 dots. The two triangles together have 1,000 X 1,001 dots. One triangle has half of this number, that is, a total of (1,000 X 1,001)/2 dots.

We can also produce an algebraic demonstration of the same result, thereby showing the exact coherence between spatial and algebraic reasoning, and between spatial and algebraic techniques of enumeration. Consider the sum of the first 5 integers:

$$1 + 2 + 3 + 4 + 5$$

Now write the sum in the reverse order:

$$5 + 4 + 3 + 2 + 1$$

The additions will come out the same no matter what order we choose, because of the faithfulness, consistency, rationality, and beauty of God.

Now write the two sums one under the other:

$$1 + 2 + 3 + 4 + 5$$
$$5 + 4 + 3 + 2 + 1$$

Add by columns instead of rows (this procedure again changes the order of addition, relying on the faithfulness of God).

$$1 + 2 + 3 + 4 + 5$$
$$5 + 4 + 3 + 2 + 1$$
$$\overline{}$$
$$6 + 6 + 6 + 6 + 6$$

The total sum of all the numbers is then 5 X 6. The sum within one row is half of this, or 5 X 6/2.

This procedure generalizes, because of the harmony and coherence in God's word. Suppose we have the sum of the first 1,000 integers:

$$1 + 2 + 3 + \ldots + 1,000$$

We repeat the same rearrangement:

```
1      +     2 +     3 + . . . + 1,000
1,000 +   999 +   998 + . . . +      1
```
_____

```
1,001 + 1,001 + 1,001 + . . . + 1,001
```

There are 1,000 copies of 1,001, for a total of 1,000 X 1,001. Either row by itself is half of this, or 1,000 X 1,001/2. In general, for the addition of the first n natural numbers, the sum is n X (n+1)/2.

We can obtain the same result in another way, by mathematical induction. Mathematical induction relies on the fundamental intuition about the integers, that we can obtain the integers by repeatedly adding 1 to the last one we have obtained. (As we saw, this idea of "generating" integers is analogically based on the "generation" of an image, based on the Trinity.)

A proof by mathematical induction starts by establishing the truth for the integer 1. For a triangle whose base has only one dot, that is, for n = 1, the number of dots should be n X (n+1)/2 = 1 X (1+1)/2 = 1. It checks out. The formula is true for n = 1.

Now observe that the triangular numbers can be described as a row of numbers whose differences form an earlier row that is simply the succession of integers:

```
1   2   3   4    5    6    7    8    9
  1   3   6   10   15   21   28   36
```

The first row is just a list of the integers in succession. The second row begins with 1, and then we add the corresponding number from the first row in order to get the next number in the second row. The difference between two successive numbers in the second row is the corresponding number in the first row. The second row clearly is the list of the triangular numbers.

Now, what property will allow this result? Let us test the formula n X (n+1)/2 and see whether it is compatible with this result. 100 X 101/2 and 101 X 102/2 are two successive numbers in this "row." When we factor out the common factor (101/2), we can see that the difference between them is

101 X 102/2 - 100 X 101/2 = (101/2) X (102-100) = (101/2) X 2 = 101

In general, k X (k+1)/2 and (k+1) X (k+2)/2 are two successive numbers in this row. The difference is

(k+1) X (k+2)/2 - k X (k+1)/2 = [(k+1)/2] X [(k+2) - k] = [(k+1)/2] X 2 = k+1

(The "+1" is needed because the differences are always one greater than the position in the series.)

Now the formula n X (n+1)/2 works for n = 1, as we have already checked. It must therefore also work for n = 2, because the difference between the formula for n = 1 and the formula for n = 2 is just the right size (namely 2). We have just checked that the difference will *always* be the right size. So we can conclude that the formula works as far out as we want to go, that is, for any natural number n. Mathematical induction allows us to deduce the general case, because we understand how the natural numbers are generated by the repeated process of adding 1. Corresponding to this, we just repeat the reasoning process: if true for 4, true for 5; if true for 5, true for 6. Our minds, thinking God's thoughts after him, can see that the reasoning applies for all natural numbers, and hence the formula is universally true.

Still other approaches can be constructed to arrive at the same result concerning triangular numbers (see appendix 2 for three more). The diversity in the different approaches derives from the diversity in the word of God, which specifies each approach. The unity in the different approaches, expressing the unity of mathematical truth, derives from the unity in the word of God. In Christ "all things hold together" (Col. 1:17). The coherence of approaches displays the beauty, faithfulness, and rationality of God. Mathematics should stimulate praise!

This one example by itself is not so important. But it is important that we grasp that, even with fairly elementary mathematical reasoning, we constantly rely on the coherence of God's word and the beauty and harmony of analogies. Reasoning from n = 5 to n = 6 is *analogous* to reasoning from 4 to 5, or from 3 to 4.

FINAL EXAMPLES

We may close off our illustrations with two examples that involve still other arithmetical beauties. First, consider the procedure of "casting out nines." This procedure can be used to check for mistakes in a paper-and-pencil arithmetic problem. Consider the multiplication problem:

```
     548
   X  83
   _____

   1644
   4384
   _____

   45484
```

After a person has worked out a problem like this one on paper, he can use the procedure of "casting out nines" as a quick check. This procedure says that instead of doing the original multiplication problem, 548 X 83, we substitute a simpler problem. There is a specific recipe for producing a simpler problem, and this recipe is what is called "casting out nines." Instead of 548 we take the result of adding up the digits in 548, namely $5 + 4 + 8 = 17$. After this step, if there is *still* more than one digit, as there is with the number 17, we repeat the procedure with 17. So we add the digits in 17, and obtain $1 + 7 = 8$. 8 is a single digit, so 8 is the first number to use in the new multiplication problem. This reduction from 548 to 8 is called "casting out nines," because the same result (8) can also be obtained by "casting out" or throwing away 9 any time the sum reaches 9 or more. For example, $5 + 4 = 9$, and we can "cast out" the 9, leaving us with 8. If we were to end up with a single digit that was a 9, we could "cast out" this 9, and we would be left with 0.

Now we must do the same with the second number in the original multiplication problem, namely 83. $8 + 3 = 11$. 11 is still two digits, so we repeat the procedure: $1 + 1 = 2$. 2 is therefore what we use as the second number in our *new* multiplication problem. The new problem has two new numbers, 8 and 2. 8 is the result of "casting out nines" from 548, while 2 is the result of "casting out nines" from 83. We can show the relation as follows:

Original multiplication problem:	548	X	83	=	45484
New (simplified) problem:	8	X	2	=	16

So now we do the new multiplication problem: $8 \times 2 = 16$. We then "cast out nines" in the result, 16, and obtain $1 + 6 = 7$.

The final check now consists in comparing the result from the *original* problem, namely 45484, with the result from our *new* problem, namely 7. Cast out nines from 45484. $4 + 5 + 4 + 8 + 4 = 25$. Then we reduce 25 to $2 + 5 = 7$. 7 is the same final result as we obtained from the new, reduced multiplication problem. If the original problem has been done correctly, the results from these two routes should always agree.

This way of checking multiplication (and analogous procedures for addition and division) seems almost magical. Why does everything harmonize when we drop out the 9s and add digits? The result depends on a deep analogy (or harmony) between ordinary arithmetic and "modular" arithmetic, or what we might call "clock" arithmetic. On an ordinary 12-hour clock face, the hour hand moves progressively up from 1 to 2 on up to 12, increasing by one unit each hour. But then instead of going up to 13, it goes around to 1 again. One can study this as a self-consistent system in which "addition" automatically never goes past 12, but goes around the clock in a circular motion. In this new arithmetical system, 11+ 3 = 2, because one always subtracts away 12 when the result becomes more than 12. It turns out that casting out nines represents a kind of new "arithmetic" in which the clock has 9 numbers instead of 12. Addition and multiplication can be consistently defined on this new "clock." This clock always subtracts away 9 when the result becomes more than 9. Because 10 is one more than 9, 10 is equivalent to 1 in the new system. Likewise, 20 is equivalent to 2. Hence the placeholding function of the decimal system is ignored, and one just adds up the digits in a multi-digit number. Casting out nines works because the new clock arithmetic remains in complete harmony with the original arithmetic taking place with ordinary numbers written in the decimal system.[4]

Our second example concerns the problem of sums of squares. 3, 4, and 5 form a "Pythagorean triple," such that $3^2 + 4^2 = 5^2$. It is called "Pythagorean" because Pythagoras originally discovered the geometric theorem that in a right triangle, the sum of the squares of the sides is equal to the square of the hypotenuse:

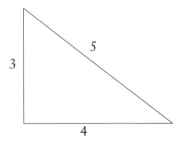

---

[4] For further exploration of these properties, one can consult any number of treatments of modular arithmetic, which is a subdivision of elementary number theory.

Do any other integers have the same property? We can find an infinite number of such triples: $5^2 + 12^2 = 13^2$; $7^2 + 24^2 = 25^2$; $9^2 + 40^2 = 41^2$. A simple recipe can generate all such triples. If a and b are positive integers, and a is greater than b, then the three numbers $a^2 - b^2$, $2ab$, and $a^2 + b^2$ form a Pythagorean triple. This one example is but one of a multitude of beauties that await the investigator.

In about 1630 Pierre de Fermat claimed that though one could find an infinite number of Pythagorean triples, one could find no positive integer solutions at all if one changed the problem from finding squares (a^2) to finding cubes (a^3) or any other power n with n>2. That is, for any integer n>2 there are no positive integers a, b, and c such that $a^n + b^n = c^n$. Fermat wrote in the margin of a book that he had discovered a proof of this result, but did not write it down. It is likely that Fermat made an error in reasoning somewhere in this still unknown proof. For several centuries mathematicians sought a proof in vain, until finally in 1994 Andrew Wiles presented a proof based on extremely sophisticated mathematics, developed only in the twentieth century. One can read the story of the quest in Simon Singh, *Fermat's Enigma*.[5]

FOR FURTHER EXPLORATION

Fortunately, a book on a Christian view of mathematics already exists that explores these riches more fully, namely James Nickel's *Mathematics: Is God Silent?*[6] I need not duplicate here its more extended discussion. The examples that I have given may suffice to show that mathematics offers a wonderful display of God's wisdom for those who are awake to its beauties and to God who ordained these beauties.

---

[5] Simon Singh, *Fermat's Enigma: The Quest to Solve the World's Greatest Mathematical Problem* (Toronto: Penguin, 1996).
[6] Nickel, *Mathematics: Is God Silent?* (see note 2, above).

23

CONCLUSION:
SERVING GOD

We return to the point that we made at the beginning. Scientists rely on God, who ordains and sustains the laws that they study. Ordinary people rely on God, not only for the air that they breathe but whenever they rely on the products of technology. But for many, the reliance is unconscious, and sometimes at odds with a heart that is in rebellion against God. We will serve God one way or another, because it is inevitable for creatures. We will serve him willingly, or else unwillingly and in spite of ourselves. But how much better to serve him as those who have been reconciled to him, and who can not only live in peace with him but praise him for his benefits! Science is intended to be a task pursued and carried out in a spirit of praise. In science, we think God's thoughts after him, and praise rises in our hearts as we see more of his wisdom.

This is the way it was meant to be, from the way that God created the world. But through the depth of human rebellion, what was meant to be has become strange and contrary to what is usual. We need the renewing and energizing of the Holy Spirit, who is a gift to those who come to Christ, if we are to discover again the way of freedom and the way that opens freedom to others.

This book is intended as a contribution to promoting that freedom. But it is only one contribution, because within this life we are all only on the way to the full freedom, "the freedom of the glory of the children of God," for which we hope (Rom. 8:21, 25). God has more to show us, and more with which to bless us, in the realms of science and mathematics. "It is the glory of God to conceal things, but the glory of kings is to search things out" (Prov. 25:2).

APPENDIX 1

THE FRAMEWORK VIEW

OF GENESIS 1

In the chapter on the analogical day theory (chapter 10), I briefly compare the framework view with the analogical day theory, and express a preference for the analogical day theory. But the framework view has some more detailed arguments in its favor that deserve attention.

THE SEVENTH DAY AS ETERNAL

For one thing, the framework view argues that the seventh day of God's rest is eternal. I agree. This argument does not really separate the framework view from the analogical day theory.

THE STRUCTURAL PATTERN OF 3 DAYS AND ANOTHER 3 DAYS

Second, the framework view argues that the arrangement into six days shows a correlation between the first set of three days and the last set of three days. On the first three days God creates the various regions of the world, and on the last three days he creates "rulers" over those regions. Thus the sun and moon (day 4) rule over day and night (day 1). The birds and the water creatures (day 5) rule over the air and the water, respectively, both of which derive from day 2. The land creatures (day 6) rule over the dry land, which was created on day 3.

This correlation is indeed suggestive. But it stretches its pattern at a few points. The division on day 2 creates waters above the expanse, called "Heaven," while on day 5 the birds "fly above the earth across the expanse of the heavens" (the sky), but do not seem to be conceived of as "ruling" over the heaven. If the creatures from the last three days are conceived of not primarily as ruling over the regions but as filling the regions, then the plants on day 3 might be reckoned, along with the land animals, as filling the dry land. I think that the correlation between the days is real. But it does not seem to be perfect or so emphatically obvious as to control everything else.

More important, the existence of a structural correlation is still compatible with an underlying chronological progression. The correlation between regions and rulers may build on top of chronological progression rather than repudiating all chronology. In fact, the creatures created on days 5 and 6 require for their well-being the previous existence of the regions that are created on days 2 and 3. Hence, the structural pattern seems to confirm that days 5 and 6 follow days 2 and 3.

GENESIS 2:5-6

The framework view usually appeals to Genesis 2:5-6:[1]

> When no bush of the field was yet in the land and no small plant of the field had yet sprung up—*for* the LORD God had not caused it to rain on the land, and there was no man to work the ground, . . . (Gen. 2:5).

According to the framework view, the remark about the absence of rain and man implies that there was a fairly long period between the creation of plants (day 3) and the creation of man (day 6) (for why otherwise would one be concerned about whether there was any rain or man?). And it implies that, once plants were created by supernatural action, God would sustain their existence through normal means, including rain and human cultivation.

These observations with respect to plants are then extended in order to conclude that after initially creating any of the various particular creatures, God used ordinary means to sustain them. If God used ordinary means to sustain the oscillation of day and night (day 1), those ordinary means would include the movement of the sun and its shining to provide light. Therefore the events of day 1 must be basically simultaneous with the creation of the sun on day 4. Day 1 and day 4 describe overlapping events from two points of view.

---

[1] Meredith G. Kline, "Because It Had Not Rained," *Westminster Theological Journal* 20 (1958): 146-157; Mark D. Futato, "Because It Had Rained: A Study of Gen 2:5-7 with Implications for Gen 2:4-25 and Gen 1:1–2:3," *Westminster Theological Journal* 60/1 (1998): 1-21.

These arguments are suggestive; but I personally am not persuaded. For one thing, there are some difficulties in understanding the picture in Genesis 2:5-6 in detail. The word for "mist" in 2:6 is uncommon, and may possibly denote a spring or a source of water from underground. Irons and Kline argue that it is a "rain-cloud."[2] Whatever may be the meaning, it appears, as Kidner argues, that there is already a lot of water even before the rain.[3] Hence, the problem, if there is one, may involve not the absence of water for nourishing plants but an abundance, perhaps even an overabundance. Kidner suggests that in 2:5-6 the narrative is returning to the situation of overabundant water that occurred in Genesis 1:2. The narrative takes away the later developments in order now to tell some parts of the story from the standpoint of God's purposes as they relate to the creation of man. Hence, the taking away of man and of rain is not really a statement about the presence of ordinary providence during the days of creation, but an invitation to go back again in time to the situation before there was either post-creation providence or a highly ordered creation.

Still another alternative presents itself. The language in 2:5b about rain and man may not be so much a comment on what principles God used in sustaining plants during days 4 and 5, but a comment looking forward to the rest of Genesis 2, where man and the garden will be prepared and an ordinary providential order for sustaining the garden will be in place. In fact, it is quite possible that Genesis 2:5-6 is not talking about the situation in the whole expanse of the earth but is focusing on the situation in the area where the garden of Eden will later be planted.[4] Plants had not yet sprung up within this limited area. God is planning a transition to a time when ordinary providence will have its role, and in that context we find a natural mention of rain and man.

Kidner's view or the focus-on-Eden view may or may not be right. Though some parts of verses 5 and 6 are reasonably clear, its overall thrust

---

[2] Lee Irons with Meredith G. Kline, "The Framework View," in David G. Hagopian, ed., *The Genesis Debate: Three Views on the Days of Creation* (Mission Viejo, Calif.: Crux, 2001), 231-232.

[3] Derek Kidner, "Genesis 2:5, 6: Wet or Dry?" *Tyndale Bulletin* 17 (1966): 109-114. Offering their own translation of verse 6, Irons and Kline interpret it as a response to the lack of rain: "So a rain-cloud began to arise from the earth . . ." (Irons and Kline, "Framework View," 232). But in Hebrew the beginning of verse 6, with "and" (*w*) plus noun ("mist/spring/rain-cloud") plus imperfect verb, in that order, does not yet begin the backbone of the narrative but is still describing circumstances in the setting, leading up to the beginning of the main part of the narrative in verse 7 (which has the normal structure for narrative backbone, namely *waw*-consecutive plus imperfect). Thus a translation that sees verse 6 as a continuation of the setting seems more natural: "and a mist was going up from the land and was watering the whole face of the ground" (verse 6, ESV).

[4] See the discussion in C. John Collins, *Genesis 1–4: A Linguistic, Literary, and Theological Commentary* (Phillipsburg, N.J.: Presbyterian & Reformed, 2006), chapter 5.

is debatable. This very debatability suggests that we exercise caution, rather than putting too much weight on it in the crucial debate about the overall structure of the days of Genesis, which after all belong to Genesis 1:1–2:3 rather than the account in Genesis 2:4–4:26.

GENERALIZING ABOUT PROVIDENTIAL PRESERVATION

Finally, even if the framework view is right in its interpretation of Genesis 2:5-6, those two verses talk about the growth of plants. They say nothing about animals or the sun. The principle in those verses does not necessarily generalize to include all other kinds of providential sustenance for all other creatures. It is still possible that God created light on the first day, and that the light came in some way other than through the shining of the sun. Accordingly, when God creates the sun and moon and stars on the fourth day, these heavenly lights do not produce the *initial* separation of light from darkness (which occurred already in Gen 1:4) but function as rulers to control and maintain that separation in a regular way. The impression of chronological succession in Genesis 1 has suggested this possibility to a number of interpreters, both ancient and modern.[5]

TWO-REGISTER COSMOLOGY

We must also consider the significance of "two-register cosmology," as expounded in Meredith Kline's article, "Space and Time in the Genesis Cosmogony."[6] The Old Testament shows us scenes in which God sits enthroned in the midst of angelic servants (1 Kings 22:19-22; Job 1:6-12; Ezek. 1; Dan. 7:9-10; etc.). In Kline's terminology, such scenes show us the "upper register," whereas events on earth belong to the lower register.

---

[5] For example, Calvin says:

[concerning day 1] It did not, however, happen from inconsideration or by accident, that the light preceded the sun and the moon. To nothing are we more prone than to tie down the power of God to those instruments, the agency of which he employs. The sun and moon supply us with light: and, according to our notions, we so include this power to give light in them, that if they were taken away from the world, it would seem impossible for any light to remain. Therefore the Lord, by the very order of the creation, bears witness that he holds in his hand the light, which he is able to import to us without the sun and moon (Calvin, *Commentaries on the First Book of Moses, Called Genesis,* trans. John King, 2 vols. [reprint; Grand Rapids, Mich.: Eerdmans, 1948], 1:76; commenting on Genesis 1:3).

[concerning day 4] God had before created the light, but he now institutes a new order in nature, that the sun should be the dispenser of diurnal light, and the moon and stars should shine by night. . . . For Moses related nothing else than that God ordained certain instruments to diffuse through the earth, by reciprocal changes, that light which had been previously created. The only difference is this, that the light was before dispersed, but now proceeds from lucid bodies; . . . (ibid., 1:83; commenting on Genesis 1:14).

[6] Kline, "Space and Time in the Genesis Cosmogony," *Perspectives on Science and Christian Faith* 48/1 (1996): 2-15.

The idea of God's heavenly dwelling is indeed taught in Scripture, and was undoubtedly part of the mental furniture of pious Israelites. Moreover, the pictorial comparison between God as king and human kingship belongs together with many analogical comparisons between God and man. The analogical day theory, as well as the framework view, would acknowledge this much.

But in addition Kline says that the days of creation are upper-register days. Does such an appeal to a heavenly register offer a satisfying explanation of *time?* Here there are difficulties.

First, the existence of an invisible spatial realm in the form of a heavenly scene with angels does not imply the existence of a distinct time dimension with little or no relation to our own. In Job 1:6-12 and 1 Kings 22:19-22, the events within the two spatial realms seem to mesh seamlessly within *one* time continuum. God makes decisions in heaven, and these are then executed on earth. There is doubtless much mystery here, and the mystery ultimately goes back to God's incomprehensibility and his eternity. But the depiction in Scripture does not suggest that we need to postulate two distinct *created* time dimensions, each linked to a distinct created spatial realm. Rather, the power of the depiction depends on our seeing that a tight correlation exists between God's commands in the heavenlies and their execution on earth. This correlation is depicted as being temporal. God issues a command, at an earlier time, and then it is executed by an angelic being on earth, at a later time.

Second, though Kline finds hints of theophany and an angelic council in Genesis 1:2 and 1:26 ("us"), their significance is debatable. (The heavenly cherubim also appear in Genesis 3:24.) The throne room picture does not play a prominent explicit role in Genesis 1, though it has a bigger role (by way of allusions) in Psalm 104:1-4. We must accordingly be cautious about overplaying its role *exegetically* in Genesis 1.

CONCLUSION

All in all, I find the framework approach suggestive, but, because of the remaining questions about 2:5-6 and its generalizations, not nearly as attractive as the analogical day theory. It would take stronger and more obvious evidence, I believe, to overturn in the mind of an Israelite the sense of progression as one moves through the days.

But, as noted in the discussion in chapter 10, the two theories (or some of the other attractive theories) do not generate any major theological differences, so we may the more easily live with the remaining disagreements.

Appendix 2
More on Triangular
Numbers

In the chapter on mathematics (chapter 22) we explored the triangular numbers, that is, numbers representing the number of dots in a triangular array.

The number of dots in a triangle that has n dots at its base is n X (n+1)/2.

Mathematical Induction Using Algebra

We can confirm this result in another way, by mathematical induction. As explained in chapter 22, a proof by mathematical induction starts by establishing the truth for the integer 1. For a triangle whose base has just one dot, that is, for n = 1, the number of dots should be n X (n+1)/2 = 1 X (1+1)/2 = 1. It checks out. The formula is true for n = 1.

Now we do what is called the "inductive" step. Assume that the formula is true for a particular value of n—say, for n = 8. Can we prove the formula for the next n, for n = 9? Consider the sum of the first 8 integers:

$$1 + 2 + \ldots + 8$$

Assuming that the formula is valid for n = 8, we know that

$$1 + 2 + \ldots + 8 = 8 \times (8+1)/2$$

Now we are trying to determine what happens for the sum of the first 9 integers:

$$1 + 2 + \ldots + 8 + 9$$

This sum is just the earlier sum (1 up to 8) plus an extra term, 9. So

$1 + 2 + \ldots + 8 + 9 = [1 + 2 + \ldots + 8] + 9$
$= 8 \times (8+1)/2 + 9$ (because we have assumed that the formula is valid for
      the sum $1 + 2 + \ldots + 8$)
$= (8/2 + 1) \times 9$ (factoring out a factor of 9)
$= [(8 + 2)/2] \times 9 = 9 \times 10/2$ (rearranging the order of the two factors)
$= 9 \times (9 + 1)/2$

Thus the formula works for n = 9.

This kind of reasoning allows us to move from the truth for n = 1 to the truth for n = 2, and then for n = 3, and so on indefinitely. We can see then that it must be true for all n.

Here is the reasoning written out for the general step. Suppose that the formula is true for n = k. That is, suppose we know that

$$1 + 2 + \ldots + k = k \times (k+1)/2$$

Can we prove it for n = k + 1? That is, can we show that

$$1 + 2 + \ldots + k + (k+1) = (k+1) \times [(k+1)+1]/2$$

Here is how we do it:

$1 + 2 + \ldots + k + (k+1) = [1 + 2 + \ldots + k] + (k+1)$ (grouping the first k terms)
$= k \times (k+1)/2 + (k+1)$ (using what we know about the sum of the k terms)
$= [k/2 + 1] \times (k+1)$ (factoring out a factor of (k+1))
$= [(k+2)/2] \times (k+1)$ (putting everything in k/2 +1 under a single denominator)
$= (k+1) \times (k+2)/2$ (rearranging)
$= (k+1) \times [(k+1) + 1]/2$

which is exactly the right formula for n = k+1.

Here we are depending on the coherence between algebra and arithmetic. Algebra uses letters like k as general expressions, while arithmetic looks at particular numbers one at a time. The two agree (cohere). All these expressions also cohere with the results that we arrived at through other kinds of arguments. God is consistent with himself, and so the results agree with one another.

We have now completed a proof by mathematical induction that the number of dots is always n X (n+1)/2. We first showed that the formula was true for n = 1. Then we showed that, if it is true for n = k, it is true for n = k+1. Since it is true for n = 1, it is true for n = 2. Since it is true for n = 2, it is true for n = 3. And so on. Our human minds, thinking God's thoughts after him, are able to see that this reasoning can be repeated indefinitely, and so we could eventually confirm that the formula is true for any n, no matter how large. The consistency of God guarantees that we can rely on this shortcut in reasoning, rather than having to check each n separately, in which case we would never finish.

A Combinatorial Approach

Let us consider another way of looking at triangular numbers, namely through combinatorial mathematics. Combinatorial mathematics develops techniques for counting all the possible ways of achieving some specified goal through choices of numbers. It is closely related to the theory of probability, and thus shows the harmony between triangular numbers and the probabilistic aspect of the world.

Suppose we have 100 balls, and we label them with successive numbers beginning with 1. We then put the balls in a bag. We draw out a first ball, put it aside, and then draw out a second. How many different combinations of two balls could we draw out? This is a laborious question to answer by trial and error, because of the large number of balls. Again, mathematical reasoning, depending on the coherence of God's word, enables us to cut down the labor. For the first ball, we have 100 choices. The first ball could be ball number 1, or number 2, or 3, or so on up to ball number 100. For the second ball, however, there are only 99 choices, because we have already put the first ball aside. The total number of different possibilities is the *product* of 100 and 99, because, for every one starting possibility, say, of drawing ball number 4 on the first draw, there are 99 separate possibilities for the second. The total number is 99 possibilities if we draw ball 1 on the first draw; another 99 possibilities if we draw ball 2 on the first draw; and so on for ball 3, ball

4, ball 5, up to ball 100. The total of all these is 99 added to itself 100 times, or 100 X 99 = 9900.

Now, suppose that we do not care which ball is drawn first. (The mathematicians use the word "combination" to denote this situation.) We are interested only in producing a second collection consisting of two balls, which we will put in a new bag. How many distinct possibilities are there? If we draw ball number 56 first, and then ball number 29 second, it leads to the same result as drawing ball 29 first and ball 56 second. The number of actually distinct possibilities then becomes half of the original number, or 100 X 99/2. We say that there are 100 X 99/2 combinations, that is, ways in which we may pick two distinct balls, when we do not care about the order in which we select them.

Now we can count up the number of combinations in another way. Suppose that, instead of focusing on the process of drawing balls out of the bag, we focus on the result, the two balls that we have in our new bag. Remember that the balls are labeled by numbers that are inscribed on them. One of the balls will have a higher number than the other. The higher number of the two could not be 1, because that leaves no smaller number. So the higher number must be at least 2.

If the higher number is 2, we have only one choice for the lower number, namely 1. Let us then record on a piece of paper the fact that this generates exactly 1 choice. If the higher number is 3, we have two choices for the lower number, namely the numbers 1 and 2. Let us record 2 choices. If the higher number is 4, we have three choices for the lower number. If the higher number is 5, we have 4 choices for the lower number, namely 1, 2, 3, and 4. And so on. The total number of choices is

$$1 + 2 + 3 + \ldots + 99$$

We stop at 99 because, if the higher numbered ball is 100, there are only 99 choices left for the lower number.

Now the total number of choices, or combinations, that we count up in this way must be the same as the total number of choices that we obtained before, namely 100 X 99/2, which was derived from looking at the process of taking balls out of the bag. Why do the two ways of reasoning lead to the same result? Because of the faithfulness of God. Thus we can write

$$1 + 2 + 3 + \ldots + 99 = 100 \text{ X } 99/2$$

This is the formula for the triangular number for a triangle with a base 99 dots long.

Once again we can see a general pattern in this reasoning, because of the harmony in God's word. We can infer that the result holds good not only when we have 100 balls in a bag but when we have any number. And so we could derive the same general result and the same formula n X (n+1)/2 by this "combinatoric" reasoning. Combinatoric reasoning coheres with the earlier reasoning using a geometric picture, the reasoning using algebra, and the reasoning by mathematical induction.

PASCAL'S TRIANGLE

We can find still another way of approaching triangular numbers using "Pascal's triangle." Blaise Pascal discovered a triangle-shaped array of numbers with special properties. This special array is now called "Pascal's triangle" in his honor. Here is the arrangement:

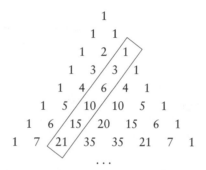

Pascal's triangle has a top row with only the number 1. In addition, 1's run down the two sides of the triangle. Each number in the interior of the triangle is defined as the sum of the two numbers that are its nearest neighbors in the preceding row.

Pascal's triangle has a number of fascinating properties, and one can read about them in the mathematical literature.[1] The sum of all the numbers in one row is a power of 2. More precisely, the numbers in the 3rd row have a sum 2^2 = 2 X 2; 4th row has a sum 2^3 = 2 X 2 X 2; the 5th row 2^4 = 2 X 2 X 2 X 2; and the (n+1)-th row 2^n. The general formula for the (r+1)-th entry in the

---

[1] James Nickel, *Mathematics: Is God Silent?* 2nd ed. (Vallecito, Calif.: Ross, 2001), 256.

(n+1)-th row is n!/r!(n-r)!, where "4!" means 4 X 3 X 2 X 1 and "n!" means n X (n-1) X (n-2) X . . . X 2 X 1.

Now let your eyes focus not on the rows but on the left-hand side of the triangle. The left-hand side is a slanted line of 1's. It starts at the top of the triangle and goes down toward the left as far as one wants to extend it. Exactly parallel to this row of 1's, but further over, is a line of integers, 1, 2, 3, 4, 5, 6, 7, . . . These are the integers in succession. And parallel to this line is a third line, which has been enclosed in a rectangle in the diagram. This consists in the triangular numbers, 1, 3, 6, 10, 15, 21, . . .

Since this line consists in numbers that are all the third number in their own horizontal row, the general formula n!/r!(n-r)! for Pascal's triangle becomes, when applied to this line, n!/2!(n-2)! (r is 2 for the third number inwards from the left end of a row).

Now notice:

n!   = n X (n-1) X (n-2) X (n-3) X . . . X 2 X 1 .
(n-2)! =   (n-2) X (n-3) X . . . X 2 X 1 .

All the factors in (n-2)! cancel corresponding factors in n! The only thing left that is not canceled is n X (n-1).

Hence the formula for a triangular number is n X (n-1)/2! But 2! = 2 X 1 = 2. So we get n X (n-1)/2. We can rewrite this as (n-1) X n/2. What happened? Before, we had the formula n X (n+1)/2. Why is this different? It just depends on where one starts counting. The triangular numbers only begin with the third row of Pascal's triangle. If we renumber, beginning with this third row, and treating it as n = 1, we are making an adjustment in n, and the formula then comes out in its familiar form, n X (n+1)/2.

SUMMARY

When we slow down the processes of reasoning, and also appreciate the variety of ways in which we may come to a coherent result, we can see a multitude of ways in which the faithfulness and beauty of God manifest themselves in the realm of mathematics.

Bibliography on
Theology of Science
Vern S. Poythress

Allis, Oswald T. "The Antiquity of Man (Gen. v. and xi.)." In *The Five Books of Moses*. Philadelphia: Presbyterian & Reformed, 1969. Appendix II, 295-298. Dependent on William H. Green.

Ambrose. *Hexaemeron*. In *The Fathers of the Church*. Edited by Hermigild Dressler et al. New York: Catholic University of America Press, 1961.

Anderson, Stephen R. *Doctor Dolittle's Delusion: Animals and the Uniqueness of Human Language*. New Haven, Conn.: Yale University Press, 2004.

Aquinas, Thomas. *Summa theologicae*. New York: Blackfriars & McGraw-Hill; London: Eyre & Spottiswoode, 1964.

Augustine. *Confessions*. Vol. 1 of *A Select Library of Nicene and Post-Nicene Fathers of the Christian Church*. Edited by Philip Schaff and Henry Wace. Reprint, Grand Rapids, Mich.: Eerdmans, 1979.

———. *The Literal Meaning of Genesis*. In *The Works of Saint Augustine*. Translated with notes by Edmund Hill; edited by John E. Rotelle. Vol. 1 Hyde Park, N.Y.: New City Press, 2002.

Bahnsen, Gregory L. "A Conditional Resolution of the Apparent Paradox of Self-Deception." Ph.D. thesis, University of Southern California, 1979.

Barbour, Ian G. *Religion and Science: Historical and Contemporary Issues*. (A Revised and Expanded Edition of *Religion in an Age of Science*.) New York: HarperCollins, 1997. Barbour favors process theology.

Basil. *Hexaemeron*. Vol. 8 of *A Select Library of Nicene and Post-Nicene Fathers of the Christian Church*. 2nd series. Edited by Philip Schaff and Henry Wace. Grand Rapids, Mich.: Eerdmans, 1978.

Bavinck, Herman. *In the Beginning: Foundations of Creation Theology*. Edited by John Bolt. Grand Rapids, Mich.: Baker, 1999.

————. *Reformed Dogmatics*. Grand Rapids, Mich.: Baker, 2003.

Behe, Michael. *Darwin's Black Box: The Biochemical Challenge to Evolution*. New York: Free Press, 1996. Evidence for design from the improbability of obtaining biochemical systems gradually. All the pieces must be in place before the system will work.

Benacerraf, Paul, and Hilary Putnam, eds. *Philosophy of Mathematics: Selected Readings*. Englewood Cliffs, N.J.: Prentice-Hall, 1964.

Berger, Peter L. *The Sacred Canopy: Elements of a Sociological Theory of Religion*. Garden City, N.Y.: Doubleday, 1967.

Berger, Peter L., and Thomas Luckmann, *The Social Construction of Reality: A Treatise in the Sociology of Knowledge*. New York: Doubleday, 1966.

Berkhof, Louis. *Systematic Theology*. 4th ed. Grand Rapids, Mich.: Eerdmans, 1941.

Bevan, Edwyn. "The Religious Value of Myths in the Old Testament." In *In the Beginning*. Edited by Samuel H. Hooke. Oxford: Oxford University Press, 1947, 149-162.

Bhaskar, Roy. *The Possibility of Naturalism: A Philosophical Critique of the Contemporary Human Sciences*. 3rd ed. London: Routledge, 1998.

————. *A Realist Theory of Science*. 2nd ed. London: Verso, 1997.

————. *Reclaiming Reality: A Critical Introduction to Contemporary Philosophy*. London/New York: Verso, 1989. Critical realism as a philosophy of science.

Bird, W. R. *The Origin of Species Revisited: The Theories of Evolution and of Abrupt Appearance*. 2 vols. New York: Philosophical Library, 1987. Repetitive but full. Skeptical about macroevolution.

Blackwell, Richard J. *Galileo, Bellarmine, and the Bible*. Notre Dame, Ind.: University of Notre Dame Press, 1991.

Blocher, Henri. *In the Beginning*. Downers Grove, Ill.: InterVarsity Press, 1984. Follows the framework interpretation.

Bloom, John A. "On Human Origins: A Survey." *Christian Scholar's Review* 27/2 (1997): 181-203.

Bloom, Neil. *How Blind Is the Watchmaker? Nature's Design and the Limits of Naturalistic Science*. Downers Grove, Ill.: InterVarsity Press, 2001. Discusses intelligent design and applies Michael Polanyi's insights about life not being reducible to physics.

Boyer, Carl B. *The History of the Calculus and its Conceptual Development (The Concepts of the Calculus)*. Reprint, New York: Dover, 1959.

Brown, Francis, S. R. Driver, and C. A. Briggs, eds. *A Hebrew and English Lexicon of the Old Testament*. Oxford: Oxford University, 1953.

Brown, Walter T. *In the Beginning: Compelling Evidence for Creation and the Flood*. 6th ed. Phoenix: Center for Scientific Creation, 1995. Young earth.

Bube, Richard H. *Putting It All Together: Seven Patterns for Relating Science and the*

Christian Faith. Lanham, Md.: University Press of America, 1995. Of seven different patterns, Bube prefers complementarity.

Calvin, John. *Commentaries on the First Book of Moses, Called Genesis*. Translated by John King. 2 vols. Grand Rapids, Mich.: Eerdmans, 1948.

———. *Commentary on the Book of Psalms*. Reprint, Grand Rapids, Mich.: Eerdmans, 1949.

———. *Institutes of the Christian Religion*. Translated by Henry Beveridge. Reprint, Grand Rapids, Mich.: Eerdmans, 1970.

Cassuto, Umberto. *A Commentary on the Book of Genesis*. Jerusalem: Magnes, n.d. 2 vols.

Clifford, Richard J. "The Hebrew Scriptures and the Theology of Creation." *Theological Studies* 46 (1985): 507-523.

Clouser, Roy. "Is There a Christian View of Everything from Soup to Nuts?" *Pro Rege* 31/4 (June 2003): 1-10. A very accessible introduction to the Dooyeweerdian view of the influence of a Christian worldview on science.

Collins, C. John ("Jack"). "Discourse Analysis and the Interpretation of Gen 2:4-7." *Westminster Theological Journal* 61/2 (Fall 1999): 269-276.

———. *Genesis 1–4: A Linguistic, Literary, and Theological Commentary*. Phillipsburg, N.J.: Presbyterian & Reformed, 2006.

———. *The God of Miracles*. Wheaton, Ill.: Crossway, 2000. Examination of different views of providence and miracle.

———. "Reading Genesis 1:1–2:3 as an Act of Communication: Discourse Analysis and Literal Interpretation." In *Did God Create in Six Days?* Edited by Joseph Pipa, Jr., and David Hall. Taylors, S.C.: Southern Presbyterian Press, 1999, 131-151. Collins advocates "analogical days."

———. *Science and Faith: Friends or Foes?* Wheaton, Ill.: Crossway, 2003.

Copan, Paul, and William Lane Craig. *Creation Out of Nothing: A Biblical, Philosophical, and Scientific Exploration*. Grand Rapids, Mich.: Baker, 2004.

Cornelius, Izak. "The Visual Representation of the World in the Ancient Near East and the Hebrew Bible." *Journal of Northwest Semitic Languages* 20/2 (1994): 193-218.

Crick, Francis, and Leslie E. Orgel. "Directed Panspermia." *Icarus* 19 (1973): 341-346.

d'Abro, A. *The Evolution of Scientific Thought from Newton to Einstein*. 2nd ed. New York: Dover, 1950.

d'Abro, A. *The Rise of the New Physics: Its Mathematical and Physical Theories*. New York: Dover, 1951.

Dalrymple, Brent. *The Age of the Earth*. Stanford, Calif.: Stanford University Press, 1991.

Davies, Paul. *The Mind of God: The Scientific Basis for a Rational World*. New York: Simon & Schuster, 1992. Includes a short list of divine attributes of scientific law.

Davis, John Jefferson. *The Frontiers of Science and Faith : Examining Questions from the Big Bang to the End of the Universe.* Downers Grove, Ill.: InterVarsity Press, 2002.

Delitzsch, Franz. *A New Commentary on Genesis.* Edinburgh: T. & T. Clark, 1888.

Dembski, William A. *The Design Revolution: Answering the Toughest Questions About Intelligent Design.* Downers Grove, Ill.: InterVarsity Press, 2004. Clearing up claims of intelligent design, answering critics, and planning for the future.

————. *Intelligent Design: The Bridge Between Science and Theology.* Downers Grove, Ill.: InterVarsity Press, 1999. Biological information as a sign of intelligent design.

————, ed. *Mere Creation: Science, Faith, and Intelligent Design.* Downers Grove, Ill.: InterVarsity Press, 1998.

————. *No Free Lunch: Why Specified Complexity Cannot Be Purchased Without Intelligence.* Lanham/Boulder/New York/Oxford: Rowman & Littlefield, 2002. This book encapsulates and strengthens what Dembski did in earlier books. Chapter 5 is on irreducible complexity, building on Behe. Chapter 6 is on intelligent design as a scientific research program (rather than a destruction of science, as some opponents have claimed). Chapter 4, on evolutionary algorithms and the use of "No Free Lunch" theorems, is important, and looks impressive, but is not as decisive as nonmathematicians may think it is. Dembski is aware that, if one grants the key naturalist-Darwinist assumption that all biological complexity is reachable by gradual steps that increase fitness, Darwinist selection would constitute an effective "evolutionary algorithm" (212). The design would then belong to the intrinsic natural laws, pushing things back to what Dembski elsewhere calls "front-loaded design" (343ff.).

Dembski, William A., and James M. Kushiner, eds. *Signs of Intelligence: Understanding Intelligent Design.* Grand Rapids, Mich.: Brazos, 2001.

Denton, Michael. *Evolution: A Theory in Crisis.* Bethesda, Md.: Adler & Adler, 1985. A nontheist talks frankly and in detail about the problems with evolutionary theory.

Dooyeweerd, Herman. *In the Twilight of Western Thought.* Philadelphia: Presbyterian & Reformed, 1960.

Dowe, Phil. *Galileo, Darwin, and Hawking: The Interplay of Science, Reason, and Religion.* Grand Rapids, Mich.: Eerdmans, 2005.

Feinberg, John S. *No One Like Him.* Wheaton, Ill.: Crossway, 2001.

Feyerabend, Paul. *Against Method: An Outline of an Anarchistic Theory of Knowledge.* London/New York: Verso, 1978. Taking Kuhn to an extreme in advocating rival paradigms.

Frame, John M. *Apologetics to the Glory of God: An Introduction.* Phillipsburg, N.J.: Presbyterian & Reformed, 1994. General apologetics, in the Van Tilian tradition, but more understandable than Van Til.

————. *The Doctrine of God.* Phillipsburg, N.J.: Presbyterian & Reformed, 2002. Especially pertinent are the chapters on miracle, providence, creation, and decrees.

———. *The Doctrine of the Knowledge of God.* Phillipsburg, N.J.: Presbyterian & Reformed, 1987.

———. "God and Biblical Language." In *God's Inerrant Word.* Edited by John Warwick Montgomery. Minneapolis: Bethany, 1974, 159-177.

———. *Perspectives on the Word of God: An Introduction to Christian Ethics.* Phillipsburg, N.J.: Presbyterian & Reformed, 1990.

———. "Scripture Speaks for Itself." In *God's Inerrant Word.* Edited by John Warwick Montgomery. Minneapolis: Bethany, 1974, 178-200.

Futato, Mark D. "Because It Had Rained: A Study of Gen 2:5-7 with Implications for Gen 2:4-25 and Gen 1:1–2:3." *Westminster Theological Journal* 60/1 (1998): 1-21.

Gee, Henry. *In Search of Deep Time: Beyond the Fossil Record to a New History of Life.* Ithaca, N.Y.: Cornell University Press, 2000. A frank discussion by a paleontologist about cladism and the limitations of scientific knowledge.

Godfrey, W. Robert. *God's Pattern for Creation: A Covenantal Reading of Genesis 1.* Phillipsburg, N.J.: Presbyterian & Reformed, 2003.

Gould, Stephen Jay. "Is Uniformitarianism Necessary?" *American Journal of Science* 265 (March 1965): 223-228.

———. *The Structure of Evolutionary Theory.* Cambridge, Mass.: Harvard University Press, 2002. A massive overview of the history and present complexity of mainstream evolutionary theory.

Green, William Henry. "Primeval Chronology." *Bibliotheca Sacra* 47 (1890): 285-303. Argues that the chronologies in Genesis 5 and 11 may have gaps. Doubt remains, but Green does have some interesting examples of other genealogies where they are not what they may naively appear to be.

Gregersen, Niels Henrik, and J. Wentzel van Huyssteen. *Rethinking Theology and Science: Six Models for the Current Dialogue.* Grand Rapids, Mich.: Eerdmans, 1998.

Gregory of Nyssa. *Answer to Eunomius' Second Book.* In *A Select Library of Nicene and Post-Nicene Fathers of the Christian Church.* 2nd series. 14 vols. Edited by Philip Schaff and Henry Wace. Vol. 5. Grand Rapids, Mich.: Eerdmans, 1978.

Guinness, Os. *The Gravedigger File: Papers on the Subversion of the Modern Church.* Downers Grove, Ill.: InterVarsity Press, 1983.

Hagopian, David G., ed. *The Genesis Debate: Three Views of the Days of Creation.* Mission Viejo, Calif.: Crux, 2001. The 24-hour-day view, the day-age view, and the framework view, each represented by two authors, with each view responding to the others.

Hall, David H. *Holding Fast to Creation.* Oak Ridge, Tenn.: Covenant Foundation, 2000. History of interpretation of creation.

Hall, Edward T. *The Silent Language.* Garden City, N.Y.: Doubleday, 1959.

Hamilton, Victor P. *The Book of Genesis: Chapters 1–17.* New International Commentary on the Old Testament. Grand Rapids, Mich.: Eerdmans, 1990.

Henry, Matthew. *Commentary on Holy Scripture.* 1708–1710.

Holton, Gerald. *The Advancement of Science, and Its Burdens: With a New Introduction*. Cambridge, Mass.: Harvard University Press, 1998. The complexity of interaction among experiments, bold theory-making, and cultural context.

Hooykaas, Reijer. *Religion and the Rise of Modern Science*. Grand Rapids, Mich.: Eerdmans, 1972.

Hummel, Charles. *The Galileo Connection: Resolving Conflicts Between Science and the Bible*. Downers Grove, Ill.: InterVarsity Press, 1986. Primarily historical.

Humphreys, D. Russell. *Starlight and Time: Solving the Puzzle of Distant Starlight in a Young Universe*. Colorado Springs: Master, 1994. Argues that general relativity theory plus certain reasonable assumptions about the beginnings provides a suitable model in which, because of relativistic time dilation, distant parts of the universe may appear to be old when the earth is young. This and forthcoming works based on it may come to play a role in the arguments of six-24-hour-day creationists. A flaw in the physical reasoning invalidates the argument.

Jaki, Stanley L. *The Origin of Science and the Science of Its Origin*. South Bend, Ind.: Regnery-Gateway, 1979.

———. *The Road of Science and the Ways of God*. Chicago: University of Chicago Press, 1980.

Jastrow, Marcus. *A Dictionary of the Targumim, the Talmud Babli and Yerushalmi, and the Midrashic Literature*. New York: Pardes, 1950.

Johnson, Dennis E. "Between Two Wor(l)ds: Worldview and Observation in the Use of General Revelation to Interpret Scripture, and Vice Versa." *Journal of the Evangelical Theological Society* 41/1 (1998): 69-84. On the relation of general and special revelation.

Johnson, Phillip E. *Darwin on Trial*. Downers Grove, Ill.: InterVarsity Press, 1991. A more recent book on problems with general Darwinian theory. For more elaborate treatment, see W. R. Bird.

———. *Evolution as Dogma: The Establishment of Naturalism*. Dallas: Haughton, 1990.

———. *The Wedge of Truth: Splitting the Foundations of Naturalism*. Downers Grove, Ill.: InterVarsity Press, 2000. Engaging explanation of how materialist philosophy covertly holds sway in academic circles, and has become a foundational assumption in reasoning used to defend materialistic evolutionary views. The primary focus for debate is on the assumption of naturalism.

Jordan, James B. "The Biblical Chronology Question: An Analysis." No. 10 in *Views and Reviews: Open Book Occasional Papers*. Niceville, Fla.: Biblical Horizons, 1988. Critique of the idea of genealogical gaps represented by William H. Green, B. B. Warfield, and Francis Schaeffer.

———. *Creation in Six Days: A Defense of the Traditional Reading of Genesis 1*. Moscow, Idaho: Canon, 1999. This includes critical interaction with Bruce Waltke's and Meredith Kline's versions of the framework view, and with C. John Collins's "analogical day" view.

Kelly, Douglas F. *Creation and Change: Genesis 1.1–2.4 in the Light of Changing*

Scientific Paradigms. Fern, Ross-shire, UK: Christian Focus, 1997. Defense of 24-hour-day creation by a Reformed systematician.

Kidner, Derek. "Genesis 2:5, 6: Wet or Dry?" *Tyndale Bulletin* 17 (1966): 109-114. Incisive critique of Kline's interpretation of Genesis 2:5.

———. *Genesis: An Introduction and Commentary*. Tyndale Old Testament Commentary. Downers Grove, Ill.: InterVarsity Press, 1967.

Kline, Meredith G. "Because It Had Not Rained." *Westminster Theological Journal* 20 (1958): 146-157.

———. *Images of the Spirit*. Grand Rapids, Mich.: Baker, 1980.

———. "Space and Time in the Genesis Cosmogony." *Perspectives on Science and Christian Faith* 48/1 (1996): 2-15. An update of Kline's "Because It Had Not Rained." More attention here to "two-register" cosmology, heaven and earth, and less reliance on Genesis 2:5. One of the best defenses of the framework interpretation.

———. *The Structure of Biblical Authority*. Grand Rapids, Mich.: Eerdmans, 1972.

Koehler, Ludwig, and Walter Baumgartner. *The Hebrew and Aramaic Lexicon of the Old Testament*. Leiden/New York/Köln: Brill, 1996.

Kuhn, Thomas S. *The Structure of Scientific Revolutions*. 2nd ed. Chicago: University of Chicago Press, 1970. A foundational work leading to revision of the inductivist view of science.

Kuyper, Abraham. *Calvinism: Six Stone Foundation Lectures*. Grand Rapids, Mich.: Eerdmans, 1943. The vision of Christ as Lord of all of life, leading to the challenge of reforming academic disciplines, including science.

Lambert, W. G., and A. R. Millard. *Atra-hasis: The Babylonian Story of the Flood*. Oxford: Oxford University Press, 1969.

Larson, Edward J., and Larry Witham. "Scientists and Religion in America." *Scientific American* 281/3 (September 1999): 88-93.

Lauer, Robert. *Temporal Man: The Meaning and Uses of Social Time*. New York: Praeger, 1981.

Letham, Robert. "'In the Space of Six Days': The Days of Creation from Origen to the Westminster Assembly." *Westminster Theological Journal* 61 (1999): 149-174.

Levine, Robert. *A Geography of Time*. New York: HarperCollins, 1997.

Levine, Robert, and Ellen Wolff. "Social Time: The Heartbeat of Culture." In *Annual Editions in Anthropology* 88/89. Edited by E. Angeloni. Guilford, Conn.: Dushkin, 1988, 78-81. Reprinted from *Psychology Today* (March 1985): 28-35. On different cultural approaches to time.

Lewontin, Richard C. *Biology as Ideology: The Doctrine of DNA*. New York: HarperCollins, 1993. Scientific rhetoric tends to reduce societies to individuals and individuals to genes. Political power has considerable influence on the shape of modern science.

Maatman, Russell. *The Bible, Natural Science, and Evolution*. Grand Rapids, Mich.:

Baker, 1970. One of the best books on evolution, because of the careful attention to presuppositions.

———. *The Impact of Evolutionary Theory: A Christian View.* Sioux Center, Iowa: Dordt College Press, 1993. Careful attention to presuppositions.

Maier, Gerhard. *The End of the Historical-Critical Method.* St. Louis: Concordia, 1977.

McCartney, Dan. "Ecce Homo: The Coming of the Kingdom as the Restoration of Human Vicegerency." *Westminster Theological Journal* 56/1 (1994): 1-21.

McGrath, Alister. *Science and Religion: An Introduction.* Oxford: Blackwell, 1999.

———. *A Scientific Theology.* 3 vols. Grand Rapids, Mich.: Eerdmans, 2001–2003. "Nature" is not immediately available; rather one's view of nature is culturally mediated. McGrath proposes to look at consilience between science and theology, especially in method and epistemology. He announces that he is working within orthodox theology, common to Catholicism, Eastern Orthodoxy, and evangelicalism (while he stands within evangelicalism). Interaction mostly with theological and creedal statements about creation.

Meek, Esther Lightcap. *Longing to Know.* Grand Rapids, Mich.: Baker, 2003. General epistemology explained for the ordinary person.

Migne, J. P., et al., eds. *Patriologia Graecae.* Paris, 1857–1866.

———. *Patriologia Latina.* Paris, 1878–1890.

Milbank, John. *Theology and Social Theory: Beyond Secular Reason.* Oxford: Blackwell, 1993.

———. *The Word Made Strange: Theology, Language, Culture.* Oxford: Blackwell, 1997.

Miller, Kenneth R. *Finding Darwin's God.* New York: Cliff Street, 1999.

Moon, Parry, and Domina Eberle Spencer. "Binary Stars and the Velocity of Light." *Journal of the Optical Society of America* 43 (August 1953): 639.

Moore, T. M. *Consider the Lilies: A Plea for Creational Theology.* Phillipsburg, N.J.: Presbyterian & Reformed, 2005.

Moreland, J. P. *Christianity and the Nature of Science: A Philosophical Investigation.* Grand Rapids, Mich.: Baker, 1989. Philosophical analysis of some of the limitations and uncertainties in science and ideas of scientific method.

———, ed. *The Creation Hypothesis: Scientific Evidence for an Intelligent Designer.* Downers Grove, Ill.: InterVarsity Press, 1994.

Moreland, J. P., and John Mark Reynolds, eds. *Three Views on Creation and Evolution.* Grand Rapids, Mich.: Zondervan, 1999.

Morris, John D., *The Young Earth.* El Cajon, Calif.: Institute for Creation Research, 1994. A more recent book advocating six-24-hour-day creation.

Murray, John. *Principles of Conduct: Aspects of Biblical Ethics.* Grand Rapids, Mich.: Eerdmans, 1957.

Newman, Robert C. *Genesis One and the Origin of the Earth.* Downers Grove, Ill.: InterVarsity Press, 1977.

Nickel, James. *Mathematics: Is God Silent?* 2nd ed. Vallecito, Calif.: Ross, 2001.

Noordtzij, Arie. *Gods Woord en der Eeuwen Getuigenis.* Kampen, Netherlands, 1924.

Oecolampadius, Johannes. *D. Io. Oecolampadii in Genesim Enarratio.* Basil, 1536.

Padgett, Alan G. *Science and the Study of God: A Mutuality Model for Theology of Science.* Grand Rapids, Mich.: Eerdmans, 2003. A model of dialogue in which science and theology can learn and correct one another. Padgett argues for an ontology of "dialectical critical realism."

Parker, Barry. *Einstein's Brainchild: Relativity Made Relatively Easy!* Amherst, N.Y.: Prometheus, 2000.

Pearcey, Nancy R. *Total Truth: Liberating Christianity from Its Cultural Captivity.* Wheaton, Ill.: Crossway, 2004. Discussion of worldviews and the origins of modern secularism and materialism.

Pearcey, Nancy R., and Charles B. Thaxton. *The Soul of Science: Christian Faith and Natural Philosophy.* Wheaton, Ill.: Crossway, 1994. Science originated from a Christian worldview.

Pennock, Robert T., ed. *Intelligent Design Creationism and Its Critics.* Cambridge, Mass./London: MIT Press, 2001.

Pennock, Robert T. *Tower of Babel: The Evidence Against the New Creationism.* Cambridge, Mass.: MIT Press, 1999. By a philosopher specializing in philosophy of science. Worth looking at to see how the creationist and intelligent design approaches to biological evolution might improve.

Penrose, Roger. *Shadows of the Mind: A Search for the Missing Science of Consciousness.* Oxford: Oxford University Press, 1994.

Plantinga, Alvin. "Evolution, Neutrality, and Antecedent Probability: A Reply to McMullin and Van Till." *Christian Scholars Review* 21 (1991/1992): 80-109.

———. "When Faith and Reason Clash: Evolution and the Bible." *Christian Scholars Review* 21 (1991/1992): 8-32.

Polanyi, Michael. *Personal Knowledge: Towards a Post-Critical Philosophy.* Chicago: University of Chicago Press, 1958.

Polkinghorne, J. C. *The Quantum World.* London: Longman, 1984.

Poythress, Vern S. "Adequacy of Language and Accommodation." In *Hermeneutics, Inerrancy, and the Bible.* Edited by Earl D. Radmacher and Robert D. Preus. Grand Rapids, Mich.: Zondervan, 1984, 351-376.

———. "A Biblical View of Mathematics." In *Foundations of Christian Scholarship: Essays in the Van Til Perspective.* Edited by Gary North. Vallecito, Calif.: Ross, 1976, 158-188.

———. "Christ the Only Savior of Interpretation." *Westminster Theological Journal* 50/2 (1988): 305-321.

———. "Christian-Theistic Transfiguration of Science." *The Bulletin of Westminster Theological Seminary* 29/5 (1990): 6. The general framework for understanding scientific theory.

————. "A Christian-Theistic View of the Age of the Universe." *The Bulletin of Westminster Theological Seminary* 29/6 (1990): 3, 6. A short examination of the important factors to weigh in determining the age of the earth.

————. *God-Centered Biblical Interpretation*. Phillipsburg, N.J.: Presbyterian & Reformed, 1999.

————. "Mathematics as Rhyme." *Journal of the American Scientific Affiliation* 35/4 (1983): 196-203.

————. "Newton's Laws as Allegory." *Journal of the American Scientific Affiliation* 35/3 (1983): 156-161.

————. "Reforming Ontology and Logic in the Light of the Trinity: An Application of Van Til's Idea of Analogy." *Westminster Theological Journal* 57 (1995): 187-219.

————. *Science and Hermeneutics: Implications of Scientific Method for Biblical Interpretation*. Grand Rapids, Mich.: Zondervan, 1988.

————. "Science as Allegory." *Journal of the American Scientific Affiliation* 35/2 (1983): 65-71. On the role of science in a world ruled by God.

————. *The Shadow of Christ in the Law of Moses*. Phillipsburg, N.J.: Presbyterian & Reformed, 1995.

————. *Symphonic Theology: The Validity of Multiple Perspectives in Theology*. Grand Rapids, Mich.: Zondervan, 1987.

————. "Why Scientists Must Believe in God: Divine Attributes of Scientific Law." *Journal of the Evangelical Theological Society* 46/1 (March 2003): 111-123.

Poythress, Vern S., and Wayne A. Grudem. *The Gender-Neutral Bible Controversy*. Nashville: Broadman & Holman, 2000.

Prickett, Stephen. *Narrative, Religion, and Science: Fundamentalism Versus Irony, 1700–1999*. Cambridge: Cambridge University Press, 2002.

Pritchard, James B., ed. *Ancient Near Eastern Texts Relating to the Old Testament*. Princeton, N.J.: Princeton University Press, 1950.

Ramm, Bernard. *The Christian View of Science and Scripture*. Grand Rapids, Mich.: Eerdmans, 1954. The best survey of various approaches to reconciling the Bible and science.

Rana, Fazale, and Hugh Ross. *Origins of Life: Biblical and Evolutionary Models Face Off*. Colorado Springs: NavPress, 2004.

Ratzsch, Del. *The Battle of Beginnings: Why Neither Side Is Winning the Creation-Evolution Debate*. Downers Grove, Ill.: InterVarsity Press, 1996.

————. Review of Robert T. Pennock (ed.), *Intelligent Design Creationism and Its Critics* (Cambridge, Mass./London: MIT Press, 2001). Available online at www.arsdisputandi.org, *The Online Journal for Philosophy of Religion* 2 (2002).

————. *Science and Its Limits: The Natural Sciences in Christian Perspective*. 2nd ed. Downers Grove, Ill.: InterVarsity Press, 2000.

"Report of the Creation Study Committee." *Minutes of the 28th General Assembly of the Presbyterian Church in America*. Atlanta: Presbyterian Church in America, 2000. Available online at http://www.pcanet.org/history/creation/report.html.

"Report of the Committee to Study the Views of Creation." *Minutes of the Seventy-First General Assembly . . . of the Orthodox Presbyterian Church*. Willow Grove, Pa.: Orthodox Presbyterian Church, 2004, 193-350.

Ridderbos, Nicolaas H. *Is There a Conflict Between Genesis 1 and Natural Science?* Grand Rapids, Mich.: Eerdmans, 1957.

Ross, Hugh. *Creation and Time: A Biblical and Scientific Perspective on the Creation-Date Controversy*. Colorado Springs: NavPress, 1994. By an evangelical astronomer. Contains data on the church fathers' views on the timing of creation days (chapter 2, 16-24). He advocates a day-age view. He includes refutations of the main evidences for young earth (chapter 10, 103-118).

———. *The Creator and the Cosmos: How the Greatest Scientific Discoveries of the Century Reveal God*. Colorado Springs: NavPress, 1993.

Ruse, Michael. *But Is It Science? The Philosophical Question in the Creation/Evolution Controversy*. Buffalo, N.Y.: Prometheus, 1988.

Sayers, Dorothy. *The Mind of the Maker*. New York: Harcourt, Brace and Company, 1941.

Schaeffer, Francis. *The God Who Is There: Speaking Historic Christianity into the Twentieth Century*. Chicago: InterVarsity Press, 1968.

Scott, Eugenie. "Creationism, Ideology, and Science." *Annals of the NY Academy of Science* 775 (June 24, 1996): 505-522.

Seely, Paul H. "The Firmament and the Water Above. Part I: The Meaning of *raqia*' in Gen 1:6-8." *Westminster Theological Journal* 53 (1991): 227-240.

———. "The Firmament and the Water Above. Part II: The Meaning of 'The Water Above the Firmament' in Gen 1:6-8." *Westminster Theological Journal* 54/1 (1992): 31-46.

———. "The Geographical Meaning of 'Earth' and 'Seas' in Genesis 1:10." *Westminster Theological Journal* 59 (1997): 231-255.

———. "The GISP2 Ice Core: Ultimate Proof that Noah's Flood Was Not Global." *Perspectives on Science and Christian Faith* 55 (2003): 252-260.

———. "Noah's Flood: Its Date, Extent, and Divine Accommodation." *Westminster Theological Journal* 66 (2004): 291-311.

Setterfield, Barry. *The Velocity of Light and the Age of the Universe*. Adelaide: Creation Science Association, 1983. Proposes that the velocity of light has decreased over time, accounting for apparent age. An unlikely route.

Shanks, Niall. *God, the Devil, and Darwin: A Critique of Intelligent Design Theory*. Oxford: Oxford University Press, 2004.

Simpson, George Gaylord. "Uniformitarianism: An Inquiry into Principle, Theory, and Method in Geohistory and Biohistory." In *Essays in Evolution and Genetics in Honor of Theodosius Dobzhansky*. Edited by M. K. Kecht and W. C. Steere. New York: Appleton-Century-Crofts, 1970.

Singh, Simon. *Fermat's Enigma: The Quest to Solve the World's Greatest Mathematical Problem*. Toronto: Penguin, 1996.

Steinmann, Andrew E. "אחד as an Ordinal Number and the Meaning of Genesis 1:5." *Journal of the Evangelical Theological Society* 45/4 (2002): 577-584. "One" in Genesis 1:5 is a cardinal rather than an ordinal. Steinmann thinks that this supports 24-hour days, but see Sterchi.

Sterchi, David A. "Does Genesis 1 Provide a Chronological Sequence?" *Journal of the Evangelical Theological Society* 39/4 (1996): 529-536. Syntactical evidence for a list rather than a chronology.

Strauss, D. F. M. "Is a Christian Mathematics Possible?" *Tydskrif vir Christelike Wetenskap [Journal for Christian Scholarship]* 39 (2003): 31-49. Dooyeweerdian approach to foundations of mathematics.

Stroes, H. R. "Does the Day Begin in the Evening or Morning." *Veus Testamentum* 16 (1966): 460-475.

Thaxton, Charles B., Walter L. Bradley, and Roger L. Olsen. *The Mystery of Life's Origin: Reassessing Current Theories*. New York: Philosophical Library, 1984. Negative evaluation of theories of prebiotic evolution leading to life.

Torrance, Thomas F. *The Ground and Grammar of Theology*. Belfast: Christian Journals, 1980.

————. *Reality and Scientific Theology: Theology and Science at the Frontiers of Knowledge*. Edinburgh: Scottish Academic Press, 1985.

————. *Space, Time, and Incarnation*. Oxford: Oxford University Press, 1969.

————. *Space, Time, and Resurrection*. Grand Rapids, Mich.: Eerdmans, 1976.

————. *Theological Science*. Oxford: Oxford University Press, 1969.

Van Til, Cornelius. *Christian-Theistic Evidences*. Classroom syllabus, Westminster Theological Seminary, 1961. Van Til's seminal treatment of the presuppositions of modern science and its treatment of evidence ("data, facts"). Van Til's discussion is most intelligible when you understand that he is for the most part discussing unbelieving science, and looking a good deal at the "antithesis"—what would happen if scientists consistently held to their unbelieving presuppositions.

————. *The Defense of the Faith*. 2nd rev. ed. Philadelphia: Presbyterian & Reformed, 1963. The classic statement of Van Til's apologetics.

————. *An Introduction to Systematic Theology*. Philadelphia: Westminster Theological Seminary, 1966. Especially "Present General Revelation About Nature," 75-85.

————. "Nature and Scripture." In *The Infallible Word*. Philadelphia: Presbyterian & Reformed, 1946, 263-301.

————. *A Survey of Christian Epistemology*. N.l.: den Dulk Christian Foundation, 1969.

Waltke, Bruce K. "The Literary Genre of Genesis, Chapter One." *Crux* 27/4 (December 1991): 2-10.

Warfield, Benjamin Breckenridge. "On the Antiquity and the Unity of the Human

Race." In *Biblical and Theological Studies*. Edited by Samuel G. Craig. Philadelphia: Presbyterian & Reformed, 1952, 238-261. Reprinted from *The Princeton Theological Review* 9 (1911): 1-25. Dependent on William H. Green, and parts are now dated in his interaction with historical anthropology.

———. *The Inspiration and Authority of the Bible*. Philadelphia: Presbyterian & Reformed, 1967.

Wenham, Gordon. *Genesis 1–15*. The Word Biblical Commentary. Vol. 1. Waco, Tex.: Word, 1987.

Westminster Theological Seminary, *The Infalliable Word: A Symposium*. Philadelphia: Presbyterian & Reformed, 1946.

Whitcomb, John C., Jr., and Henry M. Morris. *The Genesis Flood: The Biblical Record and Its Scientific Implications*. Philadelphia: Presbyterian & Reformed, 1961. The standard text for flood geology and a young earth.

Wigner, Eugene. "The Unreasonable Effectiveness of Mathematics in the Natural Sciences." *Communications on Pure and Applied Mathematics* 13 (1960): 1-14.

Witsius, Herman. *Sacred Dissertations on What Is Commonly Called the Apostles' Creed*. Reprint. Escondido, Calif.: den Dulk Christian Foundation, 1993.

Woodward, Thomas. *Doubts About Darwin: A History of Intelligent Design*. Grand Rapids, Mich.: Baker, 2003.

Young, Davis A. *The Biblical Flood: A Case Study of the Church's Response to Extrabiblical Evidence*. Grand Rapids, Mich.: Eerdmans, 1995. Survey of thinking on geology and the flood of Noah in past centuries.

———. *Creation and the Flood: An Alternative to Flood Geology and Theistic Evolution*. Grand Rapids, Mich.: Baker, 1977. A thoughtful alternative to flood geology and young earth, defending old-earth progressive creationism.

———. "Scripture in the Hands of Geologists. Part I." *Westminster Theological Journal* 49/1 (1987): 1-34.

Young, Edward J. *In the Beginning: Genesis Chapters 1 to 3 and the Authority of Scripture*. Edinburgh/Carlisle: Banner of Truth, 1976.

———. *Genesis 3: A Devotional and Expository Study*. London: Banner of Truth, 1966.

———. "The Relation of the First Verse of Genesis One to Verses Two and Three." *Westminster Theological Journal* 21 (1959): 138-139.

———. *Studies in Genesis One*. Philadelphia: Presbyterian & Reformed, 1964.

Young, William. *Foundations of Theory*. Nutley, N.J.: Presbyterian & Reformed, 1967.

General Index

Scripture Index